40 OCEAN 80 120 160 160

ARCTIC OCEAN

80 — — 80

Bering Str.

1768-71 **1a** ___ Cook
1772-5 **1b** ___ Cook
1776-9 **1c** _._._ Cook (with Bligh
            and Vancouver)
1779-80 **1C** ..... Gore and King
            (after Cook's death)

Bering Sea
Unalaska
Aleutian Is.   1c

EUROPE

ASIA

1C

40 — — 40

PACIFIC OCEAN

1C

Sandwich Is.
(Hawaiian Islands)

AFRICA

Cook killed Feb. 14th 1779

Philippine Is.   Ladrone Is.
                      (Mariana Is.)
Mindanao   Marshall Is.

Caroline Is.   Gilbert Is.

INDIAN
OCEAN

Sumatra   Phoenix Is.
            Borneo   New   New   Ellice Is.
                          Britain Ireland Bougainville
            Celebes   New   Choiseul
                               Guinea   Solomon Is.
      Java   Louisiade   Santa Cruz Is.
                                                          Samoa
                          Gt.   New   Friendly Is.
                          Barrier   Hebrides   (Tonga)
                          Reef   1c
                                      New Caledonia

                                              1b
      1a   Oct 1774   Oct 1773

Table bay   AUSTRALIA   1a

            1C   July 1773

C. of Good Hope
                    Botany Bay   40 — — 40

Van Diemen's Land
(Tasmania)

Kerguelen Is.   1c   NEW   Nov 1774   1b
                                       ZEALAND

1b   Dec   1b
                                            1773

                    1b

ANTARCTICA
40   80   120   160   160

THE
TRUE
GLORY

THE TRUE GLORY

WARREN TUTE

*The Story of
the Royal Navy over
a thousand years*

BLOOMSBURY BOOKS
LONDON

CONTENTS

LIST OF SPECIAL FEATURES

To all those unremembered heroes who, throughout the centuries, have given their lives at sea for the true glory of the realm.

ACKNOWLEDGEMENTS

I would like most warmly to thank Peter Kemp and Richard Hough for their advice and guidance in the writing of this book and also my daughter, Katie, for the help she gave me in the preparation of the Chronological Compendiums preceding each chapter.

Valuable assistance, regarding illustrations, was also given by Joan Horseley, D. F. K. Hodge, R. G. Todd and Joan Moore, all of the National Maritime Museum.

The author and publishers wish to thank the following for permission to quote extracts from the works listed below:

Sir Winston Churchill: *History of the English Speaking Peoples Vol. 4*, published by Cassell Ltd (UK) and McLelland and Stewart (Canada), and *Second World War Vols. 2 and 3*, published by Cassell Ltd. (UK) and Houghton and Mifflin (Canada).

Poem by A. P. Herbert, *Warships Week 1942*, taken from Captain E. Bush: *Flowers of the Sea*, published by George Allen & Unwin Ltd.

The Admiralty, copyright N. A. M. Rodger, first published by Terence Dalton Limited 1979.

PICTURE CREDITS

FOREWORD

The Royal Navy – or perhaps the idea of the Royal Navy – has permeated every level of British society stretching back through the mists of time to Alfred the Great. Latterly the Navy's impact, its influence and the way it has coloured our daily lives, have been more pronounced than that of any other institution in the land except for the Crown and the Law. The Royal Navy, in fact, is unique. It enjoys an untarnished, signal reputation not only in Great Britain but throughout the world, being held in respect, admiration and occasionally affection by its enemies ancient and modern. Maybe that is a generalised, slightly pompous statement with more than a touch of nineteenth-century chauvinism about it. Nevertheless I believe it to be essentially true. Why is this and how has it come about?

There is nothing remarkable in pointing out that the British are an island race. However, we have to start from that point. The sea is in our blood and for over a thousand years our freedom, the main stream of our commercial life and our resulting common wealth have depended upon a successful understanding and use of both near and distant waters. The longitude of Greenwich, a few miles south east of the City of London has long been accepted by the world as the prime meridian from which all time is measured. English has been adopted as the world language for navigation by sea and air and the 3,500 Admiralty charts, kept up to date by some 3,000 Notices to Mariners every year, still comprise the basic working documents on which global shipping goes about its business.

For a century after the Napoleonic wars the Royal Navy maintained a presence in every ocean of the world thus securing for all the freedom of the seas. Peter the Great of Russia worked for a time in the early eighteenth century as a shipwright at Deptford and later for close on a hundred years British Admirals and Captains organised and controlled the Imperial Navy of Russia.

Until the Second World War the Royal Navy served as a model for other national maritime forces, the most notable of these being the Imperial Japanese Navy. Naval uniforms throughout the world bear at least a resemblance to those introduced for officers of the Royal Navy in 1748 and for ratings in 1857.

Western laws, the customs and usages of the sea in modern times now under international discussion if not, as yet, under international control may be traced back in part to the Black Book of Admiralty which, in 1336, codified the laws of Oléron enacted by Eleanor of Aquitaine after her marriage to Henry II of England in 1152. Without detracting from the proud record of other great seafaring nations, it can fairly be said that British naval tradition has been for centuries a paradigm for the world.

Again, I am not arguing perfection or any like state of affairs. Such a claim would be impertinent. I am, however, saying that over the centuries the British did become exceptional seamen, that they did take a major role in opening up and charting the oceans of the world and that in seeking principally to trade they found themselves in the nineteenth century in a position of dominance with responsibility for policing the world.

Now that we live in an age of the guided missile, modern science has made it impossible for any one nation to control the oceans of the world in the way the Royal Navy did in the nineteenth century and the early part of the twentieth century. But threats of regional interference in unfettered use of the sea continue to lurk in the shadows today. Nations depending on a maritime strategy are still at risk and all recent conflicts have shown that, for them victory on land not supported by control of the seas can only be shortlived. Battles may be won or lost in any environment. For maritime powers wars can only be lost at sea and Jellicoe, the British Commander-in-Chief at the Battle of Jutland in 1916, was the only Admiral who could have lost an Empire in an afternoon. And what an Empire it then was!

These and other essential facts have been continually appreciated by the Royal Navy since the time of Drake. In spite of this trumpet voluntary, therefore, I proffer this story of the British Navy over a thousand years with no boastful intent. No new spirit of mastery, no rekindling of national ambition at the inevitable expense of world peace is implied in this record of the trials, tribulations and achievements of our naval forbears.

However, now that the age of materialism shows signs of drawing to a close; with earlier and more noble values being in part restored, I hope that this partial record of British seamen, their successes, their failures, their character, their reliability and their steadfastness in the face of great odds may inspire in those with a feeling for the sea a possible drawing together or at the least an increased understanding of a story remarkable by any criterion. This I have ventured to call 'The True Glory' after the prayer concocted from Drake's letters home whilst blockading Cadiz in 1587.

This prayer which General Montgomery pinned up in his caravan throughout the Desert Campaign of the Second World War serves well as the keynote to all that follows . . . 'Oh! Lord God, when Thou givest to Thy servants to endeavour any great matter, grant us also to know that it is not the beginning but the continuing of the same until it be thoroughly finished which yieldeth the true glory.'

CHAPTER I

THE ANGLO-SAXONS, NORMANS AND PLANTAGENETS

896-1485

CHRONOLOGICAL COMPENDIUM

General

The greatest threat to Anglo-Saxon England came from the Vikings. The expansion of the Northern Kingdoms and, in particular, the Danish, together with the weakness of the Old English Kings prior to Alfred resulted in fairly continuous Viking attacks until the tenth century. These attacks developed from pirate-like raids into the conquest and settlement of the land itself.

The Norman Conquest connected England with Europe. The problems and cost of holding England, Normandy and other French lands under one ruler were enormous. Until the end of the Hundred Years War (1337–1453) and the virtual loss of French lands, the English Kings were mainly concerned to retain and consolidate conquests in Normandy, Gascony and Brittany. Englishmen, well aware of the advantage of such conquests to their commerce, shipping and defence were prepared to pay for them. English administrative abilities developed greatly in response to the requirements of such widespread government. The Crown's continual demand for tax built up the counter-balancing power of Parliament.

By the fifteenth century the possible alliance of the Scots and the French became the greatest threat to English security, whilst the retention of claims over France absorbed much of England's energy.

Naval

No Navy or fleet existed in English water, even in embryo, until the reign of King Alfred (871–901). Small oared boats were used for river work and for inshore fishing but the art of sailing and navigating out of sight of land had been lost almost entirely during the Dark Ages (c.450–c.600). Such knowledge of the sea as there was remained local and was passed on by word of mouth.

By the end of this period, i.e. the beginning of the reign of Henry VII (1485), English sailing ships such as the cog, the carrack (adapted from ships of Genoan, Spanish or Portuguese origin) and the dogger, a fishing vessel which took its name from the Dutch word for a cod-fishing boat, were trading and fishing in the North Sea, the Baltic, the English Channel, the Bay of Biscay (for the Bordeaux wine trade) and occasionally into the Mediterranean. Fore and after castles were added to these ships when required to transport soldiers or for archers to fight the ships at sea. The King possessed a few ships which were basically trading vessels but which could be adapted for war. A Lord High Admiral was first appointed in 1391 and, when necessary, fleets, such as the Cinque Ports Fleet, would be assembled to meet a specific crisis such as the war against Scotland (1299–1300) when fifteen cogs, eight ships, two esneccas or 'snakes' and five other miscellaneous vessels were employed.

The steerboard had been replaced by the rudder, primitive compasses were in use and gunpowder had been invented, naval guns first being used in Louis de Mâle's attack on Antwerp in 1336. But by the end of this period, no permanent fleet as such existed nor was there any naval organisation, the captain and crew of any ship being subordinate to the knight and his fighting men wherever they were borne.

People, events and dates

790   First Viking invasion.

851   First recorded naval battle in English history: Athelstan of Kent defeats Danish force off Sandwich.

871   Accession of Alfred the Great.

882   Alfred defeats four Danish ships at sea.

895/7   Alfred builds longships to own design and defeats Danes off Essex and in Thames Estuary

959/975   Reign of Edgar. During this reign a royal progress was made by rowing round the kingdom. To be rowed was a mark of dignity: to be rowed by kings – the height of majesty. Hence tradition of a departing Commander-in-Chief being rowed ashore by brother Admirals.

1042/1066   Edward the Confessor. Establishment of the Cinque Ports – most ancient maritime institution still extant. Its purpose was quick mobilisation of merchant vessels into navy against pirates and enemies.

1066   Norman Conquest. Harold's defensive and William's invasion fleets never meet.

Post Conquest   Advent of chivalry: feudal superiority of Knights over seamen. Officer ranks – French; seamen – Anglo-Saxon.

1095   First Crusade.

1147   Second Crusade via Portugal. Wooden castles built on ships 'de la Tour' i.e. temporarily 'H.M.S.' to accommodate knights, horses and archers.

1189/1199   Richard I (Coeur-de-Lion). Third Crusade. First encounters with Saracen galleys off Messina. Ramming.

1199/1216   John. Loss of Normandy makes English Channel first line of defence.

1214   French invasion fleet destroyed at Damme in Flanders.

1215   Magna Carta.

1293   First instance of a ship being licensed by 'Letter of Marque' later described as 'Privateer'.

13th C.   Development of wine trade from Bordeaux: tuns and tunnage. Development of the cog: rudder, lodestone and early compasses come into use.

14th C.   First naval guns (?) 1336 Antwerp.

1336   Black Book of Admiralty. English codification of the laws of Oléron plus list of ancient customs and usages of the sea.

1340   Battle of Sluys. First naval battle fought in ships, the English being commanded by Edward III in person.

1377/1399   Richard II. Correspondence with Master of Prussia attempting to regulate pirates and privateers.

1391   Earl of Rutland appointed as first Lord High Admiral.

14th C.   Portolan Charts first made in Mediterranean in 13th century begin to be used in north-west Europe. These early charts are typified by the extensive use of compass roses and extended rhumb or direction lines closely covering an entire goat or sheep skin used for the chart.

15th C.   Henry the Navigator (1394–1460) establishes school at Sagres to teach navigation, astronomy and mathematics and inspires long succession of Portuguese seamen to make voyages of discovery. This leads after his death to the discovery of the Cape of Good Hope and the sea route to India.
Development of ships especially built for war.

1415   Agincourt. English invasion force carried across Channel in 1500 ships and boats. Henry V builds the "Jesus" first ship of 1,000 tons plus two others, the "Holigost" (760 tons) and the "Trinity Royal" (540 tons) followed by Huggekyns of Southampton's masterpiece the "Grace Dieu" of 1400 tons. Though modelled on Mediterranean carracks, the "Grace Dieu" was clinker-built (her remains – she was struck by lightning and burnt in 1439 – are still in the Hamble River.)

1453   Fall of Constantinople to the Turks. This disrupts the spice trade from the east and greatly encourages the discovery of new sea routes and, later, the opening up of the world.

Our story begins with Alfred. This king – the only English king to be dubbed 'the Great' by historians – is traditionally credited with forming the first English Navy in the last decade of the ninth century A.D., his achievements including the blocking of the river Lea against the Danes in 895 and his subsequent expulsion of the invaders from London. In fact, although a remarkable man with many diverse qualities, Alfred's nautical achievements scarcely rank on the scale of Trafalgar and, indeed – if we accept him as the father of the British Navy – it must also be remembered that in the first battle which this first English Navy fought, Alfred's whole fleet ran smartly aground on a falling tide. This suggests something amiss in the seamanship and boat handling department.

Alfred, however, was a man of ideas, a self-taught scholar and a leader of genius. He inspired and led as no Anglo-Saxon king had done before. His vision shone like a beacon through the fog of barbarism, death and destruction which the perennial Norwegian and Danish invasions had caused to descend on the various petty kingdoms of England towards the end of the Dark Ages. Alfred united these weak and warring monarchs south of the Humber. He partly rebuilt and re-established London, regenerating in it the mysterious power the City has had ever since.

Alfred stands as the only contemporary Christian king who proved a fair match for the disciplined and ferocious Vikings, for a time driving them out of his domain. In so far as the sea is concerned, he gave birth to a simple and clear idea which has animated the British Navy ever since. This was that an island folk can best preserve itself from invasion by taking on the aggressor afloat. Drake and Nelson respectively advanced this strategy. They demonstrated that it is invariably less costly and more effective to fight a war off the enemy's coast than off your own, attack being ever the best form of defence.

Alfred must, indeed, have had extraordinary determination. His father Egbert 'King of the English' had taken him to Rome as a boy. This was an unusual and dangerous journey to have made in those days. One effect of this journey was that Alfred and his deeply religious elder brother Ethelred (the First not the Unready) who preceded him as King of Wessex until 871, became fired by Christian zeal. They must also have been exposed to Mediterranean civilisation at a tender age or at the least have gained an idea of the non-barbarous art of living in cities. Thus Alfred sensed the importance of building 'burghs' or walled towns similar to Lucca or Rome itself as essential centres for trading, self-protection and the continuity of a stable and moderately prosperous life. Alfred may also have cast an eye on the efficiency of the Mediterranean oared galley which could out-manoeuvre and ram a clumsier ship under sail.

However, although possible, it is doubtful if Alfred did see a Roman galley on his visit to Rome. By this date there were not many of them around and Alfred would have been appalled by their size and number of crew, both beyond the range of possibility for the England of his day. Roman galleys then had a length of about 240 feet, a beam of 110 feet over the outriggers and carried a crew of about 1,200 excluding the soldiers.

Undoubtedly, though, Alfred did modify and import other Mediterranean ideas into 'the sea-defended green spot' which Celts and Anglo-Saxons called 'Clas

Merdin' or Britain. However he built his ships on the longship pattern, appreciating that this design was much better suited to north European waters than any galley.

Whether or not Alfred really thought and acted like that is, of course, conjecture. Our knowledge of those far distant times still remains opaque. Documents suggest dubious, sometimes unbelievable and often erroneous facts.

What is significant about Alfred in the story of the Navy is that in 1740 two Scotsmen, Mallet and Thompson, the former described by Dr Johnson as 'the only Scotsman whom Scotsmen did not commend', put together a Masque in honour of the birth of Princess Augusta entitled 'Alfred' in which 'Rule Britannia' first appeared. This became as popular as the story of the hot cakes Alfred is alleged to have burnt and has been part of naval mythology ever since. So for the last 250 years Alfred has been accepted as the first British king to make any serious attempt to rule the waves. For that reason, as I said, our story begins with Alfred.

What sort of Navy did Alfred create? The *Anglo-Saxon Chronicle* records that in 896, when the Danes from East Anglia and Northumbria were harassing the south coast of Wessex, King Alfred ordered warships to be built to confront the Danish ships. These vessels were almost twice as long as the Danish ones, having up to sixty oars. They were faster and steadier and had more freeboard: they are thought not to have been built after the Frisian or Danish designs but in a way King Alfred thought would be more effective. This meant that they were probably clinker-built* oared galleys, possibly armed with rams in the Mediterranean fashion. If so they were certainly purpose-built warships and may well have been superior, when working fairly close inshore, to the Viking longboats which had had to sail and/or be rowed across the North Sea.

The Vikings, of course, knew how to sail, though to what extent other than downwind is again a matter of conjecture. Generally speaking the art of sailing had been lost or largely forgotten in north-west Europe and certainly in the British Isles during the Dark Ages. This is understandable. The Dark Ages are conventionally understood to be the period from approximately A.D. 450 to 600 i.e. between the Teutonic Conquest and the conversion to Christianity, during which period writing virtually disappeared. Until the Viking era Anglo-Saxon England took the sea to be an almost uncrossable area behind which its people felt themselves more or less safe. The Romans had left their colony with certain roads which could still be used, even if only partially, for internal communication and they could move about rivers and estuaries by rowing in their coracles. The Vikings were to change all that. From 792 when the Norsemen sacked Lindisfarne off the Northumbrian coast the sea became a hostile arena from which ruthless enemies appeared over the horizon every year, to be temporarily bought off with Danegeld. The moat had thus turned into a highway controlled by alien barbarians. This then became an added reason for not venturing to sea except for purely local voyages under oars. Alfred's claim to fame is that he was the first to apply a corrective with his warships.

This 'corrective' did not survive Alfred's reign and in any case its application seems to have been accidental and partial. It is sometimes assumed that medieval and pre-

* *Clinker-built* means a method of boat building in which the lower edge of each side plank overlaps the upper edge of the one below. In *Carvel-built* boats the side planks are all flush.

medieval kings such as Alfred and Harold operated their Navies so as to intercept and fight the enemy out at sea. However, a moment's thought will show the virtual impossibility of such an event given the manpower and the communications then available.

Indeed nearly two hundred years later, when William the Conqueror landed at Pevensey, he did so unopposed. He was able to do this as the result of an overlong wait for a favourable southern wind and also because Harold's fleet had tired of delaying for an enemy who failed to appear and had dispersed. Moreover, hands were urgently needed for the harvest. In those primitive days it was a fact of life that unless the harvest could be got in, you might not survive the winter.

So as medieval Navies developed, they were assembled in the main not for battle out at sea but to transport knights and their fighting men. Apart from the eruptively aggressive Vikings who did fight each other in their ships – but only in their home fiords – and barring the individual activities of pirates, there were virtually no fleet encounters at sea until gunpowder changed the scene in the sixteenth century. Ships could not be sunk with bows and arrows. The rudder and compass did not come into use in northern Europe until the mid-thirteenth century and early sailing ships continued to be dependent on suitable weather. Where the wind blew so the ship went with the men or the goods it carried.

Indeed during that strange summer of 1066 which began just after Easter with the sighting of the comet later to be named by Halley and ended with the only conquest of the British Isles for over 900 years, almost the only relaxation the few lonely watchers on the cliffs could allow themselves to take would be when northerly winds had begun to blow.

The size of vessels, too, must be remembered. Ships as we were later to understand them scarcely existed. Most seagoing craft in southern England in those days were no more than large open boats, built to be hauled ashore on rollers. They rarely risked lying at anchor in creeks or in the open sea. Crews would cook their meals on land and sleep under the sail in the boats they had hauled up on shore.

In the end it was a question of manpower and the limited use to which it could be put. The four thousand ships, therefore, with which King Edgar a century before is supposed to have guarded his kingdom and which presumably were available to Harold in the summer of 1066, neither belonged to the King nor had been constructed, with one or two exceptions, for anything other than fishing or the transport of goods.

One of the main themes in this naval story will be manpower, its acquisition, its training and its management. In the early days manpower really meant the use of physical muscle: now in the electronic age it is more a question of mental skill. But at no time has there been more than a temporary surfeit of either. Classical Greeks, Romans, Vikings, Moors and Arabs all ran their ships and indeed their economies on slaves. The early Portuguese and Spanish explorers of the fifteenth and sixteenth centuries who opened up Africa and the Americas set out initially for God and for gold but came back with a more valuable living gold in the form of black labour. To exploit the new dominions beyond the seas later explorers then found it expedient to import into those territories African slaves by the million.

In the British Isles the form of servility differed. There was no slavery as such but life in post-Norman conquest conditions amounted at first to little more than survival. Anglo-Saxon peasant cultivators in their more or less democratically organised villages found their new feudal French-speaking masters much more demanding and oppressive. They now became serfs or villeins to the local lord of the manor who in turn derived his power from the King. This power required such lords to deliver fighting men on demand, and nowhere was this more important than in the seaport towns forming the front line should there be another invasion. Hence came about the Confederation of the Cinque Ports, the most ancient maritime institution in the land, which had been originated by King Edward the Confessor just before the conquest.

The Common Seal of Hythe, dating from the late twelfth or early thirteenth century, presents a somewhat imaginative view of an early type of ship, clinker-built, with rudiments of fore and after castles, a well-stayed mast and a square sail.

Hastings, Romney, Hythe, Dover and Sandwich comprised the first confederation. Winchelsea, Rye and other towns from Sussex to the Thames were added later. All undertook to provide the King with a fleet of ships for an agreed period each year. In medieval times the monarch himself never owned more than a handful of ships and his Navy, such as it was, comprised not only those few ships specifically built for fighting but also ships of any kind which loyal subjects would hire to the King and which could be mobilised as warships in times of crisis.

In the later middle ages the Cinque Ports provided some fifty-seven ships free of charge for fifteen days a year and then, if they were required for longer periods, there would be a fixed charter fee. In return the Cinque Ports were absolved from tax and had other legal privileges, and freedom from jurisdictions – incomprehensible to us today – such as sac and soc, tol and team, blodwit, fledwit, tumbrel, mundbryce and ligan – to say nothing of Uncle Tom Cobley and all.

Ships from the Cinque Ports became the main suppliers of cross Channel transport for the King's armies bound for the Crusades or other trouble spots abroad. Today the Lord Wardenship of the Cinque Ports, though stripped of power, still remains one of the most cherished and honoured posts in the land. The Duke of Wellington and Sir Winston Churchill were recent holders of the office and Queen Elizabeth, the Queen Mother, was installed as the current Lord Warden on 1st August 1979.

Another key factor operating throughout this story will be those attitudes, traditions and customs which together comprise the outward expression of certain dominating and generative ideas. The Norman kings and to a lesser extent their Plantagenet successors had a contempt for commerce. They were men of the field. They lived and took their pleasure by force of arms. This was in striking contrast to the Anglo-Saxons who ennobled merchants having two or more successful overseas voyages to their credit by making them Thanes or Thegns. William and his successors would have none of that. However, as most rulers and all dictators discover sooner or later, money is indispensable. For that reason William brought over the Jews of Rouen. These were so successful in bridging the gap between the native merchants and the conquering King and his nobles that they ended up owning a sizeable part of the kingdom. As a result they were universally execrated, subjected to the most shameful and brutal pogrom England has ever known and were then expelled for four centuries.

This feudal attitude to commerce extended to the sea. The era of chivalry, which

ALFRED'S NAVY

The staple ship of Alfred's navy was the longship and English warships continued to be longships until and after the Norman conquest of Britain in 1066.

The Norse or Viking galley was developed as a longship between the years A.D. 600 and A.D. 1000. They varied in size from forty to eighty oars and sported a mast, housed in a step and lowered aft when under oars. A single square sail was hoisted on a yard and braced by means of bowlines and bearing-out spars, known as bei-tass, to enable the ship to be sailed slightly to windward as well as for straight running.

Longships were built without decks or keel. Their flat shape enabled them to drive up on shallow beaches and disgorge raiding parties against defenceless coastal villages but there was no protection against the weather for their crews and in the early years they were indifferent seaboats and were therefore not operated in winter when rough seas might be expected. To begin with the Vikings had it all

their own way, ranging across the North Sea and down the English Channel to the coasts of western France and northern Spain, raiding, plundering and holding for ransom much as they pleased.

After Alfred, the Norsemen raised their freeboard a foot or two, added more longitudinal strakes and thus enabled their crews to fire arrows and hurl darts downwards into any attacking ship. This added freeboard made the longships into much better seaboats and enabled them to risk longer voyages into the stormy waters of the northern Atlantic, reaching Iceland, Greenland and possibly the coast of North America.

Alfred's claim to be the real founder of the English navy has a somewhat shaky foundation because naval actions had been fought against the Danes before Alfred built his warships and because, after his death, there were long periods when the petty kingdoms of England had nothing which could be called a navy. Kings such as Cymbeline, Egbert, Offa,

Alfred, Edward the Elder, Edgar, Canute and Harold were essentially pirates who saw that it paid them to build up the strongest force of ships they could manage in the seas around Britain.

William the Conqueror, indeed, has been described as the last of the pirate kings of England. Certainly he followed the example of Alfred in maintaining a fighting fleet whilst consolidating his conquest and establishing his dynasty.

These Norman longships of 1066 depicted on the Bayeux Tapestry are basically Transports. Some carry horses and others troops who are obviously equipped to fight ashore with shields too clumsy to be handled comfortably at sea. The aim of the expedition is to cross the Channel, preferably without trouble. The sea is a means to an end. In one sense at least it has always remained so.

lasted for some 350 years, based itself on the knight and his horse, both of whom disdained the sea. This assumed superiority of the knight and the soldier over the sailor lasted until the twentieth century. Seafaring became a menial trade suitable only for conveying 'the quality' to the nearest land battlefield across the Channel, for taking wool to Flanders and for bringing back wine from the English possession of Bordeaux.

Indeed even when humble merchant ships were co-opted into the King's service and had the words 'de la Toure' (of the Tower of London) added to their ordinary names – as H.M.S. is today – they were also required to have wooden castles built on them fore and aft, hence the words 'forecastle' and 'aftercastle', for the better housing of the knights, their horses, archers and retainers whilst at sea. Moreover the sailors who worked the ship were kept firmly subordinate to the military supercargo

embarked. This social inferiority, enforced until Drake's circumnavigation of the world in 1577–80, is still reflected in naval ranks today. Able Seaman, Boatswain, Coxswain and Master are Anglo-Saxon lower deck words: Lieutenant, Captain and Admiral – the officer ranks – are French, which was the language of the Court, although Admiral is a corruption of the Arabic Emir al Bahr, the Prince at sea.

To appreciate those distant times, the stark simplicity of everyday existence has to be visualised. People's lives were often, 'nasty, brutish and short' illuminated only by the hope of a better world after death. Hardship blighted every life, differing but little ashore or afloat. Knowledge and skill stood at a premium and those who possessed either or both guarded them as the priceless secrets they were.

However things began gradually changing towards the end of the baronial age. English law sets its memory as starting with the accession of Richard I – Coeur-de-

Lion – in 1189. Magna Carta was to follow a quarter of a century later.

At sea the laws of Oléron became codified into the Black Book of Admiralty. A Charter given by Henry II between 1162 and 1169 established a livery or uniform for the crew of the Esnecca which was a longship, propelled by oar or sail, belonging personally to the King, the twelfth century equivalent of a Royal Yacht. They also allowed twelve pence a day to the Nauclerus or Keeper of the Royal Ships in Hampshire and Devon. Richard Coeur-de-Lion's reign records the first naval appointments, listed variously as 'Leaders and Governors of all the King's Navy', 'Justices of the King's Navy' or 'Leaders and Constables of the King's Ships going to the Holy Land'. Then a century later came the establishment of the offices of 'Admiral of the North' and 'Admiral of the South'. These in turn, yet another ninety years on, were united in 1391 when Edward, Earl of Rutland (not exactly a maritime county) found himself appointed Admiral of England, a post later crystallised into 'Lord High Admiral', the ninth of the nine great officers of state of the Crown. The Navy at that time could not be described as the Senior Service. Yet naval organisation of a sort had begun.

Richard Coeur-de-Lion became the first English king since Alfred to lead a fleet into battle. He also acquired in the island of Cyprus the first English possession overseas. This he achieved during the Third Crusade. Allied somewhat uncomfortably with his erstwhile enemy, Philip Augustus of France, under the overall command of the Emperor Frederick Barbarossa, Richard assembled in Sicily a fleet of 24 busses, 39 galleys and 156 ships of other kinds, a number of which had set sail from England.

In May 1191 this fleet, after rowing on from Sicily, first subdued the Emperor of Cyprus and then, on sighting the Holy Land near Acre, found itself in the presence of a vastly superior ship with three masts, lateen sails and towering sides such as none had seen in northern waters. The English King sent a galley to enquire as to the provenance of this mighty vessel. 'We are a ship of the King of France,' came the reply. But it neither flew a Christian standard nor had the look of a French ship. So the King sent a second galley and this time the ship claimed to be Genoese. Doubts grew on the English side, the matter being firmly settled after the despatch of a third galley which rowed past the great ship without bothering to salute whereupon it was treated to a shower of darts and arrows. Accordingly and without further delay a desperate battle began in which the English, who had previously only fought ships of their own size in northern waters, tried ineffectively to grapple and board, and when this failed at last hit on the ancient idea of ramming at full speed with their iron-tipped beaks.

This proved an instant success. The great Saracen ship, stove-in below the water line, at once started to sink, the reported toll being seven Admirals, a hundred camel loads of slings, bows, arrows and darts, a quantity of the deadly 'Greek fire' in bottles and two hundred 'serpents' which were a kind of primitive firework – all designed to embarrass the Christian forces besieging Acre. The entire Turkish crew drowned or were slain bar fifty-five who were spared 'from no worthier motive than that they would be useful in the construction of military engines'. Acre surrendered and King Richard concluded a treaty with Saladin.

By the time another English king, Edward III, led a fleet into battle in 1340 at Sluys, many developments in ships and seamanship had begun to take place. Once again, though, a decisive battle was fought in enemy as opposed to home waters and once again the importance of at least a temporary control of the local seas proved to be essential before an English army could be landed on the continent of Europe.

The young King's interest in the Navy – and he was to reign for fifty years – had early won for him from Parliament the title 'King of the Sea' and he had then further ventured to assume the title of 'King of France'. This, of course, led to war. Edward III, therefore, needed all the help he could get. As later monarchs discovered to an even greater degree making war requires money and money, in those days, was only forthcoming for such prestige purposes if merchants – and especially the wool staple – saw that there might be profit to be had from supporting the venture.

Edward III had great ambitions which drove him to embark on a sort of reverse Norman conquest of France. This later became known as the Hundred Years War. At the battle of Sluys, where the defending French fleet outnumbered by about three to one the heterogeneous English force of 250 vessels, Edward struck a decisive note in opening up an essential supply line for the invading English army. Although gunpowder is alleged to have been discovered in Europe in 1313 by a German Grey Friar called Berthold Schwarz (the Chinese had perfected it around A.D. 1000) and had been used at sea by Louis de Mâle in an attack on Antwerp in 1336, the battle of Sluys was an archery affair followed by grappling, boarding and hand-to-hand fighting of such ferocity that the French fleet was almost entirely destroyed, King Edward himself in the cog "Thomas" being wounded in the process.

Yet another thread which will weave its way through this story is that of royal concern with the sea in general and the Navy in particular. This, of course, waxed and waned according to the temperament and character of individual monarchs. Early Norman and Plantagenet kings took little direct interest in the Narrow Seas, its pirates and the policing necessary for some semblance of control. In those who were personally subject to seasickness and the lack of dignity this entailed, the royal involvement diminished even more. Edward III, however, saw the importance of the sea and so did his son the Black Prince who was ten when the battle of Sluys took place. Ten years later the heir to the throne and his father were both present at the only other notable sea battle of the reign, that given the engaging name of 'Les Espagnols sur Mer' in 1350.

The battle can be taken as one of the first genuine fleet actions at sea. Edward put out from Dover when a Spanish fleet came down Channel from Flanders impelled by a convenient north-easterly wind. The larger and faster Spanish ships could no doubt have avoided battle but on sighting the interfering English altered course so far as possible to meet them. The result was that the two fleets converged downwind off Winchelsea. Edward had no oared galleys with which to manoeuvre so, displaying his usual impetuosity, he decided to ram. Panache is one thing, a clinker-built cog another and such a vessel was far from ideal for the purpose to which it was put. On impact Edward's cog split in two and was only kept afloat by bailing, a menial task in which he caused even his reluctant knights to join. His son, the Black Prince, followed suit in another ship with even more dismal results. His cog rammed a

SAILING-SHIP GUNNERY

Although guns made in Tournai were aboard ships sent by Louis de Mâle to attack Antwerp in 1336, these were probably small calibre, anti-personnel guns such as the Serpentine. During the next two centuries the Low Countries emerged as the premier source of artillery in Europe and Henry VIII was the first English king to bring Flemish gun makers to England (in 1543).

During the fifteenth and sixteenth centuries muzzle-loading guns in a great variety of types and sizes were manufactured in thousands, initially in bronze but later in cast iron to save costs.

These shipborne guns can be broadly grouped into four classes:

The cannon Of large calibre, medium length and range, subdivided into the 'whole' cannon of approximately 7-inch calibre, 11 ft in length and firing a 50 lb ball and the 'demi-cannon' of much the same length but of 6-inch calibre and firing a 32 lb shot. Approximate range 1,700 yards

The culverin Of smaller calibre in relation to its length and therefore having a greater range, varying from the 5-inch culverin proper firing a 17 lb shot, via the demi-culverin, the saker and the minion to the falconet which delivered a 1 to 2 lb shot. Full culverin range about 2,500 yds

The perier or cannonperier Which fired a medium-sized stone for a comparatively short distance from a short barrel. A typical one would have been 8-inch calibre, 5 ft long and capable of firing a 24 lb stone 1,600 yards

The mortar An even shorter gun of conical bore which fired quantities of small pieces of iron, stone or bullets to deter would-be boarders on an enemy deck

A steady improvement in the quality and strength of gunpowder, its quicker combustion and an increasing accuracy in the guns themselves permitted smaller charges to be used and the length of barrel reduced, the guns being mounted on low wooden wheeled carriages firing through gunports cut into the ship's sides as in the galleon. This brought in a new feature of naval warfare – the long range broadside – the effectiveness of which was first demonstrated in the defeat of the Spanish Armada in 1588.

Except for the carronade which used a small propellant to fire a relatively heavy shot for a limited range, naval guns changed very little until the industrial revolution, although refinements were made in absorbing the recoil and the flint-lock was introduced in place of the slowmatch and linstock.

This carronade of about 1828 marks the high point of muzzle-loading weaponry. Its wheeled carriage allows for recoil, which will be taken up by the various restraining devices (these also prevent it running amok in stormy weather). A kind of slip hook allows it to be rolled back for swabbing out and reloading.

Spanish ship and promptly sank. However, before this happened, his stalwart men did succeed in boarding the Spaniard, throwing the crew overboard and capturing the ship.

Except for the royal presence this action differed little from that of common piracy at which the English became adept and for which they were vilified in medieval Europe. Of course piracy and the more technically respectable privateering had existed virtually ever since man first put to sea. Indeed medieval nautical history is from one point of view, little more than a running tally of brigandage afloat. There was, however, one positive quality in piracy which gave a continuing incentive to both seamen and shipbuilders and that was the simple fact that to survive a pirate had to be more skilled and his ship faster and more manoeuvrable than his victim. The paradox, therefore, is that although piracy undoubtedly scourged the cross-Channel

trade of the Middle Ages, it also played no small part in improving the quality of English seamanship.

One of the most notable events in the reign of Edward III was his capture of Calais in 1347 after nearly a year's siege. This did not end the 'curse of the Channel' caused by pirates and privateers, it did however put both sides of the straits of Dover into English hands for over two centuries and the wool staple, on which England's prosperity so greatly depended, was finally fixed in Calais as the port of access to France and the Flemish weavers. Indeed the London-Calais merchants, with whom the King had to bargain for loans and levies as if with a fourth estate of the realm, became the great breeders of English capitalism. This followed the expulsion of the Jews in 1290 and the subsequent exclusion of the Florentines who replaced them and it brought into being a new race of war financiers, commercial speculators, army

'Carrack' was originally a description of ships of Spanish or Genoan origin calling at English ports. In its earliest days in the Mediterranean the carrack was a two-masted ship, with one square sail on the mainmast and a smaller sail on a mizen stepped well aft, fairly bluff in the bows with a rounded stern ending in a square counter. In the Mediterranean her hull was carvel-built (planks fixed edge-to-edge) whereas north European carracks still retained clinker construction.

purveyors and wool monopolists. To this day the Lord Chancellor sits upon a woolsack in the House of Lords as a reminder of the importance of the wool industry, the woolsack first being placed there in the reign of Edward III.

The English have always had an ambivalent attitude to piracy and privateering. The last pirate was executed in England in 1840 and privateering was not abolished officially until the Declaration of Paris in 1856. It is not hard to see why. Piracy is defined as the act of taking a ship on the high seas from the possession or control of those lawfully entitled to it. But all maritime nations have their own codes of law at sea. There were no internationally accepted standards until recent years and certainly none in medieval times except when individual kings made treaties with each other which never lasted long.

Before regular navies came into being who was then to interpret legality, the more so since merchant ships and their cargoes rarely belonged to the crews sailing them, unless they were very small? Moreover such crews in the Middle Ages were rarely prepared to defend their ships at the expense of their lives. They surrendered and hoped for the best. Some pirates, such as Chaucer's Shipman, did of course take the easy path of chucking their victims into the sea to drown. 'Of nice conscience took he no keepe, If that he faught and hadde the hier hond, By water he sente him hoom to every lond.' Most, however, took the crews prisoner and later negotiated a ransom.

Until the concept of sea power began to come into focus in Tudor times, piracy in the English Channel was seen by the common run of Englishmen as something of a sport. In 1399, for instance, John Hawley brought 1500 tuns of claret into Dartmouth in which port it was said 'the streets ran red with it'.

Such piracy was indulged in as an open secret not only by ruffians but also by conniving citizens of repute. Fighting for King and Country was one thing and no brave man would shirk that responsibility. On the other hand helping yourself to the King's property or perquisites or to those of the rich Guilds of London could be seen as a fair gamble.

This sporting conspiracy provided a new and refreshing alternative to the somewhat dated pursuits of medieval chivalry. Aristocrats, gentry and common folk alike began indulging a personal interest in the sea, correctly sensing at least one way in which their lives could be enriched. Indeed it was not until the sixteenth century, when English home waters were effectively policed by the Navy of Henry VIII, that piracy started to lose the glamour it was never to regain except briefly a century or so later in the Caribbean when the 'brethren of the coast' harassed the Spanish main and gave rise to the 'Treasure Island' armchair image which Robert Louis Stevenson created in the nineteenth century and which even now grips the imagination of both young and old. Drake in the Pacific was another matter. So are the pirates of the South China Seas today as those Vietnamese 'boat people' who have survived are well able to declare.

Seapower and the trade it protects both depend primarily on ships and the men who work them, though seapower even in its most elementary form could scarcely be said to have existed in the Middle Ages. So what did go on? Specific warships apart, what kind of ships sailed the medieval seas? The simple answer, of course, is a large variety of types and sizes conditioned by medieval trade requirements and the waters in which ships had to operate. Everyday ocean or trans-ocean sailing had yet to occur and in the early days in northern Europe there was no general purpose 'world type' of vessel such as the Arab dhow or the Chinese junk. Moreover conditions in the enclosed Mediterranean differed to a degree from those obtaining in the more demanding Baltic, Bay of Biscay, English Channel and North Sea. The fast and flexible lateen rigged Phoenician and Arab ships of the Mediterranean could not stand up against harsh northern storms or at any rate were less suitable for the great open oceans than the square-sailed Hanseatic cogs. The Mediterranean-trained Columbus on his first epic voyage west into the Atlantic set out with two of his ships, the "Santa Maria" and the "Pinta" rigged as caravelas redondas i.e. with a square sail on the main mast. These were so obviously more efficient that he caused the third and smallest "Nina" (of about 50 tons burthen) to be rerigged in the same way before leaving the Canaries.

During the six hundred years which elapsed between the reigns of Alfred and Henry VII, kings and the countries they controlled made almost continuous war on each other and, in an occasional and intermittent banding together, on the infidel Turk. The profligate expense this caused could only be met from the profits of trade. Wars could and did bankrupt those who made them, but no country, as Benjamin Franklin observed in the eighteenth century, has ever been ruined by trade.

In medieval times such prosperity as there was in north-western Europe depended in the main upon the merchant venturers of the Hanseatic League, a confederation of North German ports dating from about 1240, and on their counterparts in Amsterdam and London. Apart from the flat-bottomed barges and sluyts in which the Dutch specialised, it was the cog 'short, of great breadth and like a cockleshell' which from the thirteenth century on carried the maritime trade of northern Europe. Sturdy and capacious, their tonnage set by the number of barrels or tuns they could carry, they were in no way built for speed – a factor which only became of importance in the nineteenth century – but they could and did stand up against vile North Sea weather, served all purposes of trade and could easily be adapted to carry soldiers and archers in a war emergency. The helmsman or swain in charge of such a boat became known as the cog's swain or coxswain of today.

A little later the 'carrack' came on the scene. This started as the description of a Spanish or Genoan ship calling at English ports but later was applied to any ship of large size used as a trader. In the fishing department the 'dogger' came into being. This took its name from the Dutch word for a cod-fishing boat operating in that area of the North Sea soon to be called the 'Dogger Bank'.

After the thirteenth century trade both in the Mediterranean and in north-western seas began to be dominated by Venice, whose merchants called the tune and which became the chief maritime power in Europe. This supremacy lasted until the fall of Constantinople and the Byzantine empire to the Turks in 1453. The practical result of this disaster was that the spice route from the east was cut, though spices were essential to the preserving of meat for winter use in Europe. Coincidental with this event came the astronomical and mathematical researches and their application to navigation carried out at Sagres on the south-western tip of Portugal by Henry the

This model of a cog of about 1450 shows that they were, indeed, 'short and of great breadth, like a cockleshell, whence they are said to have derived their name'. Unlike the Hansa cog, the English ship had the traditional curved stem with the three castles at bow, stern and masthead. Designed as a sturdy and capacious merchant ship, the cog was frequently called up for war in an emergency and at this period formed the major constituent of a fleet.

Navigator. This extraordinary Prince, and the unique team he assembled, inspired and patronised the discovery of the Atlantic Islands, the West Coast of Africa and, later on, the Cape of Good Hope and the sea route to India.

The great age of exploration, initially dominated by Spaniards and Portuguese, opened up the world from the second half of the fifteenth century. These navigational feats were mainly achieved in caravels. The focus of progress at that time was on the Mediterranean heartland. England and the other countries of north-west Europe lagged behind in this great sea renaissance deriving from the rediscovery of ancient knowledge such as Ptolemy's 'Geographia'.

Northern seafarers, however, did adopt 'modern' practical aids to seamanship and navigation. These included the rudder in place of the steerboard, rutters or sailing directions for coastal pilotage (from the French word 'routier'), Portolan charts when they could be obtained and above all the compass which evolved from the lodestone or piece of magnetic iron ore on which in the early days a needle was rubbed and then stuck in a cork to be floated on a bowl of water. This needle would then point to the north as a guide for use in fog or when the Pole Star could not be seen. Pivoting needles on cards were in use in northern Europe at the end of the fourteenth century, vide Chaucer who mentions them obliquely in a treatise of 1391. Use of the compass, however, took some time to be accepted by practical Anglo-Saxon seamen as it was thought to smack of magic. Some infernal spirit had control of it, they thought, and the lodestone could better be employed for the cure of gout or the bringing of pressure to bear on wives to confess their infidelities.

This long overture to the story of the Royal Navy – not yet Royal and scarcely a Navy despite the continuing appointment of a Lord High Admiral – ends with the Wars of the Roses and the advent of the Tudors. The main theme has yet to declare itself. French-speaking overlords who had taken possession of the land in the wake of the Norman conqueror had had little use for the sea.

There were no great sailors at Court and although, as Churchill puts it 'a gleam of splendour falls across the dark, troubled story of medieval England' in the crowning of Henry V at the age of twenty-six in 1413 (he was the first King to write home in English which he did from the battlefield of Agincourt), it was not until 1436, fourteen years after Henry V had died, that Adam de Moleyns, the Bishop of Chichester, first expounded the doctrine of seapower in a privately circulated work in Latin called *De Politia Conservita Maris* and he, poor man, met his death ironically enough at the hands of sailors rioting for their pay.

De Moleyns exhorted the English to 'keep the sea . . . shewing what profit cometh thereof, and also (since he was a churchman) what worship and salvation'. No one paid attention and it was not until the following century when Hakluyt and Purchas were setting the country alight with new adventures and nautical ideas that 'the necessity of maintaining the sovereignty of the seas, whereof the peace, plenty and prosperity of the island depends' came to be understood and two more centuries were to elapse before those unfamiliar words were to find their way into the preamble of the Naval Discipline Act.

CHAPTER II

THE TUDORS

1485–1603

CHRONOLOGICAL COMPENDIUM

The Reigns and their character

Henry VII Slow establishment of Tudor dynasty and recovery from Wars of the Roses.
1485–1509

Henry VIII Expansion. The Reformation and the break with Rome.
1509–1547

Edward VI Protestant minority rule.
1547–1553

Mary Return to Catholicism.
1553–1558

Elizabeth I Expansion, establishment of the Protestant ethic, overseas development, wars with Catholic
1558–1603 Spain.

General

Throughout this period France remained the main enemy. The Tudor monarchs' overriding concern was to preserve the northern coastline of Europe, including Flanders, from overbearing French influence. The rise of Spain acted as an effective counterbalance to this growing French power. Only when the focus of the French/Spanish rivalry moved from north Italy to the Netherlands during Elizabeth's reign, did the invasion of England become a real threat.

Both Henry VII and his grand-daughter Elizabeth were 'good housekeepers'. They were also aware of the country's vulnerability and sought to avoid continental involvements. Henry VIII, on the other hand, was determined to assert English strength.

Henry VII set about putting his own house in order both financially and administratively. He left a full treasury and a country at peace. Henry VIII's aggressive foreign policy once more depleted the coffers. Meanwhile Parliament, as the greatest legislative body, slowly established and improved its position during the Tudor regimes and in particular after Henry VIII's reliance on parliamentary authority for his break with Rome and his establishment of the Church of England.

Naval

This was the great age of discovery and the beginning of world expansion. The oceans of the world came to be known and used, which also entailed an elementary understanding of seapower.

The discovery of the New World made Spain and Portugal the richest countries in Europe and the intense rivalry between Catholic Spain, Portugal and France on the one hand and the Protestant nations such as England and Holland on the other resulted in intermittent and frequent hostilities. These conflicts were fired both by religion and by a lust for gold. As the age proceeded, the Catholic kings, urged on by the Pope, determined to use their growing power to re-establish the Catholic faith in Britain and the Netherlands. This warfare came to a climax with the attempted invasion of England by the Spanish Armada in 1588 and its decisive defeat which marked the beginning of English supremacy at sea.

Ships and the guns they carried grew in size and range and great ocean-going ships were built by all the principal maritime nations. Some ships were now specifically built for war. Navigational knowledge and the cartography (mainly Dutch) on which it relied increased as exploration continued. There was also a growing national interest in seafaring and the sea, the national imagination being set alight by Hakluyt, Purchas and Shakespeare. The first dockyards were built at Portsmouth, Plymouth and in the Thames. Trinity House was inaugurated by Henry VIII to develop navigational aids such as lighthouses, buoys and beacons. The use of privateers and letters of marque grew apace and at the end of the era the great overseas trading companies such as the Muscovy Company and the East India Company came into being. Drake established the supreme authority of the captain at sea (as opposed to any knights or soldiers borne for fighting) and was the first Englishman to circumnavigate the world, being also captain of the ship he owned.

Organisation

1509–1547 The three Royal Dockyards – Chatham, Portsmouth and Plymouth – established. Navy Board (including Victualling Board at Deptford) established by Henry VIII, the original Commissioners being Lieutenant of the Admiralty, Treasurer, Comptroller, Surveyor, Master of the Ordnance and Clerk of the Ships – all being under the Lord High Admiral. Trinity House founded 1517 in the Deptford parish of St Clement 'for the relief, increase and augmentation of the shipping of this our realm of England' responsible for lighthouses, lightships, buoys and other seamarks and also for the licensing of pilots.

1547–1603 Hawkins as Treasurer and Comptroller of the Navy develops the 'low-charged' ship (which could sail closer to the wind), improved pay and conditions and established the Chatham Chest in 1590 into which seaman paid sixpence a month for the benefit of the wounded and the widows of those killed in action.
As yet there were no regular officers or men in the naval service.

Ships and Guns

16th century Multi-decked warships of over 1,000 tons being built with gunports (the "Mary Rose" being swamped through her gun ports sank off Portsmouth in action against the French and in the sight of Henry VIII in 1545).
Cast iron replaces bronze (too expensive) for guns classified into four basic types:
Cannon – 'Whole' 7-inch calibre, 11 ft length, 50 lb ball.
– 'Demi-Cannon' 6-inch calibre, 11 ft and 32 lb shot.
Culverin – smaller calibre/length and longer range.
Perier – short barrelled for short distance with medium-sized stone, 8-inch calibre, 5 ft length, 24 lb shot – max. range 1,600 yds.
Mortar – even shorter and originally conically bored. Shot comprised small pieces of iron, stone often in bags. Used against enemy decks and boarders.
Early Tudor guns were mounted on timber scaffolds or on two and four wheel high carriages. Later small wooden wheels or trucks.
The Galleon with sides pierced for gunports led to new form of naval warfare relying on broadsides, effectiveness proved at Armada. "Henry Grâce à Dieu" ("Great Harry") largest warship in world launched Erith 1514. Accidentally burnt 1553, 21 heavy guns, 231 light weapons and carried a complement of 700 men.

Navigation and Cartography

1483 Pierre Garcie *Le Grand Routier et Pilotage* for west coast of France.

1521 First printed Routier – woodcut views and information on tides.

1541 Richard Proude *New Rutter of the Sea for the Northern Partes*.

16th century Buoys come into use in European waters. 1538 First buoys in Thames. Anyone destroying seamarks on land fined £100 or outlawed.

Lightships begin to be used on shoals or banks where the building of a lighthouse impracticable.

Beacons (stakes or erections on shore) come into use. News of the Armada's arrival off Plymouth signalled by means of lighting beacons and the news went from Plymouth to London to York in twelve hours.

Astrolabe or Armillary Sphere comes into use and was supplied to Frobisher for his first expedition to discover the North-West Passage. Purchas claims Martin Behaim was first person to use Majorcan astrolabe.

1538 Mercator (1512–1594) much influenced by Ptolemy produces first map in two spheres.

1551 Mercator's Celestial Globe.

1584 Wagenaer (1534–1605) – *Pilot Book Zuiderzee to Cadiz* translated into English by Anthony Ashley.

1569 Mercator first projection of world in 18 sheets.

1570 Ortelius (1527–98) – *Theatrum Orbis Terrarum* – 53 maps – Antwerp goes into 25 editions.

1594 Hondius (1563–1611) comes to London and illustrates Drake's circumnavigation of world.

People and Events

1482–6 Diogo Cam first European to explore mouth of Congo River and south to Walvis Bay.

1487 Diaz (1455–1500) discovers Cabo Tormentose, later renamed Cape of Good Hope.

1492 Columbus (1451–1506) makes landfall at San Salvador, Bahamas.

1493 Pope Alexander VI divides world between Spain and Portugal on north/south line 370 leagues west from Cape Verde. All to the west to be Spanish: all to the east Portuguese (Treaty of Tordesillas).

1493–5 Columbus makes second voyage to Americas.

1497 Cabot (1450–98) discovers Newfoundland and Grand Banks cod fisheries.
Vasco da Gama (1460–1524) rounds Cape of Good Hope and reaches Malabar coast (1498).

1498 Cabot makes second voyage to north America and never returns. Columbus third voyage to Americas.

1499 Pinzon discovers Brazil with Cabral (1467–1530) by accidentally sailing too far west in Atlantic en route to India.

1504 Columbus fourth voyage to Americas.

1520 Magellan (1480–1521) discovers Magellan Strait and Pacific, continues on to Philippines where he is murdered. Voyage continued by Juan Sebastian del Camo and becomes first circumnavigation of world. Only contemporary account written by Antonio Pigafetta (1519–22).

1523–4 Verrazzano (1485–1528) discovers east coast of north America. 'America' named after Amerigo Vespucci (1451–1512) whose self-generated claims to have been first person to discover America are now doubted.

1536 Alvaro Nuñez Cabeza de Vaca (1490–1564) discovers Mississippi and Mexico City.

1544 Cartier (1491–1557) discovers St Lawrence in attempt to discover N.W. Passage.

1553–6 Willoughby (d. 1554), Chancellor (d. 1556) and Borough (1525–84) make two voyages to White Sea in search of North-East Passage, visiting Ivan the Terrible in Moscow (1554 Siberia discovered) and start Muscovy Company. Borough was first Englishman to sight the North Cape.

1562 Hawkins (1532–95) of Plymouth and cousin of Drake makes first voyage to Hispaniola (Haiti) via West Africa for slaves.

1567	Drake (1543–96) together with Hawkins makes 'triangular' voyage to Hispaniola via West Africa and is nearly slaughtered through Spanish treachery at San Juan de Ulloa. Thereafter privateers and in 1572 crosses Isthmus of Panama and sights Pacific.
1577	Hawkins succeeds Gonson as Treasurer of the Navy and becomes responsible for designing and building new ships to replace those inherited by Elizabeth from Henry VIII.
1577–80	Drake, backed by Elizabeth, circumnavigates the world returning with plunder worth over half a million pounds in the currency of the day. Is knighted by Elizabeth who thenceforth calls him 'her pirate'.
1585–7	Davis (1550–1605) makes three voyages to try to discover North-West Passage via Greenland. Also Frobisher (1535–94).
1578–83	Raleigh (1552–1618) and Gilbert (1539–1583) set up first British colony in North America and St Johns, Newfoundland.
1587	Drake 'singes King of Spain's beard' at Cadiz and delays sailing of Armada by a year.
1588	Drake and Hawkins serving under Lord Howard of Effingham defeat the Armada.
1591–4	Lancaster (1555–1618) makes three important voyages to Achin, Sumatra and Pernambuco and in 1601–3 commands first East Indian expedition of five ships to Achin to set up factory and trading post.
1598	Adams (d. 1620) sails with five ships Texel to India via Straits of Magellan. Adams's own ship was sole survivor of this and reached Kyushu, Japan where he was kept by the Shogun, being given a wife and an estate.

Battles

1545	French try to take command of Channel by sending a fleet into the Solent ("Mary Rose" sinks). Skirmish off Shoreham and French then retire.
1558	Gravelines. English fleet helps Flemings defeat Spaniards. Lord Clinton's expedition to burn Conquet in Brittany.
1562	Expedition to occupy Le Havre in support of Huguenots.
1568	San Juan de Ulloa.
1585–6	Vigo and St. Domingo in West Indies attacked by Drake.
1587	Cadiz – Drake sacks the port.
1588	Armada.
1589	Corunna. Drake and Norris try to take Portugal with 150 ships and 180,000 men. They sack Corunna but fail to take Lisbon.
1590	Drake, Hawkins and Frobisher make indecisive expedition to Spanish coast.
1591	Azores. Spaniards capture the "Revenge" and Grenville is mortally wounded.
1592	Burrows captures Portuguese galleon with £850,000 at Flores.
1594	Anglo-French force recaptures Brest from Spaniards but Frobisher mortally wounded.
1596	Howard of Effingham and Essex sack Cadiz and prevent another Armada being sent against England.
1597	Essex and Raleigh capture Fayal in Azores but otherwise fail.

The Tudors were the real founders of the English Navy. During the century and a bit which included the accession of Henry VII in 1485, the defeat of the Spanish Armada in 1588 and the death of Elizabeth I in 1603, the known world became transformed out of all recognition. This process also involved changes in the European balance of power, in the ships which now began to venture across great oceans, in the cartographic and navigational knowledge which enabled them to undertake breath-taking explorations including two circumnavigations of the world (Magellan and Drake), and indeed in the very dimensions of the world itself which turned out to be considerably larger than had previously been thought.

So far as everyday European life was concerned, the pattern of trade on which in the end all else depends suffered a basic shift from Venice, Genoa and the Mediterranean ports to the Atlantic states of north-west Europe.

Pope Alexander VI, a Spanish Borgia notorious amongst other things for the scandalous orgies of his papal court, divided the discovered and discoverable world between Spain and Portugal east and west down a mid Atlantic line[1], a notion which the Protestant English and Dutch were, over many years, at some pains to correct.

Henry VII built the first dry dock at Portsmouth in 1495/7 and his son inaugurated Trinity House in 1514. Henry VIII inherited a Navy of 7 warships which he increased by another 24 in the early years of his reign and set up a Navy Board to service them in 1546 which was to continue more or less unchanged for 300 years. At the start of the Tudor era the rate of pay for a seaman took an upward leap of eighteen pence a month to six shillings and eight pence and by the time Queen Elizabeth died had reached a dizzy ten shillings a month but only in periods of national emergency. Meanwhile Drake, on his return in 1580 after circumnavigating the world and plundering the Spanish plunderers, had been able to send to the Tower treasure worth half a million pounds in the currency of the day. This neatly paid off the entire national debt, Drake himself being rewarded with £10,000 and a knighthood. If we set our story as beginning with Alfred, the next great advance, therefore, took place in the reigns of Henry VII, Henry VIII and Elizabeth I.

In Tudor times the country which later became known as the mother of Parliaments and also as 'a nation of shopkeepers' began to exhibit a flowering of energy and of qualities which created the specifically English way of life we know today.

Comparatively speaking ordinary Englishmen became freer under the Crown and the Law than the inhabitants of any other country in the world. Perhaps this is an overstatement given that all social freedom is and always has been limited and circumscribed. But this burgeoning sixteenth century freedom in England, illuminated by Shakespeare, does stand as a separate and noticeable fact. This derived from the accident of our 'scepter'd isle' being isolated from a warring continent. It was also helped by our growing domination of the great oceans upon which ever since the British have come to rely. A mere three decades after Gloriana's death the Lord Keeper of the Seal was declaring that 'the dominion of the sea, as it is an undoubted *right* of the Crown of England (my italics) so is it the best security of the land. The wooden walls are the best walls of this kingdom.'[2] This could not have been claimed when Henry VII came to the throne in 1485 after twenty-five turbulent years of the Wars of the Roses.

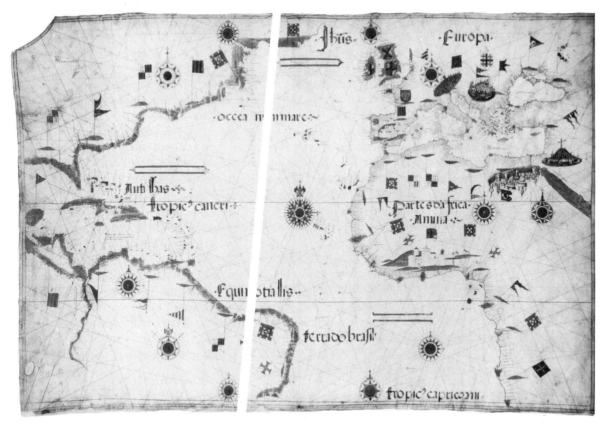

In 1485 England lay crippled in chaos. Henry's title to the throne remained shaky and disputed. He had seized power by conquest and relied only in a secondary sense on the approbation of Parliament. In the early years, therefore, his every day was beset by uncertainty and threat. Moreover his realm was virtually bankrupt.

At such times the first task of a monarch is to unite his country, heal its wounds and, if possible, give it a period of settled government. This Henry did, marrying Elizabeth of York and thus combining the white and red roses of York and Lancaster. Henry VII has been adjudged by later historians as a despot but he governed effectively and by general consent. He had a firm touch. Undoubtedly proud and determined, he was also restrained, calculating and cautious. Though shattered by the death of his elder son, Arthur, as a young man, another son remained to him and this heir became perhaps the most famous King in English history – Henry VIII.

During the sixty-two years covered by the reigns of Henry VII and Henry VIII – from 1485 to 1547 – the enduring and essential structure of the Navy came into being. Father and son differed, however, in the way they regarded the Navy's composition. Henry VII's sense of economy which enabled him to leave a full treasury to his expansive son, drove him to concentrate on building a merchant fleet. Henry VII 'could not endure to see trade sick'. This idea met a happy conjuncture in that trade and world exploration were about to take giant strides in growth. He saw

On this Portuguese chart of the North Atlantic, the 'Tordesillas Line' has been superimposed. This 1494 Treaty, the result of a 1493 Bull by the Spanish Pope Alexander VI, gave Spain exclusive rights on lands discovered or discoverable, west of a north-south line 370 leagues west of the Cape Verde islands, all to the east being Portuguese. Portugal thus established claim to the so far undiscovered Brazil. However the Treaty was never accepted by the other Atlantic powers.

to it, therefore, that his seven royal ships, although designed for war, could also be chartered out to merchants for trade.

These ships included the four masted "Regent" which in 1486 was the largest vessel yet built in England. Henry VIII improved on this in the first years of his reign by constructing the "Henri Grâce à Dieu" popularly dubbed the "Great Harry" which, displacing about 1,000 tons, was huge by any previous standard and included an innovation to be embodied in warships for the next 400 years. This was the heavy gun.

Hitherto warships with their mountainous fore and after castles had been designed for medieval archers, for grappling and for the hand to hand fighting which followed. Any naval guns on board were comparatively light breech-loaders. From now on the entire technique of warfare at sea began to change. This required time, care and much experiment. Henry VIII had, in Sussex, the best gun founders in Europe. However, the new heavy guns they made needed, because of their weight, to be mounted on the lower decks so that they could be fired through ports cut into the ship's sides.

Stability thus became a problem which took a lot of resolving. Forty years later when the "Mary Rose" sank a few hundred yards off Southsea Castle under the beady eyes of the King, it had still not been resolved and the explanation of this particular but ever possible disaster yet awaits the scrutiny of experts now the ship has been raised from the Solent mud where it had lain for over 400 years.

A further difficulty consisted of the fact that it was tricky if not impossible to secure the breech of a heavy gun against the premature ignition of a charge of powder, resulting in the blowing up of the gun and its crew rather than in the annoying of an enemy. Hence began an era of muzzle-loaded heavy armament which continued until after Trafalgar.

Meanwhile the world in which these ships would be used was changing at the rate of knots. When the pirates of the English Channel and North Sea had to be cleaned out during the reign of Henry VIII, it was clear that his great warships, soon to be known as ships of the line, were unsuitable for the purpose. But the small revenue cutters actually employed for this cleansing purpose were doubly effective because now for the first time there stood behind them the might of the King's ships which made the sheltering of pirates by unco-operative authorities and ports no longer the simple evasive action it had once been.

This was an early instance of what was later to become a staple of seapower – the threat of the 'fleet in being'. The peace of the world today depends upon the nuclear deterrent. Scaled down to the conditions of Elizabethan times, the Royal Navy now entered the world scene as the deterrent to irresponsible behaviour which it has been ever since. Throughout the sixteenth century, the fear of provoking reprisals on an incalculable scale began to inhibit unwise or incautious action. Control of the sea was now what mattered. Aggressive foreign powers and their mariners began to think twice before embarking on a course of action which might well provoke a disproportionate result.

Elizabethan England, several times smaller than mighty Spain, lay under a very present threat of invasion which only the defeat of the Armada in 1588 resolved.

This threat recurred in the Napoleonic war and in the Second World War. In neither case could the threat be countered without control of the sea. The Tudors first thought out the implications of this principle for themselves. They then applied it to advantage, Drake being the first English seaman not only to establish for all time that the Captain of a ship is the King afloat but also that the right place to fight a naval action is not off your own but off an enemy's coast. 'Others may use the ocean as their road, only the English make it their abode: Our oaks secure as if they there took root, we tread on billows with a steady foot.'[3] That steady maritime foot first began its tread in the ebullient hustle of Tudor England.

'This fortress built by Nature for herself . . . this precious stone set in the silve. sea' was, however, a late starter in the exploration stakes. The great opening-up of the world which took place in the century following the fall of Constantinople to the Ottoman Turks in 1453 stemmed from the inspiration and patronage of Henry the Navigator. He made exploration both popular and profitable. This was no easy task. Sagres in the Algarve became the Cape Canaveral of the fifteenth century. The superstitious seamen on whom Henry worked might agree that the earth was probably round but to begin with none would dare to cross the Equator southwards since it was well known that this was where the sea boiled and the caulking in a ship's deck would melt.

Eventually wiser counsels or perhaps greed and avarice won the day. By virtually bribing his Captains to venture a little further on each successful voyage, Henry's enthusiasm pushed back the frontiers of the known world first to Madeira and the Azores, then to Guinea and Senegal and finally, after rounding Cape Verde, to Sierra Leone in 1446. These hardy seamen went initially for gold and for God. They came back with slaves, manpower being an instantly marketable commodity at that time.

The resplendent early voyages of world exploration were all made by Spaniards or Portuguese or by Genoese who had adopted Iberian nationality. The French, the English and the Dutch came in at a later date. The key to this lay in the accidental discovery of the Americas, the existence of which, until Christopher Columbus, had not even been suspected. Indeed Columbus died in 1506 still firmly convinced that he had discovered the eastern seaboard of Cipangu or Japan. This was because, on the information at his disposal, he took the world to be very much smaller than it was.

He assumed that the distance from the Canary Islands to Japan was some 2,400 nautical miles. In fact it is 10,600 and the Cipangu he thought he had reached was in reality the Bahamian island of Guahaní which he named San Salvador.

Columbus was a proud, obstinate and arthritic man who considered himself directly under the Almighty's guidance. He could not, therefore, err. Indeed, even after his second and third voyages, when he ranged the entire Caribbean and charted the north-east coast of South America, he saw no reason to change his belief. Yet he had met no Chinese or Japanese potentates: he had not converted more than a handful of the heathen natives he had encountered – who seemed to be strangely un-Asiatic in appearance – and he died discredited without the honours on which he had insisted. However he had, as he stated in a famous letter, 'by Divine will placed under the sovereignty of the King and Queen an Other World whereby Spain, which

Prince Henry (the Navigator), a grandson of England's John of Gaunt established an arsenal at Sagres in the Algarve of which he was Governor for the last twenty-two years of his life (1394–1460). Here he attracted Arab, Jewish and other mathematicians to teach navigation, astronomy and cartography to his captains and pilots. An ardent student of geography, he established the first observatory in Portugal. Voyages inspired by Prince Henry discovered the Madeira group in 1420 and the Azores in 1427. Prince Henry made exploration profitable and popular. In 1434 Gil Eannes first rounded Cape Bojador: in 1442 Nuno Tristam passed Cape Blanco and between 1444 and 1446 Guinea, Senegal and Cape Verde were reached.

EARLY NAVIGATION

The earliest navigation in the western world was purely coastal. For several thousands of years after man first ventured to sea, seamen had no aids to navigation to help them. If blown out to sea by a storm or lost in a fog, they were helpless until next sighting the coast.

The lead line and sounding rod for measuring the depth of the water came into use about 2,500 B.C. This was the only artificial aid to coastal navigation until the Phoenicians invented the Wind-Rose or Wind-Star which served as the compass of early seamen until the introduction of the magnetic needle.

It is assumed that Mediterranean seafarers could identify winds by their characteristics of temperature, moisture content, etc. (the southern winds would often carry sand from the north African deserts) and by linking them with the sun, moon and stars. The wind-rose, however, would have been of little use in northern waters, where the seas were more open and the wind patterns less easy to pick out.

In the late thirteenth or early fourteenth century A.D., the first mariners' compasses were composed of a needle of soft iron which had been magnetised by a lodestone, floating in a bowl of water on a reed or small block of wood.

However, the real value of the compass to the inshore mariner became apparent when the first coastal charts (the Portolano in the Mediterranean and the Rutter in northern waters) were made. The Rutter was, in effect, a picture of coastal landmarks, harbours, anchorages, etc. as they would appear to a mariner sailing the coast. The Rutter also gave him distances, bearings and certain sailing directions such as depth of water, tidal streams and whether the seabed was suitable as holding ground for anchoring.

Navigational knowledge was then extended by the Portolano which, in the course of the 15th century and spurred on by Prince Henry the Navigator of Portugal, began to develop into the sort of chart used today.

From about the beginning of the fifteenth century new navigational aids were invented such as the back-staff, cross-staff, astrolabe and later the quadrant and sextant. More important to the coastal navigator, however, was the fostering of land and seamarks such as lighthouses, beacons, buoys and lightships. By continually taking cross-bearings of objects ashore, the coastal navigator became able to get a positional fix on almost every known coast.

This Portolan Chart of Weymouth and Portland Bill is well on the way to looking like a modern chart. A compass rose gives direction and there is a proper measurement scale. Only the various ships and creatures relate it to the fanciful and almost entirely decorative efforts of preceding centuries.

was reckoned poor, is become the richest of countries'. This was no less than the truth, and the news went round Europe at the speed of a fast horse.

The discovery of the Americas happened in the autumn of 1492, but it had taken Columbus 'a terrible, continued, painful and prolonged battle' lasting ten years to get his enterprise launched. Venture capital was no easier to come by in the fifteenth than it is in the twentieth century, its procurement then being entirely dependent on the whim of kings and of the hard-headed merchants on whom every court in Europe relied.

In 1489 Columbus had sent his brother Bartholomew to England to ask Henry VII for backing but en route he had been robbed by pirates. Arriving sick and destitute, Bartholomew considered himself to be in too poor a shape for the hard bargaining he knew would be necessary. So he delayed for what turned out to be an

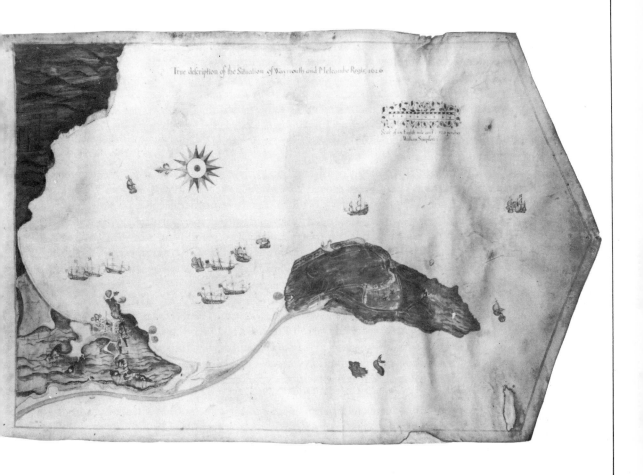

True description of the Situation of Waymouth and Melcombe Regis, 1616

unconscionable time until he had worked and made some money in order to be 'gotten somewhat handsome about him' before propositioning the King with a map of the world dedicated in Latin verse. Despite the King's acceptance of this 'with joyful countenance' and despite Bartholomew sending for brother Christopher to come to England at once, it was all too late. Queen Isabella of Spain had provided the backing required for the original expedition.

However another Genoese with similar ideas had settled in Bristol and as soon as the news of Christopher Columbus's success reached England in 1493, John Cabot planned an expedition of his own. In 1496 he petitioned the King for Letters Patent for the Discovery of New Lands. These were promptly granted. In May 1497 the first English transoceanic voyage of pure discovery set sail from Bristol making a landfall, it is thought, at Cape Breton in Nova Scotia.

What were the factors which gave this sixteenth century its particular distinction?

Firstly the fact that the population of Europe was rising. So, too, was its trade. Art, thought and science began to flourish not only in the Mediterranean states where they were cradled but all over Europe where strong secular monarchies allowed men to render unto Caesar the things which were Caesar's leaving both the decayed and reformed churches to render unto God the things which were God's.

Crucial advances in shipbuilding, navigation and weaponry enabled seapower to establish itself and fostered the growth of European influence all over the world. The latter part of the preceding century had seen rapid changes in the design of European seagoing ships without which the later extended ocean voyages would not have been possible. Of course it was not all 'plain sailing' – the teredo worm for ships and scurvy for men saw to that.

The size and reliability of ships increased. So also did their complexity. Mathematical navigation based on the quadrant, astrolabe, cross-staff and new tables for astronomical calculation, together with the magnetic compass, pilot books and marine charts, permitted the trans-oceanic mariner to calculate his latitude with fair accuracy. Longitude was another matter. The solution of that still lay nearly three centuries ahead with the invention of Harrison's chronometers. As knowledge increased so too did the making of more exact maps of the world in which the Dutch Ortelius and Mercator stand pre-eminent.

In England the royal initiative of Henry VII, Henry VIII and Elizabeth I, as dynamic as that of Prince Henry the Navigator in Portugal, created the ships and attracted the manpower on which English seapower was in future to rely. The ships were built by a new race of master shipwrights. Their design and construction were kept as closely guarded family secrets – the Pett family, for example, produced at least ten Master Shipwrights in four generations (most of them called Peter or Phineas to the confusion of historians) – and if any plans were committed to paper they have not survived. There is no direct evidence of how the early wooden walls of England were, in fact, constructed.

But to work by eye and to simple rules which were passed on by word of mouth stands as a considerable feat when it comes to designing a warship of the size of the "Great Harry". Why, for instance, did they place the point of the greatest beam not plumb amidships but further forward at about 2/5ths of the ship's length from the bow? Presumably because they had studied ducks and fish, just as centuries later Mitchell designed the Spitfire fighter aircraft by watching the flight of birds.

To man these great ships now became a problem which was to dog naval authority from the time of Henry VIII till the present day. By the middle of the sixteenth century the enduring structure of the Navy had come into being. By Letters Patent from Henry VIII there were now the ships and an organisation to look after them. But the royal fleet had, as yet, no regular body of officers and men. It is true that there existed a nucleus of 'standing officers' who acted as ship-keepers when their vessels were laid up 'in ordinary'.

These 'standing officers' – the Warrant Officers of later days – comprised the gunner responsible for the armament, the boatswain who had charge of the rigging and the running of the ship and the carpenter who took care of the hull. When commissioned, a Master – the sailing expert responsible for navigation – would be appointed together with a cook and a bursar or purser who was a civilian and acted as the ship's business manager. Fighting men and seamen were then recruited, usually by force, when and where they could be found. It was no small problem to solve.

'English sea power was the legitimate child of the Reformation' the Regius Professor of Modern History at Oxford (J. A. Froude) pointed out in the last decade of the nineteenth century, 'It grew directly out of the new despised Protestantism. Matthew Parker and Bishop Jewel, the judicious Hooker himself, excellent men as they were, would have written and preached to small purpose without Sir Francis Drake's cannon to play an accompaniment to their teaching.'[4]

To get a proper perspective, therefore, of sixteenth century life at sea, we must take a look at the outstanding leaders whom the age threw up. Certain of these men such as Drake, Hawkins and Raleigh are as familiar to British schoolchildren as Nelson himself, the arch-hero of the entire story. Others such as Willoughby, Chancellor, Borough, Gilbert, Frobisher, Oxenham, Fenton, Davis and Grenville may not be quite as well known. Each and every one, however, made his mark in a distinctive way and all built up the saga with individual exploits of tenacity and renown. All were inspired by the Crown and in some cases actively protected and partnered by the monarch of the day. What did they do and why are they so important?

The story was begun by John Cabot and his son, Sebastian, whose lives were something of an enigma. The facts are simply not available. That John Cabot made two voyages west across the Atlantic is certain but for 450 years the second one has been confused with a voyage made in 1500 by Jâo Llavrador to the east coast of Greenland mistakenly named Labrador in the belief that it was a new discovery and another one in 1501 by Caspar Corte Real to Newfoundland and the east coast of North America. Some think this second voyage, which sailed from Bristol in 1498, was never heard of again: others that John Cabot returned in 1499 to draw his pension and then soon afterwards died.

Equally difficult to establish with certainty is whether his son, Sebastian, was a pioneer, a charlatan or a man who was deliberately or accidentally forgetful. We hear nothing of Sebastian for nearly two decades until 1518 when he surfaced as Pilot Major of Spain, which means that he was examiner of all the pilots and also chief cartographer of the country. Seven years later he set out on an unsuccessful expedition to the Moluccas by way of the Straits of Magellan, unsuccessful in the sense that he never got further than the River Plate. This brought him into disgrace.

But he was evidently a glib talker. After four years' banishment he re-established himself. When over seventy he returned to England in the troubled years after the death of Henry VIII and lived on till the year before Elizabeth came to the throne, achieving the ripe age of eighty-one. During this latter period he founded at Bristol a Company of Merchant Adventurers of which he became Governor for life.

The merchants of England, especially of Bristol and London, were in the forefront of those who responded to the royal initiative in maritime affairs and the 'Mysterie and Company of Marchant Adventurers for the Discoverie of Regions, Dominions,

Islands and Places Unknowen' organised two expeditions in search of the North-East Passage in 1554 and 1555 under Sir Hugh Willoughby, Richard Chancellor and Stephen Borough. These ventures from which only Chancellor returned (and he was drowned off Aberdeen returning from a third voyage in 1556) resulted in the founding of the Muscovy Company to develop trade between England and Russia after he had paid a visit to Ivan the Terrible in Moscow. This visit was made from Archangel, St Petersburg (the present-day Leningrad) not being built for another century and a half.

The search for the North-East and North-West passages to Cathay and the Far East now began in earnest and has continued in a chiaroscuro of failure and success until the present day. This is a saga in itself equivalent to the climbing of Everest or the discovery of the South Pole. The English were among the first formally to embrace the idea. Dutch and French explorers (notably Barents 1550–1597 and Cartier 1491–1557) also joined in the search and there must have been unrecorded Russian attempts on the North-East passage but a Moscow decree of 1620 forbade trading along this route for some unintelligible reason and no Russian trading vessels returned to those waters until the 1870s.

Generally speaking it was the English who bore the brunt of these dangerous and largely unfruitful explorations and who gave their names to the bays, inlets and islands of those raw and inhospitable sub-Polar regions. The concept of these two routes – north-east round the north of Russia and north-west from the Atlantic to the Pacific via the north of Canada developed, in two distinct phases, firstly in the sixteenth and early seventeenth centuries and secondly in the late eighteenth and nineteenth centuries. In neither phase was the basic ice problem overcome and the toll of lives lost was daunting even with the coming of steam and steel-hulled ships.

However the idea that such routes were possible at all fired the imagination of seafaring peoples and especially of the English and kept the flame burning generation after generation, century after century. The prime motive was trade and of the two routes the search for the North-West Passage went on longer and had more energy devoted to it. This has even continued until today when the commercial possibilities of transporting Alaskan oil to the north-eastern seaboard of Canada and the United States still make it worth while trying to overcome the enormous natural hazards involved.

In Elizabethan times explorers searching for the North-West Passage were lone figures indeed. Seamen such as the semi-literate Yorkshireman, Martin Frobisher, the scholarly Devonian, John Davis (an expert pilot who invented the backstaff and the Davis quadrant), the poor Londoner William Baffin, the man of unknown origin, Henry Hudson, later to be deserted by his crew in the bay he named and the humorous north countryman, Luke Foxe, who called himself North-West Foxe, were all self-made men of humble birth. All were very much out on their own. Fired by a sense of adventure, they had the northern seas all to themselves. Aristocrats and middle class Englishmen who, like their Spanish and Portuguese counterparts, were equally ambitious to open the new world, chose to do so in more southerly climes, where the rewards were more immediate and somewhat easier to obtain.

The man who planted the first English colony in North America was Sir

Humphrey Gilbert. A soldier by training and a half-brother of Sir Walter Raleigh, with whose help and 'by selling the clothes off my wife's back' as he put it, he got an expedition together which sailed from Plymouth in June 1583, taking possession of Newfoundland in the Queen's name on 5th August, Gilbert's lifelong ambition had been to discover the North-West Passage to Cathay. Seven years previously he had published a treatise, 'A Discourse to prove a Passage by the North West to Cathaia and the East Indies', which so to speak scripted the centuries of searching which followed.

Patriotic, pious, learned and strangely incompetent as a leader of men, Gilbert believed that the Spanish and Portuguese did not want the Passage to be discovered and had forbidden their own navigators to explore it. The English, therefore, would have to do the job instead. This typically Elizabethan note which he struck reverberated through the years and rings out in the last sentence of the Discourse – 'He is not worthy to live at all, that for feare, or danger of death, shunneth his countrie's service, and his owne honour: seeing death is inevitable and fame of vertue imortall.' The Queen herself read the Discourse before it was published and when the first contender, Martin Frobisher, came forward gave him a licence to explore. Frobisher, as harsh a disciplinarian as Gilbert was lax, made three expeditions. During these he discovered the bay which now bears his name and brought back some black stones which he thought contained gold but which on analysis proved to be worthless mica.

Gilbert himself secured a Charter from the Queen in 1578. This was to discover the North-West Passage and plant a colony in Newfoundland of which he was to be Governor. But divided councils and lack of money got him no further than Cape Verde where he met disaster from the Spaniards. He was an ill-starred man in a number of ways and when he did plant his colony five years later in 1583, he found it impossible to impose discipline or law and regretfully set off for home, book in hand. Off the Azores his two ships ran into terrible storms on which his comment was, 'We are as near to heaven by sea as by land.' This proved to be tragically true. That night Gilbert's frigate "Squirrel" being 'ahead of us in the "Golden Hind", suddenly her lights were out . . . in that moment the frigate was devoured and swallowed up of the sea.' There were no survivors.

Another "Golden Hind" (which had started her life as the "Pelican") had already achieved immortality, at any rate so far as the history books are concerned, by being the first ship in the ownership of her Captain to circumnavigate the world. That Captain was Francis Drake, a leader of men who like Nelson three centuries later, became a legend in his lifetime. Drake is also unique in being the real and unquestioned founder of the British naval tradition. And what a man he was!

Short, stocky and red-haired, he came from a comparatively modest background – perhaps the only thing modest about him. Essentially a man of action, he was ruthless, ambitious, a bit apt to brag, generous, cheerful and deeply religious in the Protestant mould. With all his qualities and defects, he established himself in his lifetime and he remains to this day the epitome of all those subsequent Captains, Commanders and Admirals who have made the British Navy what it is. The greatest privateer of all time, he had like Nelson no need of a press-gang to man any ship he

Drake's "Golden Hind" was the only ship of five to complete the circumnavigation of the world. This later watercolour by Gregory Robinson shows a ship described as 'of near 400 tons burden, with a hundred men on board, all young and of an age for battle . . . he also has with him nine or ten gentlemen, the younger sons of great people in England. These sit at his table and he is served on silver plate with a coat of arms engraved on the dishes . . . The ship carries about thirty pieces of artillery and plenty of warlike stores.'

commanded. Men virtually queued up to come on board and though on the famous circumnavigation of the world he faced mutiny on more than one occasion, the force of his personality, his practical expertise in being able to do himself any job he might require of his seamen, allied to his consideration of them individually as human beings, gave him a power of leadership which all subsequent officers in the Royal Navy have attempted to emulate. At the time of the Armada he was at the height of his powers and whether or not the legendary game of bowls ever took place on Plymouth Hoe when the Spaniards were sighted and whether or not Drake remarked, 'There's time to finish the game and beat the Spaniards too', it is entirely typical of the way he thought.

Of course the success he achieved was phenomenal even by the sensational standards of the day and success breeds on itself. As with Nelson it is the power of leadership, the ability to make men do things from which they would normally run a mile and to continue cheerfully under his command, which is the chief feature of the man. This power of command stemmed in large measure from a basic understanding of the seamen's mentality, coupled with a sense of justice or fair play.

The Queen allowed him to keep £10,000 (a huge sum in those days) from his voyage round the world and to abstract the money before it was assessed by a Sydenham magistrate. No questions were to be asked and Drake could have taken considerably more than £10,000 had he been so minded. Instead, as the assessor remarked in a letter to Sir Francis Walsingham: 'I must say he is inclined to advance the value to be delivered to Her Majesty . . . seeking in general to recompense all men that have been in the case dealers with him. As I dare take an oath he will rather diminish his own portion than leave any of them unsatisfied. And for his mariners and followers I have seen here as eye-witness and have heard with my ears such certain signs of goodwill as I cannot yet see that any of them will leave his company. The whole course of his voyage hath shown him to be of great valour; but my hap has been to see some particulars – and namely in the discharge of his company, as doth assure me that he is a man of great government and that by the rules of God and his book, so as proceeding on such foundation, his doings cannot but prosper.'

And prosper they did. The Queen listened spellbound to his adventures, walked with him publicly about the parks and gardens, gave him a second ten thousand pounds, attended a banquet on board the "Golden Hind" at Deptford and knighted him, to the great discomfiture of Mendoza, the Spanish Ambassador, who offered to give twice as much if only such a bandit as Drake were to be properly chastised.

The Spanish faction, however, was to be further discomfited, perhaps too mild a word in the circumstances, when eight years later and after much provocation, such as 'Singeing the King of Spain's beard' at Cadiz in 1587, 'la gran empresa' of the Armada to invade and conquer England met its disastrous end. This great Enterprise, dubbed before it sailed as 'felicissima' and 'invencible', proved in the event to be neither. It did, however, mark the culminating though not the final episode in a war between little England and great Spain which had been maintained, openly and covertly, for the better part of twenty years often against the wishes and the better judgment of Philip II of Castile and Elizabeth I of England who was, after all, his sister-in-law albeit a heretic in the eyes of the Pope.

It is Drake whom history has mainly credited with this exceptional victory over the Armada which established British supremacy at sea for close on four centuries, but it was Lord Howard of Effingham (1536–1624) who in fact commanded the English fleet out of Plymouth. Drake was his Vice-Admiral and he, Hawkins, Frobisher and Fenner comprised his Council of War, Hawkins and Frobisher being knighted at sea by Howard under royal prerogative. Lord Henry Seymour had charge of the eastern squadron guarding the Thames. The reason for this command structure was that despite Drake's unquestionable seamanship, despite his feats of arms in the preceding years at Cadiz and in the Caribbean, there still remained traces of feudal thinking at Court which required a great fleet to be commanded by a great nobleman in the name of the Queen. A commoner or a mere knight was not of sufficient stature. Nevertheless the English were far in advance of the Spaniards whose Armada seamen were subordinate to the soldiers borne for landing and fighting ashore, its Commander-in-Chief never previously having been to sea. This difference proved to be fatal to the Spaniards.

In the English fleet there were 35 royal ships together with 53 'private' ships of size. In those days a rich man could still buy or build a ship, collect together a crew

THE SPANISH ARMADA

The Spanish Armada, which sailed from Spain in 1588, was designed to transport a large invading army from the Spanish Netherlands to subjugate England and re-establish Catholicism there. Command had been given to the King's cousin, the Duke of Medina Sidonia, a courageous soldier, a man of authority but one with almost no experience at sea. His 130 men-of-war were to protect troop-carrying transports which would join up with those of the Duke of Parma in the Low Countries.

Queen Elizabeth's fleet comprised 102 ships, ranging in size from Frobisher's "Triumph", considered a match for any Spaniard, to small scouting pinnaces. Supply, however, was a grave problem, no great reserves of powder and shot existing at any English port. On Friday, 19th July the Spanish fleet was sighted off the Lizard. The English fleet was in port at Plymouth and with a westerly wind blowing found itself awkwardly placed for getting to grips with the enemy now proceeding in what seemed to be a tightly disciplined, overwhelming progress.

However, some of Drake's ships, armed with local knowledge and keeping well inshore, did contrive to get to windward of the Spaniards.

An extended sea-battle had never been part of Medina Sidonia's plan. Were one to be forced on them, the Spaniards would have chosen to engage closely with their great ships and well disciplined soldiers as they had done at the battle of Lepanto in 1571. The High Admiral, Lord Howard of Effingham, and Drake knew this very well. They reacted by keeping their more manoeuvrable ships at a distance and firing their guns at their longest effective range.

During the evening of the 27th July the wind freshened and the Spaniards steered for Calais where Medina Sidonia ordered the Armada to anchor. Howard then sent in eight fireships. The result was immediate and for the Spaniards totally disastrous. Cables were cut, anchors abandoned, hulls and rigging irreparably damaged as the great Spanish galleons made for the open sea. By dawn on Monday, 29th July the entire Armada had been destroyed.

Howard abandoned the chase off Newcastle-on-Tyne and Medina Sidonia ordered his remaining ships to make their way home to Spain round the north of Scotland. They were shadowed as far as the Orkneys and were then left to the rigours of a westerly gale. The total losses of the Armada in July and August amounted to 64 ships and at least 10,000 men.

This drawing of the Spanish Armada off Calais is full of excitement, though one wonders if so much was really happening at once within such narrow limits of space. As the artist heads it with words about how this 'most celebrated' fleet 'came and perished', he obviously has a point to make. Certainly the disaster happened, though it was more spread out than depicted here.

and put to sea as its Captain, if so he chose. This made for a set of jealous, proud and unruly sea-captains of varying ability. Fleet discipline, as such, could scarcely be said to exist. Supply problems were almost insurmountable, there being a universal shortage of victuals and no great reserve of powder. 'I know not which way to deal with the mariners to make them rest contented with sour beer', Howard remarked, yet he still believed he commanded 'the gallantest company of Captains, soldiers and mariners that I think were ever seen in England.' In the Spanish ships the sailors on whom all depended were more or less despised as descendants of galley slaves.

As with the men, so with the ships, their weapons and the tactics according to which they were employed. Here again lay crucial differences in outlook. Spanish military commanders were still medievally minded. The ships they said they required were galleons with high bulwarks and massive fore and after castles. Their tactics

had a simple and age-old point – to grapple and board. The English, on the other hand, had developed the much more manoeuvrable 'low-charged' ship which could sail closer to the wind and they had long been committed to the heavy gun as the prime weapon afloat. The siege-gun had rendered castles ashore obsolete: the same result could now be achieved with ships at sea. These principles created the line-of-battle formation henceforth used by every fleet in action until the advent of the aircraft carrier.

These advances, although generally adopted by a consensus of English seafaring men, were initiated and actively developed by Drake's cousin, Sir John Hawkins (1532–1595), an equally remarkable man. Hawkins, whose father had been Mayor of Plymouth, was some ten years older than Drake, had married the daughter of Benjamin Gonson, the Treasurer of the Navy, and twenty-two years later in 1577 had succeeded to the same top job, adding to it the post of Comptroller, thus combining in himself the two most powerful and lucrative posts on the Navy Board.

Hawkins was the real architect of the Elizabethan Navy. The low-charged ships which he designed, built and put into service became the first battle fleet of modern times and although far from impeccable in business matters, he did deliberately and considerably improve the pay and conditions of the seamen and, together with the Lord High Admiral, Howard of Effingham, inaugurated the first naval charity – the Chatham Chest – for the relief of their suffering.

In all this he was fired by a sombre, calculating hatred of the Spaniards and of the Roman Catholic religion. Drake enjoyed the prime sport of the day – Spaniard baiting – in a much more light-hearted way. Drake never killed a Spaniard except in battle but loved to scare them and make them absurd and ridiculous. Hawkins's passion was of a darker hue. Both men, early in their lives, had had experience of Spanish treachery at San Juan de Ulloa but whereas Drake reacted subsequently as the pirate he was, Hawkins devoted the rest of his life to the destruction of Spanish seapower and its replacement by the seapower of England.

All in all the Navy was not to have a better administrator until the advent of Pepys a century later. 'Serve God daily', Hawkins's most famous precept ran, 'love one another, preserve your victuals, beware of fire and keep good company' – by which he meant in modern terms good station-keeping in the fleet. It was principally Hawkins who transformed the greater part of the Queen's Navy from a short haul, Narrow Seas coastal defence force into the first high-seas fleet capable of operating at long range as an ocean-going force. The blue water school of maritime strategy had come into being.

CHAPTER III

THE STUARTS

1603–1714

CHRONOLOGICAL COMPENDIUM

The Reigns and their character

James I
1603–1625

English and Scottish crowns united. Autocratic rule against the will of Parliament.

Charles I
1625–1649

Continued autocracy leading to civil war and Charles's execution.

The Commonwealth and Protectorate
1649–1660

England's first dictatorship. The Puritan ethic. Dutch wars.

Charles II
1660–1685

Restoration, relaxation of morals, the Great Plague and the Great Fire.

James II
1685–1688

Attempt to restore Catholicism.

William III of Orange and Mary
1689–1694

William alone
1694–1702

Protestant succession secured. Wars against the France of Louis XIV.

Anne
1702–1714

Union of Parliaments of England and Scotland in 1706.

General

In the early part of the seventeenth century Spain lost her predominance in Europe, now dominated by England and France, neither of whom wanted a costly war. Both James I and Charles I, however, conducted aggressive and inept foreign policies, against the will of Parliament. Particularly unpopular was Buckingham, the King's favourite, and his war on two fronts against France and Spain from 1627–9. Buckingham, Lord High Admiral from 1619, was assassinated in 1628. After the ending of the war with France in 1629, England was not to be involved on the continent (except for the mid-century Dutch wars and they were at sea) until the end of the century. Then William III and Marlborough waged sucessful campaigns against Louis XIV, the most notable victory being Blenheim in 1704. These wars were ended by the Treaty of Utrecht in 1713, Anne died in 1714 and Louis XIV in 1715.

The Anglo-Dutch wars (First 1652–4, Second 1665–7 and Third 1672–4) were caused by economic rivalry over fishing and trade. They were extremely bitter, the more so since both Protestant countries had hitherto been friendly, and were the first wars conducted almost entirely at sea.

The overriding seventeenth century problem in England was the rivalry between the House of Commons and the King. This took two forms – financial and religious. To tax their subjects legitimately brought the Stuart kings into conflict with parliament. The alternatives to this, such as Ship Money, were hated by the country. Nor was the Elizabethan church settlement satisfactory, with a growing number of Puritans confronting a Catholic king. That fear (of a Catholic king, James II) was to lead finally to the Glorious Revolution of 1688 and the succession of a Protestant line, assured by the Act of Settlement in 1701.

Naval

The planting of colonies overseas, the growth of seaborne trade and of the merchant ships in which that trade was carried, together with the increasingly powerful and efficient warships needed to protect them, are the chief features of maritime life in the seventeenth century. The Navy itself also changed. Although East Indiamen, for instance, were armed for protection against pirates and purpose-built warships could also be adapted for trade, the Navy as such and the Merchant Navy became more and more distinct.

Under Pepys and the naval-minded kings he served (Charles II and James II), the first proper organisation of the Navy took place. Articles of War and the Naval Discipline Act were brought into force, regular service naval officers, with professional examinations for the rank of Lieutenant, became a cadre making the Navy a career for life. As yet there were no uniforms and no similar long service contracts for the lower deck. At the end of a war officers would serve ashore on half-pay whereas the men, or 'the people' as they were called, were simply paid off into civilian life and recruited again by means of the press gang when the next crisis occurred. However royal interest continued to inspire the Navy and from the reign of Charles the Second, the service came to be known as the Royal Navy.

From the Restoration onwards, there was also a growing interest – again inspired by the King – in astronomy, navigation and science. The first Astronomer Royal and his Observatory were attached to the royal palace at Greenwich which was rebuilt by Wren. After the Great Fire in 1666, the City of London began to take over from Amsterdam as the premier mercantile city of Europe. A Royal Exchange was built, the Bank of England founded in 1694 and a thriving marine insurance business begun at Lloyd's coffee house which today still virtually insures the world.

The invention of more precise instruments such as the quadrant and the sextant led to a vast increase in geographical accuracy. The sea coast of the kingdom was surveyed by Greenvile Collins so that previous dependence on Dutch charts became no longer necessary and a Hydrographer to the King was appointed who produced 120 plans of harbours and coastline, the *Coasting Pilot* of 1693 going into twelve editions.

The search for the North-East and North-West Passages continued apace as did world exploration. The New Zealand, Tonga and Fiji archipelagos were discovered and in 1642 the first circumnavigation of Australia was made by a Dutchman, Tasman, sent on an expedition to the north-west Pacific by Van Diemen, Governor of the Dutch East Indies.

The first formation fighting of a line of battleships took place in the First Dutch War and with only five flags in use (the Ensign, Jack, Red, Blue and Pendant) the first primitive ship to ship signalling began.

The outstanding figure in naval affairs in the seventeenth century was undoubtedly Pepys who turned the Royal Navy into a powerful, well-disciplined force, making the office of Lord High Admiral efficient and ensuring that the dockyards and victuallers who supplied the fleet were, if not free of corruption, at least kept under a rigid surveillance. Other great personalities of the era were the Generals-at-Sea and in particular Robert Blake and George Monck, who later became the Duke of Albemarle.

Organisation

1619	George Villiers, later Duke of Buckingham appointed Lord High Admiral.
1628	Buckingham assassinated. Lords Commissioners appointed in place.
1649	Office of Lord High Admiral abolished. Replaced by Generals-at-Sea.
1660	Office of Lord High Admiral restored and James, Duke of York, appointed.
1634	Ship money first levied as alternative to taxes approved by Parliament.
1642–8	During Civil War, Navy adheres to Parliament and institutes blockade. Prince Rupert (1618–82), a cousin of the King, tries to break blockade with a handful of indifferent ships.

1649–60 Blake (1599–1657), Deane (1610–53) and Monck (1608–70) appointed Generals-at-Sea by Cromwell, the Lord Protector.

1660 Monck largely instrumental in re-establishing monarchy. Is made Duke of Albemarle.

1660 Pepys (1633–1703) appointed Clerk of the Acts to the Navy Board. Begins complete reorganisation of Navy and Dockyards.

1653 Articles of War, a disciplinary code based on ancient sea laws of Rhodes and Oléron first issued.

1660 Navigation Act makes Navy premier service.

1661 Naval Discipline Act incorporates 1653 Articles of War and adds preamble from 1660 Navigation Act 'wherein under the good Providence of God, the Wealth, Safety and Strength of this Kingdom is so much concerned'.

1664 Royal Marines established.

1671 Morgan (1635–88) ex-buccaneer, knighted and appointed Deputy Governor of Jamaica.

1673 Pepys becomes First Secretary of the Admiralty.

1684 James, Duke of York, regains appointment as Lord High Admiral and retains it on ascending throne as James II in 1685.

1688 Dethronement of James II, Pepys falsely accused of treason is forced to resign and finally retires into private life.

Ships and Weapons

1603 Phineas Pett (1570–1647) Master Shipwright Deptford and Chatham and Pett family responsible for much Stuart shipbuilding (Peter Pett 1592–1652, Peter Pett 1610–72, Christopher Pett 1620–68 and Phineas Pett 1628–78).

1637 "Sovereign of the Seas", biggest ship yet built, 100 guns, name shortened to "Sovereign" under Commonwealth and changed to "Royal Sovereign" at Restoration. Twice rebuilt, her career ended when accidentally burnt _t Chatham 1696.

1660 'Yacht' (from Dutch *jacht*) enters English language through presentation to Charles II by States General of Holland of "Mary" (100 tons, 8 guns) as a private pleasure vessel.

17th century Guns shortened as quality of powder improved. Medieval names dropped and henceforth guns known by weight of shot fired. Largest gun was Cannon Royal, weighing 8,000 lb and firing 66 lb shot. More usual guns were 42 pounders on the lower deck and 24 pounders on the upper deck.

Navigation and Cartography

17th century Astrolabe develops into back-staff, quadrant, octant and sextant.

1701 First world chart of magnetic variation.

1714 Board of Longitude (Commissioners for the Discovery of Longitude at Sea) established and offers prize for solution to the problem after consulting Sir Isaac Newton and Edmund Halley.

1662 Royal Society of London (for Improving Natural Knowledge) founded by Charles II to encourage scientific knowledge of astronomy, biology, geographical exploration, navigation and seamanship.

1675 Flamsteed (1646–1719) appointed by Charles II as his 'astronomical observator' later known as Astronomer Royal. He was succeeded by Halley (1656–1742).

1681 Greenvile Collins (d. 1694) appointed by Pepys to make a survey of sea coast of the kingdom and appointed Hydrographer to the King.

1693 Great Britain's *Coasting Pilot* published.

1687 Newton's *Principia*, basis of modern mathematics.

People and Events

1603–16 Raleigh (1552–1618) condemned to death on false accusations of plotting against James I, is imprisoned in Tower.

1616 Raleigh released to undertake mission to Guiana to discover gold mine 'without infringing any Spanish possession'. This failed and Raleigh was executed to satisfy James I's promise to Gondomar, the Spanish Ambassador in London, in 1618.

1607–11 Hudson (d. 1611) seeks North-East and North-West Passages reaching the Strait since known by his name and Hudson Bay in 1610. Mutineers put him ashore and no evidence of his fate has ever been discovered.

1620 Pilgrim Fathers sail from Plymouth in the "Mayflower".

1631 Foxe (1586–1636) attempts to find North-West Passage, reaching Frobisher Bay, Hudson Strait and Coats Island.

1631 James (1593–1635) makes similar attempt and meets Foxe in Hudson Bay. Is possibly the source for Coleridge's 'Ancient Mariner'.

1669–70 Narborough (1640–88)commands expedition to South Seas to try to break Spanish monopoly of trade. Not successful but had Greenvile Collins as his navigator.

1615 Baffin (1584–1622) penetrates Davis Strait to discover vast bay which bears his name.

1616 Cape Horn discovered and rounded by Le Maire (1585–1616) and Schouten (1590–1625).

1621–70 Penn – Parliamentary Admiral and father of William Penn the Quaker who founded Pennsylvania.

1659–1707 Clowdisley Shovel, Admiral – Dutch wars and capture of Gibraltar.

1650–1709 Admiral of the Fleet Sir George Rooke – Dutch wars and Gibraltar.

1653–1702 Admiral John Benbow – battles of Beachy Head and La Hogue, rented John Evelyn's house at Deptford later subletting it to Peter the Great of Russia on his visit to England to learn naval architecture. (1698)

Wars and Battles

England against France

1627–1629 In support of Huguenots against Richelieu. Buckingham fails to relieve La Rochelle. Nevis, one of the Leeward Islands, captured.

England against Holland

1652–1654 *First Anglo-Dutch war*

1652	Battles – off Downs
1652	– off Kentish Knock
1652	– off Dungeness
1653	– off Portland
1653	– off North Foreland
1653	– off Texel

1664–1667 *Second Anglo-Dutch war*

1664	English annex New Netherlands
1664	Fort George surrenders
1665	Battle of Southwold Bay
1665	English take St Eustatius
1666	France supports Holland
1666	English privateers take Tobago
1666	French take St Kitts

1666	Battle off Dunkirk
1666	St James Fight
1666	French take Antigua
1666	Dutch take Surinam
1667	French take Monserrat
1667	de Ruyter raids Chatham

1672–1674 *Third Anglo-Dutch War*

1672	France joins England
1672	Battle of Southwold Bay
1673	Battle of Texel
1673	Dutch capture New York

1688–1697 England and Holland against France (League of Augsburg)

1690	Battle off Beachy Head
1692	Battle off La Hogue
1694	English expedition to Brest fails

1702–1714 England and Holland against France (Spanish Succession)

1702	Cadiz
1702	Vigo Bay
1704	Capture of Gibraltar
1705	Capture of Barcelona
1708	Capture of Minorca and Sardinia
1710	Capture of Port Royal (Annapolis)

After the Armada the English might and did legitimately claim to be dominant at sea. However another two hundred years were to pass before the world could no longer deny this fact and throughout the Stuart century, roughly speaking the seventeenth, the hardy islanders had almost continuously to defend their claim to dominion, both in trade and war, against the French, Dutch, Spanish and Portuguese.

It began badly enough. King James I, dubbed 'the wisest fool in Christendom', could scarcely have differed more from his predecessor had he arrived from outer space which, perhaps, was how the north was regarded by Londoners of the time. Uncouth yet sharply intelligent, James never understood his English subjects and indulged himself in delusions of grandeur based on the divine right of Kings and the notion that his experience in Scotland had turned him into a skilful ruler. It had not and his fatal predilection for a succession of male favourites at Court, notably George Villiers whom he elevated to the dukedom of Buckingham and also, to the distress of the Navy, appointed Lord High Admiral, permitted a corrosion to creep through the country in general and in particular through the fleet.

In a rapidly expanding world the monarch's dangerous obstinacy, fatal partiality and murky indecision proved totally inadequate to the solving of organic problems in an emergent England and Scotland linked together uneasily under a single crown but with two separate and disparate Parliaments.

Principal of these problems became the physical provision of a fleet and the large-scale administration this entailed. James found himself the first British King in early modern Europe to be faced with the fact that a Navy had become the largest, costliest and technically most advanced organisation of the day.

Unfortunately for themselves and the country, both James I and Charles I were up against some of the most powerful and uncompromising men in England. Neither King had the strength of character of Henry VIII or Elizabeth (Charles has been described as a 'small, stammering Scotsman with inflexible ideals but without the will to impose them')[1] and both had to deal practically with the fact that a professional fighting service rarely spends much of its time actually at war. A Navy nevertheless requires to be kept in being, trained and ready for action through long periods of peace.

In the seventeenth century the merchants of England and especially of London resented the cost of what they considered to be royal irresponsibility at best and profligacy at worst. Anxious though they were for piracy in the Narrow Seas to be cleaned out and for Dutch fishing busses to be denied access to English fishing grounds, they had no financial control of this policing. Charles paid for this by levying ship-money when no English Parliament was sitting, and this brought him into head-on collision with Parliament when it was eventually recalled and led indirectly to the Civil War.

Pepys is the great name of the late seventeenth century so far as the Navy is concerned. In essence he created the service we know today. To understand fully the magnitude of his achievement, however, the conditions under which he had to operate must be visualised. Corruption crawled through the body politic like the plague. Great men at Court were unscrupulous, dishonest and given largely to faction. Indeed in the early years of the first Stuart King, the Treasurer of the Navy,

Sir Robert Mansell, and the Surveyor, Sir John Trevor, practised fraud to a degree seldom matched in the long, sorry tale of peculation.

As an instance of this, they had a ship built (the "Resistance") in a royal dockyard using nothing but the King's own materials and labour. They then chartered her to the Crown as a storeship. Laden with the King's stores, she parted company with the squadron to which she was attached on her first voyage, proceeded profitably abroad on her own account, sold her cargo and then freighted another back to England.

Everyone knew what went on but as long as the Lord High Admiral, Lord Howard of Effingham, who after all had commanded the fleet which destroyed the Armada, retained the King's favour, nothing could be done to remedy 'the very great and intolerable abuses, deceits, frauds, corruptions, negligences, misdemeanours and offences' besetting the naval service. As in a latterday banana republic, nothing could move without authority, itself obtainable only after bribes had been slipped to an army of petty officials, each with a finger in the pie.

These official customs and practices, though purged and corrected from time to time, continued to be the norm until the great reforms of the mid nineteenth century. After the Restoration Pepys began the slow process of change. Pepys himself accepted the necessity of perquisites but stamped on dishonesty, misappropriation and theft. In that sense he became, perhaps, the first incorruptible. He was certainly the first civil servant to impose standards of quality and behaviour not only on seagoing naval officers but also on shipbuilders, chandlers and victuallers ashore. He inaugurated a fair system of advancement for professional skill at sea, despite strong opposition from the establishment of the day, composed as it was of buyers and sellers of patronage.

However the idea of promotion through merit in civilian life continued for a further three centuries to be all but unthinkable. Office was regarded as a piece of property to be bought, sold, bargained for, inherited, mortgaged and bequeathed as if it were real estate. It remained as difficult to sack an official for misconduct as it was to dispossess a landowner for mismanaging his estates. In 1618 the Duke of Buckingham, whose power was then waxing, caused a Royal Commission to enquire into the naval administration. There was no altruism in this. The Duke had his own interests in mind. Although the catalogue of graft and jobbery this Commission revealed could scarcely have been more devastating, no heads fell on the block.

In that same year of 1618 Raleigh was executed. A naval hero of the calibre of Drake and Hawkins, his exploits and daring had made him popular with the common folk but an object of jealousy to rivals at Court.

The British North American connection, in the starting of which Raleigh and his half-brother, Sir Humphrey Gilbert, had played major roles, really forged itself in 1620 when the Pilgrim Fathers set sail from Plymouth in the "Mayflower" with results which are now well known. The voyage itself can no longer be classed as epic in the sense that those of Columbus, Magellan and Drake were categorised – indeed fishermen from the United Kingdom, France and Portugal were now making regular trips back and forth across the Atlantic to the cod banks of Newfoundland – but the "Mayflower" exploit has become legendary in the political and social history of Britain, the United States and, at one remove, of the civilised world itself. It started an era. Ironically enough 1620 is also the year when British naval enterprise reached its lowest ebb.

In the Far East the English were in full retreat from the Dutch, Amsterdam and not London was acknowledged as the commercial capital of the world, no English ships had sailed the Pacific for thirty years, in the Mediterranean an English squadron of eighteen ships had utterly failed to extirpate Algerian piracy (Moorish buccaneers had become so daring as to raid the Thames and southern English ports, coolly removing the inhabitants into slavery) and in the Narrow Seas local pirates enjoyed more freedom of action than the King's ships whose officers would in any case be thwarted by cozenage ashore.

In slight mitigation, however, it should be borne in mind that the sea, ships and sailors – and more especially the naval establishment – comprise an esoteric world not easily penetrated nor readily understood in any age by landlubbers be they military leaders such as Napoleon or Hitler or ordinary accountants and business men ashore. The sea has a language of its own and the Navy a routine and practices not easily understood by an investigating auditor. Naval affairs, therefore, throughout the ages have been regrettably marked by endemic thimblerigging and a variety of nefarious practices more obviously flagrant than in other more accessible departments of public life.

In Stuart times the higher direction of the Navy was one thing, the seagoing fleet another. At least it can be said that a few ships were actually built. This business of getting a fleet into service undoubtedly added to the ever-present financial troubles of the first two Stuart Kings and more especially Charles I. But ships were constructed pre-eminently by that family of Master Shipwrights at Deptford – the Petts. Among the vessels built during the reign of James I were two great ships, one for the East India Company, the "Trade's Increase" of 1100 tons (plus a smaller vessel the "Peppercorn") and another for the King's service, the "Prince Royal".

This latter ship cost nearly £20,000, a vast amount for those days, which included £1,309 for painting and carving. A previous vessel of similar proportions had come out at £3,600 and perhaps because of this discrepancy in cost, the Petts were not bidden to construct another ship of size on the royal account until 1635 when Charles I, impelled by a craving to possess and display the largest and most impressive ship afloat, caused the "Sovereign of the Seas" to be laid down. Her tonnage was 1637, which was also the year of her launch, and she fulfilled a double purpose, being not only the foremost fighting ship in the world but also a superb expression of the majesty of the realm. She was, moreover, the first complete three-decker to carry over one hundred guns. As to magnificence her gilded carving and general ornamentation was more sumptuous than that of any ship before or since.

The "Sovereign of the Seas", shortened to "Sovereign" under the Commonwealth and then renamed "Royal Sovereign" after the Restoration, enjoyed a full and active career of nearly sixty years, taking part in all three Dutch wars (1652–4, 1664–7) and 1672–4) in the last of which she served as Prince Rupert's flagship. Rebuilt in 1684, she engaged in the battles of Beachy Head and Barfleur in 1692 and only met her end when accidentally burnt at Chatham in January 1696. A century later, another "Royal Sovereign" was to serve at Trafalgar.

SOVEREIGN OF THE SEAS

When launched in 1637 (which was also her official tonnage) Charles the First's "Sovereign of the Seas" was the biggest ship ever to be built in Europe. Ornately embellished she was a 1st rate of 100 guns built at Woolwich by Peter and Phineas Pett and she became the first true English three-decker in that she was the first warship to have three covered gundecks. She also marks a notable step forward in warship rig, stepping only three masts instead of the four which had hitherto been more or less standard in all large warships.

The "Sovereign of the Seas" had a double purpose. Not only was she a great fighting ship, she also expressed in a unique way the majesty of the realm. Nothing of like magnificence had been seen before. She was caparisoned all over in gilded carving, from the equestrian statue on her beakhead of King Edgar trampling seven prostrate kings under foot to the carved reliefs on the stern of Victory, Jason the Argonaut, Hercules with his club and Neptune astride a sea-horse. She also carried a stern lantern in which, it was said, ten men could stand upright without shouldering or pressing each other and in which Mr Pepys shut five ladies a year after the Restoration and then went in and kissed them all.

The ship had a chequered life of nearly sixty years, being twice rebuilt before being accidentally burnt at Chatham in 1696. When the Commonwealth was established in 1649, her name was shortened to "Sovereign" and as such she took part in the battle of the Kentish Knock during the First Dutch War (1652–4).

Renamed "Royal Sovereign" after the Restoration in 1660 and rebuilt to reduce her topweight, she fought in the St James's Day battle in the Second Dutch War (1665–7), the battle of Solebay (where she was the flagship of Vice Admiral Sir Joseph Jordan), the first and second battles of the Schooneveld and the second battle of the Texel in the Third Dutch War (1672–4). In the last two battles she wore the flag of Prince Rupert, Admiral of the Fleet.

Once more rebuilt at Chatham in 1684 she served as the flagship of Admiral the Earl of Torrington at the battle of Beachy Head in 1690 and again as the flagship of Vice Admiral Sir Ralph Delaval at the battle of Barfleur in 1692. She met her sad, undistinguished end when a cook left a candle burning in his cabin.

The commissioning of Charles I's "Sovereign of the Seas" points up another aspect of the esoteric maritime world mentioned above. This is the necessity of a frequent *demonstration* of seapower once claimed, even if the demonstration be merely a token. The meaning and implications of saluting have grown and been modified over seven centuries since King John first demanded that all foreign ships traversing the Straits of Dover should acknowledge England's sovereignty of the seas by lowering their sails. Now it is simpler. By the reign of Charles I this saluting at sea had been reduced to the dipping of topsails and national flags and this is still the recognised courtesy today, the inferior power dipping its ensign first.

But there is more to this than an occasional exercise of medieval manners. The salute at sea symbolises the power status of those making and returning it. Like the territorial implications of birdsong, a salute at sea is a reminder of the invisible but

Peter Pett, seen beside the "Royal Sovereign", was a member of a family of expert ship constructors (the functions of designer and builder were then one). Royalty still chose and approved warships in those times even if they did not any longer pay for them out of their own pockets. So, just as a king might till comparatively recent times design the splendid uniforms of his soldiers, ships were expected to be beautiful and highly decorative as well as efficient in protecting the realm.

demonstrable web of power which is understood by both parties to exist. A ship's ensign is a token of majesty at sea and in the seventeenth century this was very much to the point. Spain and Portugal, temporarily under one Crown, were still virtually unassailable in their wealth and power. But among the virile Protestant nations, the Dutch had already pulled ahead of the English not only in the Far East but also in the coastal trade of Europe itself. Yet there was a snag. Almost all Dutch overseas commerce had perforce to negotiate the Narrow Seas, passing within sight of Dover Castle.

It therefore became obvious that if any nation other than England commanded the Straits, the way would lie open for it to gain a stranglehold on the traffic. So far as England was concerned, the Straits of Dover and the English Channel had since time immemorial comprised an English domain. Control, therefore, must remain in

English hands, just as the Danes controlled the approaches to the Baltic and exacted Sound Dues at Elsinore. With the Dutch in mind, therefore, Charles deliberately named his great ship "Sovereign of the Seas" as a gesture of defiance. This continuing and intense Anglo-Dutch rivalry explosively fuelled by slurs and humiliations, such as the massacre by the Dutch of English traders at Amboyna in the Far East in 1623, inevitably led to war and an almost trivial insistence on etiquette on the high seas, triggered it off. In 1637 Captain Stradling of the "Dreadnought" had obliged a Dutch Rear-Admiral by lodging him in Plymouth for neglect of his duty in not dipping his ensign and in 1652 the start of the First Anglo-Dutch war was signalled by the Dutch Admiral Tromp's refusal to salute the British 'General-at-Sea', Robert Blake, off Start Point in British home waters.

'The trade of the world is too little for us two,' a contemporary sea captain put it, 'therefore one must down.' This was unfortunately true, given that Dutch and British interests clashed in every part of the world where expansion seemed likely to be profitable. Only against Spain were the two nations at one with each other, especially in the West Indies where the great buccaneering age was about to begin. Elsewhere they had perforce to carve out separate spheres of influence.

Both nations had left the medieval era a long way behind. The Dutch had finally freed themselves from Spanish overlordship by the Treaty of Munster in 1648. The English had just beheaded a King and were experiencing their first and only military dictatorship under the Lord Protector. Both nations were limbering up for a fight. So far as the English Navy was concerned the days of octogenarian Lord High Admirals were, for the moment, gone. Commissioners appointed by Parliament

The perfect formation of these ships at Skelling in 1666 during the Second Dutch War (when fireships burned the town and about 150 Dutch vessels) shows how established the idea had become that warships should now operate together as a fleet under central command. All that was still lacking was an adequate signalling system and what might be called participation planning before an action took place. Both of these were consistently improved, to achieve near perfection under Nelson.

now directed the fleet and Cromwell's military genius infused into the upper ranks of the Navy efficient and highly disciplined Army officers, the topmost of whom were called Generals-at-Sea.

Chief among these was Robert Blake, who had never been to sea at all until he was fifty. However his second-in-command, Sir William Penn, whose son became a Quaker and founded Pennsylvania, commanded a ship at 23, became a Rear Admiral at 27 and a General-at-Sea at 32. The other great General-at-Sea who began his career as a soldier of fortune and ended it as the Duke of Albemarle was George Monck. One of the most talented tacticians afloat, in addition to being a seasoned fighting man serving first the King and then the Commonwealth, he later proceeded to exercise his talents, at great personal risk, in restoring a full Parliament to the country following Cromwell's death in 1658. Two years later he helped re-establish the monarchy under Charles II.

The three Anglo-Dutch wars of the seventeenth century have been dubbed 'professional' since for the first time warships organised into fleets engaged each other at sea and at times even bombarded forts ashore. In retrospect these wars settled almost nothing at all. Except for the capture of New Amsterdam, which became New York, they were all fought out in a small area of the Channel and the North Sea, both sides relying on gunnery as their principal means to victory instead of the previous grappling and boarding. Terrible battles raged from coast to coast with, at times, over a hundred ships involved on each side and the slaughter was as fierce and cruel as in any sea battle before or since.

From now on ships would be operating in squadrons under Admirals of the Red, White and Blue and the Dutch wars also saw the beginning, in a primitive way, of flag signalling by which simple orders could be given to single ships or to the squadron as a whole. Moreover the 'professionalism' of these wars demanded ships built exclusively for fighting and thus able to deliver a much greater fire power than the converted merchant ships which had taken on the Armada. The fighting Navy and the Merchant Fleet now drew apart in that each required a fundamentally different kind of ship – a factor lost sight of since Viking times – and from then on the line-of-battle ship and the merchant vessel, even one armed against pirates, became no longer interchangeable.

As with the ships, so with the officers who fought them. During the reign of Charles II (1660–1685) the professional naval officer arrived on the scene, entering the service as a boy and remaining in it for the whole of his active life. With specialised ships and professionally trained officers, the fighting service could now claim to be an organisation with its own special identity, and it is significant that from about 1670 the service came to be known as the Royal Navy.

Although the Anglo-Dutch wars made little territorial difference to either country, at least in Europe, both nations benefited in oblique ways elsewhere. The Dutch secured a virtual monopoly of the Spice Islands for their own East India Company, the English having to confine themselves to the Indian sub-continent. On the other side of the Atlantic English colonies established themselves on the eastern seaboard of the North American continent from Nova Scotia to South Carolina. The colonial era had begun to quicken. Moreover after the first Dutch war had ended in England's

Robert Blake (1599–1657) was, perhaps, the best known General-at-Sea during the Commonwealth period. Basically a soldier, he never went to sea until he was fifty when, in company with Deane and Monck, he was given the job of chasing Prince Rupert's squadron and captured the Scilly Islands. In the First Dutch War (1652–4) he commanded in the Channel and defeated Tromp and de Ruyter (despite Tromp lashing a broomstick to his mast and claiming he would sweep the English from the seas). From 1654–7 he operated in the Mediterranean and off Cadiz, capturing a Spanish treasure fleet. Blake laid the foundations of naval discipline and tactics in the English Navy and fully deserves Lord Clarendon's tribute as 'the copy of naval courage'.

favour in 1654, Cromwell used the 160 ships in commission for a substantial clean-up of piracy in the Mediterranean. These ships also came in handy when Spain declared war on England in 1656. They were then used for the blockading of Cadiz and the destruction of a Spanish West Indian fleet at Santa Cruz, Tenerife, as well as for the capture of Jamaica (this expedition under Sir William Penn and General Robert Venables having failed to secure the more important island of Hispaniola or Haiti).

In effect, Cromwell, above all a master of strategy, by concentrating on Spain as the prime enemy, refurbished and put back into practice the mainstream policies of Elizabeth I, policies which had been reversed for half a century by the first two Stuart Kings with no noticeable benefit to the country. Previously only temporary lodgments had been made in Spanish Caribbean territory. Now in Port Royal, Jamaica, the British had acquired a key base of enormous value at a time when the importance of overseas forts and dockyards was just beginning to be realised by colonising European nations.

History is not events, as Dr. Jacob Bronowski pointed out, it is people and people, in essence, are powered by ideas. The latter half of the seventeenth century saw a burgeoning of ideas – at all events in the Protestant countries. Moreover there is nothing so powerful as ideas which have found their time, and this concept has never been more explicitly demonstrated than in the quarter century when Samuel Pepys had the supply, conduct and well-being of the Royal Navy in his expert hands. What a sharp control those hands exercised and how appropriate was the timing!

Born in 1633, three years after the King he was to serve so well, Pepys had witnessed, as a boy of fifteen, the execution of Charles I, and throughout his youth had had almost nothing to do with ships and the sea. But in 1660 Fate took charge of his life when his cousin, the Earl of Sandwich, who commanded the fleet bringing Charles II back from exile, secured him a place in the Navy Office. From that moment on Pepys never looked back and although Fate did from time to time give him a nasty jolt, he came to know more about sea affairs in general and the Royal Navy in particular than anyone else alive during that period – not even excepting the royal brothers Charles and James who allowed very few details concerning the fleet to escape their attention.

Pepys's official title was Clerk of the Acts to the Navy Board, a post which would later come to be called Secretary of the Admiralty. As such he was one of the 'Principal Officers' of the Navy. Born the son of a somewhat threadbare Fleet Street tailor, Pepys initially relished the exalted company he was henceforth to keep. However, being what would now be called a 'self-starter', vigorous and energetic with a penetrating mind, he soon saw through the pretensions of his elders and betters, progressively discovering their foibles and weaknesses and noting them down as knaves, sots, counterfeit rogues, rotten-hearted false vapourers and incompetent idlers. 'Chance without merit brought me in', he wrote in his famous diary, 'and diligence only keeps me so, and will, living as I do among so many lazy people.'

In fact he worked incessantly to find everything out at first hand for himself, rising at four in the morning or working through to the same time at night once he got to grips with a problem. He became expert in mathematics, took lessons in ship design and found out all there was to know about the different qualities of timber, tar and rope. Since the world understood in those days that it was not the salary of a placeman which yielded the true wealth but rather the opportunities for making money in the course of day-to-day business and the granting of favours to others, Pepys used everything which legitimately came his way to this end and thereby made himself a fortune in the accepted manner.

However, in addition, he was always a good, loyal and honest servant both to his King and to the Navy and so remained even at the height of his powers: he believed in value for money and fraud, laziness and incompetence became anathema to him. Like many an Admiral since, he would descend at short notice or even without warning on a ship or dockyard establishment, examine their books, check their stocks and deal ruthlessly with any malpractice he found. Moreover he applied this technique not only to underlings but also to bribe-taking seniors whom he threatened to expose whenever their peculation got out of hand. All this was done virtually single-handed, a fact almost unbelievable in the bureaucratic twentieth century when we may not have much of a seagoing fleet but certainly have a Ministry of Defence. In 1687, two years before Pepys surrendered his office, his staff amounted to six – four clerks, a messenger and a doorkeeper.

Lord Barham, First Lord of the Admiralty at the time of Trafalgar, and himself an administrator of mark, declared Pepys to have been 'a man of extraordinary knowledge in all that related to the business of the Naval Department, of great talents and the most indefatigable industry'. What, then, were the informing ideas which animated this great man and what effect did they have? First and foremost Pepys understood and applied a principle, later encapsulated as a precept at sea, that 'There is no such thing as a bad sailor, only a bad officer.' To ensure the supply of good officer material, therefore, Pepys directed that no one should become a Lieutenant in the Royal Navy without passing a rigorous professional examination which he was only allowed to sit after several years of actual seagoing service.

No longer could the rich and well-born simply buy themselves into command at sea. Now they had not only to be trained but also to be of demonstrable competence, a reform fully supported by Charles II as well as by his brother James, a most practical and intelligent Lord High Admiral. Pepys had the ear of both these royal sailors and the example they set established standards for all time.

Immediately after the Restoration (in 1661) the Articles of War, originally based on the ancient sea laws of Rhodes and Oléron and up-dated by Cromwell in 1653, were incorporated into the first English Naval Discipline Act and ever since the pre-eminent status of the Senior Service has rested on the preamble to that Act which declares that it is the Royal Navy 'whereon, under the good Providence of God, the wealth, safety and strength of the Kingdom do chiefly depend'.

Of course there is nothing like royal interest, if genuine, for getting things going in the British way of life. In the second half of the seventeenth century constitutional monarchy was on the way in and both Charles and James found themselves far more controlled by Parliament than their father and grandfather had ever been. Yet they were still autocrats to a degree unthinkable today and Pepys used their power, at one

A portrait of Samuel Pepys by J. Hayls, 1666. Pepys was the finest administrator the Navy had had to date, the equivalent of a latter-day top industrialist. No Puritan himself, he nevertheless purged and reformed every department of the service to which he gave his attention both ashore and afloat. In this he was fully backed by Charles II and James II, both vitally interested in making the Royal Navy, as it was henceforth to be called, professional and cost-effective. Pepys established the rule that efficiency, judged by examination, rather than wealth and position would now condition promotion and he drew a firm line between perquisites which were legal (and indeed desirable as incentives) and dishonesty and corruption.

EARLY NAVAL ADMINISTRATION

The administration and operational direction of the navy were separated as long ago as the reign of Henry VIII when the Navy Board came into existence in 1532 for supply and administration. A century later and after the Lord High Admiral the Duke of Buckingham had been assassinated in 1628, Lords Commissioners for Executing the Office of Lord High Admiral were appointed to take over naval administrative duties.

The original Commissioners were the Lieutenant of the Admiralty, who supervised all activities of the Board, the Treasurer, Comptroller, Surveyor, Clerk of the Ships and Master of the Ordnance for the Ships. Later the post of Lieutenant of the Admiralty lapsed and the Treasurer became the chief administrative officer. The Clerk of the Ships became the Clerk of the Acts and it was to this post that Pepys was appointed after the Restoration in 1660. At that time the fleet consisted of 109 ships which cost £40,000 a month to run and in the midsummer of 1660 the navy owed £678,000, nearly half being unpaid wages to seamen.

In June 1673 Pepys left the Navy Board to become the first Secretary to the Admiralty, the new Admiralty Board functioning much like a Privy Council committee. King Charles II and his brother James, until then the Lord High Admiral, continued their personal direction of the navy through Pepys and his clerks and the service began to enjoy the best administration it had ever had. Examinations were introduced for midshipmen, pilots, masters and lieutenants. Captains were forbidden to carry freight or absent themselves from their ships without permission. A system of rates, standardising ships and guns, was introduced. The first steps towards a permanent corps of officers were taken, with financial reforms and the introduction of pensions. Though much of his work was undone by subsequent neglect and dissension, Pepys left as his monument an example and a tradition of single-minded service to the Navy.

The next great reformer in the mid eighteenth century was Anson. On becoming First Lord of the Admiralty in 1751, Anson reformed the royal dockyards, attacking the waste, inefficiency and corruption which for generations had been endemic. He introduced a regular uniform for officers, rewrote the Articles of War and reconstituted the existing marine regiments into the Royal Marines. He also codified the rating of sailing warships into six divisions according to the number of guns they carried, a classification subsequently adopted by almost all other navies of size.

One of the places where good naval administration will bear fruit is a naval dockyard. This is Deptford in 1779. The construction and repair of ships employs a host of trades, requiring an almost infinite number of separate items of equipment. The men have to be chosen, paid and supervised to make sure they work efficiently. Every item of equipment has to be vetted for cost, suitability and ease of replacement. Administration may start and end with figures, estimates and accounting, but in between it is all hard fact.

remove, to the full. He also never lost sight of the fact that both Kings were keen sailors on their own account. Charles introduced yachting (the word comes from the Dutch) into the Kingdom to satisfy the skill in sailing small boats which he had acquired during his exile across the water, and the States General of Holland presented him with a private pleasure vessel, the "Mary" of 100 tons and 8 guns, which he used for racing and cruising in the Thames estuary.

In the greater world of the open sea both Charles and James thirsted for naval glory and kept a sharp eye on Louis XIV – far more of an autocrat than either British King was permitted to be – whose Minister of Marine, Jean Baptiste Colbert, in addition to lending his name to a particularly delicious way of cooking a sole, brought the French Navy to a level of excellence never before achieved, rebuilt Toulon and Rochefort and set up naval schools at Rochefort, St Malo and Dieppe. Even today

certain French naval officers regard their service as royal and refer to the British Navy as 'l'autre royale'.

Both English Kings married Catholic wives. Charles wed Catherine of Braganza who brought him as dowry Tangier and Bombay and James's second wife was an Italian princess said by unkind critics to be a daughter of the Pope. James remained a practising Catholic all his life and this lost him the throne. Charles, the 'merry monarch' with a more than ample supply of wry humour, dissembled more yet proved to be the first Stuart King beloved of his subjects despite all his obvious faults. He also contrived to foster and encourage that peculiarly English genius which, like Spring, was about to burst into full flower. Pepys understood his master's qualities and potentials and involved him in an almost daily attention to the Navy, to the affairs of Trinity House of which Pepys became Master and to those of the

The discovery of the Longitude at Sea (for which Commissioners were appointed by Act of Parliament during the reign of Queen Anne in 1714) proved to be impracticable and inaccurate until John Harrison (1693–1776), a self-taught mathematician and clockmaker from Yorkshire, constructed the first sea-going timepiece which remained accurate despite a ship's movement and great temperature changes. Harrison completed four timekeepers between 1735 and 1760, the first a massive mechanism of brass and wood weighing 72 lb, the last a watch about twice the size of a pocket watch. A copy of Harrison's watch by Larcum was used by Captain Cook on his second Pacific voyage, and gave an error of less than 8 miles after circumnavigating the world.

Royal Society of which Pepys became President. Perhaps the most permanent and least considered mark which Pepys made on maritime affairs lay in cartography.

Until Pepys the English Navy had perforce had to use Dutch charts even of the coasts of England. This was dangerous, humiliating and to Pepys's eyes a little absurd, since it was neither patriotic nor practical. So Pepys, who could spot talent as well as any modern 'head hunter', bided his time. In 1681 he found the man he wanted. He commissioned a naval officer called Greenvile Collins, who had been Master (or Navigating Officer) to Sir John Narborough on his 1669–71 expedition to the Pacific, to make a survey of the sea coast of the Kingdom, Charles II granting him the title of Hydrographer to the King. Accordingly, with inadequate funds and equipment but with compensating energy and enthusiasm, Collins prepared 120 plans of harbours and open coasts, 48 of which were embodied in 1693 into Great Britain's first Coasting Pilot.

This work which ran into twelve editions became the first survey of the British coast ever made and led, a century later, to the establishment of the Hydrographer's Department of the Admiralty. It also led to the extraordinary fact that in the nineteenth and twentieth centuries the entire seafaring world navigated on British Admiralty charts.

Improvements in navigating instruments such as the quadrant and its later development the sextant brought greater accuracy into ocean navigation but did nothing to solve the gnawing problem of calculating longitude. This required a time-keeping instrument which could be relied on for accuracy under conditions of great heat or cold and in the roughest of seas. Little or no progress in solving this problem had been made by the time Pepys was forced into retirement on the dethronement of James II in 1688. However the matter was at least under intensive study by mathematicians and astronomers of the calibre of Newton and Halley and in 1714, eleven years after Pepys had died following a long illness and in shameful obscurity, Commissioners for the Discovery of the Longitude at Sea were appointed by Act of Parliament and this Board of Longitude offered a prize of £20,000 – a fortune in those days – for a solution to the problem correct to an accuracy of thirty miles. This was not awarded until 1765 when John Harrison's chronometer was proved to have lost only 15 seconds on a voyage from Britain to Barbados and back taking 156 days. How Pepys would have relished this feat!

The departure of Pepys from the naval scene and the accession of an intensely patriotic Dutch Protestant to the throne of England marked a new direction in British foreign policy and in the nature of seapower on which that foreign policy perforce relied. Control of the home waters was no longer enough. Empire building called for strategically placed bases overseas with full dockyard facilities so that ships could be kept in commission without returning to the United Kingdom for maintenance and from which distant areas such as the Mediterranean and Caribbean could be policed. Those factors apart, British foreign policy had had to come to terms with the threat constantly posed by Louis XIV, then the mightiest autocrat in Europe, who aimed, as did Napoleon a century later, at a complete supremacy on the continent. This led to the well known doctrine of 'the balance of power' in the pursuit of which Great Britain, variously allied, came to be at war either with France

– or with Spain acting as the French King's catspaw – or with the two countries together for long stretches of the eighteenth century.

In each succeeding war, as we shall see later on, the Royal Navy played an increasingly vital role. This culminated in the battle of Trafalgar which ushered in what has been called, perhaps euphemistically, the Pax Britannica of the nineteenth century. However before Queen Anne died in 1714 two important and timely events had taken place. One was the union of the Parliaments of England and Scotland in 1707 by which the United Kingdom became united in fact rather than in theory, financial control of the country's affairs being settled in London where a Scotsman, Paterson, had successfully established the Bank of England twelve years previously.

The other event was the Treaty of Utrecht in 1713 which ended the eleven years War of the Spanish Succession and by which Great Britain acquired Gibraltar and Minorca with the invaluable fleet base facilities they provided. Meanwhile how had the Navy fared since the abrupt departure in 1688 of the last King of England to hold not only the title but the active office of Lord High Admiral? (This office was later maintained in commission by the Lords Commissioners of the Admiralty until the founding of a Joint Services, Ministry of Defence in 1964. The title of Lord High Admiral was then resumed by the Crown in the person of Queen Elizabeth II.)

When James II in exile became for the Jacobites the 'King over the water' (in part allusion to his former naval prowess) the fleet which he and Pepys had built, cherished and directed more wisely than any other department or function of the Kingdom, failed him in his hour of need. There were two reasons for this. One was the contrary 'Protestant wind' which blew in William of Orange as it held James's fleet imprisoned in the Thames. The other was the bafflement of Lord Dartmouth, the Commander-in-Chief, at the contradictory orders he received from the Admiralty. Behind these orders lay the well-founded fear that officers of the Royal Navy might prove to be less loyal to the person of their Catholic King than to the Protestant faith, for which their forbears from Drake onwards had fought so valiantly and which had, over the preceding century and a half, proved to be the mainspring of the country's somewhat creaky mechanism of freedom and well-being.

Reserved, suspicious and not exactly of a humorous disposition, 'King Billy', who never mastered the English language, found himself as exasperated as his father-in-law, the exiled King, in dealing with a tough restrictive Parliament and an underpaid – or at times not-paid-at-all – fleet. Of his two principal Admirals, Edward Russell, Earl of Orford, was described as having a face like a map of jolly ignorance and the other, Arthur Herbert, Earl of Torrington, as a one-eyed debauchee who conducted a private life so shocking, even in that wildly licentious age, that Pepys wrote of him, 'Of all the worst men living, Herbert is the only man that I do not know to have any one virtue to compound for all his vices.' However with James invading Ireland, backed and impelled by the French King, these were the best, indeed the only men William could find to carry out his strategy. They did their best and professionally speaking their best turned out to be reasonably impressive.

William himself went over to Ireland and defeated his father-in-law at the battle of the Boyne. In that same year Louis XIV's attempt to reverse the trend of events at sea failed with what might be described as a drawn match off Beachy Head in 1690, for which Torrington was court-martialled and replaced by Orford. This was followed by a defeat of the French two years later off Barfleur in May 1692, a disaster observed from on shore by James who remarked wryly to his natural son, the Duke of Berwick, 'None but my brave English tars could have done so gallant a deed.'

William died in 1702, to be followed by the luckless Anne, who bore eighteen children of whom thirteen were stillborn and none of whom survived into adult life. All these children were sired by her consort, Prince George of Denmark, described at the time as the one person at Court even less interesting than the Queen. Whatever the wits might say – and Anne has been described as an oasis of mediocrity in a reign of outstanding martial and literary achievement – some of the greatest military victories in British history against the Spanish and the French were won during her reign, on land by John Churchill, first Duke of Marlborough, and at sea by Admiral Sir George Rooke. Rooke first of all took a cool eleven million pieces-of-eight off a Spanish treasure fleet at Vigo, supposedly protected by a French squadron, and then in 1704 made his spectacular capture of Gibraltar. This was followed in 1708 by the taking of Minorca by Admiral Sir John Leake, son of a Master Gunner, with the result that its splendid harbour, Port Mahon, became available to the British Mediterranean Fleet for the greater part of the eighteenth century, only being finally restored to Spain in 1802.

The Treaty of Utrecht in 1713, secured the Protestant succession in Great Britain. The death of Anne in 1714 and that of Louis XIV in 1715 (to be succeeded by his infant great grandson Louis XV) ended an era as distinct from the one which followed as it was from the Tudor century which preceded it. The Royal Navy as such had come into being. It was no longer run by an autocratic Lord High Admiral but somewhat more clumsily by Lords Commissioners of the Admiralty and was supplied and victualled by a Navy Board organised by Pepys. There had now come into existence a cadre of professional naval officers and a fleet of line-of-battle ships, together with faster sailing frigates for look-out and communication work, which would have surprised and delighted Hawkins and Drake.

France had replaced Spain as the traditional enemy and there had been a very fair proportion of naval successes against both countries. More important, however, both for Britain and the world at large was that naval energy was now being directed into maritime matters over and beyond those directly connected with war.

British seamen, backed and encouraged by the prestigious Royal Society of London for Improving Natural Knowledge, founded by Charles II in 1662, now began to exhibit an almost altruistic interest in research. They sought scientific knowledge in astronomy, biology, geographical exploration, navigation and seamanship and the fruits of this vigorous, thrusting research were made available to the world. 'It was indeed a lucky chance', as David Howarth remarks,[1] 'that the British at sea who proved to be the most effective in battle were also the most inquisitive in research and the most ingenious in invention. Their wars at sea were fought through dynastic quarrels or rivalries in trade – one might say for power or riches. But their research was unselfish.'

This and the continuing royal interest which inspired both aspects of the Navy's work formed a legitimate cause for pride.

CHAPTER IV

THE
HANOVERIANS

1714 · 1763

CHRONOLOGICAL COMPENDIUM

The Reigns and their character

George I
1714–1727

Peace and recovery. German stolidity in place of Stuart extravagance.

George II
1727–1760

Walpole and the Whig years. Slow awakening to the age of reason, and constitutional monarchy.

General

The accession of William III (Dutch William) had meant changes in the direction, priorities and underlying assumptions of British foreign policy. The link with Holland had brought England firmly to the forefront of European politics, had involved her in protracted land wars and had also led to a determination to preserve the Protestant succession against French Catholic support for the Jacobite cause.

Despite Marlborough's great victories at Blenheim and Ramillies, by 1714 the opinion of English country gentlemen, the political heart of the nation, set firmly against continental land campaigns and in favour of a 'blue water' policy. Since the Civil War England had greatly feared a standing army. On the other hand a strong navy meant that battles were fought away from home. It could also promote trading advantages over France and Holland in the colonies. It was to protect these advantages that an enthusiasm for war arose in 1739 and in 1756 after at least two decades of peace.

The first half of the eighteenth century saw unusual political stability with Walpole in power from 1721 to 1742. The office of Prime Minister was emerging. A united England and Scotland prospered as the result of enormous expansion of trade and of the early effects of the agricultural revolution. Meanwhile Britain was becoming more politically aware as 'Grub Street' flourished after the lapse of the Licensing Act in 1695. The Whig and Tory parties developed. The South Sea trading company crashed in 1720 (the 'South Sea Bubble'), the London poor discovered gin, early empire building began.

Naval

Thanks to Pepys the Royal Navy was now an organisation of complexity and power, one held in great public esteem. Through the long years of peace, the Navy, kept in being for the protection of trade, was also mobilised at the Prime Minister's whim to act as a threat or deterrent. The first Royal Naval Academy was founded at Portsmouth in 1733, uniforms for officers, designed by George II, were authorised in 1748 and studies of health at sea were undertaken with the object of eradicating particular diseases such as scurvy.

Anson, one of the founders of the naval profession as it was later known, circumnavigated the world and ended his life as First Lord of the Admiralty, having transformed the navy into the most powerful and efficient fighting instrument at sea which the world had ever seen. In turn the following generations of Captains and Admirals developed Anson's ideas so that the navy of the Seven Years War and the later Napoleonic Wars became supreme.

Warships were listed in six divisions and rated according to the number of guns carried. A first rate line of battle ship such as the "Victory" (later to become Nelson's famous flagship) which was laid down in 1759 would displace over two thousand tons and would be a three-decker mounting a hundred guns. Fifth and sixth rate ships were generally known as frigates.

Signalling between ships at sea developed into a numbered code with 28 flags and, later, 57 signals in the *Fighting Instructions*.

An oil-burning light with parabolic mirrors was first installed in the Mersey in 1763 and between 1735 and 1760 Harrison (1693–1776) developed the chronometer to an accuracy of 1/10th of a second per diem.

People and Events

Admiral of the Fleet Sir John Leake 1656–1720	forced the boom at Londonderry 1689, commanded the "Eagle" at Barfleur 1692, took part in the capture of Gibraltar 1704, later became Commander-in-Chief in the Mediterranean and captured Sardinia and Minorca.
Admiral Edward Vernon 1684–1757	known as 'Old Grog' because of the grogram boat cloak he wore, captured Portobello on the isthmus of Darien from the Spaniards in 1739 but failed to capture Cartagena. Was one of the first Admirals to practise his Captains in naval manoeuvres and their ships' companies at gun drill. In 1740 brought in the watering down of the rum ration henceforth known as grog.
Admiral the Hon. Edward Boscawen 1711–61	commanded the "Namur" in decisive victory over the French at Cape Finisterre in 1747, made a Lord Commissioner of the Admiralty 1751 and signed the order for Byng's court martial 1756. Defeated French at Lagos Bay 1759 and blockaded Quiberon Bay 1760. Always showed concern for health and comfort of his seamen.
Admiral of the Fleet Lord Edward Hawke 1705–81	defeated French Admiral Conflans in shattering victory at Quiberon Bay 1759, 1766–1768 First Lord of the Admiralty.
Admiral Sir Charles Saunders 1713–75	was naval commander-in-chief of expedition to capture Quebec 1759 with General Wolfe and brought his fleet up the St Lawrence in a brilliant feat of navigation.
Admiral of the Fleet Lord George Anson 1697–1762	circumnavigated the world 1740–44 bringing back treasure of more than half a million pounds. Defeated French squadron off Cape Finisterre 1747. Did two separate spells as First Lord of the Admiralty reorganising the Royal Marines, the rating of ships, and the Articles of War.
Admiral John Byng 1704–57	son of Viscount Torrington, Admiral of the Fleet, who had helped capture Gibraltar in the year of Byng's birth, was given command of a fleet to bring support to Minorca at the start of the Seven Years War (1756). He fought an indecisive action with the French fleet covering the invasion and then returned to Gibraltar leaving Minorca to its fate. Courtmartialled and sentenced to death. Was shot on the quarterdeck of H.M.S. "Monarch" on 14 March 1757.

Wars and Battles

1718–20 Quadruple Alliance

1718 Battle of Cape Passaro.

1719 Spanish expelled from Sicily.

1727–8 War begins without formal declaration through Spain's siege of Gibraltar. This siege is lifted in March 1728

1739–48 War of Jenkins's Ear and Austrian Succession

Caused by Spaniards pillaging Captain Jenkins's ship in 1731 and cutting off his ear. 1739 England declares war on Spain. November 1739 Admiral Vernon captures Porto Bello. Expedition to Carthagena and Cuba 1741. Battle of Toulon against combined Franco-Spanish fleet 1744. British take Cape Breton Island and Louisburg at mouth of St Lawrence 1745. French and Spanish break blockade of Genoa 1747.

1756–63 Seven Years War

Britain declares war on France 1756. French take Minorca 1756. British driven from Great Lakes 1756. British take Louisburg 1758. Battle of Cape St Vincent 1759. Battle of Quebec 1759. Battle of Quiberon Bay 1759. British take Montreal 1760. British take St Vincent, Martinique and Grenada 1762.

During the fifty years following the death of Queen Anne on 1st August 1714 great and subtle changes took place in the British realm. The accession of a German king who spoke no English changed the temper and style of the Court, increased the power of Parliament and of the elected government whose head now became known – initially as a term of abuse – as the 'Prime Minister', and ensured that there would be no Popery, no disputed succession, no French invasion and no civil war.

Most important of all, the Hanoverian kings claimed no Divine Right to rule: they were there by express sanction of Parliament and the switch from an Anglo-Scottish to an Anglo-German line, dull and dowdy though it was to begin with, came about because the direct heir to the throne, James Edward, the 'Old Pretender', son of the deposed James II, was a Catholic.

The union of England and Scotland had by now become an established fact and poverty-stricken Scots in great numbers began to invade the south, continuing on in many cases into the outposts of Empire, whilst the Whig and Tory country gentlemen of England developed their estates, improved agriculture and extended the market for a growing variety of products from overseas trade on which the country has ever since depended.

A Norfolk squire, Sir Robert Walpole, who hunted five days a week and who had been Chancellor of the Exchequer for three years after the death of Anne, became Prime Minister after the 'South Sea Bubble' had burst in 1720. Walpole stabilised the finances, avoided a major war through non-intervention in European politics, decreased the National Debt, did his best – which was not much – to limit corruption and although jeered at by those who remembered the glories of past ages, nursed the country into security and an expanding prosperity for twenty-one years.

As for the Navy, the Jacobite threat, distant but by no means trivial, persuaded both Whig and Tory administrations to keep a strong fleet in being. The Navy had balked the Stuarts in 1690 and might well have to do so again. To a certain extent the decay of the first half of the seventeenth century crept back into the first half of the eighteenth but the seagoing Royal Navy, the Admiralty which directed it and the Navy Board which supplied it, had by now coalesced into a world on its own. Patronage still ruled the day, yet the Navy had reached a stage of growth where it could only suffer intermittent and partial badgering by even the most powerful and corrupt of politicians.

The Navy was now held in the public esteem as an organisation of complexity, size and skill unrivalled by any other department of state. Incompetence could no longer be afforded. The professionalism instituted by Pepys had begun to pay a significant dividend. Unworthy officers promoted by influence were seen to discredit their patrons and perforce had to give way to men of ability who prospered and whose success encouraged a more honest and intelligent sponsorship. In effect the Navy generated its own professional patronage influenced by but shielded from the high wind of politics.

At the centre of naval affairs stood an increasingly able and powerful Admiralty Board. This ability and power owed as much to the foundation of the Bank of England in 1694 and to the funding of government debt by way of the issue of the 'first perpetual annuities' in 1715 as it did to the ruling politicians of the day. Navy

Bills became debt instruments much in demand by investors and the Navy thus effectively created its own transferable notes. 'In the immensely expensive business of running a fleet, the financial strength of Britain and the solid political will to exploit it were the Navy's greatest assets.'[1]

The Navy operated in a changing world, but one of comparative peace, as it did after the Napoleonic wars a century later. Diplomacy at least in part replaced active hostilities. During this period only one fleet action was fought. Yet throughout Walpole's twenty-one years of power this more or less incorruptible Prime Minister operating in a highly corrupt age never bothered to find out much about the sea. However, he not only kept a large fleet in being but was also in the habit of mobilising it at the drop of a hat in order to impress or to overawe the continental powers.

That one naval battle mentioned above in the years between the ending of the War of the Spanish Succession and the beginning of that of the Austrian Succession in 1739, took place in 1718. The Spanish had been far more distressed than the French by the Treaty of Utrecht. Everything, it seemed, was to be at their expense. So they took a unilateral decision at least to recover Sicily which had been ceded to Austria, despatching thither a fleet to forestall the change of sovereignty.

To counter this, Sir George Byng (father of the less fortunate John) who had helped capture Gibraltar in 1704 and who had successfully denied supplies to the Old Pretender in 1715, took a fleet of 21 ships from Minorca, found and engaged the Spanish fleet of 45 ships off Cape Passaro and won a decisive victory in which the Spanish flagship surrendered, 16 ships were captured and 7 burnt. This did wonders for British morale. Byng was elevated to the peerage as Viscount Torrington and later became First Lord of the Admiralty. The effect on the seagoing fleet was equally pronounced, perhaps even a little heady. The Royal Navy now began to consider that, given approximate parity in numbers, it could always master the French whilst against the Spaniards it could do far better in the face of far worse odds. However

As sailing warships became more sophisticated and costly, it became more difficult for the Admiralty to be sure that it was getting what it paid for. This 1725 model of a ship of 100 guns (to a scale of 1 to 48) shows one of the ways used to check supply. Although parts of the model are planked, much of the interior construction can be verified. Actual sailing quality when completed, however, varied greatly with individual ships as it does even today with racing yachts in the age of tank and aerodynamic testing.

this Britannic thrust to rule the waves had an in-built danger. Its very success led to a certain amount of overconfidence and a revival of the belief, originating with Drake and Hawkins that any Spanish possession overseas could now be had for the plucking.

This aggressive self-esteem, increasingly generated by successful commanders such as Rooke, Leakey and Byng, did something – though again not very much – to help solve the perennial problem of manning. Throughout the eighteenth century the Navy was undermanned both in numbers and in quality of personnel. The plain fact is that at no time of crisis was there ever enough first-rate human material available. Prize money lured in the volunteers: the Press Gang supplied the rest. It was not a happy blend but then life at sea has never been a pleasure cruise for those before the mast.

Nor for that matter was it much better in the eighteenth century for officers of the wardroom when compared with the life a gentleman could lead ashore. Dr Johnson's caustic pronouncement in 1759 might well be applied to the whole sailing era, 'No man will be a sailor who has contrivance enough to get himself into a jail; for being in a ship is being in jail with the chance of being drowned . . . a man in jail has more room, better food and commonly better company.' It was scarcely an aid to recruitment.

What, then, made men go to sea and what was life like for those 'that go down to the sea in ships, that do business in great waters', as the Psalmist put it, 'seeing the works of the Lord and his wonders in the deep?' The short answer was that life was rough, cold and gusty above deck; cramped, foetid and miserable below and the wonders of the deep were usually extremely perilous to endure. Food was execrable, disease endemic, the only amelioration being alcohol in such quantity that almost no sailor at sea was ever completely sober.

Yet the nature of the seaman's work with its unending exposure to the vagaries of wind and sea made him contemptuous of danger. 'The bredth of an inch-boorde is betwixt him and drowning yet he sweares and drinkes as deeply as if he were a fathom from it', William Braithwaite had written in 1631, 'His familiarity with death and danger hath armed him with a kind of dissolute security against any encounter.' Seamen slept hard in any nook or cranny into which they could wedge themselves although after 1586 when Hawkins had observed Indians taking their siestas in string contraptions slung from trees, the advent of the 'hammacoe' made life somewhat easier if not any healthier.

The perpetual complaint at sea centred on food and drink. Pepys, perhaps, put it best in declaring that 'Englishmen and more especially seamen love their bellies above everything else and therefore it must always be remembered in the management of the victualling of the Navy that to make any abatement of them in the quality or agreeableness of their victuals is to discourage and provoke them in their tenderest point and will sooner render them disgusted with the King's service than any other hardship that could be put upon them.'

A century later life at sea had but little improved. Sailors had still to clothe themselves with slops purchased from the Purser and this continued until the mid nineteenth century. Those who were ill had to pay the Surgeon to cure them if he could, an extra fee being charged if the disease happened to be venereal. Cleanliness was virtually unknown until disciplinarians like Admiral Vernon (1684–1757) and Admiral Boscawen (1711–61) began to investigate disease, ordered a little washing to take place and caused the lower decks to be fumigated and aired. Even the lemon juice cure for scurvy, although first discovered by Captain Lancaster a century and a half before and then proved by Dr James Lind in 1753 in the first controlled dietetic experiment, had nevertheless to wait for compulsory introduction into the service until 1795. For the greater part of the eighteenth century a seaman who was poorly sick would be liable to have tobacco smoke blown down his throat on the assumption that it would clear his veins, and one Surgeon reported that 'the only way known in the Navy to remove a bad smell in a ship is to produce a worse one to take its place'.[2]

Behind all this lay deeper instincts and beliefs. It became part of naval lore at an early date that illiterate seamen preferred a strong disciplinarian as a Captain rather than a superficially easier man. Anson, of whom more anon, remarked that 'A tightly disciplined ship was more often than not a happy ship', and to this precept were added the twin forces of religion and patriotism. The Elizabethan sailor could slit a Spaniard's throat, capture his ship, throw the crew overboard, buy and sell negro slaves and all with a prayer of thankfulness to God for his munificence.

Two centuries later the eighteenth century sailor was of the opinion that 'Two skinny Frenchmen and one Portugee – one British sailor can beat all three.' These deep certainties continued in the collective naval unconscious until at least the end of the Second World War in 1945 during the course of which and despite the many terrible disasters which befell the Royal Navy, I doubt if there was an officer or rating at sea who was not completely sure in his marrow that the enemy *would* be defeated. It simply could not be otherwise.

Throughout the mid eighteenth century and even more so during the Napoleonic wars 'Deep down in the sailor's consciousness – and frequently brought back to memory in song and story – was the knowledge that his forbears had won ascendancy at sea over the Spanish and the Dutch. It was a knowledge that bred in him an almost subconscious confidence in his own similar ascendancy over the sailors of France, the present enemy.'[3]

Into the above psychology was woven a greed, or at any rate a lusting, for prize money. This reward, available only to warrior seamen, can be likened to the football pools or premium bonds of today. An Able Seaman's share of any prize taken might be microscopic compared with that of a Captain or an Admiral, it was none the less more than he would ever get in a shoreside billet and without those educated officers on the quarterdeck, there would have been no opportunities for prize money at all.

'Good mariners grow not up like mushrooms without care or culture' wrote Barnaby Slush, a cook on Vernon's expedition to take Porto Bello in 1739 (during the war of Jenkins's Ear), 'It is morally impossible, nay and it's naturally impossible, too, to have a brave, active, skilful, resolute body of sailors without just and generous as well as understanding officers.' So a successful Captain would have volunteers queueing up to join his ship without benefit of the Press Gang, the mainspring to it all being prize money and the heroism necessary to acquire it.

In this connection the only comparable loot gatherers at that time were the

Brethren of the Coast, the buccaneers of the Caribbean. However they, like tax avoiders today, found it inexpedient to return to a civilised homeland to spend their ill-gotten gains. They remained beyond the Pale. On the other hand the taking of a rich prize into a Devon port had Cup Final overtones. If the fountains no longer ran with wine, it was nevertheless bonanza time not only for Jolly Jack himself but for the vulture gang of pimps, prostitutes, innkeepers and trinket salesmen who preyed on his new, unkeepable wealth. 'When storms and tempests all are o'er, And Jack receives his prize on shore, then for his doxies all he'll send, What's dearly earned he'll freely spend.'

All the great Admirals of the eighteenth century, in addition to their fighting qualities, took intelligent care of the men under their command. This was not so much altruism as practical common sense. The irascible Vernon, for instance, when at Port Royal, Jamaica in August 1740 after successfully capturing Porto Bello with only six ships, reported numerous desertions caused by men 'stupefying themselves with spirituous liquors'. There was nothing unusual in that. How then to remedy the situation without reducing the essential work force? 'Old Grog', so nicknamed from the grogram boat cloak he habitually wore, used his popularity – and it was then at its height – to venture a frontal attack on 'that formidable Dagon Drunkenness'.

He did this by ordering the daily Admiralty allowance of half a pint of rum per man to be mixed with a quart of water 'in one Scuttled Butt kept for that purpose and to be done upon Deck and in the presence of the Lieutenant of the Watch'. This ensured that no man could be cheated of his proper allowance. 'Grog' had arrived and its daily issue continued in all H.M. Ships until long after the Second World War.

Later eighteenth century Admirals such as Hawke and Boscawen also substantially exerted themselves to improve life at sea, the latter being a shining light in the health care department, whilst Hawke was blessed throughout the fleet for an all-round bettering of the rations. Basically this new 'officer responsibility' revolved round the business of seeing justice done both on board ship and on shore, though the pinning down of rascally purveyors demanded a more difficult and complicated process. The reward was instant and considerable. Men would do almost anything for an Admiral or a Captain whom they trusted to take genuine care of their welfare however primitive that welfare may seem by present day standards.

Outstanding by far in this first half of a brilliant naval century is Vernon's contemporary, George Anson (1697–1762). Not since Drake, a century and a half before, had there been a sailor so apt at setting the imagination of the country alight nor one who combined in himself the talents of Drake and Hawkins and who put those talents to work in a re-organisation from top to bottom of the naval service. Anson did all these things and in addition encouraged later naval officers such as Saunders, Keppel, Saumarez, Piercy Brett and Howe to continue the good work in their own individual ways.

Accordingly Anson goes into the record as the first British Admiral to realise that although possessed of resolute leadership himself, this was no longer enough. It had now become essential to have subordinate officers of education and intelligence who could be trained to avoid lethargy, to prepare always for the unexpected and thus to be ahead of the enemy through the use of foresight, judgment and attention to detail in meticulous planning. This realisation led to the inauguration of the first naval academy for the training of officers at Portsmouth in 1733. Nelson alone was to excel Anson as a trainer of officers, and Nelson neither circled the globe nor had to run the entire Navy as First Lord of the Admiralty for a total of over ten years.

Anson's circumnavigation stands as an extraordinary feat in itself. Like Drake, he faced and survived disaster on several occasions. Also like Drake he was essentially a man of action who talked little and wrote less. Horace Walpole called him 'reserved' and Anson himself admitted to being 'awkward in ceremony and correspondence'. He was seventeen when the first Hanoverian came to the throne and like Roderick Random's uncle, Lieutenant Tom Bowling, grew up 'defying the Pope, the Devil and the Pretender'. It was a coarse, quarrelsome age, vide Smollett and Hogarth. (At the height of the 'gin era' between 1740 and 1742, there were twice as many burials in London as there were baptisms.)

But it was also the age when 'Rule Britannia' first saw the light of day (1740). Garrick sang it at Drury Lane together with his own 'Heart of Oak' after which it became an immediate hit and at about the same time the British National Anthem in its present form was also first heard. Patriotism came in on the flood (fuelled always by Prize Money) and in 1743 George II achieved renown as the last British monarch to lead his army personally into battle against the French at Dettingen.

In 1739, after Richard Jenkins, Master of a Glasgow brig, had displayed his ear in a jar of pickle to a committee of Parliament, claiming it had been cut off by a Spanish coastguard, an 'outraged' England declared war on Spain. In the following year, a harassed Admiralty appointed Captain George Anson to command a small squadron of six ships, with the rank of Commodore. This squadron was ordered to the Pacific to annoy Spanish possessions and, if possible, capture one of the treasure ships which sailed annually across the Pacific from Acapulco to Manila.

This was easier said than done. Orders were issued in November 1739 but it was not until September 1740 that the ships were fitted out and manned sufficiently to sail. Even then they were short of 200 seamen. Of the 500 soldiers authorised on the complement to attack Spanish Pacific ports, only 259 actually came on board and the majority of those were Chelsea Pensioners in their sixties, some even over seventy. To make matters worse 210 Marines were then drafted at the last moment but these turned out to be country yokels unable even to fire the muskets they had been given. Over aged or callow, illiterate, ill fed, disaffected and diseased, these ships' companies – still short-handed – were completely inadequate to the tasks they were ordered to undertake. And when tropical flux and scurvy attacked, they naturally died like flies. In a voyage lasting nearly four years, four men were killed in action, over 1300 died of scurvy and other diseases.

The voyage is epic if only for the suffering these reluctant heroes endured. The weather in the South Atlantic had been bad enough; once into the Pacific that supposedly calm, empty ocean belied its name. For three whole months tempestuous seas and southerly storms blasted them apart at the beginning of the southern hemisphere winter. The timing could scarcely have been worse. Anson in the 'Centurion' made the agreed rendezvous at Juan Fernandez, Robinson Crusoe's

A map of Anson's heroic
circumnavigation of the
world (Sept. 1740–June
1744). Idiosyncrasies in
place names and spelling,
retained from an earlier
map, indicate a maritime
world in which much still
remained to be discovered
and regulated.

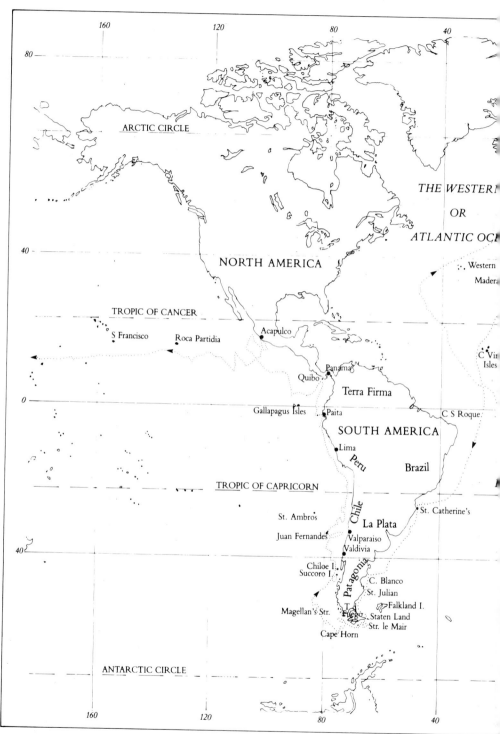

ARCTIC CIRCLE

THE WESTERN

OR

ATLANTIC OC

NORTH AMERICA

Western

Mader

TROPIC OF CANCER

S Francisco   Roca Partidia   Acapulco

C Vir
Isles

Panama

Quibo

Terra Firma

Gallapagus Isles   Paita   C S Roque

SOUTH AMERICA

Lima

Peru   Brazil

TROPIC OF CAPRICORN

St. Catherine's

St. Ambros   Chile   La Plata

Juan Fernandes   Valparaiso

Valdivia

Chiloe I.

Succoro I.   C. Blanco

Patagonia   St. Julian

Falkland I.

Magellan's Str.   Fuego   Staten Land

Str. le Mair

Cape Horn

ANTARCTIC CIRCLE

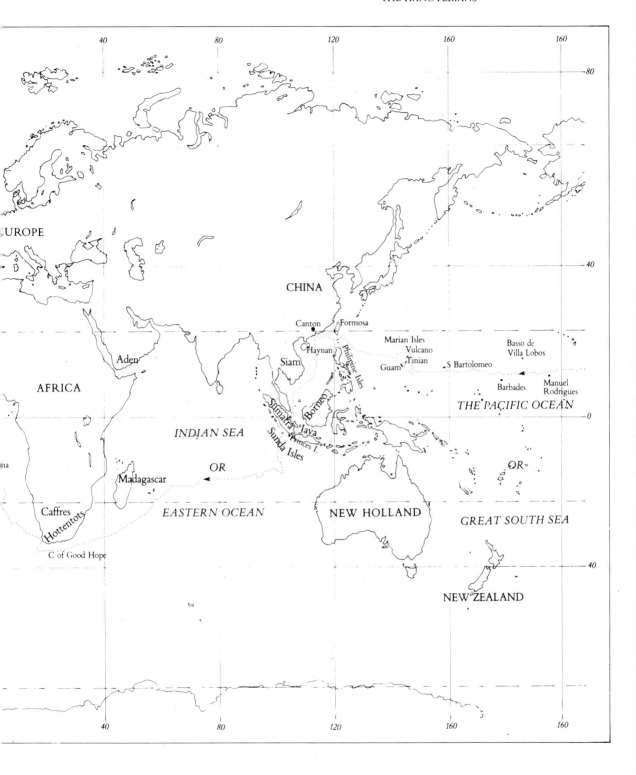

40   80   120   160   160

80

UROPE

40

CHINA

Canton   Formosa

Marian Isles   Basso de
Vulcano   Villa Lobos
Haynan   Tinian
Aden   Siam   Guam   S Bartolomeo

AFRICA   Barbades   Manuel
Rodrigues

THE PACIFIC OCEAN

Borneo   0

Sumatra Java
INDIAN SEA   Sunda Isles Princes I.

Madagascar   OR   OR

Caffres   NEW HOLLAND   GREAT SOUTH SEA
Hottentots   EASTERN OCEAN

C of Good Hope   40

NEW ZEALAND

40   80   120   160   160

island, with only thirty men fit for duty. Two more of the squadron reached him later, two were wrecked and one returned to England.

Yet those who were left never gave up. 180 sick men were carried ashore in their hammocks, a task shared by Anson himself and his officers. A long slow recovery began with no one in this desperate situation having the slightest doubt but that their Commodore, still immaculate in his wig and three cornered hat, would know in any given circumstance what was best to be done. No one even thought of abandoning the mission and when, after three months, the sick had sufficiently recovered, they sought out and took their first prize. This they brought back to the island and fitted out with guns from one of the victualling ships which had had to be destroyed. 'And now', Richard Walter, Anson's Chaplain wrote, 'the spirits of our people being greatly raised . . . by this earnest of success, they forgot all their past distresses, resumed their wonted alacrity and laboured indefatigably in completing our water, receiving our lumber and in preparing to take our farewell of the island.'

Anson then attacked Spanish settlements on the west coast of South America, afterwards taking station off Acapulco on the look-out for the treasure galleon, the capture of which would by itself have justified the entire voyage. Forewarned, perhaps, the ship never appeared. So Anson decided to cross the Pacific and attempt a capture at the Manila end. In the course of this voyage, Anson's fleet had now been reduced to a single ship and after spending six months in Macao and Canton, the first British man-of-war to visit a Chinese port, this ship sailed westward, ostensibly for home, in actual fact to intercept and capture the Philippine treasure ship "Nuestra Señora de Covadonga", whose treasure was so enormous in the currency of the day, that it made Anson rich for life and was later paraded through the City of London in thirty-two wagons loaded with over £500,000. Unmoved by peril though certainly assisted by luck, Anson had brought his "Centurion" home in the face of great odds, as when, on the last leg, he sailed inadvertently through the middle of a French fleet, being saved only by a providential fog.

After Anson's return in 1744 his story is one of almost uninterrupted success. Promoted to Flag rank in 1745, the year the Young Pretender led the second disastrous Jacobite rebellion, Anson was advanced two steps to Vice Admiral of the Blue in April 1746, created a peer after his resounding victory over the French at Finisterre in 1747 and promoted Admiral of the Blue in 1748. It was at Finisterre, when Anson captured the entire French fleet, that the Commander of "L'Invincible" struck to Anson and on delivering his sword is reported to have said, 'Monsieur, vous avez vaincu l'Invincible et la Gloire (another French ship) vous suit.' In 1748 Anson married Lady Elizabeth Yorke, daughter of the Lord Chancellor Hardwicke, an event which he regarded as the happiest of his life. He was just fifty-one and thenceforth spent the rest of his life in the corridors of power. He put this time to excellent use, the spur to all this activity being the memory of the needless disasters he had suffered on his great voyage, caused by inefficiency in the dockyards at home and the folly of ordering him to the Pacific by way of Cape Horn at the onset of winter.

At the Admiralty Anson proved to be as cool and formidable as he had been at sea. Officers were given uniforms in 1748. Ships were standardised to the extent that the six-rates (by number of guns carried) were divided into two – battleships 'fit to stand in the line' and cruisers or frigates too weak for the line but faster and thus able to shadow an enemy fleet and also fight their own kind. Existing marine regiments were replaced by a single corps of marines: the Articles of War were rewritten and in general Anson 'used his patience and tenacity to reform the Navy's administration, as Pepys had reformed it a hundred years before: he dragged it up to a state of honesty and capability which it maintained on the whole until its supremacy over its rivals had been won.'[4]

Anson could be said to have set the tone and to have provided the main driving force for most of what happened in the Royal Navy, and in the shoreside establishments on which the fleet depended, during the last fifteen years of the reign of George II. It was altogether a lively time. The stagnation of the first four decades of the century had yielded abruptly to movement and an activity at times frenetic and some of it far from successful. Anson's last triumph at sea in 1747 had been preceded in 1744 by an indecisive battle off Toulon which resulted in the court martial of Thomas Matthews, the Commander-in-Chief, and of Richard Lestock, his second-in-command, who had been sent home for failing to do his utmost to engage the enemy. Lestock was acquitted on a technicality in the rigid wording of the old Fighting Instructions. He was also a Whig with powerful friends in the Government. Matthews, an Admiral of temper (nicknamed 'Il Furibondo') was dismissed the service because he had broken the Fighting Instructions through closing in to attack before forming the line and also because he was a Tory. Reasonably-minded people were outraged. This led to recriminations which did the service no good and stultified initiative in battle for the next twenty years.

This was the more unfortunate because, thanks to Pepys at the start and to Anson at the end of this period, the Navy had become a well-equipped, integrated service as never before. The service was now accepted by both political parties as the principal *permanent* force by which British foreign policy could be effected. There has never been the prejudice against a regular Navy that there was against a standing Army, if only because the King's Navy could never be used to dominate and suppress the British people as could an army and as, indeed, Cromwell's Ironsides had been.

The Navy looked outward, so to speak, and the King's concern with it was wholly approved by the country at large. Indeed George II took a decision in 1758 which has had beneficial repercussions ever since. He sent his son, Prince Edward, to sea as a Midshipman under Captain Howe (later to become an Admiral and an Earl) with no special privileges of any sort. Howe reported, 'I was not told how to provide for His Royal Highness and all the answer I could obtain from ministerial authority respecting the treatment of and conduct towards the Prince was limited to an instruction that I was to act respecting him just as if I had not any such person on board the ship. He came not only without bed and linen of almost every kind but I paid also for his uniform clothes which I provided for him with all other necessaries at Portsmouth. I made no enquiries how I was to be indemnified for every requisite attention to the then presumptive heir to the Crown.' This novel and healthy idea, that princes should serve at sea, has been observed by reigning monarchs ever since, to the astonishment of certain foreign potentates such as the Khedive of Egypt who

THE RATING SYSTEM OF SHIPS

Although certain notable ships such as H.M.S. "Resolution" launched in 1610 are described, for convenience, as first rates (she carried eighty guns) the rating system of classification did not come into general usage until Anson's first term as First Lord of the Admiralty (1751–6). Nowadays warships are more generally graded by their tonnage and complement. From the middle of the eighteenth century, however, sailing warships were grouped according to the number of guns they carried.

From then on the rates were as follows:

First   100–110 guns
Second   84–100
Third   70–84
Fourth   50–70
Fifth   32–50

Sixth   Any number of guns up to 32 provided the ship was commanded by a Post-Captain.

Only ships of the first three rates were considered to be sufficiently powerful to be in the line of battle in main fleet actions. Ships of the fifth and sixth rates were generally known as frigates equivalent to the latter-day cruiser and although able to give a good account of themselves did not take part in fleet actions but were used as the eyes of the fleet and for the conveying of intelligence because of their greater speed. For instance, frigates would be stationed off a blockaded enemy port to alert the main battle fleet, usually held beyond the horizon, that the enemy was leaving port. Fourth rate ships, of which few were built, did not form part of the line of battle except occasionally in the smaller fleets. Carronades (short range mortar guns), first introduced into the navy in 1779, were not counted in the number of guns determining the rating of a ship until after the Napoleonic Wars in 1817.

The eyes, ears and messenger of the Fleet, the frigate. In this case H.M.S. "Glasgow", an engraving from a painting by F. Williams in 1814.

visited one of H.M. Ships at Alexandria in the 1880s to discover a grandson of Queen Victoria coaling ship.

We have now entered the era of the great eighteenth century Captains and Admirals, those 'immortals' who form the heart – and what a heart it is – of Rule Britannia. These men make as magnificent a *corpus navalis* as ever the world has seen, each a splendidly differentiated individual in his own right whilst shaped by and in turn shaping the Royal Navy itself. There has been nothing to touch them in the present materialistic age through which we have lived and to no other period is a panegyric more suited.

Warts and all – and the defects of its heroes matched the scale of their qualities – this was a period in British history better dealt with in poetry than in prose, its tone admirably caught in Boscawen's letter to his wife, Fanny, from the "Royal George"

off Brest on 30th July 1756 immediately before the outbreak of the Seven Years War: 'I beg my dear will not be uneasy at my staying out so long. To be sure I lose the fruits of the earth but then I am gathering the flowers of the sea.' The flowers of the sea and the men who gathered them decorate the next sixty years from the beginning of the Seven Years War in 1756.

By 1815 Europe had been finally freed from the overlordship of France, England's 'ancient enemy'. It was a long drawn out struggle, in its context titanic, and it certainly began badly enough with the loss of Minorca and the execution for negligence of the Admiral responsible. This has been described as the worst legalistic crime in the nation's annals. *'Dans ce pays-ci'*, wrote Voltaire, *'il est bon de tuer de temps en temps un amiral pour encourager les autres.'*

However far from encouraging anyone at all, this judicial murder had the opposite effect. Byng had been acquitted of cowardice or disaffection and for George II not to exercise the royal prerogative of clemency for the 'text book' default of negligence – of 'not doing his utmost to take or destroy the enemy's ships' outraged the Navy and dismayed the common folk who, initially, had put up the hue and cry. The inscription on Byng's monument at Southill, Bedfordshire conveys what the country thought: 'To the Perpetual Disgrace of Public Justice the Hon. John Byng Esq, Admiral of the Blue, Fell a Martyr to Political Persecution March 14 1757 when Bravery and Loyalty were insufficient Securities for the Life and Honour of a Naval Officer.'

What happened was that at the start of the Seven Years War Minorca had come under siege from a French squadron commanded by Admiral Galissonière. Admiral Byng, son of the victor of Passaro in 1718, was ordered to relieve the island. And so he might have done had he abandoned at an early stage the rigid line formation called for by the Fighting Instructions. His Flag Captain suggested this action but Byng, who had sat on the Matthews-Lestock court martial, replied 'Remember the misfortunes of Mr Matthews' and played it by the book. Unfortunately he misjudged events and was later forced to leave the line anyway in a desperate attempt to remedy the situation. He failed. Later still the French, having inflicted much damage on the English ships, retreated and this was where Byng made his final mistake.

Instead of risking all and pursuing the much larger French fleet, Byng called a Council of War, decided to save his own ships and get them to Gibraltar for repair, leaving Minorca to its fate. At the court martial it was of no avail to plead that not a ship was lost and that Gibraltar, too, was under acute threat. Minorca had had to surrender. Undeniably Byng had done less than his utmost to prevent this disaster, even allowing for the fact that, badly outnumbered, he might in the event have lost his entire fleet. Under the Article of War in question, guilt was punishable by death with no alternative. The court martial had no discretion to modify the sentence but its members unanimously recommended mercy. 'We cannot help laying the Distresses of our Minds before Your Lordships on this occasion', they said 'in finding ourselves under a Necessity of condemning a Man to Death from the great severity of the 12th Article of War part of which he falls under, and which admits of no Mitigation, *even if the Crime should be committed by an Error in Judgment only*. And therefore for our Consciences' sake, as well as in justice to the Prisoner, we pray Your Lordships in the most earnest manner to recommend him to His Majesty's Clemency.' All were horrified when their advice was disregarded and it took another twenty-two years for the Article in question to be amended to read, 'Death or to inflict such other punishment as the nature and degree of the offence shall be found to deserve.'

The Navy has abhorred this execution ever since and with such a start it might well be thought that the country scarcely deserved to prosper in a war which significantly changed the European world and its empires for two centuries. However the execution of this luckless Admiral did demonstrate in a brutal way that more was now expected of senior naval officers than mere courage and loyalty. Tactical judgment allied to strategic understanding had now become a *sine qua non*. Fortunately these were qualities in good supply among the Navy's 'top brass' of the day and they were also present in William Pitt the Elder who had pleaded for Byng.

'The House of Commons, sir, is inclined to mercy', said Pitt to the King. 'You have taught me to look for the sense of my people elsewhere than in the House of Commons', the King replied.

Pitt had taken office in 1757 as Secretary of State and was to prove himself in the years immediately following to be the greatest War Minister Britain had ever found. 'Walpole', Dr Johnson remarked, 'was a Minister given by the Crown to the people. Pitt was a Minister given by the people to the Crown', and in 1757 Pitt regarded himself as the saviour of England, making no bones about it. 'I was called to the administration of affairs by the voice of the people: to them I have always considered myself accountable for my conduct, and cannot therefore continue in a situation which makes me responsible for measures I am no longer allowed to guide.' There were no two ways about that. Now a strong, incorruptible politician had arrived at the centre of power, one whose outlook was to be duplicated a few decades later by Napoleon himself. 'J'ordonne ou je me tais', Napoleon said, 'I give the orders or I keep my mouth shut.' Two years after Pitt had taken over the reins of power, the results of his political, and naval leadership were so successful that 1759 has gone down into British history as an *annus mirabilis*.

In opening the first Parliament after the Peace of Aix-la-Chapelle in 1748, George II had said: 'Our signal successes at sea must ever be remembered to the glory of the British fleet and entitle it to the particular attention and support of this nation.' In other words he was drawing attention to the fact that it was command of the sea which had brought that particular war to an end just as it was a strengthening of that command of the sea which enabled the subsequent Seven Years War to be brought to an even more striking conclusion.

However all was by no means plain sailing. Across the Atlantic Britain had made a bad error in 1748 by returning Louisburg on Cape Breton, Nova Scotia, to France. From Louisburg the approach to the St Lawrence river and to French Canada could be controlled. Louisburg could also be used – and was so used – for attacking the large volume of shipping which plied between the United Kingdom and the eastern seaboard of North America. Moreover the French had begun building a chain of forts between Louisiana and the Great Lakes along the Ohio which would effectively hem in the million or so British colonists east of the Allegheny mountains. Since this would inhibit expansion westward over the vast continent, hostilities were in a state of perpetual flux long before the formal declaration of war.

Today we think of Combined Operations as a product of the Second World War. Broadly speaking that is true but this tricky, risky and expensive science really began in modern form during the Seven Years War. The most notable Combined Operation during this war was the capture of Quebec in 1759, entailing among other hazards, the almost incredible scaling by night of the Heights of Abraham. Part of the success of this operation was due to the fact that General Wolfe, who was in command and who died in the battle, had previously carried out two other amphibious landings – one at Rochefort in 1757, which totally failed in spite of the efforts of Hawke and Howe, and the other at Louisburg which was recaptured in 1758. Louisburg opened the way to Quebec and Montreal.

At the Louisburg assault the military commander was Lord Amherst, Wolfe being

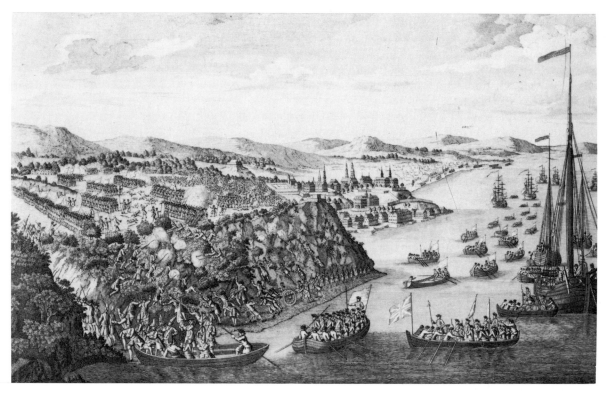

The capture of Quebec in 1759 was an early example of a brilliantly successful combined operation and demonstrated one aspect of seapower which is the ability of its possessor to choose the time and place for each strike. Control of the St Lawrence seaway 300 miles up from its mouth, aided by some accurate charting by the young James Cook, enabled Admiral Saunders and General Wolfe to plan and execute a surprise attack from the Plains of Abraham after scaling seemingly impassable cliffs in the Anse de Foulon, and led the Army Commander afterwards to detail in his despatch 'the great share the Navy has had in this successful campaign'.

second-in-command and the naval commander, Admiral Edward Boscawen. At Quebec Admiral Sir Charles Saunders, who had been a Lieutenant under Anson on the famous circumnavigation, commanded the naval forces, overcoming navigational difficulties previously thought insurmountable and essentially relying upon a remarkable survey of the unknown river by a young sailing master, James Cook, recently promoted from the lower deck. Also present was a twenty-five-year-old recently promoted Post Captain called John Jervis who covered under heavy fire the passage of troops across the fast flowing St Lawrence and who was later to become, as Earl St Vincent, the most famous naval officer of the Napoleonic wars, Nelson alone excepted.

The ship and boat handling at Quebec can be seen not only as an exceptional feat in itself but also as an early instance of a particular attitude of mind which has distinguished the Navy ever since. This was a determination not only to do what the Army expected but to go one better and make a joke of it. In this they were undoubtedly inspired by young General Wolfe, a mere thirty-two at the time, who had written after the disaster two years previously at Rochefort that 'experience shows me that in an affair depending upon vigour and despatch, the generals should settle their plan of operations so that no time may be lost in idle debate and consultations when the sword should be drawn: that pushing on smartly is the road to success and more particularly so in an affair of this nature: that nothing is to be reckoned an obstacle to your undertaking which is not really so on *tryall*: that in war something must be allowed to chance and fortune, seeing it is in its nature hazardous, and an option of difficulties; that the greatness of an object should come under consideration, opposed to the impediments that lie in the way.'

Meanwhile in Europe the French were known to be preparing yet another invasion of Britain and on a greater scale than before. 'The two greatest battles at sea in this war were fought to prevent invasion of the United Kingdom. This invasion got further than most; and at sea the moves and countermoves were so like Napoleon's and Nelson's that they have the air of a dress rehearsal.'[5] Anson, First Lord of the Admiralty, and Pitt, the Prime Minister, decided to tackle this danger at source.

One French army was assembling in Normandy with transports being built and marshalled at Le Havre. Another operation was being prepared near Ostend. To cover these armies the main French fleets at Toulon in the Mediterranean and at Brest in the Atlantic were intended to combine, sail west of Britain, land a force on the Clyde, continue round the north of Scotland and down to Ostend, pick up the army there and ferry it across to Essex. By this time the Normandy army would have crossed the Channel and Britain would then be effectively reduced by a three pronged attack. To attacker and defender alike command of the sea therefore became imperative during the summer of 1759.

The means necessary to acquire and maintain total seapower were becoming more sophisticated with each passing decade. Anson, now at the end of his life and rich in experience, knew that blockade was no longer enough. The enemy's battle fleet might be pinned down in its own harbours by Boscawen in the Mediterranean and by Hawke off Brest, but it was still essential to have lighter and faster cruiser forces available to protect lines of communication to the British Isles. Anson accordingly stationed one such force at the Downs under Commodore Sir Piercy Brett (another ex-Lieutenant on the circumnavigation) and he also set about organising an expedition to destroy the transports being assembled at Le Havre. This was later referred to as 'Anson's project' and was entrusted to a forty-year-old recently promoted Rear Admiral, George Rodney, who was also to become one of the most famous names in British naval history.

In July 1759 the first of three great victories took place. After a long delay through bad weather, Rodney entered Le Havre with a small squadron of ships and six bomb-ketches and for the next fifty-two hours systematically destroyed transports, magazines and stores. That achieved he then blockaded the port for the rest of the year.

The second victory was won by Boscawen. 'Old Dreadnought', or 'Wry-necked Dick' as the Cornishman came to be nicknamed after a severe neck wound, had been appointed to command in the Mediterranean following his successful siege of Louisburg the previous year. His orders were to prevent the French Toulon fleet under Amiral de la Clue from joining up with the main fleet at Brest, intended for the invasion of England. This was no easy task, given that the nearest base for supplies was Gibraltar, whither Boscawen repaired in July to take on food and water.

In August, de la Clue, seeing that the blockade had been temporarily lifted, slipped out of Toulon with twelve ships and passed through the Straits of Gibraltar at night, hoping to do so undetected. But a frigate spotted them and although the British fleet

THE SEVEN YEARS WAR
BATTLE OF QUIBERON BAY 1759

Quiberon Bay rates as the outstanding, culminating achievement of Admiral Sir Edward Hawke, then fifty-four years old. The French Admiral, Conflans, had escaped from Brest and sailed south east for Quiberon and Vannes to pick up the French invasion army.

Wild and changeable weather, affecting both fleets, continued until the 20th November when the two fleets sighted each other. It was a dark November afternoon and Conflans, who had local pilots, at once made inshore. Hawke hoisted the signal 'Form as you chase'.

It was already beginning to get dark before Conflans' leading ships had passed between Le Four Shoal and the rocky Cardinals into waters where he might well consider himself safe. But Hawke, with no local pilots, simply followed him in. A rising sea off a lee shore might have caused a more prudent admiral to pause but Hawke was determined to destroy the French fleet.

Hawke's line was led by Lord Howe in the "Magnanime". Then followed closely the "Torbay", "Dorsetshire", "Resolution", "Warspite" and Hawke's own flagship the "Royal George". As soon as Conflans realised Hawke's intention, he tried to head out to sea once more. However an encounter with the "Royal George" made him change his mind and anchor off Le Croisic, to the sound not only of gunfire but also of the ominous thunder of breakers on the rocky coast nearby.

Captain Keppel in the "Torbay" sank the first French ship, the 74 gun "Thésée" which was laid on her beam ends by a sudden squall and flooded through her open gun ports. Next was the "Héros" which surrendered to Howe after the loss of 400 killed or wounded. Shortly after four o'clock with darkness upon them, the "Royal George" put two broadsides into the "Superbe" which foundered almost at once. Another French ship, the "Formidable", struck her colours and was made prize.

It was an extraordinary situation.

The two fleets anchored in close proximity throughout a dark, stormy night with the sound of signal guns from ships aground or in distress adding to the confusion. When dawn broke Conflans in the "Soleil Royal" found himself within range of Hawke's guns. Making no attempt to fight it out, he tried to escape, ran his ship on to the Rouelle Shoal, ordered it to be set alight and then escaped ashore with his crew.

Thus was won a remarkable victory which not only put any invasion of Britain out of the question at that time, but irrevocably humbled France's navy under the eyes of her watching soldiers.

An artist's impression of the battle gives a claustrophobic feeling of these enormous sailing ships manoeuvring – almost on top of one another – in enclosed waters and failing light.

was rerigging, in just over two hours Boscawen got them to sea, signalling a General Chase. In the running action off Lagos, lasting two days, three ships of the line the "Centaur", the "Modeste" and the famous "Téméraire" were captured, the "Ocean" and the "Redoubtable" were destroyed and the remainder ran for safety into Cadiz where they were closely blockaded for the rest of the year by Broderick, the second-in-command, Boscawen being summoned back to England by Anson and told to bring with him ten ships.

The Lagos action was a timely success. The invasion threat had now become present and real, perhaps even imminent and it was in no way lessened by Pitt's steely refusal to withdraw any ships from across the Atlantic where the assault on Quebec was being prepared. Pitt was determined to conquer Canada and that came first even if England had to be exposed in the process. So when the news of

Boscawen's triumph reached England in early September, the church bells rang out and the country gave a collective sigh of relief. 'I own I was afraid of invasion till now', the Duke of Newcastle said in a letter to Anson's father-in-law, the Lord Chancellor.

The church bells rang again after Hawke's definitive victory at Quiberon Bay in late November. This, according to Smollett, a contemporary, must be seen as 'one of the most important actions that ever happened in any war between the two nations'. Certainly for daring and risk with all at stake after the stormiest summer and autumn on record, the battle at Quiberon Bay has never been matched in the sailing era, except perhaps by Trafalgar half a century later. For England at that time, the outcome was just as decisive.

The French lost six ships of the line in the engagement itself and of those which

An oil painting by R. Paton showing the taking of Morro Castle during the capture of Havana between 7th July and 14th August 1762. During this last year of the Seven Years War British seapower secured the capture of the following French and Spanish colonies: St Vincent, Martinique, Grenada, Havana and Manila.

escaped four broke their backs and only three were ever fit to go to sea again. Five ships under the Chevalier de Beauffremont-Listenois got away to Rochefort but Keppel who chased them reported that they had been taken right up the river Charente. The French Admiral had fled ashore half-drowned. 'When I consider the season of the year, the hard gales on the day of action, a flying enemy, the shortness of the day and the coast they were on', Hawke wrote in his report, 'I can boldly affirm that all that could possibly be done has been done.'

To quote Smollett again: 'It gave the finishing blow to the naval power of France', and although the war itself was to continue for a further two years, the threat of invasion had been lifted and the French fleet had ceased, for the time being, to exist as a coherent force.

CHAPTER V

GEORGE III

1763–1815

CHRONOLOGICAL COMPENDIUM

General

The involvement of the American colonies in the Seven Years War and the need to make them pay their way were to trigger off a momentous debate on the colonies' relationship with Britain. By 1776 all understanding had broken down and the colonies had declared independence in the midst of war. They had the support of France.

By the end of the century Europe was shaken by the French Revolution and the outbreak of war against France. Napoleon's rise to power, his virtual conquest of Europe and his attempt to undermine England's economic and political superiority meant nearly continuous war from 1793 to 1815.

Constitutional arguments and attempts to limit the crown's powers, especially after George III's illness, were indicative of the instability of politics. George III found trusted 'Prime Ministers' in Lord North and the younger Pitt.

The effects of the agricultural and early industrial revolution, as well as the continuing growth of rich trading bases in the East, made England the wealthiest nation in Europe and so in the world.

Naval

The latter part of the eighteenth century saw the Royal Navy supreme both in its ships and in the officers and men who manned them. British seapower had now become one of the prime factors in international politics.

Sailing battleships had approximately doubled in size over the preceding century and their equipment was increasingly sophisticated. The steering wheel had taken the place of the overlong, unwieldy tiller and a ship's rigging had become a matter of fine art.

Ships were now organised into fleets of heavy fighting vessels in a line of battle, with frigates – of which there were never enough and which were faster sailers – acting as the eyes and intelligence gatherers for the commander-in-chief. Communications, too, were steadily improving both from ship to ship and between the Admiralty and the main dockyard ports.

Adequate victualling and the health of ships' companies during long periods at sea, as, for instance, in the blockading of French and Spanish ports, still remained a problem. However the answer to scurvy had at last been found by Captain Cook in his issue of lemon juice and 'portable soup'.

During the first part of this period, the Pacific Ocean, the last great area of the world to be opened up, was explored and charted by Captain Cook who lost his life on the third of his three great voyages. The colonisation of Australia and New Zealand began.

Although the Royal Navy was now officered by a cadre of highly trained professionals who made the service their career for life, no similar arrangements were devised for the lower deck. 'The people' were still recruited in the main by the press gang, although there was an increasing voluntary element and great leaders, such as Nelson, could always pick and choose their subordinate officers and their ships' companies.

Organisation

John Montagu, Earl of Sandwich 1718–92 and **Charles Middleton, Lord Barham** 1726–1813 were outstanding administrators as First Lords in a period, inspired by Anson, which matched skill at sea with expertise ashore.

John Jervis, Earl of St Vincent
1735–1823

was probably the finest First Sea Lord (as the post was later known) whom the Royal Navy has ever had.

Other great fighting admirals who served the Board of Admiralty during this period were Richard, Earl Howe (1726–99), Augustus, Viscount Keppel (1725–86), Samuel, Lord Hood (1724–1816) and Sir Thomas Troubridge (1758–1807).

Principal Commanders (in addition to the above)

John Byron
1723–86

Admiral, known as 'Foul Weather Jack' and grandfather of Lord Byron, the poet, made a fruitless circumnavigation of the globe in search of Terra Australis Incognita in 1764 and later commanded a fleet during the War of American Independence.

William Bligh
1754–1817

Vice Admiral, famous for the open boat voyage of 3,600 miles from the Friendly Islands to Timor, near Java, made as a result of the mutiny on the "Bounty". Later commanded ships at the battles of Camperdown (1797) and Copenhagen (1801) and later still became governor of New South Wales.

Sir Home Popham
1762–1820

Rear Admiral, served as a young man with the East India Company, then in 1806 seized the Cape of Good Hope from the Dutch. Known principally for his scientific interest in signalling. In 1803 the Admiralty adopted his system of a vocabulary code which vastly extended the range of orders and instructions available to an admiral at sea. Nelson used Popham's code to send his famous signal to the fleet at Trafalgar. Popham was his mother's twenty-first child.

George Rodney, First Baron and Admiral
1719–92

blockaded Le Havre in Seven Years War, later C. in C. of Leeward Islands, taking Martinique, St Lucia, Grenada and St Vincent from the French, relieved Gibraltar 1780 and principal victory was that over the French Admiral de Grasse off Dominica at the battle of the Saints.

The Hood family

(In addition to Samuel) 1. Brother Viscount Bridport (1726–1814) – one of Howe's admirals at battle of the 'Glorious First of June', later commanded the Channel Fleet and blockaded Brest 1798–1800. 2. Alexander, Captain, served on Cook's second voyage of exploration. 3. Vice Admiral Sir Samuel, at the Saints 1782, the Nile 1798, Copenhagen 1801 and later C. in C. East Indies.

Sir Edward Codrington
1770–1851

Admiral, trained under Howe and Nelson and was present at battle of Glorious First of June and Trafalgar. 1827 C. in C. Mediterranean – Battle of Navarino.

Sir William Cornwallis
1744–1819

Admiral and lifelong friend of Nelson. Succeeded St Vincent in command of Channel Fleet 1801 and defeated Napoleon's strategy for invasion of Britain by preventing Admiral Ganteaume from coming out of Brest in year of Trafalgar.

Cuthbert Collingwood
1748–1810

Vice Admiral and First Baron, another great friend of Nelson's – Glorious First of June, St Vincent and Trafalgar where he was Nelson's second-in-command.

Sir Thomas Hardy
1769–1839

Admiral and present at all three of Nelson's victories (Nile, Copenhagen and Trafalgar). Was at Nelson's side when he died.

Sir Henry Blackwood
1770–1832

Vice Admiral and probably best known of all Nelson's captains. Commanded the frigate "Euryalus" keeping watch on Cadiz and two days before Trafalgar warned Nelson that the enemy ships were weighing anchor. Ended his career as C. in C. The Nore.

Explorers

Captain James Cook
1728–79

son of a day labourer in Yorkshire, volunteered for the Royal Navy as a seaman, quickly promoted to Master (i.e. responsible for navigation), served on expedition to take Quebec and surveyed the St Lawrence river, enabling the big ships of the fleet to ascend it. After Seven

Years War returned to Newfoundland which he surveyed and charted for five years. Then backed by the Admiralty and the Royal Society made his three famous voyages of exploration to the Pacific, on the last of which he was murdered at Hawaii.

Philip Cartaret
1738–96

Rear Admiral with Byron on his circumnavigation of the world 1764–6 and made a second one himself the following year returning to England in 1769. Served with Rodney in West Indies and retired in 1794.

Samuel Wallis
1728–95

Captain R.N., discovered Tahiti which led to Cook's three voyages. Helped to find the cure for scurvy.

George Vancouver
1758–98

navigator and explorer, served as Midshipman under Cook and took part with Rodney in battle of 'The Saints'. In 1791 undertook voyage of discovery of the north-west coast of America and the Pacific. Accepted the ceding of Hawaii to Great Britain 1794.

Matthew Flinders
1774–1814

navigator and explorer, entered Royal Navy in 1789 and was at battle of Glorious First of June. Known principally for his survey of Australia and Tasmania with his friend, the surgeon, George Bass.

Others

Thomas Cochrane,
Tenth Earl of
Dundonald
1775–1860

contemporary of Nelson, later liberated Chile, Peru, Brazil and Greece.

Sir Samuel Greig
1735–1788

Served as Lieutenant under Hawke in Seven Years War, then invited to Russia by Catherine the Great to help reorganise the Russian Navy in 1763, later became Commander-in-Chief.

The Immortals

It is customary at Trafalgar Day dinners to drink a toast to the 'Immortal Memory' and certainly Horatio Nelson (1758–1805), First Viscount and Vice Admiral, is by far and away the country's outstanding hero. Brilliant, capable, versatile, loyal and generous, his character and achievements have, perhaps, been matched only by Sir Winston Churchill's.

He was born on 29th September 1758 at Burnham Thorpe in Norfolk and was the third surviving son of the Rector, the Reverend Edmund Nelson. Short in stature (5 ft 1 in) and somewhat sickly (he suffered from seasickness all his life) he went to sea at the age of twelve in H.M.S. "Raisonnable", commanded by his uncle Captain Maurice Suckling.

After some years at sea in the Arctic and East Indies, he was made a Lieutenant at nineteen in 1777, his first command being given him during the War of American Independence when he was first captain of a brig and then of a frigate. Shortly before he was twenty-one, he was promoted post-captain and distinguished himself in Nicaragua where he became the senior officer of a joint expedition to capture the Spanish fort of San Juan.

In 1793 when the war with Revolutionary France began Nelson was given command of H.M.S. "Agamemnon" (64 guns) and appointed to Lord Hood's fleet in the Mediterranean. Helping the army to secure Corsica from the French, he was blinded in the right eye and in 1795 took a distinguished part in the actions of 13–14 March and 13 July against the French fleet, being one of the few captains to show initiative and a thirst for battle.

Promoted to Commodore and given command of H.M.S. "Captain" he took part in the battle of Cape St Vincent on 14 February 1797 between Sir John Jervis's fleet of fifteen ships and a numerically superior but less efficient Spanish fleet. He was promoted Rear Admiral of the Blue six days after the battle.

The following year he was seriously wounded (losing his right arm) in an unsuccessful attempt to capture a Spanish treasure ship at Santa Cruz, Tenerife, in the Canary Islands. Invalided home, he remained there until April 1798 when he hoisted his flag in H.M.S. "Vanguard" and rejoined Jervis, now Earl St Vincent, off the Portuguese coast. Jervis at once gave him command of a detached squadron, whose individual captains became collectively known as 'the band of brothers' to search for and destroy the French fleet and army under Napoleon Bonaparte known to have been assembled for an unknown destination.

This blind and initially unsuccessful search resulted in the destruction of the French fleet at Aboukir Bay at the mouth of the Nile on 1 August 1798. This was the first of Nelson's great victories and afterwards he went to Naples where he was hailed as the saviour of Italy and was cared for by Sir William Hamilton, the British Minister, and his wife, Emma, with whom Nelson fell deeply in love.

Back in England, Nelson was appointed second-in-command to Admiral Sir Hyde Parker on a Baltic expedition to defeat a coalition of the northern Powers. This resulted in the battle of Copenhagen on 2 April 1801 where Nelson defeated the Danish fleet, refusing to break off the action on orders from Sir Hyde Parker, by putting his telescope to his blind eye.

Sir William Hamilton died in London on 6 April 1803 and on 16 May, Nelson now a Vice Admiral of the Blue, was appointed Commander-in-Chief of the Mediterranean Fleet, flying his flag in H.M.S. "Victory". On 21 October 1805 the last great action of the sailing era was fought off Cape Trafalgar between twenty-seven British ships of the line and thirty-three French and Spanish. Nelson won a comprehensive victory but was struck down by a bullet from a marksman in the fighting top of the French "Redoutable". A few hours later he died.

Nelson's brilliant successes, which stamped him as a master tactician, were not due to rashness but to a shrewd appraisal of the forces he faced. He was a supreme example of a leader who could trust his captains, take them fully into his confidence and leave them to exercise their own initiative. As a result he received not only personal devotion but also a quality of service in battle which few other admirals have ever inspired.

The other Immortal of the Napoleonic wars was John Jervis, Earl St Vincent, and Admiral of the fleet, without whose critical support and affection, Nelson could never have become the man he was. In his breadth of vision, great humanity and unceasing quest for naval efficiency, Jervis is unequalled as the pattern of all that was best in the eighteenth century naval officer. Both Jervis and Nelson had harsh things to say of each other but whatever their feelings of temporary distress, their mutual understanding and respect resulted in an extraordinary working partnership. 'God bless you, no man loves and esteems you more truly,' St Vincent said and this was matched by Nelson's remark: 'Without you, I am nothing.'

St Vincent never became a public idol like Nelson. However his presence was as splendid and even dramatic, since he could intimidate at will or appear irresistibly genial and amusing. His epitaph is best expressed by something he said in his old age: 'I have never yet forsaken any man who served well under me.'

Ships and Weapons

Anson established the rating and nomenclature of ships for the remainder of the sailing age. These were as follows:

Ships of the line	First rate	100–110 guns
	Second rate	84–100 guns
	Third rate	70–84 guns
	Fourth rate	50–70 guns
Frigates	Fifth rate	32–50 guns
	Sixth rate	Up to 32 guns if commanded by a post-captain. If not they were called sloops.

Sloops   Lieutenants in command were not posted until after experience in sloops. This led to the rank of Commander.

All battleships had three masts and were square-rigged. Sloops had one mast and Brigsloops two.

The Carronade   (so named from the Carron Iron Foundry) came into use in 1779 and was first proved in the battle of the Saints. It came to be known in the Royal Navy as the Smasher, its only defect being a lack of range which showed up badly in the war against the United States in 1812.

During the eighteenth century the recoil absorption of guns was refined and the flint lock took the place of the slow match and linstock. All guns remained muzzle-loaded, their maximum range being approximately one mile. Most fleet actions took place at ranges of one to two hundred yards, or less if conditions allowed.

Communications

By 1782 signalling was conducted by a system of twenty-eight flags, used in a numbered code devised by Howe, Kempenfelt and Sir Charles Knowles (1754–1828). This system was first used in Howe's relief of Gibraltar and led to the Admiralty's *Signal Book for the Ships of War* (1799) which remained in force for thirty years.

From the eighteenth to the mid-nineteenth century, night signalling was conducted by four lanterns, rockets, blue Bengal lights and false fires. In fog, guns were fired.

Sir Home Popham and the Reverend Lord George Murray developed the Semaphore and in 1796 Murray's invention was accepted by the Admiralty and installed in fifteen stations London to Deal. A signal could be made and acknowledged on this route in two minutes and its successs led to a further ten stations being set up between London and Portsmouth. In 1806 twenty-two stations were built extending the system to Plymouth when a message could be sent and acknowledged in three minutes. Each hilltop repeating station had two rooms, one eight guinea clock and two twelve guinea telescopes. The snag was that the system could only read one way.

In 1816, however, Popham invented a system which swivelled and could be read from any direction.

Popham's *Telegraphic Signals or Marine Vocabulary* of 1803 led to the *Fleet Signal Book* of 1816. The following year Captain Frederick Marryat (1792–1848), the well-known writer and among other things captain of H.M.S. "Beaver", Guardship at St Helena in 1815 until Napoleon died there in 1821, devised an 'International Code of Signals' for which he was made a Fellow of the Royal Society.

Navigation and Cartography

The success of Harrison's chronometers allowed the problem of discovering longitude at sea to be solved in the latter part of the eighteenth century. This led to much more accurate chart making in which Captain Cook excelled.

In 1795 the Admiralty established its Hydrographic Department and since then most hydrographic knowledge has come from the world's navies and in particular the Royal Navy.

In 1801 Alexander Dalrymple (1737–1808) who had been a Writer with the East India Company and had been the Admiralty Hydrographer since 1795, issued the first Admiralty chart and in 1807 the Naval Chart Committee came into being.

In 1818 the Admiralty accepted responsibility for the Royal Observatory at Greenwich and this lasted until the Scientific Research Council took over in 1965.

In 1819 permission was given for the Admiralty to sell charts to the Merchant Marine and since then the world has navigated almost entirely on British Admiralty charts.

Wars and Battles

1775–1783   **American War of Independence**

Battle off Ushant 1778 against the French – indeterminate resulting in courts martial of Admirals Keppel and Palliser
Battle of St Vincent 1780 during siege of Gibraltar (1779–1782)
Battle of the Saints (between Guadeloupe and Dominica) 1782. Rodney saves the West Indies for Britain.

Battle of Lake Champlain 1776
Battle of Chesapeake Bay (1) 16 March 1781; (2) 5 September 1781 between Rear Admiral Thomas Graves and Vice Admiral the Comte de Grasse resulting in British defeat and surrender at Yorktown.

1792–1815 **French Revolutionary and Napoleonic Wars**

Battle of the Glorious First of June 1794: First major sea encounter of the war between Admirals Lord Howe and Villaret de Joyeuse
Battle of Cape St Vincent 1797 between Admiral Sir John Jervis and Admiral Don José de Cordova
Battle of Camperdown 1797 between Admiral Lord Duncan (1731–1804) and Dutch Vice Admiral Jan de Winter (the Dutch had been forced to become an ally of France by Napoleon)
Battle of the Nile (Aboukir Bay) 1798 between Rear Admiral Nelson and Admiral François Brueys
Battle of Copenhagen 1801 between Admiral Sir Hyde Parker (with Nelson second-in-command) and the Danish Prince Regent
Battle of Trafalgar 1805 between Vice Admiral Lord Nelson and Admiral Pierre Villeneuve. Except for the battle of Navarino 1827 this was the last major fleet encounter of the days of sail

1812–14 **War between Britain and United States**

Action off Boston 1813 between USS "Chesapeake" and H.M.S. "Shannon" – one of the best known frigate actions in naval history
Battle of Lake Erie 1813, Lake Champlain 1814,

Between 1763 when the Seven Years War ended and 1815 when the defeat of Napoleon concluded the long centuries of animosity and war between England and France, the Royal Navy achieved new and dramatic peaks of renown. All remaining triumphs of the sailing Navy are spaced out in this sixty year span of George III's reign. A galaxy of naval talent – not always victorious in the short term – illuminated the carving out of empire, witnessed the sombre realities of the French Revolution and eventually overwhelmed the military dictatorship which followed in twenty years of war.

In the United Kingdom itself the advent of steam and the industrial era changed daily life in the land for ever. War, and especially war at sea, was conducted on a code of gentlemanly conduct – a derived chivalry if you like – such as the world had rarely seen before and which has only been intermittently practised since. Honour and glory still had meaning and the fighting, though bloody and brutal as ever, was as yet on a man-to-man scale. Machines had not yet taken over. In the Seven Years War the Navy was directed for the greater part of the time by Anson who had been alive in the previous century: Nelson, from whom the age sometimes draws its name, was born into a Norfolk parsonage in 1758 and the Duke of Wellington, who brought the Napoleonic wars to an end, did not die until 1852 when Victoria had been on the throne for fifteen years. Altogether the second half of the eighteenth century stands as perhaps the most remarkable fifty years in the country's whole history.

The winter of 1759 marked the ultimate sovereignty of the Royal Navy at sea to date. Three major victories in four months had secured the grudging but unquestioned admission of that supremacy from Britain's only possible rivals – Holland, Spain and France. The Dutch had been dropping behind for years, the Spaniards were paralysed by material greed and spiritually had turned in on themselves. The French had been shattered at sea in straight combat and from then on never really recovered their self-esteem. This in itself was odd. Generally speaking the French had better ships, better guns, well trained crews and equally competent officers. What they lacked, however, was confidence and for that there were two simple reasons going back to Drake and Hawkins. One was the aristocrat–peasant gap between French officers and their men, which resulted in the latter being treated as little better than animals. However harsh the discipline in British men-of-war, British sailors were always considered to be human beings.

The second reason was that it was always the British who sought out and pressed home a fight. The French and the Spanish would avoid action if they could, because in their hearts they knew they would lose. The Royal Navy had become accustomed to command of the seas and the whole civilised world had begun to recognise this fact. Indeed the only war which Britain lost during this period – the War of American Independence – was brought to an end by a temporary loss of seapower to an alliance of American, French, Spanish and Dutch fleets on the other side of the Atlantic. By the time Napoleon surrendered, the British were not only the paramount power at sea, they had given mankind the priceless idea that henceforth the oceans of the world were to be freely available to the ships of every nation regardless of power and size and that the Royal Navy would be there to police this freedom.

George III was the first Hanoverian to be born and bred in England and the first to speak English as his native tongue. He was a simple, homely man to whom historians since have tended to condescend. In recent years, however, he seems to have received more of his due. He had wanted to marry an English girl but his dominant mother forced on him an obscure German princess to whom he nevertheless became devoted and who bore him fifteen children. His detractors describe him as a limited young man with full lips and a large nose, but Dr Johnson who was allowed to use the excellent Palace Library thought him cultivated and eager to learn. Certainly the young King's enthusiasm for navigation and exploration, which he exercised through the Royal Society, led to a vast increase in European knowledge of the Pacific. In this the Royal Navy played an essential and, in the context of the times, a somewhat surprising role.

Exploration was now thought to be a proper use to which the Navy could be put in peace instead of paying off ships and men to moulder in idleness until the next crisis arrived. Moreover the success of men like Byron, Carteret, Flinders, Bass, Wallis, Vancouver, Broughton, and above all, Captain Cook, set the imagination of the country alight, much as the Elizabethan navigators had done two centuries before. Exploration and what was later known as the cult of the noble savage became the fashion of the day and, because no other Navy had used the sextant and the chronometer for discovery and chart making, the opening up through British endeavour of the Pacific, the surveying of Australia, New Zealand, Polynesia and the fringes of Antarctica made British exploration into a global status symbol. The Admiralty Hydrographic department was formed in 1795 and ever since the world's shipping has navigated, in the main, on British Admiralty charts.

The orotund phraseology of the orders given to Captain John Byron of the frigate "Dolphin" in 1764 conveys admirably the feeling of that operatic age, an age of all-round crescendo: 'Whereas nothing can redound more to the honour of this Nation as a Maritime Power, to the dignity of the Crown of Great Britain and to the advancement of the Trade and Navigation thereof, than to make Discoveries of Countries hitherto unknown: His Majesty taking the Premisses into His Royal Consideration and conceiving no conjuncture so proper for an Enterprise of this Nature as a Time of Profound Peace which His Kingdoms at present happily enjoy, has thought fit to make those Attempts which are specified in the following Instructions . . .'

When Cook sailed on his last voyage, the War of American Independence (1775–1783) had already begun. Cook met his end in Hawaii then called the Sandwich Islands after his sponsor Lord Sandwich. He was killed in 1779 a year after France had entered this first colonial war on the insurgents' side. Spain and Holland then joined in, declaring war on Britain in 1779 and 1780 and the combined effect of all this caused the shortest and, in fact, the only interruption to British world exploration which otherwise continued, through peace and war, until there was nothing of further importance left to discover. That is a saga in itself.

Cook's main claim to fame is the map of the world's largest ocean, the Pacific (see endpaper map). His extraordinary achievements resulted in Australia and New Zealand being populated by men and women of British stock and he was to extend the British Empire far beyond the range of any of his predecessors although he died

THE VOYAGES OF CAPTAIN COOK

Captain James Cook was without question the most famous and successful sailor of his era and perhaps remains to this day the most competent and inspired navigator and cartographer there has ever been. Although of humble birth and accorded little enough recognition by his jealous contemporaries, his exploration and charting of the Pacific Ocean stands as the single most outstanding feat in the whole story of man and the sea (see map endpapers).

Cook made three voyages between 1768 and 1779, when he was murdered in Kealakekua Bay in the Sandwich Islands. Each voyage had mixed motives, some of them known only by the Admiralty and by Cook himself. The first voyage, for instance, from 25th August 1768 to 12th July 1771 was ostensibly to make a scientific observation of the passage of Venus between the earth and the sun, on 3rd January 1769, from an island in the centre of the Pacific. However when Cook opened his secret orders, he found that he was afterwards to sail south from Tahiti to search for Terra Australis Incognita and explore the coast of New Zealand, discovered by Tasman in 1642 but still thought to be part of a great southern land mass. Each expedition, of course, being sponsored by the Royal Society as well as the Admiralty, carried botanists and astronomers and indeed when the "Endeavour" sailed in 1768 she had a complement of seventy-one crew, twelve marines and eleven scientists and their servants. Among the more notable of these scientists were the astronomer Charles Green and Joseph Banks, a wealthy Fellow of the Royal Society.

On the first voyage, after Tahiti, Cook charted the two New Zealand islands. He then went on to cover the east coast of Australia. On the second voyage he was the first navigator to cross the Antarctic Circle. Convinced by now that no Terra Australis Incognita existed in reality, Cook went on to New Zealand, Tahiti and Tonga and returned eastwards via Cape Horn and the Cape of Good Hope, thus being the first navigator to circumnavigate the globe in an easterly direction. On the third voyage Cook had instructions to go via Cape Town to Tahiti and, touching at Tasmania and Queen Charlotte's Sound, discovered the Cook and Palmerston islands and after Tahiti the Polynesian-inhabited Hawaiian group. He then sailed on to the north-western coast of North America discovering the deep inlet Nootka Sound, and surveyed the southern coast of Alaska in search of the Pacific end of the will-o'-the-wisp North-West Passage.

unaware of this potential fact. 'The world will hardly admit an excuse for a man leaving a coast unexplored he has once discovered', Cook wrote and his insatiable curiosity lived on in the generations of explorers who followed him, linked in a self-perpetuating chain which ensured that every commander of subsequent expeditions had sailed before on at least one as a junior officer.

William Bligh (of the "Bounty") and George Vancouver, who had voyaged with Cook, commanded Pacific expeditions of their own in the 1780s. During the following decade, William Broughton, who had been a Lieutenant under Vancouver, charted the north-east coasts of the Pacific and Matthew Flinders, who explored the Australian coastline from 1795 to 1803, had been a Midshipman under Bligh. In turn one of Flinders' Midshipmen was John Franklin who was to make his name in yet another attempt on the North-West Passage during Queen Victoria's reign, in the

Captain Cook's "Endeavour" encounters three waterspouts near the coast of New Zealand. Something that can too easily be forgotten when reading of naval warfare is the war that all ships must perpetually wage against the elements. For this reason questions of training and of suitability and availability of equipment have an extra urgency at sea and demand first-class administration.

process losing his life. The point is that no matter how stretched naval resources might be at any given time in peace or war, from Cook onwards the Admiralty could always spare a few ships to continue exploring, surveying and chart making for the benefit not only of Great Britain but of the world at large.

The Navy as a whole saw the pendulum inevitably swinging against it after the high success of the Seven Years War. Peace entailed a wholesale paying off of ships, half pay for officers and the callous injection into civilian life of thousands of jobless, half-starved sailors who at times formed themselves into city mobs. This naval adversity was reflected in the political life of the country, with its bitter division between Whig and Tory and a ruthless determination on the part of the propertied classes to coerce the 'have-nots'. Burke in England and Voltaire and Rousseau in France helped to create a climate of revolution. Across the Atlantic the untaxed

'Proprietaries' such as the Duke of York, Lord Baltimore and the successors of William Penn found themselves sitting on a boiler of resentment without a safety valve. The fire beneath the boiler was stoked by the refusal of the British Government to conciliate or concede.

Small wonder, then, that the abrupt consignment into Boston harbour of a few cases of tea in December 1773 was seen by John Adams (later the second President of the United States) as 'so bold, so daring, so firm, intrepid and inflexible . . . that I cannot but consider it as an epoch of history'. And so it was.

Thus the American War of Independence began. The Patriots in Massachusetts had about 10,000 men in the colonial militia as opposed to General Gage's 4,000 British troops. Cannon were stolen from government establishments. Agents were sent to Europe to buy arms and Dutch merchants shipped gunpowder to the Americans in large glass bottles labelled 'Spirits'. An eight year struggle on land had begun. The outcome, however, would be decided at sea.

Once France, Spain and Holland had entered the war Britain was left without a single ally. Moreover there was no unanimity at home that the war should be waged at all. However, continue it did, the Royal Navy being engaged all over the world except in the Pacific. There were four main areas of operation – the Channel and its approaches, Gibraltar, the Far East and the Caribbean together with the east coast of North America.

Naturally, though, it was on the west side of the Atlantic that the most significant naval events took place. Here the great names are Howe, Rodney and Samuel Hood. Nelson was given his first command during this war. He had been promoted a Post Captain at twenty-one and led a courageous expedition up the river San Juan in Nicaragua where he nearly died of malaria. Other young naval commanders who would later become members of Nelson's 'band of brothers' such as Cornwallis, likewise a Post Captain at twenty-two and Collingwood, ten years older, also saw active service in this saddest of wars between members of the same national family. Civil wars always produce the most bitter and internecine fighting and Admiral Earl Howe, whose brother was the General Commanding at New York and who arrived on the station with a conciliatory letter to Benjamin Franklin, together with books, parcels and letters from Franklin's friends in England, resigned his command in 1778 in acute disagreement with Lord North's disastrous administration. He then refused to accept a command at sea till 1782 (and then only in the Channel Fleet).

Admirals and Captains like Howe were fully prepared to fight the French and Spanish when these ancient enemies entered the war, with, it must be remembered, the prospect of prize money to back up their patriotism; they were far from eager to fight colonials who, until 1775, had been as British as themselves. Indeed, had there not been an exceptional man as First Lord of the Admiralty from 1771 until 1782, there might well have been other individuals like Howe who felt themselves unable to bring force to bear on their American cousins for the benefit of a corrupt and incompetent Tory administration and 'the sacredness of their property', as Chatham called it.

The Earl of Sandwich, whose great grandfather had been Pepys's patron, carried the Navy through those troubled times with panache and success. A large, jovial, good-natured man whose careless gait, an observer remarked, 'made him seem to be walking down both sides of the street at once', he appears to have been a man of tact and charm, adroit and nerveless both in society and in affairs of state. He was also the epitome of the eighteenth century aristocrat, a member of the notorious Hellfire Club and a gambler who once spent twenty-four hours at the gaming table in Brooks Club with no other food than beef between two layers of bread, thus bringing 'sandwich' into the language. He was also a classical scholar, adept in both oriental and European languages, a patron of exploration and of such unconventional sports – at that time – as fishing, yachting and skittles. He was also a leading cricketer and a tireless organiser of amateur theatricals. He had a wife who went insane (like George III) and a mistress whom he adored and whom he kept at Admiralty House. This did not go down too well in non-conformist circles. Earlier in his life he had fought against the Pretender under the then First Lord, the Duke of Bedford, and to round off the picture he had, during his term of office, a brother and two sons serving at sea in the Royal Navy.

Sandwich was a total amateur in administration when he first became a Lord Commissioner of Admiralty in 1744 but during his last eleven years as First Lord from 1771 to 1782, it was stated by Horace Walpole, a bitter opponent of North's government, that 'No man in the Administration was so much master of his business, so quick or so shrewd.' Dr Rodger adds: 'Lord Sandwich was universally admitted to possess eminent talents, great application to the duties of his office and thorough acquaintance with public business . . . in all his official functions he displayed perspicuity as well as despatch. No naval officer who stated his demand with becoming brevity ever waited for an answer and he was accustomed to say "If a man will draw up his case and put his name at foot of the first page, I will give him an immediate reply. Where he compels me to turn over the sheet, he must wait my leisure".'[1]

Sandwich mastered the Admiralty and the Navy as no civilian First Lord had ever done before or was ever to do again. By 1778 he was in effect the Minister for War, with the same capacity for professional and political detail that had so distinguished Anson in the previous generation. There was, however, a darker side to the picture, best illustrated, perhaps, by the fact that in that same year of 1778 it took the combined efforts of the Admiralty, the Navy Board, the Treasury and the Secretary of State seven months to ship two hundred butts of vinegar from Deptford to New York. 'Not less than four departments each had its own sea-transport service; the Navy Board, the Ordnance Board, the Victualling Board and the Treasury which chartered Army Victuallers. In 1779 the Treasury relinquished this charge to the Navy Board, leaving only three departments bidding against one another, pushing up prices which were already increased by the shortage of shipping and leaving the Navy Board, whose credit was the weakest, in the worst position.'[2]

His Lordship may indeed have been the undisputed Czar of the operational Navy: the organisation and the administration of the whole concern remained slipshod, askew and hugger-mugger. This was basically because no one had real control of the Navy's financial resources. The Treasury formally approved the Navy Estimates but had neither the power nor the information to check on expenditure. Only the Navy

Board of all the other departments kept any accounts at all and these were singular in the extreme. For example in 1780 the Navy Pay office had only managed to clear its books to 1758. In that same year of 1780 the heirs of Viscount Falkland owed to the Navy £27,611 on account of their ancestor who had left office in 1689. Chaos ruled and there was only one man who considered he could cure it.

This was Charles Middleton and he at least made a start. In August 1778 Middleton became Comptroller, Head of the Navy Board and what was in effect the principal administrative assistant to the First Lord. He was highly competent, equalling Sandwich, who admired him, in energy and ability. However the First Lord's respect was not reciprocated and it is a tribute to Sandwich's restraint and tact that they were able to work together at all.

Middleton, later Lord Barham, was without question one of the greatest civil servants the Navy has ever had. He was not a likeable man. The son of a minor Scottish customs officer, he was called by his enemies a 'canting Methodist' who believed in 'God and himself and thought obstacles to either were obstacles to the other'. He regarded incompetence and immorality as walking hand in hand. This point of view found little support in the clubs of St James's Street. More unfortunately still, Middleton could scarcely conceal his contempt for Lord Sandwich and had no hesitation in telling the First Lord, to whose post he aspired himself, how best to dispose of fleets and commands. 'The cause of every disorder, my lord, is in the Admiralty and till a reformation is begun there, no good can be expected from any other quarter. For want of plan, for want of men of professional knowledge used to business to assist at the Admiralty and for want of method and execution, one error has produced another, and the whole has become such a mess of confusion, that I see no prospect of reducing it to order. All I can do at the Navy Office will avail but little if the Admiralty continues what it is at present.'[3] Thirteen years after Sandwich died in 1792 and six months before Trafalgar, Middleton at last achieved his lifelong ambition and took office himself as First Lord with the title of Lord Barham. He was seventy-nine.

Both Sandwich and Barham in their different ways were devoted to improving the Navy in every way they could devise. Apart from day to day operations, Sandwich is remembered for introducing copper-bottoming to H.M. Ships. This inhibited the growth of weed and barnacles and improved sailing performance. He also brought in the carronade, a short gun mounted on a light carriage. This could fire a heavy shot over a limited range and showed its value in the 'yard-arm to yard-arm' fighting at which the British came to excel. This gun first proved itself in Rodney's Battle of the Saints in 1782, becoming known in the Royal Navy as the 'smasher'. On a more elegant note Sandwich was responsible for giving classical names to Royal Naval ships, a practice which has continued ever since and in token of the support he received from Sandwich through the Royal Society, Captain Cook named the group of Hawaiian islands in his honour the Sandwich Islands.

Apart from Howe the two great fighting Admirals at sea were Rodney (1719–92) and Hood (1724–1816) his second-in-command on the North American Station. The two men differed greatly in temperament and in the way their careers developed. Rodney had influential connections and had become a Post Captain at the age of twenty-three. Hood, like Nelson, was the son of a country parson and did not reach Post Captain's rank until he was thirty-two. Both were commanders of resolution who gained their experience in the Seven Years War but whereas Hood was ranked by Nelson as one of the greatest Admirals of all time, Rodney invited no confidences. He was feared rather than liked by his subordinates, for whom he held a general contempt, and he possessed an avidity for prize money above all else. Because of his arrogance and his inability to take underlings into his confidence, he failed to make his instructions fully understood at crucial points in a battle.

Apart or together, however, both Admirals achieved significant victories. Rodney relieved Gibraltar in 1780 and together they won the Battle of the Saints in the Caribbean in 1782, a decisive triumph which enabled Britain to conclude better peace terms with France in 1784 than had been thought possible. As a result both Admirals were made peers. Thus in his last ten years Rodney was able to enjoy the enlarged circumstances and wider social life which he found so congenial and for which he had hankered throughout his career. Rodney had had to flee the country to avoid his gambling debts and lived in Paris from 1775 to 1779 by which time France and Britain were at war. Nevertheless, such was the spirit of the age that when Sandwich invited him back to take over the West Indian Command, the French Marshal Biron, after checking with the Minister of Marine, loaned him the money necessary for his return and got Louis XVI to allow him to leave France. This extraordinary gesture stemmed from Marshal Biron's contempt for naval actions in general. 'It is piff-poff on one side and the other and afterwards the sea is just as salt', he is recorded as saying, thus confirming yet again that France has always rated her Navy a bad second to her land forces.

In this painting by T. Whitcombe, the "Formidable" is seen breaking the line at the Battle of the Saints on 12th April 1782. This definitive victory by Admiral Rodney over the French Admiral de Grasse effectively saved the West Indies during the last year of the American War of Independence and provided a good bargaining counter in the peace preliminaries between Britain and America. Britain lost the American colonies basically because the combination of French, Spanish and Dutch fleets with the rebelling Americans defeated British seapower along the North American seaboard. As Washington wrote to Lafayette, 'In any operation . . . a decisive naval superiority is . . . the basis upon which every hope of success must ultimately depend.'

Although Great Britain had lost the war in the sense that the American colonies did secede, turning themselves into the independent United States, the Battle of the Saints – and great battles are the milestones of naval history – extinguished French naval power in the Caribbean for a decade and secured Jamaica in the south as well as Canada in the north. Indeed it could well be argued that it was the French who lost all round. Louis XVI had loaned or given twenty-six million francs to the nascent republic, thanks to the skilful diplomacy of Benjamin Franklin, at a time when French finances were on the downward slope leading to the revolution seven years later. 'If we may judge of the future from what has passed here under our eyes', the Comte de Vergennes wrote to the French Minister in America, 'we shall be but poorly paid for all that we have done for the United States and for securing to them a national existence.' This turned out to be true and French support of the revolution across the Atlantic became in fact one of the final nails driven into the coffin of the French monarchy by the monarchy itself.

This war, moreover, proved to be the last period when the Navy of de Grasse and Suffren could act chivalrously at sea. After the French revolution in 1789 which convulsed the country and sent their best officers to the guillotine, the French Navy was reformed *au fond*. Henceforth it was to fight in a quite different spirit guided by political commissars put on board ship, as in the Russian Navy of today, to ensure that officers and men did their duty according to the revolutionary precept. As a result there were few if any 'happy ships' in the French Navy during the next Anglo-French contest which began on 1st February 1793 eleven days after Louis XVI had been executed.

The War of American Independence had provided the Royal Navy with an invaluable exercise period for what now lay ahead. The Lieutenants and Captains who had fought under Howe, Rodney and Hood, themselves became the Admirals of the Napoleonic wars. These included Saumarez; Cornwallis, Collingwood and Nelson, not forgetting Prince William, Duke of Clarence, later to be the last Lord High Admiral afloat and to be dubbed 'the Sailor King' on ascending the throne as William IV.

Although this definitive war against France which with one fourteen month break in 1802–3 continued for twenty-two years, did not break out until 1793, a scare arose in 1790 when the Fleet was mobilised on a threat of war with Spain. This 'Spanish Armament' concerned a dispute over Vancouver Island claimed by Britain, Russia and Spain. In the event both Spain and Russia retreated from the brink, admitting the prior right of British settlement in that remote area. On June 17, 1579 Drake is alleged to have erected a plate of brass on a stout post near to what is now San Francisco claiming western North America for Queen Elizabeth of England. This plate was rediscovered in 1936 and has since been described as a hoax by the distinguished American historian, Samuel Eliot Morison. However further tests in 1979 and the later discovery of a 1567 sixpenny piece, pierced to form part of the plate, now tend to authenticate the original plate, a final decision on which awaits the ability of science to age-date brass. A facsimile of this plate, presented to Queen Elizabeth II on her coronation in 1953, can be seen at Drake's home, Buckland Abbey, in Devon. How differently the course of history would have run on the

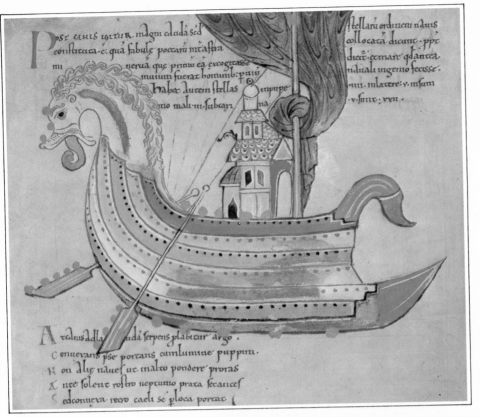

Post eaius igitur. magni caiida sed
constituta e. quâ fabule poetarū in astra
mi nerua que primū eâ excogitasse
muium fuerat hominib: paiu
haber autem stellas in pupe
mo mali in subcari na

stellarū ordinem nauis
collocata dicunt. ppc
dicit ecmare qd antea
nduali ingenio fecisse.
iiii. in latere. v. in sum
v. sunt. xvii

A redius adla da serpens plabitur argo.
Conuerans pse portans cumlumine puppim.
Non alie naues ut malto pondere proras
Ante solent rostro neptunio praxa secantes
Sedconuexa retro caeli se ploca portat

Norse dragon ship, from an Anglo-Saxon manuscript.

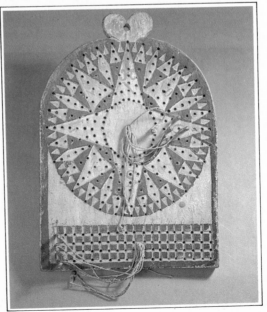

Wooden traverse and wind rose used with an hourglass to record changes in direction and speed.

Top left: Drake
Top right: Anson
Below: Cook
Right-hand page: Nelson.

Four great men of the
British Navy.

The Glorious First of June, 1794, by P.J. de Loutherbourg.

The Battle of Trafalgar, 1805, by J.M.W. Turner.

western seaboard of North America had Drake's claim to California for the British Crown been substantiated!

John Pitt, Earl of Chatham, and brother of the Prime Minister became First Lord of the Admiralty in 1788. On being replaced in 1794 by Earl Spencer hundreds of unopened letters were found at his home. Although not completely inept he was 'surely the laziest man ever to hold a British Cabinet office' according to Middleton who wanted the job himself. However, the seagoing Navy was in reasonably good shape for what was soon to be seen by the entire country as a war of survival against the terrible power of Revolutionary France, now on the point of overrunning Europe. Two veteran Admirals were still available for high command. Both were exceptional. Howe, George III's favourite Admiral, had been a leading spirit in three separate wars, had preceded Chatham for five years as First Lord where he had ensured that the Navy's budget was fully kept up and at the King's insistence had taken command of the principal fleet in home waters even though he was sixty-six years of age and was on record as saying that at sixty a man was too old for operational service. The other, Samuel Hood, was nearly seventy but, uninhibited by modesty, had no worries about his age or ability and was appointed Commander-in-Chief of the Mediterranean Fleet. Among his Captains was Horatio Nelson who at the age of thirty-four was given command of the "Agamemnon", 64 guns. So the long struggle began.

Little of note happened at sea during the first year of the war, whilst on land the French terror was at its height with forty to fifty men and women being guillotined every day. An attempt to take Dunkirk failed lamentably and an inadequate army under the Duke of York was defeated in the Netherlands. In July, however, Hood put an occupying force into Corsica and this held the island until 1796. At the end of August, moreover, the British fleet seized Toulon in support of the French Royalists who were trying to build up a counter revolution from that port. If only the British had been able to land more trained soldiers at Toulon, the whole course of the war might have been changed.

As it was they came up against a young artillery Lieutenant who had the courage to disobey the ill-drafted orders of the fearsome Committee of Public Safety in Paris and thereafter captured Fort l'Aiguilette on the promontory which commanded the entrance to the harbour. The following day the British fleet left before the trap could be sprung and the city surrendered to the Revolutionaries who wreaked vengeance on thousands of helpless captives. All further resistance then ceased. On this being reported to Robespierre and the Committee in Paris, they enquired further into this singular Lieutenant who had taken Toulon. His name was Napoleon Bonaparte and the Directorate which put an end to the Terror immediately sensed his value both whilst assuming power itself and later in appointing him to command the ragged and famished troops attacking the Austrians in northern Italy. From then until the débâcle of Moscow in 1812, there was no looking back for France.

In the summer of 1794 Howe undertook a series of operations which culminated in the battle known as 'The Glorious First of June'. This demonstrated that what had been true of individual Captains of valour could now equally be applied to the fleet as a whole. In seamanship, tactics and gunnery the British could prove themselves superior to any opponent likely to be encountered. Moreover no divided loyalties now caused them to hesitate as they had done in the War of American Independence. 'We are at war with those who would destroy the whole fabric of our Constitution', Pitt said in the House of Commons, 'Our enemies in this instance are equally enemies of all religion . . . and desirous to propagate everywhere, by the force of their arms, that system of infidelity which they avow in their principles.'

Under Howe's command there was an assembly of talent such as had not been seen since the Dutch wars of the Commonwealth and Restoration periods. Admiral Graves of the Chesapeake action in the American War of Independence was second-in-command. Alexander Hood, Samuel's younger brother by two years, had been at Quiberon Bay. Bowyer, Caldwell and Gardner had all served as Captains under Rodney. Then there was the Captain of the Fleet, Sir Roger Curtis, who had played a prominent part in the great siege of Gibraltar. Against them stood the French commander, Admiral Villaret-Joyeuse, 'one of the lightning promotions caused by the Revolution', but, alas, sadly hampered by Jean-Bon Saint-André, a man with the dubious reputation of being the ablest political representative in the fleet, and of whom the British said: ' . . . he fled full soon /At the First of June /But he bade the rest keep fighting.'

This first sea encounter of the Revolutionary War took place far out in the Atlantic and, curiously enough, was claimed as a victory by both sides. So in a sense it was. Tactically Howe could declare an undoubted success. He seized six prizes and sank a seventh ship of the line without a single British loss. Strategically, though, the French could assert that this was a small price to pay for the safe arrival in starving France of a very considerable cargo of grain from neutral America. George III both rejoiced and was mortified. The arrival of the prize ships at Spithead, however, gave the country the sort of tonic always needed at the start of a gruelling war.

Despite the Glorious First of June, however, things went badly for the British as they always seemed to do in the early stages of a major contest. In the Mediterranean, Hood was replaced by the sixty-year-old Sir John Jervis, fresh from the capture of Martinique and Guadaloupe in the West Indies. Old Jervie, Nelson's 'dear Lord', was a natural leader, a tough fighter and a severe disciplinarian. He quickly appreciated Nelson's ability in expelling French garrisons from Corsica – where Nelson had lost the sight of his right eye – and promptly gave him an independent squadron with which to blockade the Italian coast. However naval strategy had, perforce, to be geared to events ashore and there the French were sweeping the board. In 1795 Spain switched sides, declaring war on Britain, and the combination of Spanish hostility with Napoleon's advance through Italy caused the Royal Navy to withdraw from the Mediteranean to Gibraltar in 1796, Nelson's last duty being to evacuate troops and stores from Bastia in Corsica and then from Porto Ferraio in Elba.

Newspapers at home were pointing out the likelihood of invasion (which was, in fact, attempted on a small scale in Pembrokeshire and Ireland but without success) and, as the press has often done since, of this being 'the darkest hour in English history'. It was certainly a time of great crisis. Habeas Corpus had been suspended and the Bank of England was churning out paper money no longer cashable for gold, a practice it continued for twenty years. Then in 1797 came the mutinies at Spithead

and the Nore when the Channel Fleet refused to put to sea. The shadow of the French Revolution, which had happened only eight years previously, lay across the country, as did that of the Russian revolution over a century afterwards in 1917. In both years long standing grievances came to the boil. It was a sombre time.

However in the blackest of periods there has usually been some enlivening event at sea. In 1797 this turned out to be the Battle of Cape St Vincent. Here, off the Sagres headland where Henry the Navigator had had his school and where English fleets since Drake had awaited their prey, Jervis with fifteen ships of the line took on double that number of Spanish ships en route to join up with the French at Brest for another classic attempt at invasion of the British Isles. This rendezvous was decisively prevented by Jervis. Four ships of the line were captured, two of them with 112 guns being bigger than any ship then in the Royal Navy. The British suffered no losses although many ships were seriously damaged. The Battle of Cape St Vincent, after which Jervis was created a peer and from which he took his title (this being suggested by George III) was further remarkable for the unprecedented action by Nelson in disobeying orders, wearing out of the line away from the enemy and then rounding on the Spanish van alone. Although soon followed by his friends Troubridge and Collingwood, Nelson at one time took on seven enemy ships in succession. Had he failed, he would have been court-martialled and possibly excuted as Byng had been:

An oil painting by R. Clevely of the Battle of Cape St Vincent. Until the mid nineteenth century the art of naval gunnery consisted principally of the broadside, i.e. throwing the greatest weight of shot from muzzle-loaded smooth-bore cannon in a simultaneous discharge against the enemy. Maximum range was about a mile but effectively most ships preferred to fight at about one hundred yards, known then as 'the half pistol shot'.

An aquatint of Nelson boarding the "San Nicolas" during the battle of Cape St Vincent on 14th February 1797. It was this occasion which Nelson later described as his 'patent bridge for capturing enemies' and it should be remembered that the point of spreading death and destruction by gunfire was not to sink an enemy ship but rather to facilitate its boarding and capture both for the prize money and so that the ship, after being repaired, could be used again by the winning side.

in the event, like Jervis, he was honoured by promotion to Rear Admiral, receiving also the Knighthood of the Bath.

For the next eight years these two great men, Jervis and Nelson, dominated the naval scene. Both were now heroes in fact and in the popular imagination. Both had exacting standards of excellence, were strong disciplinarians and had a swift answer to those who could not keep up to the mark. Both were not only respected and admired but loved, in the case of Nelson, to the point of adoration. Though frequently and strongly critical of each other, both understood and worked along the same lines, at times as if telepathically united, their close association really declaring itself to the fleet at the start of that first crucial year of 1797 at the Battle of Cape St Vincent in February. A comparison of the logs of Jervis's and Nelson's ships during that battle shows that at exactly the same moment that Jervis was ordering all ships to leave their regular stations and attack where they could, Nelson without waiting for orders was leaving his station and driving hard at the Spaniards – proof of their unanimity of mind without the need of formal communication. Log H.M.S.

"Victory" (St Vincent) 14 February 1797, 12.51 p.m. General signal: Take out suitable stations *and Engage Enemy as Arriving up in succession.* Log H.M.S. "Captain" (Nelson) 14 February 1797, 12.50 p.m.: The Commodore ordered the ship to be wore when she was immediately engaged with the "Santissima Trinidad" and two other 3-decked ships.

After Jervis had helped the aged Howe to deal with the mutinies at Spithead and the Nore in April and May and after Nelson had lost his right arm in an unsuccessful attempt to capture a Spanish treasure ship at Tenerife in July, the two men came together again in April of the following year, 1798. Nelson hoisted his flag in H.M.S. "Vanguard" and rejoined St Vincent off the Portuguese coast, being promptly detached and sent on into the Mediterranean with a squadron of the best ships Jervis could spare to search out and destroy the French fleet which it was guessed was to sail for an unknown destination. It was now that the individual Captains of this squadron – Nelson's first independent command of a fleet – became known as 'the band of brothers'. This closely-knit consortium of fighting men has remained unique in naval history.

It was now also, as David Howarth observes,[4] that the Navy and the country began to take account of Nelson's other quality 'beyond his courage and his tactical skill – the way men loved him. Nobody at second hand has ever quite defined the reason for it. In letters that other men wrote, one can find his innumerable acts of thoughtfulness and kindness, great and small; one can see that however busy he was, tired, weighed down by responsibility, worry and ill-health, he never neglected old friendships or failed by some instinctive touch to make new ones. Yet one cannot hope to recall the irresistible charm his presence certainly had; one can only imagine it from the way that hard-bitten sailors of every rank took pens and paper and more or less laboriously wrote about their love of him – love, not respect or admiration, was the word that all of them used – and from the amazing outburst of grief throughout the Navy when he died. "Men adored him" as the sailor wrote at Trafalgar, "and in fighting under him, every man thought himself sure of success". Historically that is the salient fact: no commander was ever more loved, and love bred confidence. Fleets under Nelson's command had a loyalty and coherence no other had ever equalled.'

Great leaders before and since have all been privy to the same secret. No one, however, has ever been as successful as Nelson in blending authority with friendship based on appreciation and respect. Nelson always took his band of brothers fully into his confidence. He kept them fully in the know as to what he intended to do in any given set of circumstances. He rehearsed and rehearsed. It is an axiom of leadership that the Captain must never be seen to falter and Nelson never did. He had a sure touch and demonstrated not only an unassailable confidence in himself but also a trust in every officer and sailor in his fleet. He made it clear that all were brave and intelligent men capable of using discretion in the heat of battle, a discretion he would always support. 'Nelson was the man to *love*', said Sir Pulteney Malcolm who knew most of the naval commanders in that extraordinary era, and that is perhaps why H.M.S. "Victory" at Portsmouth and his tomb in St Paul's cathedral continue to be places which people feel compelled to visit.[5]

The foray into the Mediterranean which climaxed in the Battle of the Nile came about because Napoleon had begun to brag that Europe, soon to be almost completely under French domination, had already become too small to furnish him with enough glory. He would have to go east. This idea was confirmed by exceptional activity in French Mediterranean ports so that the news reaching England suggested that some big operation was imminent if not already under way. Thus it was that Rear Admiral Nelson at thirty-nine sailed into the enclosed sea which had seen no British naval presence for two years and which yielded scant intelligence of any reliability other than that gleaned from merchantmen haphazardly encountered.

Nelson's expedition, moreover, barely survived an early disaster. This was a storm off Sardinia in which the "Vanguard" was dismasted and nearly sank. His subsequent trans-Mediterranean search became the proverbial attempt to find a needle in a haystack with little but instinct to serve as a guide. In the event Nelson brought off a brilliant coup but only after more than three months of to-ing and fro-ing, of frustration and of acute anxiety.

This scratching about for Napoleon's fleet and the huge convoy for Egypt which it protected was rendered even more difficult by the fact that Nelson disposed of no frigates with which to scout. The storm had dismasted the "Vanguard" and had separated the frigates from the fourteen ships of the line but not before so much damage had been done that the frigate captains considered that the flagship must either have been wrecked or would be forced back to Gibraltar for repairs. So the frigates returned to the Rock and Nelson was left without the essential 'eyes of the fleet'.

In fact the "Vanguard" carpenters achieved the exceptional by re-masting the ship at sea and Nelson sailed on to Naples where he thought that Sir William Hamilton, the British Minister to the Court of the Two Sicilies, might have news, if anyone did, of the French fleet and its progress east. It was here that he first met Emma Hamilton, but that apart gleaned nothing except that the capture of Malta might be a part of Napoleon's plan. This proved to be so.

By 1798 there was little of the crusading spirit left in the Knights of St John who had held Malta since 1530. They were now corrupt and effete and they surrendered to the French by a somewhat shabby pre-arrangement. Napoleon rewarded them by removing as much of their silver and gold as he could take away and then, after leaving a garrison at Valletta under Vaubois, sailed on to Alexandria determined to conquer the Middle East. Nelson followed him, overtook him without in fact knowing that he had done so and found the Egyptian port bare and untouched. What was he now to do? Perhaps he had got it all wrong. He decided to sail back to Sicily and thus, unknown to either, the two fleets crossed each other's tracks. Replenished with water and fresh meat, Nelson then decided on another cast to the south of Greece and there captured a French brig from which he learnt that Napoleon's fleet had been sighted off Crete steering south-east. His instinct had been right after all.

On the afternoon of 1st August 1798 the French fleet under Admiral François Paul Brueys was discovered at anchor near the Rosetta mouth of the Nile. The French with a stronger force than Nelson's felt securely protected by shore batteries, gunboats and above all by the treacherous shoals of Aboukir Bay. They thought it inconceivable that Nelson would risk an encounter that evening because they knew he had no charts. How wrong they were! Nelson and his Captains, well briefed on what they were likely to have to do, attacked at night, each individual Captain being trusted to do whatever was necessary without further orders. By dawn the entire French fleet had been annihilated except for two ships of the line and two frigates under Rear Admiral Villeneuve which managed to get away.

Napoleon's army was thus marooned and later surrendered after its leader had escaped back to France in a Venetian ship. For the time being Italy had been saved. Nelson had gone into the battle forecasting for himself either a peerage or burial in Westminster Abbey. In the event he was showered with honours, including a Sicilian Dukedom and returned overland to England with the Hamiltons via Trieste, Vienna and Hamburg. He was now a national hero on the scale of Drake, his reputation marred only by the scandalous affaire with Lady Hamilton.

Seapower, when actively exercised in war, is almost always resented by neutral countries. It is as if the policeman must only be allowed to patrol his beat; should he ask you to open your bag then that is unpardonable interference with the liberty of the subject. This resentment had become apparent during the War of American Independence when Russia in 1780 had declared a state of armed neutrality in order to prevent 'the haughty British' from searching neutral vessels for contraband of war. Russia had then secured the support of Sweden, Denmark, Prussia, Austria and Spain in this growl of protest which was both ironic and embarrassing since the Imperial Russian Navy of Catherine the Great had been restored to working order, and was currently commanded, by a British Admiral, Sir Samuel Greig.

Nothing much resulted from this protest. Indeed the declaration had been nicknamed at the time the 'armed nullity'. But in 1800 resentment was revived by Tsar Paul I who got the backing of Denmark, Sweden and Prussia to an embargo on British vessels visiting Russian ports until such time as Britain should restore Malta to the Knights of St John, at that time somewhat curiously under Russian protection. Tsar Paul was to be assassinated four months later but in the meantime there were obvious dangers should the Baltic navies come to be used by France against Britain. A fleet was therefore organised to forestall any such possibility, just as Force H was brought into being after the collapse of France in June 1940 in order to prevent the French Atlantic Fleet from being used by Hitler against Great Britain. Both actions, in 1801 and 1940, resulted in pre-emptive strikes which were greatly disliked at the time and have been questioned ever since.

In 1801 command of this fleet was entrusted to Sir Hyde Parker, a son of the Admiral who had begun his career under Commodore Anson and who had distinguished himself against the Dutch off the Dogger Bank in 1781. The less notable son was not a happy choice and this was made worse by the appointment of Nelson some eighteen years his junior (Hyde Parker was sixty and Nelson forty-two) as second-in-command. Nelson persuaded his Commander-in-Chief to let him lead the assault on the Danish fleet at Copenhagen. This action was later described by Nelson as the hardest of his life. Neither Hyde Parker nor Nelson enjoyed attacking the Danes but political expediency required it to be done. The decision once taken, however, Nelson was determined to see it through: Hyde Parker was not. This resulted in perhaps the most famous of the stories about Nelson. 'Leave off the action?' he said when Hyde Parker, who was not at the time engaged, hoisted the signal at the height of the battle, 'Now damn me if I do! You know, Foley', he added to his Flag Captain, 'I have only one eye – I have a right to be blind sometimes', whereupon he applied his telescope to his blind eye and said, 'I really do not see the signal.'

A break in the war which had already gone on for nearly ten years took place in 1802 when on 27th March the Peace of Amiens was signed. The preliminaries to this treaty 'to pacify the whole of Europe' had been signed six months before. Neither side, however, believed it would last. The British had more cogent reasons for this than the French because anyone with a telescope and a sharp eye could see the encampments of Napoleon's Grand Army on the hills across the Channel from Dover, while Boulogne and other harbours were packed solid with specially built invasion barges. Indeed Nelson's last act before peace broke out – and it was one of his few failures – was to organise a raid on this shipping across the Channel. Perhaps because he did not lead the attack himself, perhaps because it was discovered that the boats were unexpectedly moored with iron chains instead of with more easily severed ropes – the operation miscarried and a great many British lives were lost.

On 18th May 1803 hostilities were renewed, ostensibly because Britain refused to hand over Malta, in reality because Napoleon now felt himself ready to invade. Nelson was appointed Commander-in-Chief, Mediterranean in the recently rebuilt "Victory" (then over forty years old). Sir William Cornwallis (1744–1819) took over the Western Squadron whose principal task was the blockading of Admiral Ganteaume's fleet at Brest and Rochefort. Of the two assignments the Atlantic watch was the tougher one and seakeeping in the highly dangerous Bay of Biscay called for skill and patience of a high order.

Cornwallis, fifteen years older than Nelson and now a lifelong friend, had served in the Navy since the age of eleven, had been promoted, like Nelson, to Post Captain at the the age of twenty-two and by 1803 was acknowledged as one of the most experienced Admirals afloat. A severe disciplinarian and reserved in character, Cornwallis was nevertheless popular on the lower deck as evidenced by the number of nicknames he had been given – 'Billy Blue' being the favourite from the frequency with which he hoisted the Blue Peter, the signal to make sail – others such as Coachee or Mr Whip deriving from his florid complexion. But in reality he was liked and respected because he did all he could to improve the daily life of his ships' companies.

Cornwallis has no great battle associated with his name but is typical of that breed of Admiral content to take on the day to day hard slog, the careful planning and the unglamorous seawatch no matter the weather, all of which added to the incessant strain of always being ready for action. Both Cornwallis and Nelson shared a grim determination to bring matters to a head with the French and this required endurance. Front line endurance depends on the maximum back-up it can get, and it was characteristic of Nelson that in the early days he transferred his flag to a frigate in the Mediterranean, generously leaving his powerful three-decker, "Victory", to Cornwallis in the Atlantic until that fleet could be suitably reinforced.

In 1804 Pitt was recalled to power. There was now no doubt whatever of the invasion threat nor of the frantic war effort required to combat it. Napoleon had for the moment cowed the entire continent, in the process compelling the Pope to crown him Emperor of the French. Great Britain stood alone. However, Napoleon lacked one essential and that was naval control of the Channel for long enough to ferry across his invasion army of two hundred thousand men. 'As before and since in her history', Churchill wrote, 'the Royal Navy alone seemed to stand between the Island and national destruction.' The task was daunting and in essence the storm-tossed ships of Cornwallis in the Atlantic and of Nelson in the Mediterranean not only secured the safety of the realm from the Grand Army which never saw them but also stood between Napoleon and his domination of Europe. For two long anxious years Nelson never stepped ashore. Cornwallis fared little better except that once in a while his ships could return to Plymouth to revictual, repair, land the sick and gather news from home. Nelson off Toulon had no nearer base than Malta or Gibraltar each some six to seven hundred miles away. His fleet, therefore, had to become self-reliant and in practice watered and took on such fresh provisions as were obtainable from the barren northern end of Sardinia.

The blockade affected the two navies in different ways. It hardened the British both physically and in their will to win: it rotted the French and Spanish through enforced idleness and lack of experience at sea. Moreover the French were further handicapped by serving an autocrat who, whatever his genius on land, had no real conception of what was required at sea. Napoleon's scheme for the invasion of England was grandiose. Its execution depended on orders to his Admirals impossible to obey. Napoleon thought that the British were wearing themselves to shreds with their debilitating blockade whereas his ships were conserving themselves in harbour. He was totally wrong on both counts. Not only had few of the French crews ever been to sea at all in the ships they manned, the ships themselves were in disrepair and virtually the entire officer class had gone to the guillotine. And just as no one dared to tell Hitler the truth during the Second World War, so no French Admiral would stand up to Napoleon at the risk of his head. Whilst corruption continued to plague the dockyards of England and to endanger supply, the seagoing fleets had never been better led nor, all things considered, in more efficient shape. And both navies knew that truth.

Napoleon's plan – made apparently without considering the implications of his disastrous Egyptian expedition – relied upon the two main fleets emerging from Toulon and Brest, joining forces with the Spaniards from Cartagena and Cadiz and then sailing for the West Indies. There the armada would be reinforced by a squadron from Rochefort and then sweep back to the Channel, dominating it long enough for the Grand Army to cross unmolested. Once ashore in England, Napoleon had not the slightest doubt that he would carry all before him, dictating his own terms in London where a G.H.Q. was being prepared for him in Edwardes Square, Kensington.

The French Admiral charged with executing this grand design thought otherwise. Comte Pierre de Villeneuve (1763–1806) had gained rapid promotion after the revolution. A Captain in 1793 and a Rear Admiral in 1796, he had had previous experience both of Napoleon's plans and of Nelson's panache at the Battle of the Nile

SIGNALLING AT SEA

The language of naval signals was born when ships first found themselves working together beyond shouting range.

Flag signals were created primarily to convey tactical instructions during fleet or squadron encounters with the enemy. In 1653 Admiral Blake used the five most prominent parts of his ship to hoist some twenty-five different manoeuvring signals. From then on flags of different colours and designs appeared, until in 1780 there were fifty flags conveying some 330 instructions.

A complete revolution in signalling methods, however, was inaugurated by Admiral Howe in 1776, at the start of the American War of Independence. Howe introduced a signal book in which the total number of flags was twenty-one, many of new design. In this book he grouped and numbered each instruction so that it could be signalled simply by quoting the number and page on which it appeared. Improvements and variations in flag design were later developed by Kem-penfelt and Knowles. Soon it became customary for Flag Officers to draw up and print their own signal books on taking over command. Howe's signal code, however, continued in use in the fleet until the battles of St Vincent and the Nile.

In 1795 a new form of signalling called semaphore was devised by the Rev. Lord George Murray and in the first place consisted of a screen with six shutters which could be operated to give numerous combinations. Semaphore stations were established on hilltops between the Admiralty and Portsmouth and the Nore, essential messages being relayed in a matter of minutes. The semaphore language was later adapted for use at sea by a man positioning his arms like the arms of a clock to convey letters of the alphabet.

By 1812 Sir Home Popham had produced his second and enlarged edition of telegraphic signals (his first of 1,000 words had been in use at Trafalgar), giving a vocabulary of 30,000 words.

Then in 1844 the American Samuel Morse devised his code on the 'make and break' principle for use with the electric telegraph and this was adapted for use at sea by Captain Colomb when in 1867 his flashing signal lantern appeared. Finally in 1895 Admiral Jackson got together with Signor Marconi and three years later astonished the sceptics by tying an insulated wire to a flagstaff at Bournemouth and transmitting a morse message which was received fourteen miles away at Alum Bay in the Isle of Wight. From then on, there was no looking back, one sad casualty being *The Handbook of Homing Pigeons for Naval Purposes*, published that same year.

Dominating this painting of the Battery at Portsmouth in about 1830 is the semaphore which could signal to the Fleet in harbour or to the nearest of a chain of relay stations reaching to the Admiralty in London.

when, with the greatest difficulty, he had managed to lead out of harbour the only four ships to escape after the holocaust. Promoted Admiral and appointed to Toulon in November 1804, Villeneuve was a brave man in a terrible dilemma. His respect for Nelson and his other British adversaries had in no way diminished, whilst his basic doubts about Napoleon had increased to an alarming degree. When it came to the point Villeneuve felt that his prime duty must lie in preserving the fleet. Indeed when the Trafalgar climax came on 19th October 1805 Villeneuve refused to obey orders to leave Cadiz, only being induced to sail by the news that Napoleon had appointed a successor who was at that very moment en route to take over his command. There was never a better prescription for disaster and this for him Trafalgar turned out to be.

To go back, however, to the events leading up to the Battle of Trafalgar, the story

really began on the dark night of 30th March 1805. Whilst Nelson was standing off Sardinia, Villeneuve with 11 ships of the line and 8 frigates slipped out of Toulon unobserved and then headed west. When the news did reach Nelson, he had first to make sure that the French fleet was not heading once more for the Near East. This done, Nelson set sail for Gibraltar. Strong westerly gales delayed his arrival until 4th May. He then learnt that Villeneuve had slipped through three weeks before, being joined in the Atlantic by six Spanish ships of the line. The long haul across the Atlantic had begun but Nelson could only guess at this, piecing the French design together from chance reports from merchantmen and frigates.

Nelson promptly gave chase. Villeneuve and his combined fleet reached Martinique on 14th May. Nelson made Barbados on the 4th June, a false lead causing him to miss Villeneuve in the Caribbean. Villeneuve, however, got the news of Nelson's arrival only three days later and on 8th June again set sail, this time back to Europe. On 12th June Nelson reached Antigua which island Villeneuve had left four days previously. But what was his destination and what was Nelson now to do?

Although much inferior in numbers to the combined Franco-Spanish fleet, such an imbalance never lost Nelson a wink of sleep. His total confidence in the superiority of his own ships and the men who manned them left him with only one concern – how best to find and destroy the enemy. Where had they gone? Were they en route to Europe or were they playing cat and mouse among the West Indian islands? It was a crucial decision and Nelson opted for Europe, noting in the despatch he sent home to the Admiralty in a fast sloop, 'So far from being infallible like the Pope, I believe my opinion to be very fallible, and therefore I may be mistaken that the enemy's fleet has gone to Europe; but I cannot think myself otherwise, notwithstanding the variety of opinions which a number of good people have formed.'

In fact he was right, except that Villeneuve was heading for Brest whereas Nelson thought he would make for Cadiz and the Straits of Gibraltar. For that reason Nelson set sail thither himself. By a stroke of luck the sloop carrying Nelson's despatches overtook the combined Franco-Spanish fleet in mid Atlantic on 19th June, noting its position, course and speed. This was an invaluable piece of intelligence which wise old Barham, having at last become First Lord of the Admiralty a few months previously, put to immediate advantage by detaching Vice Admiral Sir Robert Calder, with a squadron from Cornwallis's fleet blockading Brest, to intercept Villeneuve off Finisterre. Due to thick fog this action on 22nd July was indecisive, Calder only succeeding in cutting off two ships but at the same time and in spite of direct orders from Napoleon, Admiral Ganteaume at Brest failed to break out and Villeneuve, harried by Calder, took refuge in Ferrol. The Trafalgar campaign had entered its final phase of three months.

Nelson reached Cadiz on 18th July. There was no sign of Villeneuve but Collingwood was on guard and therefore after replenishing in Morocco Nelson sailed for home waters on 23rd July. That same day Napoleon arrived at Boulogne. For England the greatest crisis since the Armada was about to break. Outlying units of the Royal Navy now gathered at the western end of the Channel for the defence of the whole United Kingdom. Calder rejoined Cornwallis off Brest on 14th August and the next day Nelson arrived in the Channel with twelve more ships. The sea barrier against Napoleon now totalled some forty ships of the line. Nelson continued on in the "Victory" to Portsmouth. Napoleon believed that the British fleets were still dispersed and therefore the moment had come to invade. He was to be badly disillusioned. The climax was at hand.

On the 13th August Villeneuve and his crippled fleet (the French and Spanish components had no common language, no unified training and not even a joint signal book) sailed north from Ferrol in a dispirited attempt to join Ganteaume and force the English Channel. On 21st August Ganteaume was observed to be leaving Brest but Cornwallis at once closed in with his whole fleet whereupon the French turned back. So, too, did Villeneuve. Only too desperately aware that his ships full of sick men and dangerously short of supplies could never stand up to the British, Villeneuve made south for Cadiz. From then on the threat of invasion melted away.

But seapower derives from 'the fleet in being' being kept 'in being' and the French fleets although refusing to fight, nevertheless continued to exist. The potential threat remained. 'We have only one great object in view', Nelson wrote to Collingwood, 'that of annihilating our enemies.' Now the drama entered its final act. Collingwood had prudently withdrawn from Cadiz long enough to allow Villeneuve to enter harbour and thus be entrapped. Collingwood then despatched the fast frigate "Euryalus" to Portsmouth with the news and her Captain, Henry Blackwood, another close friend of Nelson's stopped off at Merton, on his way to the Admiralty, at five in the morning. Anticipating his orders, Nelson left Merton and his beloved Emma, 'all which I hold dear in this world', and rejoined the "Victory" at Portsmouth, passing through extraordinary scenes of hero-worship with people kneeling down in the mud to bless him.

On 15th September Nelson in H.M.S. "Victory" sailed for Cadiz, his arrival there a fortnight later being greeted by 'a sort of general joy'. Collingwood, ten years older than Nelson and that eighteenth century rarity – a man who had succeeded without influence or patronage, was none the less a somewhat dour, puritanical Northumbrian, respected not loved. Although a good strategist and administrator Collingwood had no use for the hospitalities which Captains and Wardroom officers in H.M. Ships love to exchange and which Nelson always encouraged as an antidote to the boredom of long days of blockade. Nelson always kept the wheels well oiled and the magic of his return has never been better described than by David Howarth in his *Sovereign of the Seas*:

'At once he wrought his miracle of command. In the next few days he invited all the Captains to dinner, brought them personal messages, from home, attended meticulously to their private worries, exerted his utmost tact to soothe any hurt that Collingwood might have felt – and above all explained to them exactly the revolutionary tactics he had devised to 'annihilate' the enemy fleets as soon as they dared to leave port. Boredom vanished and pride spread through the fleet. In the next few days, all the ships that had not served with him before had men overside in bosuns' chairs, repainting in the colours that had been an emblem of his Mediterranean fleet, yellow bands with the gunports black, so that the hulls looked chequered.'[6]

Matters came to a head when Napoleon withdrew the Grand Army from the Channel and ordered Villeneuve at Cadiz to take his fleet back to Toulon and later to Naples in support of the next venture he had in mind. To make sure these orders were obeyed, the Emperor sent a replacement Commander-in-Chief to Cadiz and it was this dire 'Hobson's choice' which caused Villeneuve to change his mind, against his better judgment, and leave harbour on the 19th October. The most crucial naval battle in history was about to begin.

Napoleon never hesitated to send men to their deaths provided some sort of heroic gesture could be claimed. At Trafalgar his direct orders to leave harbour and fight whatever the odds contained the ominous phrase, 'His Majesty counts for nothing the loss of his ships provided they are lost with glory.'

Two days later it was all over. The 33 French and Spanish ships manned in many cases by riff-raff from the streets, with 1500 on the sick list and driven to sea as a sacrifice to Napoleon's thwarted ambitions were opposed by 27 British ships of the line. In spite of a numerical superiority, the French and Spanish were unfit for sea, untrained to fight and unwilling to engage in a battle they all knew they would lose.

Between the 19th and dawn on the 21st Nelson had kept out of sight beyond the horizon but his frigates, under Blackwood, maintained a close watch on Cadiz and signalled every enemy movement. Once Villeneuve realised that he could not slip away unseen, he tried hard – and against his orders – to get back to Cadiz. He was too late. In almost windless conditions Nelson nevertheless cut him off and forced him to fight in the open sea. By late afternoon of 21st October 1805, 18 French and Spanish ships had surrendered and the rest were in full flight, 11 attempting to enter Cadiz with 4 more being captured off the Spanish coast. However at 1.15 that same afternoon an event occurred which turned this total victory at sea into a national disaster. Nelson was shot whilst pacing the quarterdeck with his Flag Captain, Hardy. 'They have done for me at last', he said, as they carried him below, 'my backbone is shot through.'

Partial firing continued for another three hours, as the log of H.M.S. "Victory" records 'when a victory having been reported to the Right Hon. Lord Viscount Nelson KB and Commander-in-Chief, he then died of his wound'.

The triumph was complete and final, resulting in a century in which the prestige of the Royal Navy stood so high that sea warfare all but ceased. However, 'on such terms', as Captain Blackwood wrote that night to his wife, 'it was a victory I never wished to have witnessed.' When the news reached London in early November the entire country went into mourning in a way unprecedented before and never equalled since.

CHAPTER VI

FROM WATERLOO TO THE CRIMEA

1815-1856

CHRONOLOGICAL COMPENDIUM

The Reigns and their character

George IV
Prince Regent till
death of George III in
1820 then 1820–1830

Aftermath to Napoleonic Wars: civil unrest after demobilisation. Extravagance at Court.

William IV
1830–1837

Great Reform Bill 1832. Beginning of railway age.

Victoria
1837–1901

Industrial supremacy: growth of British Empire.

General

After Britain's defeat of Napoleon, her position as leading European, indeed world, power was assured. France became politically unstable after the Revolution and the Austrian Empire was badly divided. There was to be no major war in Europe until 1914. Conflicts were 'exported'. Thus the Eastern Question and the outbreak of the Crimean War in 1854 were important not only as a result of concern for the 'Holy Places' in the Turkish Empire but also, more crucially, as a means to check Russian expansion in the East, and insist on the closure of the Dardanelles in time of peace to foreign ships of war. Nor did the Crimean War solve the Eastern Question which continued until the First World War.

The underlying concern of foreign policy was to safeguard Britain's world trade, and particularly the lucrative Eastern trade; hence the Burmese and Chinese (or 'Opium') wars.

In Britain itself the fight for political reform had begun, marked by the Great Reform Act of 1832. The political parties strengthened their identities and divisions; the role of the Prime Ministers, Grey, Peel and Palmerston, and their cabinets, was now assured and vital to parliamentary government. Chartism and the fight to improve working conditions, free trade and Irish pressure for Home Rule dominated the first half of the nineteenth century.

At the same time newly dug canals covered much of England, the mining of coal greatly increased, and the railways spread fast. The Metropolitan Police force was established and the Penny Post inaugurated. Voyages of exploration, mainly to the Arctic and the Antarctic, took place and scientific discovery in all fields continued to advance. Communications greatly quickened and the steam engine replaced animal and human muscle power.

Naval

The year 1818, three years after the Napoleonic Wars came to an end, saw the first iron passenger ship plying on the Clyde and in the following year a 'steam-assisted' ship, the "Savannah", crossed the Atlantic in twenty-six days. *The Times* headlined the event with the words 'Great Experiment' and it was certainly an augury of things to come. The Admiralty, however, continued to rely upon the 'wooden walls of England' and it was to be another twenty years or so before Their Lordships reluctantly set up a Department of Steam Machinery.

After Trafalgar the Royal Navy had no rivals afloat but there was a price to pay for the heavy reduction in numbers both of ships and of men, which the economy of the country required in peacetime conditions. Vast numbers of sailors, some of them crippled and ill, were thrown callously on to an almost non-existent labour market. For those who remained on active service, living conditions somewhat improved but the prospect of promotion, indeed of useful employment, diminished. Lieutenants of sixty and admirals of eighty formed part of the naval scene. The service became sluggish and its higher direction somewhat complacent.

Now that the last great ocean, the Pacific, had been opened up by Cook and the generation of explorers which followed him, attention turned once more to the discovery of a North-

West Passage and in general exploration concerned itself with the Arctic and Antarctic. Interest in hydrography and meteorology increased and the charting of the oceans and coastlines of the world was actively pursued by the Admiralty.

Except for the battle of Navarino during the liberation of Greece in 1827 and the Burmese and Chinese wars of 1824 and 1839 respectively, few hostilities other than those of a local nature took place and the Royal Navy's main role became the control of piracy and of slave running and, in general, the policing of the oceans – primarily for the benefit of British trade but also for that of the world at large.

The office of Lord High Admiral was specially revived in 1827 for the Duke of Clarence (later William IV). This was intended to be nominal and honorific. William, however, embarked in the "Royal Sovereign" in 1828, hoisted the Lord High Admiral's flag and assumed military command of the fleet during manoeuvres. This resulted in strong protests from the Prime Minister and the King and as a consequence Prince William resigned his naval post.

In 1832 the Navy and Victualling Boards were absorbed into the Admiralty and from then on the direction and administration of the Royal Navy was conducted by the First Lord, the five Sea Lords, the Civil Lord responsible for dockyards and a Parliamentary Secretary for finance.

In essence the nineteenth century saw the British nation, and the life it led, change out of all recognition. Naturally the Royal Navy followed suit. In effect, however, and in the first half of the century, the nation and the navy drew apart. For the previous three centuries the Royal Navy had been uniquely valuable to the nation both in peace and war. Generally speaking the service had been the largest and most expensive of the government employment agencies. It had saved the state at the Restoration and in the revolution of 1688. Since the times of Queen Elizabeth I, no generation of sea officers had come and gone without battle experience against enemy fleets. No administration had failed to maintain a navy which, generally speaking, had been stronger than that of any potential enemy. The country depended for its prosperity on a powerful navy and instinctively the gentlemen and the merchants of Britain knew this well.

All this was now to change. The nation became the mightiest in the world whilst the Royal Navy shrank absolutely and, relatively to foreign powers, to a degree not seen since the reign of James I. Whilst the country's influence increased, the Royal Navy's horizons contracted. Critics, who saw the situation clearly, observed that the fiery torch which had blinded Napoleon, was now diminishing into a candle. The heroes of Trafalgar had now to be content with chasing Arab dhows and burning villages in the obscure and unhealthy backwaters of the distant parts of empire. The country might have gained an empire: the Royal Navy no longer had a very glamorous role.

Organisation

Reduction of numbers:

1813   98 sail of the line, 130,000 officers and men.

1817   13 sail remained 20,000 officers and men.

1832   Navy Board merged into the Admiralty which thus became the single organisation responsible for every aspect of the naval affairs of the nation.

1835   First Chief Engineer and Inspector of Machinery appointed.

1837   First Comptroller of Steam Machinery.

Ships and Weapons

1822   First steam vessels brought into use: the tugs "Comet" and "Monkey" used for towing ships of the line out of harbour when the wind was unfavourable.

Communications, Navigation, Hydrography

1801   First Admiralty Chart

1807   Hydrographer takes over Naval Chart Committee

1810–19   Hydrographer also responsible for Board of Longitude

1818   Admiralty takes over Royal Observatory, Greenwich

1819   Permission given to sell charts to Merchant Marine

1823   First *Sailing Directions* published by British Hydrographic Office

1829   First *Light List* published

1833   First *Tide Tables* published

1834   First 'Notices to Mariners' issued. By this year there were 2,000 charts in existence

1842   Admiralty Compass Department set up by Sir Francis Beaufort (1774–1857), a Rear Admiral who had been a boy of thirteen at the battle of the Glorious First of June, was the Hydrographer for twenty-six years and gave his name to the scale used for wind and weather

        Tide tables were henceforth published annually

        Beaufort also inaugurated Scientific Branch into the Admiralty which included the Hydrographic Department, the Royal and Cape Observatories, the *Nautical Almanac* and the Chronometer offices

1849   Admiralty *Manual of Scientific Enquiry* issued to guide observers especially Medical Officers

Signalling and Telegraphs

1796   Rev. Lord George Murray invents semaphore

1806–25   Admiralty sets up telegraph stations on hills between London and Portsmouth, Plymouth, Deal and Yarmouth

1837   Wheatstone patents electric telegraph

1844   Samuel Morse (1791–1872) invents his code for use on telegraph line between Washington DC and Baltimore and by 1858 this was in general use all over the world

Exploration and development of empire

1787   Arthur Phillip (1733–1814) Vice Admiral takes first fleet of convicts to Botany Bay, New South Wales, later becoming first governor. Convicts still went to Sydney until 1840

1806–7   Beaufort surveys River Plate

        Arctic exploration during the post-Napoleonic period was stimulated and promoted by Sir John Barrow (1764–1848), Secretary of the Admiralty from 1807, and he encouraged the following:

        Sir John Franklin (1786–1847). Sir John Ross (1777–1856). Sir William Parry (1790–1855). Sir Edward Sabine (1788–1883). Matthew Flinders (1774–1814). George Bass (1771–1802). Philip Parker King (1793–1856). George Vancouver (1758–98). Robert Fitzroy (1805–65), Commanding Officer of the "Beagle" of Darwin's expedition of 1831–6. Sir Edward Belcher (1799–1877). Sir George Back (1796–1878). F. W. Beechey (1796–1856).

Wars and Battles

1824–6   Anglo-Burmese war

1827   Battle of Navarino Bay – Turkish and Egyptian fleets destroyed by combined British, French and Russian fleets. Last fleet action under sail

1839–42   War against China ('Opium' war) – Hong Kong taken by British and Canton and Shanghai opened to British trade

1854–6   Crimean war

Seapower, heroic endurance and a national determination combined to defeat Napoleon and ushered in a century of peace. All wars, of course, are finally concluded on land and the Napoleonic war did not end until ten years after Trafalgar. However, it was control of the sea which decided it. Napoleon once said 'the Spanish ulcer killed me', and that was true, but it was the Navy which kept Wellington's armies supplied in the Peninsular war and which enabled him to win in the end.

On the 15th July 1815 – four weeks after Waterloo – Napoleon surrendered to the Captain of H.M.S. "Bellerophon" in the Biscay port of La Rochelle and that night at dinner remarked, 'If it had not been for you English, I would have been Emperor of the East; but wherever there is water to float a ship, we were sure to find you in our way.'

In general terms seapower in those days meant control of the seas by a fleet dominating each area but those final ten years of the war which included a second North American campaign in 1812–14 (the War of 1812) were by no means 'plain sailing' for the Royal Navy. Indeed, had Napoloen acted on the advice of Robert Surcouf (1773–1827), perhaps the most successful French privateer there ever was, hostilities might well have been prolonged and the convoy and escort system overstrained to the point of collapse.

Surcouf said to Napoleon, on opting to remain a corsair rather than be appointed to command of a warship: 'Sire, in your place I should burn all my ships of the line and never give battle to the British Fleet or show fight to British cruising squadrons; but I should launch on every sea a multitude of frigates and light craft which would very soon annihilate the commerce of our rival and deliver her into our hands.' Surcouf was a shade over-optimistic but the echo of that advice can be heard in the German U-boat campaigns in the two world wars of the twentieth century.

In the summer of 1815 Great Britain stood at the head of Europe and it was on the skilful conduct by Castlereagh of the Congress of Vienna that the general peace of succeeding generations depended until the outbreak of the First World War in 1914. Throughout these peace negotiations Castlereagh and Wellington stood between France and her restively vindictive enemies. As Churchill remarks: 'Unrestrained, Prussia, Austria and Russia would have divided between them the states of Germany, imposed a harsh peace upon France and fought each other over the partition of Poland. The moderating influence of Britain was the foundation of the peace of Europe.'[1] Localised wars did, of course, break out throughout the nineteenth century but none was on the scale of the Napoleonic contest.

Ironically enough, however, the first half of the nineteenth century saw the Royal Navy diminish into the smallest, weakest and least efficient service both absolutely and in relation to foreign powers that it had ever been at any time since the reign of James I. The early years of the Pax Britannica, therefore, relied on a mixture of diplomacy and bluff. Paradoxically, as Great Britain's influence – and its Empire – grew to be the greatest in the world, so the Navy's horizons, at any rate until after the Crimean War, shrank to an almost absurd degree. How did this come about?

By the end of the Napoleonic Wars, the Royal Navy had no rivals afloat. It had demonstrated to the world a fine working tradition of valour and victory. But twenty years fighting had all but bankrupted the nation and, as always happens after a major war, the rundown was abrupt, inevitable and cruel. An army of occupation might still be required for a year or two in Europe. No one wanted a fleet. In 1813 there had been some 600 ships in commission manned by 130,000 officers and men. By 1817 only 20,000 remained. Of 98 ships of the line only 13 remained in commission. At the battle of Navarino against the Turks in October 1827, the British component of the combined British, French and Russian fleet comprised only 4 ships of the line, 3 frigates and 4 other vessels.

The reason for this sudden upheaval was simply that the role of the Navy changed overnight from waging a war into keeping the peace. Maritime conquerors were now required to become policemen with a subsidiary call to be explorers and scientists. Glorious as it had been to win the war, it was now both wise and honourable to compel the peace. However, there were two snags to which no one in authority had the answer or anything approaching it. There could now be little seatime and less promotion for those who stayed: for those thrown on the beach there was no employment, with consequent hardship amounting to beggary.

The immediate post-war years show up as grey and ugly in the extreme. During the nineteenth century and nationally speaking the British advanced out of all recognition, the Navy naturally being a part of that progress. But this advance was bought at a price. By the time of the Crimean War there were Lieutenants of sixty and Admirals of over eighty. There was also an inbuilt resistance to innovations such as steam and iron and a defiant clinging to sail and the wooden walls of England which, looking back now, seems to be all but ludicrous.

On the lower deck there did come about a basic amelioration in sailors' lives. After 1815 the Press Gang became a thing of the past. All were now volunteers and that especial camaraderie unique to the messdecks of a warship began anew. The riff-raff and dirty, dishonest, ignorant and miserable shoreside criminals were no longer sent

'Saturday Night at Sea' by George Cruikshank gives an idea of lower deck life around 1810. Sailors generally messed on hanging tables round or near the guns they fought, slinging their hammocks overhead at night. For two hundred years the ration scale of the Navy remained unchanged at 1 lb of salt pork or 2 lbs of beef on alternate days, 1 lb of biscuit (usually complete with weevils) and 1 gallon of beer (more often than not sour) plus a weekly issue of 2 pints of pease, 3 of oatmeal, 8 ounces of butter (rancid) and 1 lb of cheese (bonehard). The only real amelioration was liquor.

to sea. Living conditions also improved though to begin with this was scarcely perceptible. Violent punishments declined, the impulse for this having been given by Nelson who preferred to rely on loyalty and respect, although flogging was not suspended until the 1870s.

Food slowly got better. One of the mutineers' demands in 1797 had been for fresh vegetables whilst in port and twenty-five years later H.M. Ships began to get an occasional supply. Canned meat from the Dartford Iron Works made the diet more edible and no one minded that bully beef was, like so many other innovations, a French idea, the name being corrupted into English from 'boeuf bouilli'. No sailor as yet had any official entitlement to leave but more and more captains were taking the risk of allowing men ashore. Naturally they returned on board drunk but at least they came back, the punishment for drunkenness being one of the lightest in the book – the mulct of a day's pay.

Increasingly men took their wives or girl friends to sea. There had always been women on board during the Napoleonic Wars and at least one baby had been born during the Battle of the Nile. Mary Ann Talbot, one of the sixteen illegitimate children of the Earl of Talbot had dressed as a man and served with distinction at sea and in 1808 someone recorded the fact that a larky lady obliged nineteen of the lower

An engraving from a watercolour by J. Moore shows the conflagration of Dalla during the Burmese War of 1824–6. During the century of the Pax Britannica, the Royal Navy virtually policed the world. Later in this period the British Empire required fleets and squadrons to be stationed at strategic points all over the globe from which bases gunboats, suitable for river and shallow water operations, would be despatched to deal with local troubles wherever arising. (Centre, E.I.C. "Diana", commanded by the famous seawriter, Captain Marryat.)

deck in one night. To a certain extent 'the People', as sailors were then known, organised that side of life in the way they saw fit. An Admiralty order, although officially ending the presence of women on board in 1817, actually did little more than decree that 'no ship was to be too much pestered with wives' and winked an eye at the custom until the advent of a young Queen to the throne in 1837.

However, women at sea, as opposed to women on board in harbour, were not as prevalent as the above might suggest. Admiralty instructions laid down that no women were to be taken to sea and all ships were to be cleared of them before weighing anchor. Most ships followed Admiralty instructions but, in some, three or four wives of senior petty officers were allowed to remain on board, though they were not victualled. Occasionally some women escaped the search and it was these few that engendered the more notorious stories. Around 1820 discipline was lax and many captains took their wives to sea with them.

As always the tone was set by the Crown and George IV, first as Regent and then as King, together with his brother the Duke of Clarence, later William IV, were not notable for their puritanism or even restraint so far as women were concerned. The poet Shelley declared that William and his brothers were 'the dregs of their dull race' and posterity has done little to improve the reputation of George III's sons. In fact, the Duke of Clarence, though at times garrulous and choleric, was a kind-hearted, well-meaning man who spent fifty years in the Navy and ended his life with seven years as King.

A Captain at twenty-one and for a brief time the last Lord High Admiral afloat, he was known as 'Sailor Billy' (also less kindly as 'Silly Billy') and spent a large part of his service career fighting the Admiralty, making rambling and intemperate speeches and doing what he could for his friends (it was said that as a result of his efforts on behalf of Nelson the latter was unemployed for five years). For twenty years he lived with a buxom Irish actress called Mrs Jordan by whom he had ten

A watercolour of the lower deck of a man-of-war at Gravesend about 1810. Women were officially banned from H.M. Ships in 1817 but the practice of taking certain of them to sea continued for at least another twenty years. A baby was born on board H.M.S. "Tremendous" during the battle of the Glorious First of June (1794) and was christened Daniel Tremendous Mackenzie. Another was born at the battle of the Nile and a woman later petitioned Nelson for a pension as 'she had assisted the surgeon for eleven weeks afterwards'.

children, before marrying Princess Adelaide of Saxe-Coburg-Meiningen in 1818.

But he never forgot or forgave the treatment he had received at the hands of the Admiralty which refused his demand for active service in the Napoleonic wars, a refusal backed up by his father and the Prime Minister. This came about because he took the side of his brother, the Prince of Wales, against the King. However, when the bizarre constitutional experiment was made in 1827 of appointing the Duke of Clarence as Lord High Admiral, his generous but wild ideas proved too much even for George IV. Having removed the Fleet against Admiralty orders for a private cruise, the man described as 'a good egg but cracked' was dismissed by the incoming government of the Duke of Wellington after the King had been forced, sadly, to express his acute displeasure and call for his resignation. In a memorandum to the Prime Minister George IV wrote: 'I am quite aware that I am fast drawing to the close of my life . . . a month, a week, a day may call the Lord High Admiral to be my successor . . . in the meantime the Lord High Admiral shall strictly obey the laws enacted by Parliament or I desire immediately to receive his resignation.' William resigned in August 1828.

In one other way the standard of life on board ship improved, though by an apparent deprivation. Until and through the Napoleonic Wars drunkenness caused most of the punishments afloat and also the majority of casualties. This was because, in a rolling and pitching ship, alcoholically bemused seamen were always concussing themselves against the low bulkheads or regularly falling out of the rigging on to hard decks or into an unwelcoming sea. In the early days ships' companies were supplied with almost unlimited beer (until it went sour) and after Admiral Vernon's time with half a pint of rum each day mixed three parts of water to one of rum. This made life slightly more bearable but it turned sailors into alcoholics and because the grog issue was seen as a sacred right no one dared to cut it down. However in 1824 the Admiralty decided, as an experiment, to halve the rum ration, replacing it with tea or cocoa in lieu – this experiment was nicknamed the 'Gorgon' (No Grog reversed) and took place in H.M.S. "Thetis", thereafter called H.M.S. "Tea Chest". Seamen bellyached for a while but then to the astonishment of all admitted that they felt the better for it. A quarter of a century later the rum ration was again halved and once more the men approved. So things remained until long after the Second World War when in 1970 the free issue of rum was finally abolished.

Other improvements in service conditions were also made, but at a snail's pace. In 1831 the idea of pensions after twenty-one years' service was mooted and five year Good Conduct badges with a small increment of pay were introduced in 1849. However it was not until over half a century after Trafalgar that a regular uniform for sailors was authorised. In 1858 a Royal Commission on Manning under the Earl of Hardwick recommended a complete overhaul of the system by which clothing, victuals and punishments were meted out. Facilities for basic training were vastly increased and long service contracts came into force.

From then on the lower deck enlisted for an initial period of 12 years with the option of staying on for another 10 plus 5 in the Reserve, a pension being payable after 22 years. Such long service contracts, varied according to circumstances, have been operated by the Royal Navy ever since. They gave sailors who would pass their entire working lives on the lower deck the same security and pride which Pepys had given to the officers nearly two centuries previously. By 1858, however, the sailing navy had all but come to an end, its death knell sounded by the Crimean War.

During the turbulent years between Waterloo and the beginning of the Victorian age, the Board of Admiralty, like the shrinking Navy it controlled, lost the political standing and power it had enjoyed during the long struggle against Napoleon. Then the First Lord had dominated the Cabinet and had virtually directed the nation's war policies. Now uninspired mediocrity became the keynote. The second Viscount Melville, First Lord almost continuously from 1812 to 1830, was described by an enthusiastic fellow Scot as 'judicious, clairvoyant and uncommonly sound headed, like his father' and by a colleague as a 'most amiable and worthy man, and very good at business.' In truth he seems to have possessed only moderate talents, and on one occasion his clairvoyance failed to prevent him appointing a second Captain to a ship he had already given away once.[2]

Stagnation was the order of the day. Palmerston, who sat on the Board for two years, described his duties as 'passing a couple of hours in the Board Room doing little or nothing'. Indeed the Boards of those early years of peace had few men of calibre to conduct their business. However, a spirit of reform had begun to sweep through the country culminating in the great Reform Bill of 1832, but the Tory government in power from the signing of peace until 1830 stoutly resisted the radical changes which eventually swept them from office.

Their outlook was exemplified by the First Secretary of the Admiralty, John Wilson Croker, who had been appointed in 1809, only being dismissed with Wellington's ministry in 1830. Croker was proud to be 'an extreme conservative in politics, able, ambitious, arrogant and autocratic. He kept a tight control on the business of the office, opening every letter with his own hand.'[3] According to a hostile observer he was opposed to everything in the shape of reform, improvement and expense.

The second secretary, in later years to be known as the Permanent Secretary, was mercifully different. Sir John Barrow held office from 9th April 1807 to 28th January 1845 and unlike Croker had been a poor boy in Lancashire rising entirely by his own ability. Described as an apt and friendly administrator, he served four sovereigns, forty Boards plus a Lord High Admiral during his thirty-eight year span of office. He also made himself a man of influence in different spheres, founding the Royal Geographical Society, becoming an authority on China and South Africa, advising the publisher John Murray, contributing to the *Quarterly Review* and, perhaps most notable of all, becoming the driving force in Arctic exploration.

1830 is the year when real changes began. George IV died and with the accession of his sixty-five year old brother William IV, 'the least known of British sovereigns during the past four hundred years', the Whigs stormed into power and with them, led by Earl Grey, a crew of reformers fired by the pent-up enthusiasm of zealots who had spent most of their adult lives frustrated by a succession of Tory governments.

Grey appointed Sir James Graham as First Lord. Graham was a young, inexperienced politician whose first instinct in the cleaning up of corruption was to reduce spending and increase the personal responsibility of individual Lords Commissioners for their subordinate branches. Graham saw the Navy Board, still distinct from the Admiralty proper, as his first target and, aided by Sir John Barrow, at once reduced the estimates by £1,200,000 to £4,650,000. 12 Commissioners, 61 Superior and 37 Inferior dockyard officers were dismissed together with over 100 clerks. Graham also introduced a system of internal audit, unthinkable before and, in place of the previous junior boards, five 'Principal Officers' were appointed – the Accountant-General, Storekeeper-General, Comptroller of Victualling, Physician and Surveyor.

Each now bore responsibility for his department to one of the Lords Commissioners of Admiralty and thus the 'ancient and redoubtable' Navy Board, first brought into being by Henry VIII, came to its end. Few grieved. In the Whig view economy was synonymous with efficiency and this might well have been so had the volume of business remained parochially small. Unfortunately it did not. During Barrow's long tenure of office the number of letters passing through the Secretary's hands each year increased from 25,402 to 47,866. The departmental duties now devolving upon the First Sea Lord with his overall responsibility for the Navy were soon to become 'so arduous and multifarious that it was with difficulty that he could get through the daily routine of office work, much less find time for the careful consideration of grave and important questions of national defence.'[4] Luckily there were no major wars or other external crises of note until the Crimean War in 1854.

Incidents and minor campaigns did, of course, take place at intervals throughout this period. The first of these occurred in 1816 when Lord Exmouth, reinforced by six Dutch ships, sailed into Algiers and forced the Dey to release his Christian slaves. Then from 1824 to 1826 a naval force decisively repelled the King of Ava in an Indo-Burmese war and thereafter installed a British Resident in Rangoon. Here for the first time in war a steam vessel was employed by the Navy. This was the "Diana" owned by the East India Company and operated under the orders of Captain Frederick Marryat, who had entered the Navy as a Midshipman under Lord Cochrane (later the 10th Earl of Dundonald) in 1806 and who, three years later, was to begin the series of sea novels, such as *Mr Midshipman Easy*, which were to rank him with Smollett as one of the foremost writers about the sea there has ever been.

Cochrane himself, the inspiration for C. S. Forester's Hornblower, had a brilliant career afloat in the Napoleonic wars. This was followed by a most chequered career ashore including a spell in prison for a somewhat debatable involvement in a Stock Exchange swindle of which he was later cleared. Cochrane then engaged himself in liberating Chile and Peru from the suzerainty of Spain. After that he repeated the process in Brazil and finally assisted the Greeks in their struggle for freedom against the Turks after Byron had died at Missolonghi. This was all very much in keeping with the spirit of the age when the cause of freedom could be certain of attracting the support of English gentlemen otherwise unemployed at home.

The Greek struggle reached a climax at the battle of Navarino, the last major action fought wholly under sail, in October 1827 when a combined British, French and Russian fleet under Sir Edward Codrington defeated a much larger Turco-Egyptian fleet under Ibrahim Pasha. Codrington (1770–1851) had been a Lieutenant under Howe at the Glorious First of June in 1794, had captained H.M.S. "Orion" under Nelson at Trafalgar in 1805 and after Navarino commanded the Channel Fleet in 1831, finishing his service career as Commander-in-Chief at Plymouth from 1839 to 1842 by which time he was seventy-two. During that same period of 1839–42 the Anglo-Chinese 'opium' war took place as a result of which Hong Kong was ceded to Britain and Canton, Amoy, Foochow, Ningpo and Shanghai were opened to British trade, consuls were established in the treaty ports and a large indemnity extorted which the Chinese, understandably, resented ever after.

The policing of distant oceans and the setting up of bases overseas which were a necessary concomitant, kept the seagoing navy in a more active state than that of its senior officers, few of whom could be persuaded to retire even when four-fifths of the Navy List were in fact living ashore on half pay with nothing whatever to do. However, one other naval activity continued to be alive and healthy, although it had been disrupted by the Napoleonic wars. This was exploration and the surveying, charting and oceanography it entailed.

By the second decade of the nineteenth century almost all habitable coastlines had been explored, so enquiring minds now turned to the desperate challenge of the Arctic and Antarctic. The ancient lure of finding a northern sea route through the icy wastes of Canada to the Pacific now revived. This search for a North-West Passage had waxed and waned during the 350 years after Cabot had reached Newfoundland in 1497, losing his life in unknown circumstances on a second voyage the following year.

The Hudson's Bay Company had been formed in 1670 primarily to trade in furs but it was also bound by its charter to continue attempts to find a North-West Passage. During the eighteenth century the Company attracted much criticism for the feeble efforts it made in this direction and various face saving minor sea voyages round Hudson's Bay together with land journeys further north took place. Parliament had offered a prize of £20,000 in 1745 to any British subject discovering a North-West Passage and in 1817 the Act was modified to provide a sliding scale of rewards for approaching the Pole and for reaching certain meridians of longitude. It was this which inspired the great nineteenth century British Admiralty expeditions, the first of which set off in April 1818 under Commodore Sir John Ross (1777–1856). Other expeditions under Sir William Parry (1790–1855), Ross's nephew James (1800–62) and Sir John Franklin (1786–1847) followed and the passage was at last discovered in 1850 by Vice Admiral Sir Robert McClure (1807–73). A fifty year pause then ensued before further attempts to navigate the passage were made in the twentieth century.

Hydrography also came into its own during the first half of the nineteenth century. The Admiralty established its Hydrographic Department in 1795, the first Hydrographer being Alexander Dalrymple (1737–1808). Dalrymple had originally been a writer with the East India Company and then became the Company's first Hydrographer. After resolving an uneasy relationship with the Naval Chart Committee, Dalrymple's judgment and initiative caused him to be appointed as the Board of Admiralty's sole adviser on all navigational matters. When he died of 'mortification' or what would now be called gangrene, his place was taken by Thomas Hurd (1753–1823) who was also Secretary to the Board of Longitude.

Hurd accepted responsibility for the Royal Observatory, Greenwich in 1818 (run by the Admiralty until 1965 when the Scientific Research Council took over) and in

1819 secured permission to sell Admiralty charts to the merchant marine. In 1823 Hurd published the first Admiralty 'Sailing Directions' and in 1829 the first 'Light Lists'. He encouraged the exchange of information with other National Hydrographic Offices (such as that of the United States in 1830), most hydrographic knowledge coming, in fact, from the navies of the world. Tide tables were first issued in 1833 and in the following year, the Admiralty having already published two thousand charts, the practice began of correcting and updating them by means of Admiralty Notices to Mariners.

Hydrographers of the Navy seem to be noted for longevity in office, the most famous being Rear Admiral Sir Francis Beaufort (1774–1857) who was Hydrographer for twenty-six years from 1829 to 1855. Beaufort had gone to sea in the navy as a boy of thirteen, had served at the battle of the Glorious First of June in 1794 and had also been on the expedition to Buenos Aires in 1806–7 when he made surveys of the River Plate. A friend of Sir John Barrow, the Secretary of the Admiralty, who supported and encouraged him, Beaufort became a Fellow of the Royal Society in 1814, of the Astronomical Society from its foundation in 1820 and a Founder Member with Barrow of the Royal Geographical Society in 1830. Beaufort kept a weather log from his earliest days at sea and his prime interest in meteorology led to the development of the wind and weather scale which bears his name. Another of his interests was in tidal theory and he instituted a Scientific Branch in the Admiralty which included the Hydrographic Office, the Royal and Cape Observatories, the Nautical Almanac and the Chronometer offices.

Beaufort was matched in distinction on the other side of the Atlantic by an American naval officer, Matthew Maury (1806–73) who, after circumnavigating the world in the U.S.S. "Vincennes" published a highly successful treatise on Navigation and then became Superintendent of the new Naval Observatory in Washington D.C. Maury's basic interest lay in the winds and currents of the North Atlantic and the classic chart he published in 1842 became of immediate use to the tough Packet Ship Captains by saving time on their regular transatlantic crossings. Maury was also the instigator of the First International Conference on Oceanography held at Brussels in 1853 and can therefore be considered the father of oceanography, that realm of today and of the immediate future in which American scientists seem always to have excelled.

The first half of the 19th century, however, saw the world come under the domination of steam. Steam and the industrial age revolutionised life at all levels in a manner and to a degree never before experienced. Today we marvel at the nuclear-electronic-silicon chip 'miracles' which assail us every time we open the paper or turn on the television. But such is human nature that we soon take them for granted. A man on the moon? The photographing of the remotest planets in the solar system? We see all this now merely as the march of events and very soon cease to react. We become 'blasé', as it used to be said when I was a boy. The wonder has somehow or other evaporated. Wonder has been defined as the *qualitative* distance which God places between man and the truth. More simply, perhaps, wonder is the gap between mankind and the great unknown and wonderment today is in surprisingly short supply. In 1825, however, when the Stockton to Darlington railway was opened and the household match had just been invented with all that this meant to ordinary folk, 'wonders would never cease'. For the first time in history, man had available new levers of power, the equivalent of muscle which he could control without a whip and which overnight rendered human and animal physical energy out of date. The possibilities of this took people in different ways, a number of them far from beneficial. But one thing was sure. Steam and the changes it was about to ring were inescapable.

Not, however, so far as Their Lordships were concerned. A few steam tugs to help sailing ships into and out of harbour were just acceptable, steam propulsion fitted to a three-decker line of battleship remained unthinkable. The "Charlotte Dundas", a small wooden vessel with a single paddle wheel fitted in the stern, had successfully plied the Forth and Clyde canal since 1802 and Bell's "Comet", the single cylinder engine of which is preserved in the Science Museum in London, had worked a passenger and cargo service on the Clyde from 1812 until 1820 when the ship was wrecked in a gale. Their Lordships were not impressed.

Lord Melville, the First Lord in 1828, put out the bland statement that 'Their Lordships feel it their bounden duty to discourage to the utmost of their ability the employment of steam vessels, as they consider the introduction of steam is calculated to strike a fatal blow at the supremacy of the Empire' – the logic of which may not be apparent though it was perhaps governed by the fact that Great Britain had a fleet of sailing ships which had for so long proved supreme that there could be little point in making them obsolete. Merchant service operators on both sides of the Atlantic thought otherwise.

Men like Cunard and Brunel were soon to demonstrate in an unassailable way that steam was no overnight marvel. Their Lordships continued to prefer the opinion of Dr Dionysius Lardner who in 1835 declared the idea of a direct steamship crossing from Liverpool to New York to be 'perfectly chimerical and that they might as well talk of making a voyage from New York or Liverpool to the moon'. It is true that there were self-evident objections to the effectiveness of paddle wheels in an Atlantic gale but even after two inventors (the Swedish John Ericsson and the English Francis Pettit Smith) had independently taken out patents on screw propulsion within six weeks of each other in 1836, Their Lordships the following year opined that 'even if the propeller had the powers of propelling a vessel' (which it had just done in a trial run with Their Lordships on board) 'it would be found altogether useless in practice because, the power being applied in the stern, it would be absolutely impossible to make the vessel steer'.

The spectacle of experts being confounded by fact has long given the British acute pleasure and the first half of the nineteenth century was rich in this department. 'Who ever heard of iron floating?' they were asking in 1830 when the first iron ships were being mooted and later when a government committee was asked to consider the possibility of telegraphing without wires, Sir Charles Wheatcroft, the eminent physicist and electrical expert, declared with absolute authority that 'there is no possibility of that whatever, gentlemen, none whatever'. Nor were these prejudices a British monopoly. Long after the steam engine had become an established fact in England, Monsieur Thiers, the Minister of Public Works in the French Government,

came across the Channel, examined the railways in daily use and returned to France to report that the *chemin-de-fer* would never be suitable for France.

The fact is that the Establishment of the day shut its collective mind against innovation, perhaps because the ruling classes were afraid of any communication device whether by sea, rail, telegraph or post which could bring noble and peasant to a common level. The Duke of Wellington never ventured a journey by train until 1843 and then only because he was attending the Queen and her Consort on a journey all the way from London to Windsor by means of this devilish conveyance. So far as the Navy was concerned what was good enough for Nelson was more than good enough for his successors, until the Crimean War revealed that the wooden walls of England were about as effective as *papier mâché*.

But the inventive and engineering genius of the British, which began flowering from the latter part of the eighteenth century and was responsible amongst a host of other things for railways, gas lighting, the discovery of electro-magnetic rotation and the inauguration of the adhesive stamp and the Penny Post, simply by-passed the Admiralty until civilians had proved that steamships were not only practicable for a regular transatlantic service but could also be made to pay. It was not until 1835 that

This coloured lithograph of the wreck of H.M.S. "Birkenhead", a frigate, in 1852 vividly brings home the terrors the sea can cause to the Royal Navy and the Merchant Marine. The Commanding Sea may not always be cruel: it is certainly dangerous and it is only in the latter part of the twentieth century that the 'depths of misery and the jaws of death' can now be avoided through the development of accurate navigational instruments at sea, up-to-date charts and the placing and maintenance of lighthouses, lightships and buoys.

THE COMING OF STEAM

Although the world's first steam vessel, the "Pyroscaphe" was invented by a Frenchman, the Marquis d'Abbans in 1783, it only worked for fifteen minutes before breaking down. The steamship age really began with the "Charlotte Dundas" which made her first voyage on the Clyde in 1802 and by towing two 70 ton barges a distance of twenty miles at a speed of three knots proved that the steam-driven ship could be a commercial proposition. By 1816 a steamship passenger service was in operation across the English Channel between Brighton and Le Havre and in 1820 the SS "Aaron Manby" with an engine designed by Henry Bell went into service between London and Paris achieving an average speed of 8–9 knots. During the previous year the American steam-assisted ship "Savannah" had become the first such ship to cross the Atlantic from west to east.

However the Admiralty adopted a cautious approach. Apart from a few steam tugs used to get sailing ships into and out of harbour, no steam-powered warships over 1000 tons were built until 1846 when three iron steam frigates of 1400 tons were built, the first with paddlewheels and the other two with propellers. But these were only used as troopships. Finally, experience in the Crimean War of 1854–6 convinced the Admiralty that steam-powered iron warships were here to stay.

The use of high pressure steam in compound engines and the invention of the armoured hull now began to dominate naval thinking. In 1860 H.M.S. "Warrior" became the first major warship in the world with an iron hull. The "Warrior" and her successors continued to be fitted with a full rig of sails and it was not until the early 1880s that British naval officers came to accept that there was no further use for their beloved masts and sails.

Finally at the end of the nineteenth century the steam turbine arrived, dramatically demonstrated by its inventor, the Hon. Charles Parsons, at Queen Victoria's Diamond Jubilee Review at Spithead in 1897 when he steamed his yacht "Turbinia" up and down the lines of anchored warships at a speed of 34.5 knots. The steam turbine was simpler to construct than the reciprocating engine, occupied much less space in the engine room and had a favourable power-to-weight ratio. The Admiralty could hardly fail to be impressed and in 1899 launched a destroyer H.M.S. "Viper" the first warship in the world to be fitted with four Parsons turbines driving two propellers and attaining a speed of 36.58 knots on her trials.

Playing her part in King George IV's voyage to Scotland in 1822 was the Royal Navy's first successful steam vessel, the tug, "Comet". Sail, however, would still be favoured for large warships for many years to come. Trafalgar and its glories were too recent memories for change to seem other than sacrilegious.

the first Admiralty Chief Engineer and Inspector of Machinery was appointed with the emolument of a Master Shipwright and not until 1837, the year Victoria came to the throne, that the distinguished arctic explorer, Sir William Parry, was recalled from Australia, where he had been Commissioner of the Australia Agricultural Company, to organise the Department of Steam Machinery which he then ran as Comptroller for ten years.

From then on elderly Admirals and second-rate politicians began to be outpaced by civilian entrepreneurs and engineers and the pages of the Admiralty Digest headed 'Inventions and Visionary Suggestions' grew more numerous each year including exotic types of armour such as indiarubber, springs (to cause the shot to bounce off), canvas, gutta-percha and old boots. All sorts of weird ships and devices came to be designed, some of which actually worked.

In criticising Their Lordships for their tardy acceptance of steam, it has to be remembered that Victorian governments and corporate bodies were by their nature reactionary, that the Fleet had, by any measure, become pitifully small and at the same time was mostly employed far overseas. In the 1840s when 'steam bridged the Channel' there were never as many as ten battleships available. In the 1844 crisis with France, when war looked like a possibility, the Mediterranean Fleet consisted of one ship. The Admiralty had reduced itself to the scale of a village shop and as late as the 1850s its Secretary, William Romaine, opened and read every incoming letter himself. It is scarcely surprising, therefore, that the Crimean War of 1854–56 might be said to have shocked the Navy into the nineteenth century.

Yet even when steam had inevitably come to stay, most seagoing naval officers despised and detested the invention and all it entailed. With coal dust covering the decks and smuts the sails, with the all-pervading smell of oil, with the infernal conditions of the stokehold and the stubborn independence of grimy engineers largely of Scottish origin on whom deck officers had now perforce to rely, how could a steam ship be as smart as a sailing ship with its scrubbed decks, gleaming brightwork and snow-white sails? The silent elegance of a line-of-battleship under sail had gone for ever.

The Crimean War brought matters to a head. By the time it ended all arguments against steam had lost any validity they had ever had and a thorough overhaul of the Royal Navy had to take place. The war itself was ineffectually and at times farcically fought by both sides at the cost of needless and appalling suffering. The reports of William Russell – the first war correspondent – to *The Times* caused a national outcry against the government. A Private Member's bill to appoint a Commission of Enquiry was carried by a majority so large as to be derisive and the government fell.

Mobilisation of a fleet for the first time in nearly forty years had revealed weaknesses which would have been comic had the results not been so tragic in human misery. The Commander-in-Chief at Plymouth was 81, that of the West Indies 79; the Admiral appointed to command of the Baltic Fleet, Sir Charles Napier, was 68 and Sir James Dundas in the Black Sea was 69. The Navy's role in the Crimean War was neither competent nor effective and the impression left on British public opinion, nurtured as it had been on memories of Trafalgar, was lamentable. *Punch* summed it up in an acid riddle by asking 'What is the difference between the Fleet in the Baltic and the Fleet in the Black Sea?' to which the answer was given 'The Fleet in the Baltic was expected to do everything and it did nothing: the Fleet in the Black Sea was expected to do nothing and it did it.'

Perhaps it was fortunate that there were to be no general wars on a world scale for another sixty years or at any rate no major wars in which Great Britain took part because, incredible as it seemed to those who understood seapower at that time, by the Declaration of Paris in 1856, the world's strongest Navy abandoned its traditional right to control the carriage of contraband goods in neutral bottoms in time of war. At a single stroke blockade had been scuppered. This extraordinary gesture was made in return for an agreement to abolish privateering. Of course this was healthy in itself and it was argued that the freedom of the seas should henceforth be inviolate. In any case, it was felt, there would be benefit to the British merchant marine, already the most powerful in the world. Such was the tenor of the times. The policy of laissez-faire stood at its height, universal peace was thought to be at hand and not until 1914, when international goodwill had plainly ceased to exist, was the weapon of total blockade again to be picked up by the belligerent powers.

CHAPTER VII

FROM
THE CRIMEA
TO
THE FIRST
WORLD WAR

1856–1914

CHRONOLOGICAL COMPENDIUM

General

The latter part of the long reign of Queen Victoria (1837–1901) saw the industrial revolution, based on steam power, reach its apogee. Britain had become the foremost trading nation in the world. This period also witnessed the British Empire at its zenith. Large areas of world maps were coloured red, to show they were British owned or governed, and it was literally true to say that the sun never set on the British Empire.

Although other European nations involved themselves in competition for colonies, Britain had India (where administration had been taken over from the East India Company after the Mutiny in 1857), Australia, New Zealand, Canada, many of the Caribbean Islands together with large areas of Africa. This expansion and prosperity depended upon the importation of cheap food and raw materials and the export of manufactures which, at the time, were acknowledged to be the best in the world. By the end of the century Britain owned fifty-two per cent of all the shipping in the world, sixty-four per cent of which had been built in British yards, Lloyds insured the world and the British gold sovereign had become the most prized coin in international currencies.

The country's political scene had long been dominated by Gladstone and Disraeli, the leading Liberal and Conservative Prime Minister respectively. The electorate gradually became better educated and informed. Compulsory primary education began in 1870 and trades unions were legalised in 1871, an immense increase in power being granted them in 1906. Factory and working hours legislation continued to improve conditions for the industrial proletariat who at the start of the industrial revolution had been in a state little better than slavery. In 1909 the Women's Suffrage Movement became militant but did not gain the vote until 1919. The Irish debate on Home Rule remained unresolved yet increasingly important.

The very success of Great Britain, however, generated envy and competition among her European neighbours and with Bismarck's consolidation of Germany into an empire under the Kaiser, an arms race and especially a naval arms race began. Tragically, and it seemed inevitably, this senseless piling up of armaments on either side resulted in the outbreak of war on the fourth of August 1914. Except for the localised Boer War of 1899 to 1902, the Great War, as it was then known, was the first major conflict undertaken by Great Britain for sixty years.

Naval

The Crimean War sounded the death knell of the sailing navy. Reforms were now seen to be urgent and the age of the ironclad began. The first ironclads were also rigged for sail, but screw propulsion, armour plating, the compound steam engine and changes in naval gunnery (from solid shot to explosive shell, from smooth bore to rifled bore, from muzzle-loading to breech-loading – with the interrupted thread breech block – and from the charge of gunpowder to that of cordite) dictated a range of purpose-built steel warships of which the big gun dreadnought battleship became the supreme example. In its time the dreadnought stood as the most powerful warship the world had ever seen. The dreadnought or battleship era was to last for the first half of the twentieth century.

Improvement in ships and their weapons was matched by a reform of the conditions of service for the officers and men who manned them. In 1857 uniforms, long service contracts and pensions were authorised for the lower deck. The gunboat era gave young naval lieutenants independent command – and the responsibilities which went with it in remote trouble spots all over the world – such as young mariners had not had since the time of Drake's 'fencibles'. All in all the Royal Navy policed the oceans of the world in an exemplary fashion whilst Their Lordships attempted – not always with success – to keep the fleet up to date with the technological advances being made. These were such that at one time a ship had become out of date between being designed and being launched.

Contrasted with the first half of the nineteenth century, the latter half saw the Royal Navy regain its glamour in the public eye. Gilbert and Sullivan might poke gentle fun at Their Lordships in *H.M.S. Pinafore*, the country was firmly of the opinion that 'all the nice girls love a sailor'. Every merchant ship and warship in the world dipped its ensign first to the White Ensign. The Royal Navy had almost total command of the seas and, at the Diamond Jubilee Review of the Fleet in 1897, displayed a range of naval might assembled in one place such as had never been seen before.

Meanwhile the invention of dynamite by Alfred Nobel in 1866, the harnessing of electricity, the arrival of the internal combustion engine, the motor car and the aeroplane, and, so far as the Navy was concerned, the development of the mine, the torpedo and the submarine, the steam turbine engine and the realisation of the advantages of oil fuel over coal all combined to change the scene which the navy would have to face after the First World War as drastically as earlier inventions had changed that with which it had to deal after the Crimean War.

Organisation, Ships and Weapons

1860 H.M.S. "Warrior" first ironclad ship built for Royal Navy (originally classified as a steam frigate of 9,210 tons). She had 4½ inch iron armour with 18 inch teak backing, full outfit of masts and sails, ten 110 pounder and twenty-six 68 pounder muzzle loaders plus four 70 pounder breech loaders.

1870 H.M.S. "Captain" had full rig of sails, steam propulsion and heavy guns in revolving turrets. Caught by a squall during the night of 7 September 1870 with all her sails spread, she capsized and sank with almost all on board.

1855–1920 Gunboat era. Nearly two hundred gunboats of 100 to 120 feet in length with 20 to 60 horse-power engines and a full rig of sails were built in 1855–6. They were usually armed with a 68 pounder forward, a 32 pounder aft and two 24 pounders amidships. Gunboats were still being built in 1900.

1867 Robert Whitehead (1823–1905) invents first torpedo which can steer under its own power.

1889 Naval Defence Act passed, bringing in 'the two power standard'. Building up of a unified modern navy begins.

1860–70 Compound (triple expansion) steam engine revolutionises propulsion and greatly reduces cost.

1889 Sir Charles Parsons (1854–1931) produces first turbo-dynamo machinery and constructs first turbine-propelled vessel the "Turbinia" which, with a speed of over 30 knots, makes a great sensation at the 1897 Naval Review at Spithead. Parsons was also interested in optics and astronomical instruments. Acclaimed as most original engineer Great Britain has produced since James Watt.

At the turn of the century the invention of the internal combustion engine, the electric motor and the Whitehead torpedo leads to development of the submarine. Early pioneers were William Bourne, Cornelius van Drebbel, David Bushnell, Robert Fulton and at this period the Irish-born American J. P. Holland who designed the first five submarines built in Britain. They displaced 105 tons on the surface, had a surface speed of 8½ knots and a submerged speed of 7 knots with an endurance of 500 miles at 7 knots using petrol driven engines. Britain entered the First World War with 74 submarines built and 31 building.

1912 Royal Naval Air Service formed unofficially by breaking away from the Royal Flying Corps. Its first director was Captain (later Admiral Sir) Murray Sueter, supported by the First Lord of the Admiralty, Winston Churchill.

Expansion of Royal Dockyards in the colonial era: Gibraltar 1704, Malta 1814, Halifax 1749, Bermuda (first floating dock) 1860, Simonstown (South Africa) early twentieth century, Trincomalee, Ceylon 1827, Singapore 1869 (after opening of Suez Canal), Hong Kong 1842.

1906 First dreadnought battleship.

1890 Sir Percy Scott (1853–1924) becomes Commanding Officer of H.M.S. "Excellent" (Naval Gunnery School), introduces telescopic sights and other refinements.

1905 Scott appointed Admiralty Inspector of Target Practice and with Arthur H. Pollen (1866–1937) pioneers fire control and gyroscopically-controlled plotting table. Ratio of hits to rounds fired rises from thirty per cent to eighty-one per cent.

1913 Sir Frederick Dreyer (1878–1956), in 1907 a dreadnought gunnery officer, had his Fire Control Table adopted throughout Royal Navy.

Communications

1867 Philip Colomb (1831–99), Rear Admiral, adapts Morse code for use with shuttered lantern. With advent of electric lighting all-round signalling from masthead becomes possible.

1874 First searchlight. Mr Wilde's electric light. 11,000 candlepower.

1880 Gramme's 'Englishman's Night Sun' – 20,000 candlepower.

1890 Sir Henry B. Jackson (1855–1929) experiments with radio and succeeds in transmitting signals over several hundred yards.

1896 Jackson meets Marconi and discovers both working on same lines.

1900 Jackson gets Admiralty to contract Marconi's radio for Royal Navy (1919 Jackson Admiral of the Fleet and Chairman of the Radio Research Board).

Early twentieth century Fessenden apparatus leads to Asdic and Sonar Radar (in early days called Radio Directional Finding).

1858 First transatlantic cable: breaks down shortly after installation (but messages exchanged Queen Victoria–U.S. President).

1866 Transatlantic cable finally established and working.

1869 Suez Canal opens: first transcontinental railway – coast to coast – completed in United States.

1914 Panama Canal opened.

1909 First cross-channel flight by aeroplane.

People

John Fisher
1841–1920 First Baron Fisher of Kilverstone, Admiral of the Fleet. The greatest administrator the Royal Navy has produced since Lord Barham.

1881 Commanding Officer, H.M.S. "Inflexible" (battleship)

1892–7 Third Sea Lord and Controller

1897–9 C. in C. North America and West Indies station

1899–1902 C. in C. Mediterranean Fleet

1902–3 Second Sea Lord – reforms entry and training of officers

1904–9 First Sea Lord – introduced the all-big-gun battleship (H.M.S. "Dreadnought" laid down October 1905 completed December 1906) – reforms manning of Reserve Fleet – reduced fleet by scrapping ships of small fighting power – concentrated main fleet in home waters. Resigned as a result of feud with Beresford 1910

1914 Reappointed First Sea Lord by Churchill: resigned after Dardanelles fiasco May 1915.

Lord Charles Beresford Admiral
1846–1919 First Baron of Metemmeh and Curraghmore

1882 Commanding Officer, H.M.S. "Condor" – bombardment of Alexandria

1884–5 Commanded naval brigade in attempt to rescue General Gordon from Khartoum

1886–8 Junior Naval Lord. Advocated passing of Naval Defence Act 1889

1899 Second-in-command, Mediterranean Fleet

1903–5	Vice Admiral, Channel Squadron
1905–6	C. in C. Mediterranean Fleet
1907–9	C. in C. Channel Fleet
1910	Placed on retired list.

Prince Louis of Battenberg
1843–1921

Later changed name to Mountbatten and became First Marquess of Milford Haven

1894	Captain and Secretary of what later became Committee of Imperial Defence
1902	Director of Naval Intelligence
1907	Second-in-command, Mediterranean Fleet
1908	C. in C. Atlantic Fleet
1911	Second Sea Lord and on retirement of Sir Francis Bridgeman became first Sea Lord
1914	Resigned because of scurrilous press campaign against his German origins.

Sir Percy Scott
1853–1924

Admiral and gunnery specialist.

Sir Charles Parsons
1854–1931

Marine Engineer and F.R.S.

Sir Frederick Evans
1815–85

Captain and Hydrographer of the Navy 1874–84

Pelham Aldrich
1844–1930

Admiral "Challenger" expedition 1872–6 Naturalist and hydrographer.

Isambard Kingdom Brunel
1806–59

Engineer and ship designer.

Sir Richard Collinson
1811–83

Admiral and explorer.

John Ericsson
1803–89

Swedish inventor. Screw propulsion and armament.

Robert Fitzroy
1805–65

Rear Admiral. Accompanied Charles Darwin on voyage of the "Beagle" 1831–6. Cartographer and meteorologist.

August Hobart–Hampden
1822–86

British naval officer and Turkish admiral. Fought in Crimean War, blockade runner to the Confederacy in American civil war and later entered the Turkish service.

Sir Francis McClintock
1819–1907

Admiral and Arctic explorer.

Sir Robert McClure
1807–73

Vice Admiral and discoverer of the North-West Passage in 1850.

Alfred Mahan
1840–1914

U.S. Rear Admiral and naval historian whose work has had great influence on all modern navies.

Sir Clements Markham
1830–1916

Naval officer, traveller and explorer.

John Moresby
1830–1922

Admiral and explorer

Sir Erasmus Ommaney 1814–1904	Admiral and Arctic explorer.
Sherard Osborn 1822–75	Admiral and explorer.
Sir John Parry 1863–1926	Admiral and Hydrographer (grandson of Sir William Parry).
Samuel Plimsoll 1824–98	Politician and instigator of the Merchant Shipping Act of 1876 which established safety regulations for the loading of ships.
Robert Scott 1868–1912	Captain and Antarctic explorer.
Sir Ernest Shackleton 1874–1922	Merchant service officer and explorer.
Elmer Sperry 1860–1930	U.S. inventor – gyroscopic compass (1907) and high intensity carbon arc searchlight (1915).
Sir Thomas Spratt 1811–90	Vice Admiral and Surveyor.
John Stokes 1812–85	Admiral and Surveyor.
Sir Murray Sueter 1872–1960	Rear Admiral – created the Naval Air Service.
Sir Bartholomew Sulivan 1810–90	Vice Admiral and Surveyor.
William Thomson 1824–1907	First Baron Kelvin – Physicist. Major work in electricity and submarine cables.
Thomas Tizard 1839–1924	Captain and Surveyor.
Sir George Tryon 1832–93	Vice Admiral.
Sir William Wharton 1843–1905	Rear Admiral and Hydrographer of the Navy.
Robert Whitehead 1823–1905	Engineer and inventor of torpedo.

H.M.S. "Calliope", a cruiser launched in 1884, is typical of the warships built in the last two decades of the 19th century when 'new ideas and inventions were coming so fast that a new naval ship could be obsolete before it was launched'. Ship designers and armament manufacturers naturally tried to seek the best of both worlds (of sail and steam) and frequently got the worst. "Calliope", however, was the only warship to escape from Apia Harbour, Samoa during a fierce hurricane in 1889. Every other warship in the harbour was wrecked.

The Crimean War began in the early summer of 1854 and on the 12th June of that same year a boy of thirteen entered the Royal Navy who was to dominate the service as it has never been dominated before or since. This was John Arbuthnot Fisher (1841–1920), later to be the First Baron Fisher of Kilverstone, Admiral of the Fleet and the most renowned and contentious First Sea Lord there has ever been.

On the following day 'penniless, friendless and forlorn' as he afterwards wrote, the boy's naval career began as a Cadet in H.M.S. "Victory" at Portsmouth when he saw eight men flogged and fainted at the sight. The Captain of the famous "Victory", Nelson's flagship at Trafalgar and then nearly a hundred years old, had recently been courtmartialled for cruelty after flogging an entire crew. This Court Martial appeared to have had little effect on Captain Day's behaviour and his Commander carried on with equal brutality, padlocking men to a ringbolt and hurling buckets of salt water at them. 'All the same I loved them', Fisher wrote much later in his life, 'and both loved me till they died. They were each of them great for war but, alas!, peace was their portion.' A strange comment in the circumstances considering that Fisher came to regard war as the ultimate madness and folly. However, peace was not the only problem which the Navy as a whole had to face during the second half of the nineteenth century.

The sixty odd years of Fisher's active service life saw the Navy change and change again out of all recognition. Jackie Fisher, born four years after Victoria came to the throne, joined a sailing navy which was only dimly aware, and at the same time suspicious, of its own future. In practical terms the Royal Navy had experienced

FISHER'S REFORMS

Even as a young Captain in the eighteen-seventies, Fisher was known as an apostle of progress who understood the growing importance of steam, armour, electrical machinery and torpedoes. However, thirty years later when Fisher became Second and then First Sea Lord, the Navy was still carrying on somewhat complacently in the spit and polish era. The study of strategy, the higher training of officers and gunnery were all dangerously neglected, the torpedo continued to be undervalued and almost no attention was paid to the welfare of the lower deck.

His reforms began with officer-training methods and the introduction of the Selborne Scheme of entry to Osborne and Dartmouth. Cadets then spent four or five years at sea when, in addition to the seamanship necessary for executive duties, they were also given an understanding of machinery and weapons. Fees at Osborne and Dartmouth were abolished and he threw naval careers open to talent, a move which was to be fully justified in later years. He also removed many of the lower deck's grievances over food, living quarters, discipline and professional prospects.

Fisher had five crucial years as First Sea Lord (1904-9), the springboard for his reforms being the emergence of Germany as a first-class naval power, with the threat this posed in the North Sea. Accordingly Fisher concentrated the main strength of the fleet in home waters. At the same time he reduced the seagoing fleet (and its cost) by ruthlessly scrapping out of date ships of poor fighting power. He followed this process by tuning up the preparedness of the navy for war by introducing the 'nucleus crew system' in ships of the Reserve Fleet, with a two-fifths complement of key ranks and ratings who lived permanently on board.

The revolutionary reform for which Fisher is chiefly remembered, however, was the introduction of the all-big-gun class of capital ship in H.M.S. "Dreadnought". At the same time he brought in a new and larger type of armoured cruiser – later to be known as battle-cruisers – which also had an all-big-gun armament and a speed of 25 knots and whose role was to act as super-scouting cruisers.

The dreadnought policy was strongly criticised on technical grounds, since by rendering all existing battleships obsolete it swept away Britain's overwhelming preponderance in numbers of capital ships and gave Germany almost a level start in the race for naval supremacy. But the all-big-gun battleship was here to stay – and Fisher knew it.

Aided by Churchill, Fisher ensured that oil would replace coal as the Navy's basic motive power. In addition he played a vital part in the development of small non-rigid airships (or 'blimps' as they were later called) to combat the U-boat menace.

The Channel Fleet as seen by Ede Martino in 1898, then the most powerful ships in the world, yet due to be swept into obsolescence in only eight years time by the coming of Fisher's "Dreadnought".

almost no action for forty years and a further five were to elapse before the Admiralty was even to lay down the first ever British warship with an iron hull. This was the "Warrior" designed to overtake and destroy any other warship afloat. In particular the designers had in mind the French "Gloire", an 'ironclad' whose wooden hull was protected by armour plating nearly five inches thick. By the time Fisher died, he had come to realise – and was considered senile and dotty in saying so – that the Dreadnought battleship age for which he was almost entirely responsible, had ended and that future warfare at sea would be dominated by aircraft and submarines. Only the Mountbattens, *père et fils*, span a period of more astonishing change.

In considering the Navy of post Crimean times, we have to begin with the Admiralty itself. 'The weakness which the men of the 1860s saw in the Admiralty was that of a large and expensive department subject to very imperfect control by

Parliament, by the Treasury and by its own Minister . . . the burden of administration on each of the Lords, especially the Naval Lords who were the only sea officers in their departments and alone qualified to judge of any question however trivial which required professional knowledge, was great enough to drive out all consideration of general policy. In the passage of thirty years, unnoticed by contemporaries in and out of the service, the central direction of naval policy had almost evaporated . . . the system was supportable so long as the Navy itself remained largely untouched by the technical changes which had overturned the social and economic fabric of nineteenth century England, so long as it remained small and so long as no great questions of naval policy demanded decision. By the 1860s all these conditions were about to pass away for ever.'[1]

The circumstances which the Admiralty and the Navy faced around 1870 need to

A coloured lithograph of a painting by R. Dudley shows H.M.S. "Agamemnon" laying part of the first Atlantic cable in 1858. The cable was just missed by a large whale. Completed on the 5th August 1858, congratulatory messages were exchanged between Queen Victoria and the President of the United States but faulty insulation caused a rapid deterioration and the line went dead on 20th October. The first successful Atlantic cable was completed in 1866.

be seen in the context of contemporary life in the country and in the world at large. In the first place communications had greatly improved. The railway had been a fact of life for nearly half a century. In 1863 the construction of the first London Underground had begun, in 1867 a railway was opened through the Brenner Pass, in 1869 the Suez Canal and in 1870 the first transcontinental railroad across the United States came into operation by which time there were 15,310 miles of railway open in England, half the world's steel being produced by the United Kingdom.

In population Great Britain at 26 million (or 31·4 if Ireland was included) had already been overtaken by the United States at 39 million, by Japan at 33 million, by France at 36 million, with Germany at 41 million heading the league. Between 1857 and 1866 transatlantic cables were laid and after heroic hazards had been overcome, instant communication between Europe and America became another fact of everyday life. During the decade from 1860 – 70 424,000 from Britain and 914,000 from Ireland had emigrated to the United States. Herr Krupp had begun arms production in Essen in 1861 and in 1866 Alfred Nobel invented dynamite. Most significant of all, perhaps, was the fact that in 1859 the first oil well had been drilled in Pennsylvania, the Standard Oil Company being founded by John D. Rockefeller in 1870. In that same year debtors' prisons were abolished in Great Britain and Charles Dickens died. By the end of the so-called Pax Britannica in 1914, electricity, the internal combustion engine, wireless telegraphy, the submarine and the aircraft were further to change out of all recognition the Navy which Fisher had joined in 1854. By then he was an Admiral of the Fleet with the first real test of it all in war lying immediately ahead. It was an extraordinary span of experience.

To this burgeoning century of materialism (Karl Marx had issued his Communist Manifesto in 1848 and the first volume of Das Kapital in 1867) the Royal Navy had perforce to adapt – through a welter of invention, mechanical progress and social change – led by officers who, with the exception of gunboat captains, had rarely if ever seen a shot fired in anger, who continued to train themselves under sail and who, despite the floundering of politicians, fulfilled their worldwide peacekeeping role with an efficiency, a cheerfulness and a constant sense of fairplay amounting to genius. The nation, and at one remove the world, rewarded them with a respect and admiration second only to that given to the Crown and the Law. By comparison no other fighting service in any country of the world came anywhere near the Royal Navy. This status, and the pride it engendered, reached its apotheosis in the Diamond Jubilee Review of 1897 when seven miles of ships assembled at Spithead, symbolising in a single place the integrity of imperial power. By the end of the century 'all the nice girls loved a sailor' and every middle class child had a sailor suit for its Sunday best. By that time, too, 52% of all shipping in the world was owned by Great Britain, the second largest owner being the United States with 8%. Moreover 64% of all tonnage afloat had been built in British yards. Ordinary folk might not be unduly bothered by Empire, they cared very much indeed about their fishing and merchant fleets and especially about the Royal Navy which protected both.

Presiding over it all in the last thirty years of her sixty-four year reign, the ageing Queen set the tone, married her progeny into the royal houses of Europe and exhibited a continuing pride in her favourite son appropriately called Alfred who served thirty-five years in the Royal Navy, rose to be Admiral of the Fleet and only ended his active service in 1893 when he succeeded his uncle as the Duke of Saxe-Coburg-Gotha. Another royal link with the Navy came about in 1884 when Lieutenant the Prince Louis of Battenberg married Princess Victoria of Hesse, a grand daughter of Queen Victoria. The Navy was 'royalling up' as never before. Yet, in spite of these growing links between the Monarch and her Senior Service, Queen Victoria had had no especial affection for the Royal Navy since the Admiralty had refused, early in her reign, to make her husband an Admiral of the Fleet. This rankled until she and Captain Fisher became warm friends and he received a standing invitation to stay at Osborne whenever she was there and he in England. This dated from her holiday at Mentone in 1882 when Fisher's command, H.M.S. "Inflexible", acted as her guardship.

The groundwork for this rapprochement, however, had been made in 1871 by Vice Admiral Sir George Tryon (1832–93) when he was Private Secretary to the First Lord of the Admiralty, Lord Goschen. Tryon was the first British admiral of the

Victorian period to begin training the navy for war and it was owing to his energy and loyalty, when confidential adviser to a fair-minded, firm First Lord, that the recognition of the Navy at Court began anew. Queen Victoria is said to have greatly admired him and Tryon's popularity at Court resulted in naval officers being again invited to levées and to retired Admirals being appointed as Colonial Governors, hitherto the exclusive prerogative of the Army.

The Admiralty, however, had immense problems to solve, outside this charmed royal circle, during the last forty years of the nineteenth century. To face this task the mid-Victorian Tories both afloat and ashore (most Flag Officers and the civilian Boards appointed by Derby and Disraeli were Tory in politics) proved generally inadequate. However, there was one man in an influential appointment from 1861 to 1871 who was a strong Liberal and that was Sir Robert Spencer Robinson, Third Lord and Controller, the name of his office having been changed from that of Surveyor in 1860. Robinson headed that part of the Admiralty responsible for the design and construction of ships and the management of dockyards and he assumed with the office a great deal of the autonomous powers of the old Comptroller.

'When Robinson became Controller, the Navy possessed only two ironclads. When he left office there were no wooden sail of the line left in the battle fleet. Iron, steam and breech-loading guns had suddenly and completely upset the tranquil and orderly technical progress of previous years. Robinson was a man of commanding intellect, familiar with the new inventions and alive to their implications as few other admirals were. He was ambitious, unscrupulous and unpopular. Like Middleton eighty years before, he made no secret of his desire to have a seat on the Board, and with it a practical supremacy. As a subordinate of the First Sea Lord he had great influence; as a colleague with the largest and most important part of naval administration at his command, he would be the real leader of the naval lords.'[2]

'Matériel', a French word adopted after 1814 as a collective term for the hulls, armour, machinery and supplies used in the Royal Navy (as distinct from 'personnel' or body of persons employed) was to generate appalling problems, difficulties and disasters until the idea of standardisation was grasped and applied ruthlessly by Jackie Fisher. But by then it was the first decade of the twentieth century. Until 1880 battleships were built in ones or twos because they were still largely experimental in face of the burgeoning advance in technology in guns, armour and naval engineering. There was also a natural reluctance to commit too many eggs to one basket until the most efficient design had been proved by experience. The first battleships built as a class were the six "Admirals" of 1880–82, followed by the eight "Royal Sovereigns" of 1889–90. The first battleship for which Fisher was responsible as Controller was the "Renown", a one-off, which was completed just in time to become his flagship on the America and West Indies station and, later, in the Mediterranean.

In the late 1860s the scene was anarchic, in no way helped by Gladstone's appointment of H. C. E. Childers as First Lord in 1868. This was the Liberal answer to reactionary Tory Sea Lords and it proved to be a catastrophe.

Childers had no previous knowledge of the Navy, was possessed of a brusque and offensive manner and an 'unconcealed belief that all power over the Navy was vested in him alone'. This could scarcely be thought a recipe for either efficiency or popularity. Moreover Childers was disinclined to seek or accept advice and within a month of taking office had virtually abolished the Board of Admiralty except in name. The Board which had foregathered 249 times in 1866 had but 33 meetings in 1870. Admiralty staff was reduced from 586 to 537 and personnel in the seagoing fleet cut down by 5,000. All communication between Board Members had to be in writing and on the rare occasions when the First Lord felt in need of advice, he summoned the adviser alone to his room. Thus co-ordination between departments, never a strong feature of Admiralty, practically speaking ceased to exist. Decisions of policy were settled autocratically by the First Lord and Board capacity to cope with ever increasing technical business virtually came to an end. The other Liberal in power, the Third Lord, Robinson, alone had the strength of character to stand up to this latter day Napoleon but proved to be 'a wayward ally and an ungovernable subordinate'. Within a year he had gone. It became clear that things could not continue in this way for long.

Matters came to a head after the "Captain" calamity. H.M.S. "Captain", the sixth warship to bear the name (the third had been commanded by Nelson at the battle of Cape St. Vincent in 1797) was a revolutionary battleship, heavily armoured, with revolving gun turrets in place of the previous fixed batteries, steam propulsion and, for good measure, a full rig of sails. She was the Liberals' answer to Tory naval architecture, designed by a naval officer, Captain Cowper Phipps Coles (1819–70) and the first to combine heavy guns with a low freeboard. She was intended to show the world the enlightened spirit of naval progress in warship design.

Built by Laird of Birkenhead, her freeboard, when launched in 1870, proved to be two feet less than the eight feet which Coles had calculated. On her maiden voyage she found herself caught in a squall during the night of 7th September 1870 with all sails spread, whereupon she capsized and sank with the loss of almost all on board including Coles himself and Midshipman Childers whom his father had sent to sea in the ship to demonstrate his faith in the design. Instead of at once resigning, Childers published an exoneration of himself 'by Command of Their Lordships' who were not even favoured with a sight of the minute until they read it in the newspapers. At the same time Childers laid the entire blame on subordinates unable to defend themselves. It was a scandal. In the political row which followed, Sir Spencer Robinson was personally dismissed by Gladstone and Sir Edward Reed, the Chief Naval Architect, resigned, 'these being the two principally blamed by Childers for the loss of a ship they had neither designed nor approved. On 13th March 1871 Childers followed them, broken in health and spirits and unlamented by all who had worked with him.'[3]

One good thing did, however, come out of all this mess. Direction of the Admiralty was taken over at that point by G. J. Goschen who proved to be as wise and skilful an administrator as Childers had been inept. Goschen removed the Controller from the Board, instituted 'Daily Meetings' to facilitate the exchange of information, encouraged discussion and improved co-ordination, generally behaving as a statesman rather than as a politician. He drafted in Sir Alexander Milne, a Tory who had last served under Disraeli, as first Naval Lord, the first senior Lord to be so appointed by the opposite party.

Goschen thus established the post of First Sea Lord as a professional rather than as a party appointment. It did little to remedy the Navy's peripheral standing in the public pecking order but it did stress the professional requirements of the service over and above the tedious, grumbling necessity of merely keeping the Navy Estimates down and of getting them through Parliament. This was a far cry from the ages of Pepys and Barham, and also from that of Jackie Fisher some two or three decades ahead. But at least a start had been made.

As we have seen, seagoing experience during the Crimean War had decisively thrown out of court any last argument against the use of steam in warships. Co-incidentally, in 1854, engineering techniques took a huge leap upwards and forwards when the compound engine first went to sea in the S.S. "Brandon". The days of costly, wasteful, low-pressure steam were over. Henceforth high-pressure boilers supplied steam which could be used not only once but two, three and later four times at progressively lower pressures. This resulted in a dramatic lowering of cost. From 1870 when the White Star company took the lead in the Atlantic from Cunard by putting compound engines to work in their ships, steam virtually banished sail from global maritime trade. In 1872 you could cross the Atlantic from Queenstown in Ireland to New York in eight days.

The Navy, still nostalgic in its regard for sail, took a long time to digest these vast technological changes. It also needed to establish the coaling bases and dockyards on which worldwide naval operations were coming to depend. Few serving officers enjoyed or even approved of the way things were going but Progress in the end proved irresistible. In one department, however, a new concept took shape. This was the construction and putting into service of the small steam gunboat.

Almost from the beginning naval officers have been divided into big ship and small ship men. In the mid-Victorian Navy the latter were now to be given a new run for their money after forty years of waiting for dead men's shoes. The gunboat provided young men with a genuine chance of early command (for which there is no substitute) together with the responsibility and challenge that went with it. Young Victorian 'bloods' lapped it up. For fifty years after the Crimean War 'send a gunboat' became an everyday phrase in British diplomacy. Not since the sea-fencibles of the Armada and Napoleonic eras, when almost any boat which could float was pressed into service against possible invasion, had young men enjoyed such opportunities. Gunboat service was dangerous and daring. It lasted till the First World War but thereafter did not recur until the Coastal Forces and Combined Operations of the Second World War were organised to meet a similar need. What, in fact, did gunboat diplomacy mean?

The Victorian gunboat was a shallow-draught vessel designed for shores and harbours unapproachable by bigger ships. 100 to 120 feet long with engines of 20 to 60 horsepower and a full sailing rig, they carried the largest possible armament which could be mounted subject only to the minimum living space for the 30 to 40 members of the crew. Early gunboats carried a 68 pounder forward, a 32 pounder aft and two 24 pounders amidships. In action everyone except the Lieutenant in command and stokers shovelling coal, manned the guns or passed up ammunition. Even then not all the guns could be fired at once. Indeed, so cramped was the space

below deck with engine, bunkers, boiler and magazines that it was said that a tall officer could only shave – as Cochrane had had to do in his first tiny command, the sloop "Speedy" – by sticking his head through a skylight and propping up a mirror on deck. Nevertheless the gunboat, purpose made for the job and the times, stands as the centrepiece in many a Victorian saga of empire and proved to be what today would be called extremely cost-effective.

    The gunboat came to be used much more for policing than as an offensive weapon. Occasionally gunboats would support military operations on the Nile or the rivers of China, but in the main the gunboat soon came to be regarded as the marine equivalent of the 'copper' on his beat. Traders, missionaries, consuls, governors and sometimes even foreign potentates would send out cries for help all over the world from New Zealand to Brazil, Jamaica to Siam. In a single year Honduras, Morocco, Vancouver and the Newfoundland fishing grounds all made urgent demands for assistance; Dr Livingstone on the Zambesi together with British prisoners in Sierra Leone and Formosa were all helped or released, very often without a shot being fired, the mere appearance of the White Ensign sufficing to dispose of the trouble.

The gunboat era lasted some sixty to seventy years from the mid nineteenth century and H.M.S. "Mutine", launched at Birkenhead in 1900 and serving until 1932, is typical of the larger ships which carried on a splendid but rigorous tradition, policing inshore waters, all over the world.

Ever since Drake, British Captains and Admirals had had to learn some of the art of diplomacy often at very short notice and with no precedents to go on. Now Lieutenants in their twenties and very much on their own were finding they had to evaluate a local situation, decide who was right or wrong and then adjust matters either diplomatically or with a few well placed shells. Senior officers were not on hand to advise or deter, being sometimes hundreds or even thousands of miles away. The responsibilities borne by a gunboat captain were immense but all carried on with a nonchalance which continuously added to the Navy's lustre. These daring young men did not always get it right – how could they – but this worried the Admiralty and the Foreign Office far more than it did the gunboat captains themselves. Apart from exceptional lapses such as the hanging of 177 negroes in Jamaica in 1865 by a Lieutenant of twenty-six, there is no doubt that gunboat diplomacy over its fifty years span did immeasurably more good than harm. Other nations occasionally resented what they saw as British arrogance, especially Americans in the early days when the Royal Navy so often interfered in the slave trade to the detriment of southern plantation owners, but in general the world considered that a little British haughtiness was a small price to pay for the ending of piracy and the uninterrupted freedom of the seas. No one questioned that the British were motivated by self-interest, but this was enlightened by the fact that the results of their arduous and often thankless policing benefited every maritime nation. From then on the oceans of the world were to be genuinely safe and free.

This Britannic ruling of the waves, although controlled by the Royal Navy, was mainly effected all over the world by the Merchant Service. The vast late-Victorian expansion of shipping, half of it sailing under the Red Ensign and almost all of it insured at Lloyds, inevitably attracted a mass of legislation, the purpose of which was to protect seamen, passengers, cargoes and the ships in which they sailed from the machinations of fraudulent ship owners. This was no easy problem to solve.

It began with the coffin-ships which Samuel Plimsoll (1824–98) so detested and it continues today when certain operators working under flags of convenience still sink their ships at sea in order to draw insurance. In 1875 after a monumental row in the House of Commons, with Plimsoll losing his temper and shaking his fist in the Speaker's face, the Board of Trade was directed to survey and register all ships under the British flag and pass them as fit for sea only if they were loaded to a certain safety mark which has been known ever since as the Plimsoll line. The provisions of this first definitive Act were extended over the next forty years until almost every conceivable activity at sea had been subjected to law, most of it – or at any rate the important parts of it – being adopted all over the world through international conventions. British law has been the model for this and although in the early years British merchants and taxpayers stood mostly to gain, the resulting benefits have been shared by the entire world. Today, a century later, when the British Empire is no more and the British merchant fleet ranks fifth after Liberia, Greece, Japan and Panama, the bulk of the free nations' shipping continues to be insured or re-insured by Lloyds of London whose rigid safety standards apply all over the globe. Samuel Plimsoll, M.P. for Derby, began his campaign against the overloading and overinsuring of ill-found ships in 1870. The Merchant Shipping (Plimsoll) Act, 1876, heavily supported by public opinion, did a certain amount to correct these malpractices but left the fixing of the load line to the shipowners. The Act of 1890 secured its enforcement by the Board of Trade and these regulations were applied to foreign ships using British ports in 1906. The London load-line convention (5 July 1930) signed by forty states, was embodied in the Merchant Shipping Act of 1932.

The last two decades of the nineteenth century saw European and American inventiveness and industrial development reach such a pitch that any 'modern' naval ship could well be obsolete by the time it was launched. Up to the turning point in 1884 the situation was virtually out of hand so far as a succession of weak, listless Boards of Admiralty was concerned. Such naval staff as existed came under the Controller who was responsible for applying the new technology and dominated the Admiralty both intellectually and in the number of his assistants, having under him the Directors of Naval Construction, Naval Ordnance, Dockyards and Stores, the Inspector of Dockyard Expense Accounts and the Engineer-in-Chief.

The Board of Admiralty itself continued to gum itself up with trivia and provided neither the direction nor the co-ordination so badly needed. Whenever possible Their Lordships resolutely shut their eyes to any and every new invention since, in their opinion, it could only make obsolete their cherished and largely useless ships.

However in 1884 a great change in public opinion began. This produced dramatic effects on the Navy. In September of that year W. T. Stead, the fiery journalist who was to become a powerful ally of Jackie Fisher, published his first article on 'The Truth about the Navy' in the *Pall Mall Gazette*. Five years later the Naval Defence Act of 1889 which brought in the 'two power standard', showed clearly the extent to which fundamental attitudes had changed. Wheezy time-worn demands for economy were now replaced by an increasing popular pressure for a larger and more powerful fleet. This reversal of attitudes can be seen as one of the shadows behind the fall of Gladstone in 1894, his long career ending in part because he refused to acknowledge this new public call for much heavier naval expenditure. How did all this come about?

The answer can be summed up in the name of one person – Count Otto von Bismarck (1815–98). This extraordinary man had been recalled from the Prussian Embassy in Paris in 1861 after William I of Prussia ascended the throne of Frederick the Great and, in the company of von Moltke as Chief of the General Staff and of von Roon as Minister of War, took up the post of Minister-President of Prussia. 'First as Chancellor of the North German Federation and finally of the German Empire, this singular genius', as Churchill called him,[4] 'presided with a cold passion over the unification and Prussianisation of Germany, the elimination of Russia's nearest European rivals and the elevation of William to the German Emperor's throne in 1871'. Three separate wars were prepared and executed by him to enable Prussia to 'fulfil her destiny of leading and controlling the German-speaking peoples'. These were the war with Denmark in 1864 by which Schleswig-Holstein became attached to Prussia, the Seven Weeks war in 1866 in which Austria was crushed and her associates in Germany eliminated and the 1870 war against France which resulted in the annexation of Alsace and Lorraine.

For nearly thirty years Bismarck was to serve and to dominate William I and his

two successors without a break, until bitter differences with the young Kaiser
William II finally provoked his dismissal in 1890. But by then Bismarck's gigantic
reforms and aggressive empire building had already passed the point of no return. A
terrifying armaments race between England and Germany got under way, a race
which was to climax in the First World War. The naval component of this Prussian
challenge, however, only took firm shape as the result of von Tirpitz's naval
expansion act of 1898, the year in which Bismarck died at the age of eighty-three.

This train of sinister events on the continent came to be watched with disquiet on
the English side of the Channel and the North Sea, soon to be regarded by Germany
as 'their' sea. The British Admiralty inaugurated its Naval Intelligence Division in
1886, the intention being that it should grow into a naval staff. It did not do so for
twenty-five years. So far as Intelligence was concerned, the N.I.D. proved itself
invaluable. The idea that it should develop into a War Staff, however, came up
against entrenched opposition, no such unit being appointed until just before the
outbreak of the First World War.

Indeed even Jackie Fisher at the height of his power considered that a staff to advise
on strategy and tactics would be only a criticism of the First Sea Lord's single-handed
rule. It would be 'a very excellent organisation for cutting out and arranging foreign
newspaper clippings' and it would also 'make excellent sea officers into very
indifferent clerks'. The country might – and did – demand a great Navy: it was still
regarded, though, as a peace-keeping force not attuned to war. This was yet another
of the soporifics resulting from a century of peace.

Nevertheless from 1884 onwards the Admiralty was compelled to adapt to the
changing world. At least Their Lordships were not as inefficient as their opposite
numbers at the War Office who in 1886 mislaid an entire Regiment in England in
time of peace. The new technology in ships and the weapons with which they were
armed, compelled the Admiralty to pioneer scientific research into such matters as
hydrodynamics and metallurgy. This was thought to be extraordinary in Whitehall.
The Times might describe the Admiralty as 'a very ancient and peculiar corporation',
it was nevertheless forced to control some of the largest and most complex industrial
organisations in the country. Moreover, and despite the popular opinion of the day,
these organisations ranked amongst the most efficient. In 1882, for instance, before
the great expansion began, the Royal Dockyards employed nearly 20,000 men,
Portsmouth alone having 6,256.

The gun, the torpedo, the submarine and the mine now dictated the kind of ships
the Navy had to build. Each weapon produced its own further problems – the gun,
for instance, needed to be breech-loading, to be able to fire explosive shells instead
of solid cannon balls through rifled barrels for long distance accuracy, to be grouped
in revolving armoured turrets and to be controlled by a central director as high up
in the ship as possible.

The immense strength of iron hulls together with the power needed and now
available to drive them through the water, led to the revival of ramming tactics and
as early as 1868 H.M.S. "Minotaur" was fitted with a specially strengthened ram
bow. How valuable this was is questionable. The Battle of Lissa between the Austrian
and Italian fleets in 1866 was hailed at the time as a vindication of the ram, though

subsequent analysis proved this to be false. Paddle wheels had long given way to screw propellers and the invention of the turbine, dramatically demonstrated by Parsons at the Diamond Jubilee Review of 1897 when his yacht "Turbinia" achieved the unheard of speed of 34.5 knots, marked the end of the reciprocating engine era. The gradual change over from coal to oil, insisted upon by Jackie Fisher in the first decade of the twentieth century against great opposition from the coal lobby (the United Kingdom possessing vast reserves of coal but at that time no known oil), the invention of wireless telegraphy and the arrival on the scene of ocean-going submarines first with petrol and then with diesel-electric technology resulted in massive complications throughout the whole naval fabric.

The cost, too, was staggering. In 1896, for instance, one fifth of all government expenditure went on the Navy. The work force directly or indirectly involved amounted to a quarter of a million people or two and a quarter per cent of all people employed in the United Kingdom. No doubt it was just as well that the Philo Remington Company had produced its first typewriter in 1873. The days of quill pen administration were over.

By the time the so-called Pax Britannica came to an abrupt end on 4th August 1914, the Admiralty was building and maintaining an enormous fleet. 'It specified, designed and often manufactured every variety of stores from chamber pots to

The task of the Royal Navy in the heyday of the British Empire was to police in peacetime, and protect in time of war, commerce on the navigable waters within its territories and on the oceans between them. The formidable nature and extent of the problem is illustrated by this map showing the principal lands of that empire.

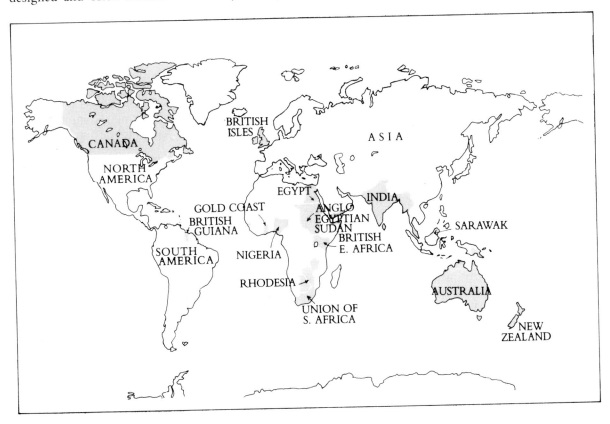

H.M.S. "Warrior" launched in 1860 was Britain's answer to the French "Gloire", the first ironclad frigate, so designated because all her main guns were mounted on a single deck. "Warrior" was the revolutionary ship which marked the enormous changes forced on the navies of the world by the Crimean War, when it was proved that ships could not survive in battle without armour on their sides to keep out shells fired by the new rifled guns. Her hull can still be seen at Pembroke in South Wales, where it acts as an oil fuelling pier.

torpedoes. It fed, clothed and supervised its officers and men from boyhood to the grave and to a considerable extent their wives and children with them. In an age when the state hardly impinged on the affairs of most of its citizens and was only beginning to interfere in the economic life of the nation, the Admiralty represented a complete society in miniature; an industrial society and a welfare state half a century before the state itself assumed that role. The Navy was remarkably self-contained. It depended on no other department of government for any essential supply, except of course money (and until 1907 in part for guns). It believed, with some reason, that there was very little it could not do and very little it should not attempt. Though there was sometimes friction between clerks and naval officers at the Admiralty, the civilians had a real affection for the Navy and a sense of belonging to a wider naval family. The Director of Victualling, for example, insisted on inspecting personally every type of stores he ordered for the fleet so that in his room samples of sailor's caps, boots, serge, raisins, sugar, chocolate, flannel strewed the table that stood under a mysterious glass case in which was a single ship's biscuit, centuries old.'[5]

Which brings us again to Jackie Fisher. Here was a man who symbolised over the span of his life every facet of naval skill and irreversible irresistible progress all of which so filled and distinguished those sixty long years between the Crimean War and the war-to-end-all-wars, as it was once known. He was an astonishing man, ruthless, quixotic, physically unprepossessing yet brilliant. Under his influence and

later his tutelage the Royal Navy changed from the dangerously complacent post-Nelsonic rigidly run and arthritic sailing fleet which it was when he first went to sea in 1854 to the prime, highly trained maritime weapon with which Great Britain entered the First World War. How did he do it? And what made him tick?

Like Nelson, whom he greatly admired, Fisher had powerful friends both when he entered the service and, at intervals when it mattered most, throughout his service career. His mother had been the daughter of a Bond Street wine merchant, one of her grandfathers had served under Nelson at Trafalgar and Emma Hamilton, as a young housemaid, had once scrubbed the steps of the house next door. This was to be Fisher's compensation for his mother's humble background in 'trade'. Both Admirals married somewhat ordinary wives, though Jackie unlike Nelson professed to adore his Katharine until the day she died – whilst at the same time enjoying what would later be called a full extra-marital emotional life. Both had charm to an exceptional degree. Both made professional enemies yet were adored – and that is not too strong a word – by those who served with them. If you believe, as I do, that talent in any profession declares itself at an early age and draws to itself the people and help it needs, then the careers of both Nelson and Fisher exemplify this idea. Whilst still a boy Fisher realised that his fascination for women would get him to the top, as indeed it did, and right up to his death he enjoyed the affection and support of all the women of influence who crossed his path. These included the Queen.

Nelson died heroically in action at 47: Fisher in his bed at 79. The driving force in both men, though, was the same – patriotic, self-sacrificing fervour to do better for the country they loved than anyone had ever done before. Both succeeded to an astonishing degree but whereas Nelson became the epitome of the fighting Admiral at sea, Fisher's merit lay in the remarkable peacetime reorganisation of the service which he carried through and which placed in the hands of seagoing commanders, such as Sturdee, Jellicoe, Beatty and Keyes, ships, squadrons and fleets that were thought at the time to have no equal in the world.

On the other hand Fisher in his zeal for efficiency was indiscreet, harsh, abusive, revengeful and damnably autocratic. 'It is difficult for any English naval officer to be cruel', an admirer wrote, 'but cruelty is part of the surgery of the great reformer . . . there is undoubtedly a useful dash of the savage in Fisher's nature.'[6] So what, indeed, did this ruthless savage achieve? What was it that made The Times say of his State Funeral: 'Lord Fisher was a stormy petrel, bringing the tempests he rejoiced in. Behind him he had, at first, no one: behind him he had, in these later years, the whole solid affection and admiration of the people. And yesterday morning the people, in its silent, stolid, reverent British way, wrote its affection and admiration for 'Jacky Fisher' upon the social history of our time.'[7]

In the course of his career Fisher served in or was concerned with three revolutionary ships. Number one was H.M.S. "Warrior" the first ironclad built for the Royal Navy in 1860. The second was H.M.S. "Inflexible" (a monster of 12,000 tons with four 16-inch guns, armour plate 22 inches thick, a speed of 14 knots and a full rig of sails) launched in 1876 with Fisher as her first Captain. The third was H.M.S. "Dreadnought", laid down in 1905 with ten 12-inch guns, a displacement of 17,250 tons and a speed of 21 knots, which Fisher, then First Sea Lord, caused to

Admiral of the Fleet John Arbuthnot Fisher, First Baron Fisher of Kilverstone (1841–1920) painted by Arthur Cope in 1902. Undoubtedly one of the greatest innovators in naval history, ruthless in getting rid of hallowed but outdated concepts, he was the greatest administrator the service has produced since Barham. He reformed ships, men and the organisation from top to bottom and his chief triumph was the introduction of the all-big-gun type of battleship in H.M.S. "Dreadnought" in 1906. At the end of his life he was one of the first to hear the knell of the Battle Fleet sound and to realise that the future lay with aircraft and submarines.

H.M.S. "DREADNOUGHT"

In 1900 Great Britain maintained a 'two-power standard' of naval strength. Numerically this meant that the Royal Navy must equal the combined fleets of any two other nations. There were good reasons for this. Britain had dominions and colonies all over the world and the British Empire depended for its survival on command of the sea routes linking them together.

The typical battleship at that time, more or less common to all navies, was a steel ship of about 17,000 tons with four 12-inch guns in two turrets and up to forty smaller guns of varying and often questionable value, with a speed of 18–19 knots. These battleships were known generally as 'mixed armament ships', and their fighting range amounted to little more than 3,000 yards.

In 1904 Admiral Sir John Fisher was appointed First Sea Lord. Fisher had made up his mind that a new battleship was essential for Britain to retain her naval supremacy. This would have to be an 'all-big-gun' ship, her guns needing to produce a much more deadly salvo at a greater range. If Britain did not build such ships, other countries would and the country's naval supremacy would have gone. Thus H.M.S. "Dreadnought" was born. The keel was laid on 2nd October 1905; four months later she was launched and this great revolutionary ship was ready for trials on 3rd October 1906.

Her cost was £1,783,883. But the gamble paid off. Built in almost complete secrecy, the "Dreadnought" mounted ten 12-inch guns in five turrets. She was protected by twelve inch armour, had a displacement of 17,250 tons and could attain a speed of 21 knots, powered by turbine engines.

This awe-inspiring ship overshadowed every other battleship afloat, and especially those of Germany, the principal challenger to British naval supremacy. Germany had already committed herself to building a series of Deutschland class battleships of 13,400 tons, with the old fashioned mixed armament. To make matters worse, the Kiel Canal could not take ships over 16,000 tons. So, while Germany digested these unpleasant facts, Britain pressed ahead with her building programme and maintained her lead – at least on paper – to such an extent that by 1918 she had completed forty-eight dreadnoughts to Germany's twenty-six. France, Italy and Russia all commissioned these new and expensive symbols of power and even South American republics ordered 'a brace or two'.

From then on the "Dreadnought" gave its name to every capital ship of a similar kind built anywhere in the world until the end of the big ship era at the close of the Second World War.

A painting by W. Fred Mitchell of H.M.S. "Dreadnought" in 1907, which even in the eighties still shows her as undoubtedly a 'modern' ship – the first of her kind.

be built in the utmost secrecy in a year and a day and which at a single stroke made every other battleship in the world obsolete. The Germans, too, were building a powerful High Seas Fleet but the conception, speed of building and successful design of the dreadnought put Britain ahead in the race. Before Germany had completed her first class of four dreadnoughts (the generic name used for capital ships for over 40 years), Britain had seven in commission plus three equally revolutionary battle-cruisers which were faster though less heavily armed and armoured than the dreadnought proper.

The idea of the dreadnought battleship came from an Italian naval architect, Vittorio Cuniberti, and was first mooted in *Jane's Fighting Ships* in 1903. Its British progenitors were the Constructor William H. Gard, the Director of Naval Construction, Sir Philip Watts and the Admiralty Committee on Designs appointed by Fisher

in November 1904 a month after he had become First Sea Lord. It included such officers, later to be so famous, as Captains John R. Jellicoe, Henry B. Jackson and R. H. S. Bacon, together with Rear Admiral the Prince Louis of Battenberg. But it is Fisher, teamed up with Lord Selbourne, the political First Lord of Admiralty, to whom the credit must mainly go.

Fisher arrived at this point of supreme power twenty-two stormy years after his captaincy of H.M.S. "Inflexible". The greater part of this period had been spent ashore in appointments where his progressive or radical ideas could most influence naval affairs so far as matériel was concerned. These shore billets included running the Navy's Gunnery School, H.M.S. "Excellent", at Portsmouth from 1883–5, being the Director of Naval Ordnance and Torpedoes 1886–91, Admiral Superintendent of Portsmouth Dockyard 1891–2 and Third Sea Lord and Controller 1892–7.

That tots up to fifteen years of pressurised work on ships and weapons which led Fisher to see more clearly and sooner than any other senior officer of his time that the Navy's weakness lay in a confusion and proliferation of design.

Ships and weapons were being produced with almost no standardisation of any kind. In today's jargon each was a 'one-off' job. Stores suitable for one ship were useless for another. British sea power was maintained by a conglomeration of individual and diverse ships all over the world, each of which required virtually a support system of its own. Few other than Fisher thought that this might constitute a fatal danger in war. The Royal Navy still proudly carried on with its 'spit and polish' era. Showing the flag ranked above strategy, the higher training of officers, gunnery and torpedoes. It was a dream world and it had to end. As Nelson with his band of brothers, so now Fisher collected round himself a small gang of reformers intent on efficiency at sea and a readiness for war. They were far from popular but, inspired by Fisher who remorselessly banged his way through all opposition with the cry 'Get on or get out', they changed the face of the Navy for ever.

Fisher returned to sea in 1897, first in command of the North America and West Indies Station and then in 1899 as Commander-in-Chief of the crack Mediterranean Fleet. Promoted to full Admiral in 1901, he was appointed Second Sea Lord in 1902 and at once applied his revolutionary ideas to the Navy's personnel. These ideas included a common entry and training of Cadets at Osborne and Dartmouth to be followed by four to five years at sea in which the new breed of officer was to become not only fully trained as a seaman but also to acquire a practical acquaintanceship with engineering techniques. He matched this idea for the lower deck by building schools ashore for seamen in the main dockyard towns. Having thus refreshed and renewed both the matériel and personnel aspects of the Navy, Fisher did a couple of years as Commander-in-Chief at Portsmouth where he 'topped out' his reforms, so to speak, and then at the suggestion, and with the support, of King Edward VII who, like his mother, had become a friend, was appointed First Sea Lord in October 1904 at the age of sixty-three 'but still the youngest man of the Navy in brain, heart and energy'.

There then followed five years of electrifying change. Reforms were driven along at a spanking pace and imposed on all with an authority which certain senior officers, notably Lord Charles Beresford, found highly offensive. Fisher let nothing stand in his way. Convinced that war with Germany was inevitable, he was also determined that it should be short, sharp and victorious.

To ensure success, he scrapped the worldwide strategy on which the Navy had relied since the Crimean War. 'Policing' went out of the window, the main fleet being brought home and concentrated in the North Sea. In any case Fisher considered that only four kinds of ship were necessary for the war he envisaged – battleships, capable of 21 knots, armoured cruisers of 25.5 knots, torpedo boat destroyers of 36 knots and submarines.

One of his prime actions as First Sea Lord, therefore, was to write 'scrap the lot' across a list of 154 ships, including 17 pre-dreadnought battleships which he described as mere devices for wasting men. Small wonder, then, that not everyone saw it his way! The dreadnought had certainly been a success, his critics said, but

The launching of H.M.S. "Dreadnought" made existing battleships obsolete, including those of the Royal Navy, and she immediately became the model for all future battleship development. She displaced 17,250 tons, had a length of 526 ft, a beam of 82 ft and a draught of 26 ft 11 in, a speed of 21 knots and was armed with ten 12-inch, twenty-four 12-pounders, five Maxims, five 18-inch torpedo tubes and carried a complement of 729. "Dreadnought" was the first battleship to have a main armament all of one calibre and the first to have steam turbine propulsion, making her the fastest battleship afloat. She served through the First World War, ramming and sinking a German submarine in 1915 and was sold for scrap in 1920.

THE ANGLO-GERMAN ARMS RACE

(1898–1914)

It used to be said that the creation of the German Navy was the main cause of the First World War. In fact until the last two decades of the nineteenth century, the German Navy scarcely existed.

The construction of the German fleet was initially a political move to preserve the balance of power in Europe but after the crowning of Kaiser Wilhelm II in 1888, the arms race started in earnest. At that time the capital ships of Great Britain ruled the seas. However the Germans, together with the French and the Russians, had already developed mines and torpedoes, weapons which at small cost could put the value of a battle fleet in question.

Then in 1897 Admiral Tirpitz was appointed Secretary of State for the Imperial German Navy. In the following year the German Navy Law of 1898 called for the building of eight battleships, twelve large and thirty small cruisers, its preamble stating

that 'as opposed to the greater naval powers, the battle fleet will have importance solely in sorties'. In other words the German ships would be designed to operate locally in the North Sea for short periods only. This affected important design features such as watertight compartments which made the living on board less comfortable but the ship itself far harder to sink.

Despite the great lead which Britain enjoyed in this armament race, by 1910 Germany had built twenty-eight battleships and nine armoured cruisers. Set against Britain's fifty-six battleships and thirty-eight armoured cruisers, the threat did not appear excessive but if the fleets of other European nations were included, various balances could be struck on paper and it had always to be remembered that Britain was an island totally dependent on seaborne trade.

The building of the dreadnought class of big-gun battleships which

began in 1906 certainly put Britain ahead and the skill and speed of our shipbuilding industry kept that lead up to and through the First World War. However – with hindsight – it is now clear that German ships, guns and matériel were superior in subtle but definite ways. Moreover when war did break out in 1914, it became apparent almost at once that the dominating weapons would be the submarine, the torpedo and the mine and that the vast effort poured into the building and maintenance of the battle fleet would turn out to be pointless.

Kaiser Wilhelm II visits Kiel, Germany's great naval port. Would Germany or any other power have built an equivalent of the "Dreadnought" had Britain not done so, or did the change to this new type of battleship in fact promote Germany to a greater degree of naval parity than she would otherwise have had at the outbreak of the First World War?

why make the rest of the fleet obsolete? Why substitute oil 'which does not exist in sufficient quantity in the world' for coal, of which substance the British Isles are largely composed? But Fisher persevered, got what he wanted and for good measure reduced the naval estimates for three successive years whilst at the same time increasing the fighting efficiency of the fleet. This was no small feat.

Opposition to the 'Fisherites', however, did build up. The British cannot stomach an absolute dictator for more than a limited time, even in an autocratic service such as the Royal Navy. In the end Fisher's conviction that he was always right and everyone else almost invariably wrong began to go to his head. He became yet another example of the well known dictum that power in any great degree does indeed corrupt. In general the Navy agreed with his reforms: it could not for ever put up with his manners and the way in which he forced things through.

A disastrous quarrel, fuelled by pride, jealousy and snobbery, blew up with Admiral Lord Charles Beresford, Commander-in-Chief of the Channel Fleet. This reached such proportions that it split the upper ranks of the service and in April 1909 compelled the Asquith government to investigate the matter. It even split the Royal Family, Edward VII taking Fisher's side and his son, later George V, Beresford's. As a result Fisher resigned after ensuring that his successor, Admiral Sir A. K. Wilson, could be depended upon to continue his policies. Fisher's departure became effective on 25th January 1910, ten weeks after he had been raised to the peerage.

But Fisher's influence continued. Winston Churchill (1874–1965) who became First Lord in October 1911 and who recalled Fisher as First Sea Lord three years later when the war had been under way for less than three months, continued Fisher's dynamic policies whilst reserving his right to criticise. Later Churchill wrote: 'There is no doubt whatever that Fisher was right in nine-tenths of what he fought for. His great reforms sustained the power of the Royal Navy at the most critical period in its history.'

Fisher's life and achievements have also to be seen against another background than that of the Royal Navy alone. In the first fourteen years of the twentieth century new alignments of national power were constantly being made. Two other powerful Navies, apart from the Kaiser's, had entered the world scene – those of America and Japan. At that time neither country threatened Great Britain in the way that Germany did. Both, however, were concerned with a global balance of power, a continuing concern which reached its climax in the Second World War.

Both navies, too, had sprung from and to a certain extent had modelled themselves on the Royal Navy, at any rate in their early days. Indeed Admiral Heihachiro Togo (1847–1934), the father of the Imperial Japanese Navy, had spent three years in the 1870s in H.M.S. "Worcester", the nautical training ship at Greenhithe and to the end of his life referred to England as his second mother country. Admired almost as much in England as in his native Japan, Togo was awarded the unprecedented honour for a foreigner of the British Order of Merit in 1906 in token, perhaps, amongst other things of the crushing victory he had achieved the previous year when the Japanese Grand Fleet, a large proportion of which had been built by the British, annihilated the Russian Baltic Fleet at the battle of Tsushima off the coast of Japan. This almost total elimination of Russian naval power allowed Fisher to withdraw all five British battleships from the China Station, despite an understandable outburst of fury from Admiral Sir Gerard Noel, the Commander-in-Chief on the spot.

Perhaps it was as well, though, that Fisher went when he did. The service needed a rest from vendetta, it needed time to adjust to the organisational changes Fisher had made, to set up the naval war staff which Fisher had opposed and to come to a working relationship with the submarine, wireless telegraphy and aircraft which, though supported by Fisher (the submarine had been called 'Fisher's Toy'), were still in their initial stages of growth. He had left an indelible mark on the Royal Navy at the apex of its power. In five short years at the top he had 'blown away a century's dust and cobwebs' and he had done so only just in time.

In 1910 King Edward VII died and with him an era. The following year Halley's comet, last seen the year before Victoria ascended the throne, reappeared bringing with it the usual auguries of change. In 1914 the first great world convulsion began.

The Right Honourable Sir Winston Spencer Churchill (1874–1965), twice First Lord of the Admiralty, on each occasion at the outbreak of a world war. Jackie Fisher first aroused Churchill's interest in the Navy and he became First Lord in the late summer of 1911 after the Agadir crisis. His very considerable achievements in both wars have been diminished only by the tragedy of the Dardanelles in 1915.

CHAPTER VIII

THE FIRST WORLD WAR

1914–1918

CHRONOLOGICAL COMPENDIUM

General

The First World War was triggered off by the assassination of the Archduke Francis Ferdinand of Austria at Sarajevo, an obscure town in the Balkans, on the 28th June 1914. A month later Austria-Hungary declared war on Serbia who appealed to Russia for help, the French President Raymond Poincaré had visited Russia, and Germany had required Russia to cease mobilisation, a requirement not obeyed by the Tsar. On 1st August Germany declared war on Russia, France mobilised, Italy declared her neutrality and a German-Turkish treaty was signed at Constantinople. On 3rd August Germany declared war on France and invaded Belgium. 'The lights are going out all over Europe' the British Foreign Secretary, Viscount Grey, observed and added sombrely 'we shall not see them lit again in our lifetime.' The next day Britain declared war on Germany and the holocaust began.

Four years later and after 6,181,000 men had been killed with a further 12,570,000 wounded, an Armistice was signed between the Allies and Germany and twenty uneasy years of peace in Europe began before the Second World War opened in September 1939.

Naval

At the outbreak of war in 1914 Winston Churchill (1874–1965) was First Lord. Admiral of the Fleet, Prince Louis Alexander of Battenberg (1843–1921) was First Sea Lord and Chief of the Naval Staff. John Rushworth Jellicoe (1859–1935), Admiral of the Fleet and first Earl, had command of the Grand Fleet with David Beatty (1871–1936), also later to become Admiral of the Fleet and first Earl, the Commander-in-Chief of the Battle Cruiser Squadron.

On 29th October 1914 Prince Louis resigned as First Sea Lord and was replaced by Jackie Fisher. When Churchill and Fisher both resigned after the Dardanelles fiasco in May 1915, Arthur Balfour became First Lord to be followed by Sir Edward Carson in December 1916 and by Sir Eric Geddes in July 1917. Admiral Sir Henry Jackson (1855–1929) replaced Fisher as First Sea Lord in May 1915 and was in turn replaced by Jellicoe in December 1916 and by Admiral Rosslyn Wemyss (1864–1933) later Admiral of the Fleet and First Baron, in January 1918.

Other prominent naval officers in the First World War were:

Alfred Chatfield
1873–1967

who was Flag Captain to Vice Admiral Sir David Beatty in the battlecruiser "Lion" during the first two years of the war, later becoming an Admiral of the Fleet and a Baron and serving as First Sea Lord from 1933 to 1938.

Sir Christopher Cradock
1862–1914

Rear Admiral, who lost his life fighting von Spee's squadron off Coronel in the south Pacific on 1st November 1914.

Sir John de Robeck
1862–1928

who as a Rear Admiral was second-in-command of the naval forces at the Dardanelles and then took over command in March 1915, later the third and second Battle Squadrons of the Grand Fleet, C. in C. Mediterranean and Atlantic and promoted Admiral of the Fleet in November 1925.

Sir Frederick Dreyer
1878–1956

One of the greatest gunnery experts in the Royal Navy; was Flag Captain to Jellicoe when C. in C. of the Grand Fleet at the battle of Jutland on 31st May 1916; later becoming an Admiral and retired when Assistant Chief of Naval Staff at the Admiralty after the Invergordon naval mutiny in 1931.

Sir John Edgell
1880–1962

Vice Admiral and later Hydrographer of the Navy.

Sir William Hall
1870–1943

Admiral and Director of Naval Intelligence during the First World War.

Roger Keyes Admiral of the Fleet and First Baron Keyes of Zeebrugge chiefly remembered for his command
1872–1945 of the Dover Patrol and the blocking of Zeebrugge and Ostend.

Sir Henry Oliver As Vice Admiral was appointed Chief of the Admiralty War Staff from November 1914 to the
1865–1965 spring of 1918 when he was given command of the First Battle Squadron, later becoming
Admiral of the Fleet.

Sir Herbert Admiral, iconoclastic member of the first naval staff at the Admiralty and sharply critical of
Richmond Fisher.
1871–1946

Sir Frederick Admiral of the Fleet chiefly remembered for his destruction of von Spee's squadron at the
Sturdee Falklands Islands on 8th December 1914.
1859–1925

Sir Reginald Admiral of the Fleet, was one of Fisher's 'bright young men' and chiefly remembered for his
Tyrwhitt command of the Harwich Force (light cruisers and destroyers) and for the battles of Heligoland
1870–1951 Bight and Dogger Bank.

Rosslyn Wemyss Admiral of the Fleet and First Baron, was First Sea Lord when Germany was defeated.
1864–1933

Battles and Events

16 December 1914	German bombardment of Scarborough, Hartlepool and Whitby
28 August 1914	Battle of Heligoland Bight
1 November 1914	Battle of Coronel (Admiral Cradock's squadron lost)
8 December 1914	Battle of Falkland Islands (von Spee's squadron sunk)
24 January 1915	Battle of Dogger Bank
18 February 1915	German submarine blockade of Britain opens
19 February 1915	Naval attack on Dardanelles begins
7 May 1915	"Lusitania" torpedoed with loss of 1,198 lives
31 May 1916	Battle of Jutland
5 June 1916	H.M.S. "Hampshire" with Lord Kitchener on board lost off Orkneys
24 March 1916	Hospital ship "Portugal" sunk
25 April 1916	Germans bombard Lowestoft
4 May 1916	German note to America undertaking not to sink ships without warning
20/24 November 1916	Hospital ships "Britannic" and "Braemar" sunk
1 February 1917	Germans begin unrestricted submarine warfare
6 April 1917	United States declares war on Germany
23 April 1917	German destroyer raid on Dover repelled
2 November 1917	British naval success in the Kattegat
22/3 April 1918	British raid on Zeebrugge and Ostend
9/10 May 1918	Ostend blocked by sinking of H.M.S. "Vindictive"
10 November 1918	German naval mutiny at Kiel
12 November 1918	Allied fleet passes through Dardanelles
21 November 1918	German High Seas Fleet surrenders

Comparative Strengths of navies at outbreak of war

	Britain	Germany	France	Russia	Italy	U.S.	Japan
Dreadnoughts	19	13	6	6	6	8	3
Pre-Dreadnoughts	39	22	20	8	8	22	13
Battle Cruisers	8	5	—	3	—	—	2
Cruisers	63	7	19	6	10	15	13
Light Cruisers	35	33	7	8	7	14	16
Destroyers	180	163	80	100	35	48	64
Submarines	44	38	75	35	20	36	14

Naval Losses 1914–18

	Dreadnoughts	Pre-Dreadnoughts	Battle Cruisers	Cruisers	Light Cruisers	Dest.	S/M
British Empire	2	11	3	13	12	64	54
France	—	4	—	5	—	13	12
Germany	—	1	1	6	17	68	200
Austria	2	1	—	—	3	6	11
Turkey	—	1	—	—	1	3	—
Italy	1	3	—	1	2	9	7
Russia	2	2	—	2	—	18	15
Japan	1	—	1	—	2	1	—
United States	—	—	—	1	—	2	2

At the end of the First World War, 'The surrender of the German Fleet, accomplished without shock of battle', the Admiralty signalled, 'will remain for all time the example of the wonderful silence and sureness with which seapower attains its ends.'

Those who had fought in and survived the preceding four years were unlikely to subscribe to the 'wonderful silence and sureness' bit. Neither in the Admiralty itself nor in the higher command at sea could such a claim be substantiated. Far from being anywhere near as perfect as they thought they were, the Navy and the Admiralty can be seen as strong in technology and administration whilst conducting the entire war at sixes and sevens so far as strategy and direction were concerned. And the bill which had had to be paid was appalling.

In just over four years of war on land and sea some three quarters of a million Britons (9% of the male population under 45) were killed and a further 1,600,000 injured. At sea 4,837 Allied merchant ships had been despatched to Davy Jones's locker, amounting in tonnage to 11,135,000. In 1914 figures this represented 38% of British tonnage afloat. Replacement launchings dropped from 58.7% in the years between 1909 and 1914 to 35% in 1920, the slack being eagerly taken up by the United States and Japan.

The financial picture darkened even more. Naval expenditure in 1914 had been £51.5 million: in 1919–20 it had reached £160 million, the cost of the war rising from £3 million to £7 million a day. Most significant of all since it was to affect everyday life for the next sixty years, the National Debt had increased from £650 million in 1914 to £7,435 million at the end of the war. In a few short years the United States found itself, somewhat against its will, as the world's greatest creditor nation, replacing Britain in many of the world markets. The pound steadily weakened against the dollar and the death knell of Empire began to toll through the twenty inter-war years, continuing through the Second World War. Today the British Empire has gone and the Commonwealth exists in little more than name.

How very differently it all began! We were going to teach the Kaiser a lesson he would never forget and the war would be over by Christmas. The nation firmly believed that almost everything lay to the British advantage. For instance it was obvious that apart from naval hardware, we had geography on our side in the blockade imposed upon Germany. From Scapa Flow 21 dreadnoughts, 8 pre-dreadnoughts and 4 battle-cruisers sealed off the northern exit of what the Kaiser was pleased to call 'the German ocean'. The southern exit was secured by 19 pre-dreadnoughts based on Portland. The locked-in German High Seas Fleet, on the other hand, numbered only 13 dreadnoughts, 16 pre-dreadnoughts and 5 battle-cruisers.

Any sortie, therefore, north into the Atlantic or south through the Channel would have to be undertaken against overwhelming odds, making it logistically all but impossible and strategically dubious in the extreme. Admittedly this conclusion was based on a numerical assessment, but that was how both sides saw the situation at the beginning of the war. The effect of unrestricted U-boat warfare had yet to be appreciated, and even when Armageddon was over, big-ship thinking still dominated the Admiralty to the detriment of those like Jackie Fisher who had begun to sense the truth.

Even after the warning implied by the battle of Jutland, the romance of the dreadnought continued to grip British Admirals, and at one remove the country, despite the obvious fact that submarines in the present and aircraft in the future were clearly going to make the big-gun battleship about as viable as the dinosaur. This conservatism, fatal though it nearly proved to be, should not be too harshly criticised nor too glibly cast aside. That was how the world thought in those days. The heart more often than the head governs the way nations are run. The dreadnoughts of the Grand Fleet were awesome and wondrous, an emblem of all that most people considered British majesty ought to be. Battleships were cherished, indeed almost loved. The fact that they were too valuable and too vulnerable to be risked in battle – and that this was a ludicrous state of affairs – took a long time to filter down into the national consciousness and had certainly not done so when I joined the Navy in 1932. The dreadnoughts of 1914 had a 'fierce feline beauty' and this gave the nation the martial confidence it needed.

Spurious as we can now see it to be, in the First World War the Capital Ship seemed to complement the skill and the spirit of the humblest Ordinary Seaman which at no time was found wanting. How else could it be? The image of the mightiest fleet in the world was there in everyone's mind. It was part of the pride of being British. Indeed in the placid decades of peace before 1914, the pride of the British or arrogance, if you like, whilst less harsh and brutal, perhaps, than that of the Prussian foe, had nevertheless come to be accepted by the world as a fact of life. The axiom of pride leading on to a fall was to be proved yet again as savagely and tragically true. A terrible awakening was about to take place, an awakening not fully to be completed until yet another world war had ravaged mankind. In 1914, however, a subtle and nagging disquiet had already begun.

Winston Spencer Churchill, a brilliant young politician whom few trusted (and that few did not include the King), had been First Lord of the Admiralty since 24th October 1911. Before that he had been an energetic Home Secretary. Asquith had appointed him to the Admiralty after a crisis in Morocco had brought the country to within an ace of war with Germany. The Agadir crisis late in August 1911 had gravely embarrassed the Establishment. When it broke, the First Sea Lord, Admiral Sir Arthur Wilson, together with most of the Board, were away shooting and on being eventually brought back to London were found to have no coherent or comprehensive plan for war of any kind. When pressed, Admiral Wilson gave vent to a few silly platitudes, devoid of serious thought, and the Secretary for War, Viscount Haldane, threatened to resign unless the Admiralty was compelled to appoint a naval staff which could and would plan for war.

Churchill had had no previous knowledge of naval affairs but at once set about becoming an expert with the zeal and application he was to exercise for the rest of his life. During his first eighteen months in office, he spent 182 days at sea. Such enthusiasm was considered extraordinary and even questionable. He also dismissed Wilson at the first opportunity, replacing him on 5th December 1911 with Sir Francis Bridgeman 'a colourless man with judgment but no force of character' and a year later with Prince Louis of Battenberg, an Admiral of very much greater all-round ability but who had the misfortune to be of German blood. At that time Churchill as First Lord was described as falling, in temperament and method, between Sandwich in the eighteenth and Childers in the nineteenth centuries – 'like Sandwich he was a politician of noble birth who made it his pride to master the technicalities of the naval world; like Childers he claimed and exercised an unlimited power of suggestion in matters which he understood, half understood or did not understand at all.'[1]

Churchill showed himself at once to be a true disciple of Jackie Fisher whom he much admired. Both were men who were apt to go overboard in pursuit of a new technical development, such as the aeroplane, however zany the idea might appear at first sight. Both greatly improved the service conditions of the seagoing fleet, especially on the lower deck. Both fought the coal lobby and Churchill had oil fuel introduced and a controlling share in the Anglo-Persian oil company bought in order to provide it. Like Fisher, however, Churchill's attitude to the urgent task of creating a proper and responsible staff remained ambivalent. The Naval War Staff which he set up in 1912 was in fact purely advisory: no one was required to pay undue attention to anything it said.

Indeed the greater part of this staff simply consisted of the Naval Intelligence Division under a new name – 'the old dog had merely been provided with a War Staff collar'. A majority of the staff officers, moreover, had been selected because they were too old, sick or incompetent to be sent to sea. Here again arrogance was at work. 'The brains and talents of the Navy had been mortgaged to Gunnery and to the Fleets at sea, and, deflected for years into technical channels, they continued to flow in the same direction.'[2] Due to the snobbery of the time, therefore, the advice proffered by Naval War Staff was discounted in advance. To some extent this outlook prevailed until the Second World War and certainly in the early thirties when I went to sea in H.M.S. "Nelson", the 33,000 ton battleship which was then flagship of the Home Fleet, Gunnery Officers considered themselves an élite, many of them being under the impression that the Navy existed for their benefit and theirs alone.

Looking back on it now, there is no doubt that the Royal Navy deserved the high tribute it was accorded for its overall achievements in the First World War. However, it is also a fact that both the nation and the Navy entered a war in the summer of 1914 for which they were wholly unprepared. 'Neither the Cabinet nor the Admiralty possessed any effective means of formulating naval policy and the Admiralty was ill equipped to execute it. The wireless aerials rigged on masts on the roof might impress the uninitiated, they scarcely betokened a directing intelligence within.'[3]

This quickly became apparent. By November 1914 the reputation and the spirit of the Royal Navy had dangerously ebbed. Barring one action in the Heligoland Bight on 28th August when three German cruisers and a destroyer had been sunk, nothing had gone right. As Fisher had warned – though the warning had fallen on deaf ears – the mine and the torpedo-carrying submarine were proving to be far more deadly than the higher command, both British and German, had ever foreseen. Three large armoured cruisers had been sunk by a single U-boat in one day alone. A single German mine had accounted for one of the very latest super-dreadnoughts. Trade in the Indian Ocean had been virtually halted by the "Emden" and the "Konigsberg" and elsewhere German surface raiders were sinking British merchant ships at will,

BREECH-LOADING GUNNERY

The use of hardened steel armour plating, improved propellants, giving higher muzzle velocity and the explosive shell began in the middle of the nineteenth century and these, together with the rifled barrel and efficient breech-loading mechanisms, set the style of naval gunnery for the next century until the self-propelled missile superseded the big gun as the principal weapon at sea.

This development had been preceded by a continuous process of competition between the means of attack and defence which culminated around 1876 in iron armour twenty inches thick and rifled guns of some 16 inches calibre, weighing 110 tons.

With the coming of steam propulsion and the ironclad battleship, it became desirable for guns to be able to fire ahead rather than being confined to broadside firing and this led to the invention of the rotating armoured gun turret. This was complemented by improvements in breech-loading mechanisms such as

the interrupted thread breech-block which increased rate of fire and the ability to open or shut the breech by the single motion of a lever. Guns steadily increased in size, the heaviest British gun of the nineteenth century being a 16.25-inch monster destined for H.M.S. "Victoria" the barrel of which weighed 111 tons and which fired an 1800 lb shell giving a muzzle energy of over 53,000 tons.

At the same time smaller guns varying in bore from 3- to 8-inches became the armament of ships such as cruisers and destroyers and were mounted in battleships as secondary armament against destroyers delivering torpedo attacks or, on high-angle mountings, against attacking aircraft.

In both the First and Second World Wars the guns of both main and secondary armaments were hydraulically or electrically operated in revolving turret-barbettes by crews inside the turrets following the settings given them by central director firing using a Fire Control Table

(introduced by Dreyer in 1913). This system included Dumaresq's machine (invented in 1902) into which was fed the ship's own speed and course, bearing to the enemy ship and an estimate of the enemy's speed and course, a range clock and spotting table, all basically set and checked by the human eye. Now, the conventional guns remaining in service are fully automatic, being loaded, aimed and fired entirely mechanically without any crew intervention.

The greatest weight of metal ever to hurtle from a gun turret of the Royal Navy used to be fired from these 16-inch guns on H.M.S. "Nelson" (or from the similar ones on its sistership H.M.S. "Rodney"). But as the sputnik took over from the aircraft when that could fly no higher, so the guided missile and the ICBM have ended the quest for the evermore-enormous gun.

a particularly dangerous German cruiser squadron being at large in the Pacific after it had destroyed without loss to itself the two armoured cruisers sent out to dispose of it. A growing public anxiety at the way the Navy was being run began to express itself, with Churchill's reputation being put increasingly at risk. This was not something he relished. A dramatic gesture was clearly required and Churchill persuaded the Prime Minister, Asquith, to make it. Prince Louis of Battenberg had to go.

The main excuse for this shabby piece of 'yard arm clearing' was Prince Louis' German ancestry. Such prejudice marched with the times, incomprehensible as it may seem today. In 1914 no orchestra would play Wagner's music and no one drank hock and seltzer any more. Even the Royal Family changed its name, henceforth to be known as the House of Windsor: Battenberg anglicised into Mountbatten and so

it went on. Hatred of all things German during the first three months of the war focussed into venomous attacks on the First Sea Lord and so, for the good of the country and with a great magnanimity and dignity, Prince Louis tendered his resignation. As replacement Asquith recalled Fisher to the central direction of naval affairs. This turned out to be a bomb with a very short fuse.

Fisher's appointment was received with great popular acclaim. It did not go down well with the King. 'I did all I could to prevent it', the Monarch wrote in his diary, 'I told Churchill that Fisher was not trusted by the Navy and they had no confidence in him personally. I think it is a great mistake and he is seventy-four. In the end I had to give in with great reluctance.'[4]

As it turned out the King's doubts were justified. They were shared by David Beatty (1871–1936), the Admiral commanding the Grand Fleet Battlecruisers. 'I cannot see Winston and Jackie Fisher working very long in harmony. They will quarrel before long', he confided to his wife and this, almost inevitably, proved to be true. After six turbulent months the relationship came to grief in a final and bitter crisis, the end music, so to speak, being entitled 'the Dardanelles'.

Before this happened, however, and very shortly after Fisher's return, one of the classic events of the First World War took place. This was a stunning victory, very badly needed, since Fisher on arrival at the Admiralty had found 'everything wrong in dispositions of ships, misuse of manpower, inadequate torpedoes and mines, weak gunnery . . . every day I find evidence of utter incapacity and no one shot!' History records the event as Fisher's finest hour, as indeed it was, and Churchill, too, recognised it as one of their 'few mutually happy moments'. The event in question was Admiral Sturdee's destruction of von Spee's cruiser force off the Falkland Islands on 8th December 1914. However the way in which this came about was ironic, combining luck, wily diplomacy by Churchill and the most daring strategy by Fisher.

Sir Frederick Doveton Sturdee (1859–1925) had been Chief of Staff to Beresford and was therefore anathema to Fisher who, on his return to power, found 'that pedantic ass Sturdee' as chief of the Admiralty's newly fledged Naval War Staff. Fisher would have none of it. He told Churchill Sturdee would have to go. But Sturdee refused. Fisher then threatened to resign himself unless he could be given a new Chief of Staff. At that moment luck and timing came to the rescue.

On 1st November off Coronel in Chile von Spee had annihilated, bar two ships, the "Glasgow" and "Otranto" a British armed cruiser force under Rear Admiral Sir Christopher Cradock. This was a moment for which Fisher, unconsciously perhaps, had been preparing the whole of his service career. There were now to be no half measures and von Spee must be instantly crushed. With Churchill's full support Fisher ordered two of the newest battlecruisers to sail from Plymouth at full speed for the Falkland Islands.

Plymouth said the ships were not ready; the boiler firebricks were being rebuilt. Fisher gave them three days and then, when Plymouth argued back, drafted all available dockyard bricklayers on board the ships and told them to finish the job en route. Meanwhile Sturdee, whose 'criminal ineptitude' – in Fisher's opinion – had caused the death of Cradock and some 1600 officers and men at Coronel was offered the job of commanding the expedition by Churchill. Sturdee, who was a good sea officer, accepted with alacrity, made the 7,000 mile journey at his own somewhat leisurely pace and arrived at Port Stanley on 7th December, his first action being immediately to refuel.

The very next day, by a piece of supreme luck, the German ships, completely unaware of the trap into which they were sailing, appeared off the Falklands, saw the British battlecruisers' tripod masts, realised what this meant and set off south-east at high speed. Sturdee followed at once and after an action lasting four hours sank four of the five German ships, the fifth blowing herself up three months later when caught unawares by two British cruisers in the port of Mas Afuera. The disaster at Coronel had been amply revenged.

This Falkland Islands success gave the country a sharp boost to morale, much as

the sinking of the pocket battleship "Graf Spee" did at a similar moment in the Second World War. Churchill generously told Fisher 'This was your show and your luck . . . your *flair* was quite true. Let us have some more victories together and confound all our foes abroad and (don't forget) at home.' Alas! it was not to be. Except for one successful action on 24th January 1915 off the Dogger Bank, a success marred on the British side by bad communication which allowed all but one of the German ships to escape, a stalemate began in the North Sea which, Jutland apart, continued for the rest of the war.

With hindsight this can now be seen as the most sensible strategy for which Britain could have opted, had there been a choice, since in that way the surface naval war could never be lost. Were the German High Seas Fleet to emerge, it would be heavily outnumbered and soon overcome; if it remained in port the victory would be Britain's in any case. The public, however, egged on by the Press found this tame, puzzling and unsatisfactory. They had been promised great deeds, so they imagined, on the scale of Trafalgar and when none appeared to be forthcoming they felt cheated. All that vast pre-war expenditure on the battle fleet had begun to seem absurd.

The first six months of 1915 with Churchill and Fisher in tandem at the Admiralty were shot through with dazzling ideas of how to change the face of the war, equally colourful rows between the two titanic leaders and an absence of creative thought, even of common sense, in the higher direction of the war. This would have provided the substance of high comedy had the results not been so patently tragic.

A painting showing the "Scharnhorst" during the Battle of the Falkland Islands in 1914. In November 1914 the German Admiral Graf von Spee's Pacific Squadron had destroyed Admiral Cradock's squadron off the Chilean coast and had then rounded Cape Horn into the Atlantic. However, the British Admiralty had despatched the battlecruisers "Invincible" and "Inflexible" in great secrecy to the Falklands where they were joined by the cruisers "Kent", "Cornwall" and "Glasgow". After a long-range action of a few hours, the "Gneisenau" and "Scharnhorst" were sunk. The remaining smaller ships also became casualties, two then, one later.

However, things could not go on in that way for long and the climax came with the Dardanelles catastrophe. This began in January 1915 when Fisher's Baltic project, which until then had been enthusiastically supported by Churchill, was abandoned by the Cabinet in favour of a new and dramatic plan to assist Russia in the south.

Fisher's Baltic project, which he had nurtured since visiting Russia with King Edward VII in 1908, envisaged the landing by the Royal Navy of an expeditionary force on the Pomeranian coast ninety miles from Berlin. This would occupy the attention of a million German soldiers, he reckoned, and would bring about a total confusion in the capital, especially if backed up by the landing of a Russian army from the other end of the Baltic. 'The Baltic project', Fisher wrote, 'meant victory by land and sea. It was simply history repeating itself. Frederick the Great for the only time in his life (on hearing the Russians had landed) was frightened and sent for poison. Geography has not altered since his time. The Pomeranian coast has not shifted and a million Russian soldiers could have been landed within 82 miles of Berlin.'[5]

Fisher had always held strong views that Britain should never become involved in a debilitating continental land war and had put up vociferous opposition to the despatch of the British Expeditionary Force to France in August 1914. By the end of the year the 'old contemptibles' had been almost wiped out. Fisher's fears had been justified but there was nothing that anyone could do about it. The country was now committed to a lengthening campaign which would soon demand a conscript army. Notwithstanding that, however, Fisher had sent Churchill a wildly imaginative plan for a combined naval and military attack on Turkey. This required bombardment of the Dardanelles forts by pre-dreadnought battleships, the landing of a powerful British Expeditionary Force south of the entrance to the Straits 'the Greeks to go for Gallipoli at the same time as we go for Besika, the Bulgarians for Constantinople and the Russians, Servians and Roumanians for Austria'.

It was a grand conception but it presupposed that Greece and Bulgaria would enter the war on the allied side. Churchill spotted this weakness but kept quiet about it. However he did latch on to the idea of forcing the Dardanelles by bombardment from ancient battleships. Here, he declared, was a chance for the Navy, heroic and alone, to strike Turkey a fatal blow. This would distract attention from the failures of the past and would at the same time bolster up his own reputation.

In fact even a cursory look at the narrow, well defended strait dividing Turkey in Europe from Turkey in Asia would have shown it to be a prescription for calamity. In mid-January Fisher suddenly realised the implications of Churchill's fantastic plan and he then began protesting in the strongest terms. The Prime Minister overruled him. At a crucial meeting of the War Council Fisher attempted to resign but was dissuaded from doing so by Kitchener. From then on it was all downhill to disaster.

Matters came to a head in May. In personal bitterness, agony of mind and anguish for his country, Fisher resigned despite advice to '*stick* to your *Post* like *Nelson*' from Edward VII's widow, Queen Alexandra, and a suggestion from Lord Esher that Fisher should revive the office of Lord High Admiral and take it himself. The Dardanelles broke Churchill, too, and ten days later he departed from the Admiralty becoming Chancellor of the Duchy of Lancaster. The débâcle of Gallipoli and the

Dardanelles dragged on till the end of the year, the only glint of redemption being the successful evacuation of the troops without loss by January 1916.

Meanwhile the blockade of Germany by Britain and of the United Kingdom by Germany continued. The great battle fleets of both nations might have been stalled into a continuing stalemate: the submarine, however, was coming into its own. Here the advantage lay clearly on Germany's side. Once again popular opinion of the day collided with some unpleasant facts. The British idea, prevalent until at least 1917, was that the Royal Navy had the measure of the U-boat, whilst British supremacy in surface ships had never been in question. This notion could now scarcely be justified by events, true though it was that after the first few months of the war German merchantmen were unable to sail except as blockade runners under a high degree of risk. It was also true that within six months of the start of the war, German surface raiders had been swept from the seven seas.

German U-boats, however, especially in the days before radar or even Asdic, had things very much the way they wanted. Worthwhile targets were to be found almost anywhere they chose to hunt. On the other hand British submarines operating in the confined waters of the Heligoland Bight, the Baltic and the Sea of Marmora, had to penetrate to their target areas against heavy odds. None the less they achieved some remarkable feats.

Both the German and British submarine services, though, were up against a general feeling that the way they went about their business was in some way shady. One British Admiral declared that submarine warfare by either side was 'underhand, unfair and damned un-English'. But then those were still the days when a gentleman

A watercolour showing H.M.S. "Queen Elizabeth" at Gallipoli. Here the concept of sea power was misunderstood and misused. The attempt by the British Mediterranean Fleet to force a passage to Constantinople through the Dardanelles and thus put Turkey out of the war failed because of lines of moored mines across the straits and also because the fleet became a 'sitting duck' for the guns of the Turkish forts guarding the channel. This was foreseen and opposed by Fisher who nevertheless gave Churchill grudging support, instead of resigning. The latter's obstinacy caused one of the worst disasters of the First World War and both Fisher and Churchill subsequently resigned.

of whatever nationality could be relied on not to 'let the side down'. The disreputable and treacherous behaviour of Burgess, Maclean, Philby and Blunt was literally inconceivable in the First World War. A gentleman's word was his bond. When the first German spy to be caught was shot in the Tower of London rather than hanged in prison as a common criminal, this was because the man in question, Karl Hans Lody, was a German naval officer, and one who spent his last night on earth in the company of Sir Basil Thomson, Head of the Special Branch, smoking and discussing German music and English literature with his captor. He wrote, 'I feel it my duty as a German officer to express my sincere thanks and appreciation towards the staff of officers and men who were in charge of my person during my confinement. Their kind and considerate treatment has called up my highest esteem and admiration regarding good fellowship even towards an enemy, and if I may be permitted I would thank you to make this known to them.' Incidentally Lody was the first man to be executed in the Tower of London for a hundred and fifty years.

Unrestricted submarine warfare – the destruction of any ship on sight without warning – was considered definitely 'off side', not only in England but also in America. It was contrary to the Hague Convention of 1907 to sink a merchant ship without first ensuring the safety of both passengers and crew. Nevertheless Germany chose to defy this international law, until the sinking of the Cunard liner "Lusitania" off Kinsale Head in Ireland with the loss of 1,198 lives in May 1915 so outraged world opinion that the German High Command felt obliged to restrain their U-boat commanders.

'Gentlemanly attitudes' lasted until after Jutland when blockade by submarine

U-boats in Wilhelmshaven 1917. The U-boat and not the battleship proved to be the dominating naval weapon in the First World War. Only the introduction of the convoy system in 1917 – and it was introduced reluctantly – helped to reduce the appalling loss of vital allied merchant shipping which had brought the United Kingdom within a few weeks of starvation by 1917.

became the only foreseeable way in which Germany could win the war. Unrestricted attacks began once more in February 1917 on the orders of von Scheer. This may well have been the principal background factor in bringing the United States into the war in April 1917. From then on the Allies suffered a 'negative cash flow' in shipping. The British merchant fleet, still far and away the largest in the world, started to lose more ships than could be replaced. By the autumn of 1917 German U-boats had sunk, under appalling conditions of suffering, two-and-three-quarter million tons of allied shipping. The peculiar vileness of twentieth century war had begun to identify itself. Not only professional fighting men but women and children were now at stake and have so continued to be until today.

As Fisher had foretold, the submarine day by day proved itself to be the dominant weapon at sea. The remedy, had more of the higher command bothered to read history, was there to hand and had been amply established in the Napoleonic wars. This was the convoy system. However, such was the inertia and wooden-mindedness induced by a century of peace that it took three years of war, catastrophic losses, and the fact that the country faced starvation in six weeks, before Their Lordships saw fit to bring the convoy system into operation and even then Jellicoe, appointed First Sea Lord in December 1916 in order to take charge of the battle against the U-boats, began by declaring himself against the idea. This was folly of a high order and it nearly lost us the war. Indeed pessimism had reached such a pitch in March 1917 that the Cabinet considered treating for peace on the best terms they could get.

By the summer of 1917 the seagoing fleet and responsible opinion ashore had lost confidence in the Admiralty. This loss of faith had been caused in part by the Admiralty's faulty handling of the crucial battle of Jutland in May 1916 both whilst the action was in progress and in the communiqués Their Lordships issued afterwards. The moral shock which Jutland gave the nation reverberated for the rest of the war and to a certain extent has continued ever since.

Jutland was the greatest naval engagement of the war. Indeed it was the set-piece where the battle fleets of Britain and Germany met for the first and last time. How was it then so indecisive? Why was it that the Royal Navy meeting at long last an opponent who was equally skilled, equally well led and perhaps in some respects better equipped, had come off worst? It was all very well for an American journalist to say: 'The German Fleet has assaulted its jailer but is still in jail'. Why had the jailer not executed summary justice on its captive? Why was Jutland not the overwhelming British victory it had promised to be?

True it was that Germany remained blockaded and that the High Seas Fleet never again ventured to sea except to surrender. True also that Jellicoe, as Churchill pointed out, was the only man on either side who could lose the war in an afternoon. The British public failed to see why he had not won it in an afternoon. David Beatty might remark at the height of the battle that 'there seems to be something wrong with our bloody ships today'. There certainly was and not only with the ships. The Nelson touch seemed to be pointedly missing. And there was never to be another chance to put it all right.

Apart from the design of ships, dud shells and other matériel factors, there were serious lapses in communication. These occurred in visual signalling at sea, in interdepartmental traffic in the Admiralty and in wireless telegraphy between Admiralty and fleet. All in all they comprised, perhaps, the main root cause of this indecisive encounter at Jutland in which the Germans lost one battleship, one battlecruiser, four cruisers and five destroyers together with 2,551 men as against British losses of three battlecruisers, three cruisers, eight destroyers and 6,097 men. These massive errors in communication were made by otherwise competent and reasonably intelligent human beings at the Admiralty. Their mistakes could not be blamed on broken cables or defective equipment and they were inexcusable. The fetish of centralisation and a matching obsession with secrecy stood at the back of these faults and the tragedies they caused. What makes it all worse was that the Admiralty had begun the war with at least one advantage which put it potentially ahead of its German counterpart and that was the Naval Intelligence Division.

In 1903 Jackie Fisher, fresh from revolutionising the training of naval officers and men, had charmed and cajoled Professor Alfred Ewing into leaving his well-paid post at Cambridge in order to become the first Director of Naval Education, a post he later expanded into Intelligence. Sir Alfred, as he became, made a notable success of the job. By the start of the war he had recruited a small group of academic friends, installed them in the Admiralty and had set them to work decyphering German naval wireless signals.

An invaluable and increasing stream of intelligence of the utmost importance began to emerge from Room 40 O.B. (Old Building). For all the use to which it was put, this information might just as well have run into the sand. The Operations Division neither valued nor trusted the N.I.D. boffins and the analyses they made. Extraordinary as it now seems, Operations were forbidden to have any contact with Naval Intelligence, their material being sent 'raw' to the War Room, without context or comment, for such use as the staff might see fit. The Director of the Operations Division despised Room 40 and all that came out of it. 'Thank God!' he exclaimed when the Germans changed their codes, 'I shan't have any more of that damned stuff.'[6]

It occurred to no one that there is little point in keeping a secret from the enemy if you do not make use of it yourself. The Admiralty did not see it that way. Secrecy was all. The Naval Attaché in Paris before the war had had to learn from his French contacts exactly what information was passing between the British and French Admiralties. Within the Admiralty, Room 40 was forbidden to communicate with the German section of N.I.D. and the enemy submarine section, so that those who knew where the enemy was could not meet those who knew where British ships were.

During the whole war the Director of Naval Intelligence's private secretary never once entered Room 40. The staff of the Operations Division themselves were not always permitted to know the positions of important British ships at sea, so that the master plot in the War Room, like Hamlet without the Prince, showed the North Sea without the Grand Fleet. As strangers ranging from Bishops to charwomen were often about the War Room, the Plot was falsified to deceive them. Naturally it deceived others as well. The War Registry, which handled all signals and telegrams, was believed to be untrustworthy, so signals were made vague and misleading, with the natural result that the recipients were misled. British ships steamed into British minefields because the mining chart was too secret to be issued to them.[7] They would have ordered things better in Ruritania.

The above state of affairs is the more reprehensible since by the end of the war the Naval Intelligence Division under Admiral Sir William 'Blinker' Hall – so called because of his habit of rapidly blinking his eyes while talking – had achieved a brilliant reputation, ahead of all other such organisations in the world. This climaxed in the 'Zimmerman telegram' which brought the United States into the war in 1917 through a disclosure of German inducements to Mexico to declare war on the United States should the United States come in on the allied side.

Hall's talent and courage, now that the facts are known, show up as the more intense since he took over what was virtually a 'non-organisation' and certainly a nice old mess. This had previously been the parish of Admiral Sir Henry Oliver (the worst dressed officer in the Navy and nicknamed 'Dummy' through a reluctance to speak or smile) who worked some fourteen hours a day, rarely took leave and considered himself, perhaps with some justification, as the man dealing single-handed with the conduct of the war. Although Oliver undoubtedly exercised a great influence on naval policy during the First World War, 'what he gained in wisdom, he sacrificed in largely failing to inspire and lead the officers and men he commanded'.[8] In essence Oliver acted as a bureaucrat, even later at sea when he commanded the First Battle Squadron in 1918. Hall, on the other hand, was a man of vision with more than a little of the Nelson touch about him. Unfortunately such men have always been in short supply, a fact especially apparent in the twentieth century.

In the First World War only Beatty, perhaps, had the jaunty self-assurance and panache we associate with Nelson and other great Admirals of the sailing era. Yet even Beatty's handling of the battlecruiser fleet at Jutland was questioned at the time and has been fully and hotly debated ever since. Moreover, when he succeeded Jellicoe as Commander-in-Chief of the Grand Fleet at the end of 1916, he found himself hampered as before, not only by German reluctance to face another big ship encounter, but also by having to devote all possible resources to defeating the U-boat campaign – as a first priority – whilst at the same time trying to remedy some of the major defects which Jutland had revealed in capital ship and shell design. At least Nelson had known where he was with his ships and his guns.

Sir John Jellicoe (1859–1935), the other outstanding Admiral of the First World War, was a very different kind of man from Beatty. Although served by officers and men throughout his career with a devotion accorded to few others, and although earmarked by Fisher as 'admiralissimo when Armageddon comes', his innate caution, his belief that an action should be fought only as a gunnery duel by a rigidly controlled line of battle and his exaggerated fear of mines and torpedo attacks gave him a pessimistic wariness, the opposite of that dogged, aggressive determination to take the war into the enemy's camp which had animated every British sea commander of any calibre from Drake to Nelson.

Jellicoe's tenure of office at the Admiralty as First Sea Lord, which began on 4th December 1916 and ended just over a year later on 10th January 1918, developed even

THE ROYAL MARINES

The Admiral's Regiment was first formed in 1664 and first referred to as the Marines in 1672. The Corps has taken part in more battles worldwide on land and sea than any other single branch of the British armed forces. George IV allowed them to use his own cypher G.IV in perpetuity together with the foul anchor of the Admiralty and the word 'Gibraltar' which fortress they had secured for the British crown in 1704. Their distinguishing badge is a globe surrounded by laurel and their motto *Per Mare Per Terram*. The Royal Marines' role – as demonstrated in the Falklands campaign – is primarily to *assault*. It was in 1802 that the great St Vincent persuaded George III to style them 'Royal' Marines.

In the early years they were constantly and inevitably disbanded in peace and then hurriedly reformed in war. It was not until Anson brought his great influence to bear in 1747, when he was First Lord of the Admiralty, that it was decided that existing regiments and all future ones were to come henceforth under the Admiralty. This was at a time when the army and the navy were paid under different systems and the Marines very often not at all.

Yet their loyalty has never been in question. Their record was unblemished in the Spithead mutiny in 1797 and also in that of Invergordon in 1931. Indeed since that first mutiny the Royal Marines have always acted as Wardroom attendants and been berthed between the officers and the lower deck. During slack times Marines have taken on other shipboard jobs such as Butcher, Barber and Lamptrimmer (extra pay twopence a day). They perform guard and sentry duties and they have for long run the navy's bands. In battleships and cruisers of the big-gun era, Royal Marines would fight a quarter of the ship's armament and until 1923 the Corps was divided into the Royal Marine Artillery and the Royal Marine Light Infantry.

Now, since the Second World War, they act primarily as Commandos. From boarding parties in the second Dutch war in 1664 to the Falklands in 1982 is a long haul but there is almost no incident, event or battle in those three centuries in which the Royal Marines have not been involved. It was only in the Second World War and afterwards at Suez and in the Falklands that their role in purely naval amphibious actions was replaced by the great tri-service operations of today in which, though helicopter and landing craft are of major importance, the trained Royal Marine has proved more valuable than either.

The Alliance of Royal Navy and Royal Marines has always been a small scale Combined Operation of a peculiarly close kind. Here are some of the marines of 42 Commando who took part in the recapture of South Georgia in April, 1982.

less fortunately. Jellicoe was described as a man of many talents but not of those most in need. A compulsive centraliser, obsessively given to the finer points of administration such as the scrutiny of Wine Bills of junior officers on distant stations, he resisted advice unless it agreed with his pre-conceived ideas, saw no point in a staff and set his face firmly against the introduction of a convoy system.

It is small wonder that his critics – and they became more numerous as that grim year of 1917 proceeded – declared Jellicoe to be 'a tired and over-conscientious man in rather poor health who could not delegate business, constantly overworked himself and always saw the black side of things clearly'.[9] The Navy might well ask what it had done to deserve such leadership – or rather the lack of it.

Nevertheless in neither war did this deadness at the top disturb, except superficially, the morale of the sea-going fleet. The Admiralty has always been distrusted, disliked

and denigrated by seagoing naval officers. But contempt is one thing, disloyalty another and there was never any question of that. Of course a 'Jellicoe versus Beatty' controversy over Jutland began, which in a sense has continued ever since. At the time the seagoing fleet simply put up with the situation it found itself in and got on with the job. Busts of both Jellicoe and Beatty were placed in Trafalgar Square after the war, and this reflects the esteem in which 'two distinguished Admirals, upholders of a proud tradition' were held. On that note, *requiescant in pace*.

A more serious argument concerning matériel rather than personalities got under way towards the end of the war. In 1911 shortly after the flying machine became a fact of life, an American aviator, Eugene Ely, had taken off and landed on a platform erected on a cruiser. Those who had eyes to see soon grasped the implications of this. In the early years of the war, spotting aircraft were regularly flown off British warships and in 1917 and 1918, flight decks were installed in H.M.S. "Furious" and H.M.S. "Argus", the latter having an unobstructed deck over her whole length. The aircraft carrier had arrived.

At the same time the Royal Navy had 43 Dreadnoughts in service keeping guard on the German High Seas fleet which had 24. Most would never fire a shot in anger. As a corollary and to make matters worse, the Navy suffered from an acute shortage of destroyers and small escort vessels and on top of all that, the Grand Fleet was forced to cut short its exercises in order to economise on oil fuel. The entry of the United States into the war had solved the escort problem but only *pro tem*. It was like borrowing more money to pay interest on a loan, it enabled the Admiralty to avoid facing this disgraceful lack of foresight and to continue with the comfortable notion that the capital ship would always reign supreme. Fisher certainly thought otherwise and said so with force. But the old warrior was discredited and in any case was soon to die. Beatty, who was later to be First Sea Lord for eight crucial years, whilst aware that aircraft might have a place in future warfare, remained irrevocably committed to the dreadnought as the nub of sea power. It was not so much a question of wishful thinking as a blind refusal to face the facts.

Ironically, however, the dreadnoughts provided the setting and in one sense the mechanism for ending the war. The German High Seas Fleet had, in fact, made one or two abortive sorties after Jutland but any younger German officer or seaman worth his salt had transferred to the U-boats. This left the ships' companies of capital ships frustrated in enforced idleness with the events of the 1917 Russian Revolution very much on their minds. Early in 1918 when it was becoming apparent that Germany no longer had much hope of winning the war, the first murmurings of mutiny began to be heard on the lower decks of German battleships. In the summer of 1917 two mutineers had been executed but this only increased the fire heating up the brew of boredom, left-wing propaganda, poor food and tactless handling – a brew which came to the boil after Hipper succeeded Scheer as Commander-in-Chief in August 1918.

At the end of October 1918 Hipper planned a sortie to cover raids on the mouth of the Thames and the Straits of Dover but this triggered off mutinies in several of the big ships first at Wilhelmshaven and then at Kiel. On 9th November the Kaiser abdicated and a Council of People's Delegates took power. An Armistice between the Allies and Germany was signed two days later and the High Seas Fleet then sailed on its final voyage to surrender to the Royal Navy off the Firth of Forth. The Great War at sea had come to an end.

CHAPTER IX

THE INTER-WAR YEARS

1918-1939

CHRONOLOGICAL COMPENDIUM

General

As it had done after the Napoleonic Wars, so now, after the First World War, the country found great difficulty in settling down to peace. Vast war debts plagued the economy, unemployment reached approximately three-and-a-half million at the height of the Depression and a feeling of resentment and disillusion both internationally with reparations and the League of Nations, and at home with the way the country was being mismanaged by an over privileged élite, turned the electorate towards socialism and in some cases to communism. The first Labour government came into power in 1924 and the second in 1929. Neither lasted long but the writing was on the wall.

When the threat posed by a resurgent Germany under Hitler (and to a lesser extent by Italy under Mussolini) began to be understood, Britain rearmed. But even this was mismanaged and too little was done too late.

Naval

The continuing debate in the disarmament period which followed the Washington treaties of 1922 and 1927 turned on whether the big-gun battleship had been outdated by the flying machine. This question was not to be settled until the Second World War. In the meantime the establishment came down heavily on the side of the battleship. Beatty and his one time Flag Captain, Chatfield, were First Sea Lords from 1919 to 1927 and from 1933 to 1938 respectively and both were battleship men. As a result, when rebuilding did begin, there was a concentration on new capital ships at the expense of flotilla craft and submarines. This was against the opinion, since justified, of younger officers who supported torpedo and air power.

The naval nadir of the interwar years was the Invergordon mutiny in September 1931. This resulted in Britain abandoning the gold standard, but morale was restored when inept handling of sailors' pay by the Admiralty was remedied and from then on communication improved both between Admiralty and fleet and on board ship between officers and men. By the time war broke out again in 1939, pay and living conditions at sea had improved and a marriage allowance for officers was inaugurated with reluctance in 1937.

Throughout the inter-war years, naval strategy continued to be based on the two-power basis, that is that the Royal Navy must always be capable of defeating the fleets of two major powers combined. On paper this concentration on size and numbers could be justified, and it certainly strengthened the battleship faction, but it also led to a dangerous lack of destroyers, escort vessels and submarines when it was recognised that a successful blockade of three weeks could starve the country into surrender. However, the look of the fleet and the importance of showing the flag continued to bemuse public opinion and certainly the Jubilee Review of the fleet in 1935, led by H.M.S. "Hood", the world's largest warship (42,000 tons), was a magnificent and impressive affair. No one could then know that only six years later the "Hood" would be sunk in a matter of minutes with the loss of all but three of her fifteen hundred officers and men.

Treaties, Organisation and Shipbuilding

Washington Naval Conferences and Treaties 1920, 1921, 1922, 1927 and 1934

Geddes Committee on National Expenditure (the 'Geddes axe') 1921

Chiefs of Staff Committee (of the Committee of Imperial Defence) 1923
H.M.S. "Nelson" and H.M.S. "Rodney" only two battleships built in the inter-war years. 33,000 tons, 45,000 H.P. mounting nine 16-inch, twelve 6-inch and six 4·7-inch high-angle guns

H.M.S. "Hermes" 1923 first ship to be built as aircraft carrier from keel up. Other carriers were H.M.S. "Argus", "Eagle" and "Furious"

Men and Events

1919	Seventy-one German warships scuttled at Scapa Flow
1919–21	War between Bolsheviks and White Russians involves Royal Navy in Baltic and Black Sea.
1919	Alcock and Brown fly across the Atlantic in 16 hours 27 minutes
1927	Lindbergh makes first solo flight across Atlantic
1931	First 'pocket battleship' ("Deutschland") launched in Germany
1935	Robert Watson-Watt builds first practical radar equipment for detecting aircraft
1926	General Strike in Britain
1929	Wall Street collapse leads to world slump
1931	Sino-Japanese war begins. Japanese in control of China 1942
1933	Hitler appointed German Chancellor
1936–9	Spanish civil war

World Disposition of Royal Navy in 1939

By the outbreak of war there were two main fleets – the Home and Mediterranean with Battle and Cruiser Squadrons. Other foreign stations (headed by cruiser squadrons) were the East Indies based on Ceylon, the Africa based on Simonstown, South Africa, the China based on Hong Kong with the Commodore, Malaya at Singapore, the America and West Indies (including the Commodore, South America Division) based on Bermuda together with the ships of the Royal Australian, Royal Canadian and New Zealand Navies, based on Australia, Canada and New Zealand.

The twenty inter-war years from 1919 to 1939 show up as a grey, troubled and undistinguished vista in our history. Almost nothing seemed to go right. The nation was exhausted, the fruits of victory shrivelled before even ripening, the first rumblings of the social revolution and of the blind, materialistic age which followed could first be detected in the Police strike of 1919, in the General Strike of 1926, in the Hunger Marches of the early thirties and in the Mutiny at Invergordon in 1931 which brought the country off the Gold Standard.

Unemployment at 323,000 in 1919 reached 2.8 million in 1932 yet the overall standard of living remained much as it had been in the nineteenth century. Right up to the outbreak of the Second World War in 1939 living-in domestic servants were paid about ten shillings a week and were not generally unhappy to have the work, although extremists today might not agree.

But the gathering storm, as Churchill called it, was a dispiriting time to live through. Disillusionment glowered as 'the-war-to-end-all wars' was soon seen to be leading to a far from golden peace. 'Never again' became the universal phrase with which everyone dismissed the holocaust, but the idealism of the League of Nations, of Disarmament and of a land fit for heroes to live in soon melted away. The noble notion of Prohibition in the United States ended by simply propagating organised crime which has never since been completely eradicated and the harsh reparations imposed on Germany by the unrelenting victors generated Hitler and the horrors of National Socialism.

Further east an even more dire slavery was being imposed in Stalin's Russia, whilst at the same time the virus of treachery associated with our top universities began to spawn. All in all the present seemed to be grim with every prospect darkening.

For the Royal Navy the breathing space turned out to be little but a time of decline

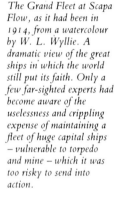

The Grand Fleet at Scapa Flow, as it had been in 1914, from a watercolour by W. L. Wyllie. A dramatic view of the great ships in which the world still put its faith. Only a few far-sighted experts had become aware of the uselessness and crippling expense of maintaining a fleet of huge capital ships – vulnerable to torpedo and mine – which it was too risky to send into action.

and decay. Unwanted, it was soon to be decimated in ships and men and then later hamstrung by disarmament treaties, whilst all the time being forced to maintain its everyday operations under dangerous and dated illusions of grandeur. Without giving it a second thought, the country continued to assume that its brave boys in blue would carry on much as before. And indeed they did. In my own childhood and youth the sun never set on the British Empire, which still comprised the greater part of the globe including Australia, New Zealand, Canada, the Indian sub-continent, the Caribbean islands and vast areas of Africa.

Naturally, therefore, the Royal Navy continued to police the oceans of the world as if nothing had really changed since Trafalgar and woe betide ships of any nationality which failed to dip their flags to the White Ensign on the high seas. Obsolescent though many of its great capital ships undoubtedly were, Britain still kept two major battle fleets in being in the Atlantic and in the Mediterranean, with business-like cruiser squadrons in the East Indies, Africa, China, America and the West Indies, Australia and New Zealand, these last two squadrons being under the control of their respective Naval Boards. Could it be, then, that the decline and decay might be more apparent than real? To this the answer is both yes and no.

Numerically speaking the Royal Navy ended the war with 438,000 men manning 58 capital ships, 103 cruisers, 12 aircraft carriers, 456 destroyers and 122 submarines. Savage cuts in defence expenditure were at once called for and what came to be known as 'the Geddes Axe' was later wielded with an appalling ruthlessness. (This was named after Sir Eric Geddes, a self-made north country railway engineer, who had been First Lord from July 1917 to January 1919 and who chaired a committee on naval expenditure in 1921.)

By 1933 shipbuilding had fallen to 7 per cent of its pre-war figure, with 62 per cent of the workforce unemployed. In three years (1929–32) steel production fell by 45 per cent and pig iron by 53 per cent. The massive slump followed by a worldwide depression hit the Navy in a number of different ways. For instance never in the nineteenth century had the country accepted even the prospect of naval *parity* with another country, let alone the limitation of her fleet by international treaty. The universal cry for disarmament and a belief in the League of Nations changed all that. Most serious of all, with huge dollar debts, exports bedevilled by tariffs and an end to the steady continuous expansion taken for granted by the Victorians, the British economy effectively clattered into something approaching veiled bankruptcy during those hapless interwar years.

In 1933 the country had a visible and invisible balance of payments deficit of £104 million and started to live on capital. We have done so ever since. A severe restructuring and modernisation both of industry and of attitudes had become an urgent necessity. Yet no one moved because no one really knew what to do. In the United States the depression did produce a quasi-dictatorial remedy in Franklin D. Roosevelt's New Deal. Great Britain could find no person of like calibre in her public life. Except for Churchill and a very few others, political leaders in the twenties and thirties remained almost complacently unaware of the depth of the problem, sure in their bones that somehow or other we would muddle through in the end. Potentially the British Empire was still thought to be the richest organisation in the world and this dangerous illusion was fostered even more by the abandonment of Free Trade in 1932 and the institution of Imperial Preference, by which the mother country got her food and her raw materials cheap in return for a guaranteed market for her manufactures. The effect of all this on Britain's potential as a first-class naval power was also disguised and at times misunderstood. It all added up, as Churchill observed, to a period of near terminal exhaustion being described as peace.

The problems the Navy had to face in 1919 were immediate and acute. To begin with, war continued in the Baltic against the Bolsheviks and in the Mediterranean against the Turks. 40,000 men had still not been demobilised by April 1919 and as these were the most experienced and consequently longest-serving, there were mutinies and unrest among the forces in Russia. Their Lordships received no clear directives from the Cabinet except for instant overall cuts in expenditure. There were no matching cuts in the responsibilities the Navy still had to bear.

Even continuity was at stake. Between 1920 and 1923 there were five First Lords, seven Parliamentary Secretaries, six Civil Lords and eighteen Sea Lords. The one rock throughout this period, however, was the First Sea Lord, Admiral of the Fleet Earl Beatty, who stuck at his post from 1st November 1919 to 30th July 1927. However, this long reign itself became a mixed blessing in many ways, especially in so far as Beatty's continued belief in the efficacy of the capital ship above all else was concerned. This and other insistent attitudes made detached observers reserve their judgment.

Beatty came to the Admiralty with as high a reputation as any Admiral in the First World War. Handsome, wealthy and able, in temperament jaunty, in character firm, he was as a result popular. At Jutland Beatty alone had exhibited a trace of the Nelson touch, attempting to engage the enemy more closely, whereas Jellicoe, admittedly bearing far greater responsibilities and for reasons properly accepted as valid, had turned away not caring to risk his fleet.

In December 1916 when the war was not going well for the Allies, the Cabinet had pulled Jellicoe in from sea and appointed him First Sea Lord. He was not a success. During the thirteen months of impending and actual disaster which followed (mainly attributable to the U-boat campaign), Beatty had commanded an almost unused Grand Fleet, becoming the first Admiral of the Fleet to serve at sea since Anson. In that capacity he accepted the surrender of the German High Seas Fleet in November 1918. By then the tired and over-conscientious Jellicoe, resisting all reform, refusing to delegate and even distrusting his own staff, had been replaced by his Deputy, Admiral Sir Rosslyn Wemyss. This event took place in January 1918. The blunt dismissal of Jellicoe, at that time described as the Navy's greatest living officer, subtly increased the dissatisfaction with which officers and men at sea, together with informed opinion on shore, regarded the Admiralty.

By November 1919, a year after the Armistice, when Beatty in turn became First Sea Lord, two political First Lords, Sir Edward Carson and Sir Eric Geddes, had come and gone leaving the job in a chaotic state. However the 'state within the state' which the Admiralty had been dubbed because of its vast administrative power and its zealously maintained independence from other government departments, did happen to enjoy the services of an outstanding Permanent Secretary, Sir Oswyn

Murray. In this the Navy and the country were lucky indeed. A man of lively intelligence, great strength of character and from whom 'it was extremely difficult to find good reasons for differing', Murray in his old-fashioned, high, starched collars set a distinct style of his own. He also assembled teams of civil servants and sailors which were unique in the way they worked together in mutual trust and confidence. Murray himself became the wise and respected friend of successive Boards of Admiralty for nineteen years until his death in July 1936.

The post-war maritime world to which the Navy now had to adapt was conditioned by the Washington Conference of 1921–2. In Great Britain the tone was set by a previous order given in August 1919 to the effect that the Navy must draft its estimates 'on the assumption that the British Empire would not be engaged in any great war during the next ten years'. This came to be known as the Ten Year Rule and enabled naval allocations to be reduced from £356 million in 1918–19 to £52 million in 1923.

In itself this economy was healthy but the implications required a fundamental reassessment of seapower in the post-war era. There were now no modern (post Jutland) capital ships under construction, apart from H.M.S. "Hood", the world's largest battlecruiser at 42,000 tons. This would not have mattered, Their Lordships observed, except that within a few years the Americans would have twelve new capital ships in commission and the Japanese eight. Naval mastery outside European waters had therefore to be abandoned and Great Britain would now be possessed of only the third most powerful fleet in the world.

A token of things to come. H.M.S. "Eagle" which had started as a British built battleship, the "Almirante Cochrane", for the Chilean navy was converted in 1920 into one of the first aircraft carriers. She had a flight deck running the whole length of the ship with her bridge superstructure, mast and funnels on the starboard side. The first ship to be built from the keel up as an aircraft carrier was H.M.S. "Hermes" launched in 1923.

TRINITY HOUSE

Foreigners frequently express surprise that the erection and maintenance of lighthouses, lightships, buoys and other aids to navigation within the waters surrounding the shores of the United Kingdom are not a responsibility of the state but are taken care of by an autonomous body of great age and distinction called Trinity House. However that is how these matters have been arranged since Henry VIII in 1514 set up a guild of shipmen and mariners 'to the praise and honour of the most glorious and individable Trinity'.

The original purpose of Trinity House was to do all things necessary for the 'relief, increase and augmentation of the shipping of this our realm of England'.

Elizabeth I extended the duties of the guild to the erection of sea-marks. As the Queen said, 'by the destroying and taking away of certain steeples, woods and other marks standing upon the main shores . . . being as beacons and marks of ancient time, divers ships have been miscarried, perished and lost in the sea.' Trinity House also became the licensing authority for pilots.

In 1604 the members of Trinity House were divided into Elder and Younger Brethren. The former were made responsible for the discharge of the Corporation's practical duties and they also act as nautical assessors in the Admiralty Division of the High Court. Eleven are elected from the merchant service and two are appointed from the Royal Navy. From time to time, persons of distinction are admitted as honorary Elder Brethren (the present Master is H.R.H. the Duke of Edinburgh and H.R.H. the Prince of Wales is one of the Elder Brethren). Younger Brethren have no responsibility for the practical duties of Trinity House but have a vote in the election of a master and wardens. In Scotland lighthouses are the responsibility of the Commissioners of Northern Lighthouses who owe their origin to an Act of Parliament passed in 1786. The Corporation of Trinity House is the general lighthouse authority for England and Wales, the Channel Islands and Gibraltar. It is also responsible for dealing with wrecks dangerous to navigation except for those occurring within port limits or wrecks of H.M. Ships.

Certain charitable Trusts are also administered by Trinity House for the relief of aged or distressed mariners and their dependants.

Trinity House is not only a foundation of great antiquity associated with many picturesque customs, it is an intensely practical and down-to-earth institution. One of its many functions is to care for buoys. Buoys of various shapes and colours mark the two (differently shown) sides of navigable channels, the resting place of wrecks in shallow water where they might interfere with navigation, the limits of sandbanks or spurs of rock in well-used waters. Some of these buoys contain lights and others bells or sirens for use in fog. All of them must be kept in good order, clearly painted in their correct colours and firmly moored in their correct places (even after storms).

This naturally struck the Navy as alarming and unacceptable. Beatty forthwith demanded the laying down in the two years from 1920 to 1922 of eight large battleships plus two new or converted aircraft carriers at a cost of £84 million and this programme was on the point of acceptance by the government when the United States President, Harding, driven by an economy-minded Congress, invited the world powers to a conference in Washington to discuss naval disarmament and the balance of power in the Far East.

The treaties resulting from this Washington Conference had far-reaching effects. The British Government accepted them with alacrity despite stunned protests from the Admiralty. Yet they made popular sense given the current climate of idealism. All naval building programmes were to be halted. The United States Navy and the Royal Navy were to have parity to the extent of 525,000 tons each of capital ships.

Japan lay next with 315,000 tons, in token of her higher naval status since her defeat of Russia's navy. France and Italy were to be content with 175,000 tons and France certainly thought she had been sold up the creek.

These disarmament provisions, although making sense at the time, and indeed being desirable for economic reasons alone, had disastrous effects on the shipbuilding industry. Apart from the two new 'treaty' battleships "Nelson" and "Rodney", each of 33,000 tons, which had in any case to be redesigned to conform to conference obligations, all work on all battleships stopped until just before the Second World War, this fifteen-year gap having a deleterious effect, to put it mildly, on building techniques, training and morale. Irreplaceable skilled labour left shipyards by the thousand and, as Jackie Fisher had pointed out as long ago as 1902, 'you cannot build ships in a hurry with a Supplementary Estimate'.

Moreover there were one or two dangerous inconsistencies disguised by establishment reliance on the supreme value of the heavy-gun ship. Get the capital ship ratio right, senior naval officers thought, and all else would fall into place, not the least advantage being that a possible arms race between Great Britain, the United States and Japan would be avoided. Moreover the status quo was backed up by a four power treaty (Great Britain, the United States, Japan, France) to respect each other's possessions in the Far East and, with the exception of Singapore and Pearl Harbor, to ban new fortifications in that same area.

On the face of it the 'parsimonious and pacific' electorate was satisfied with this new order of things. We still lived in a world of the capital ship. No one seemed to worry unduly that the submarine was excluded from all limitations (at French insistence) as to building and use. With hindsight this lapse is extraordinary yet no one bothered at the time. Although U-boats had come within sight of winning the war for Germany, submarines lacked the glamour of the battle fleet and were as suspect as the use of steam had been a century before.

Moreover Asdic, an Anglo-French underwater detection device, was thought to reduce the potential of submarines to a far greater extent than was to be proved in the Second World War. For instance Asdics were useless in surface attacks by submarines at night. Generally speaking the great battle of Jutland continued to be refought ad nauseam, whilst little consideration was ever given to the future protection of merchant shipping in another war. The principle of the convoy had at last and reluctantly been accepted, but the provision of suitable escort vessels never received more than a low priority. The battle fleet remained the prime piece of hardware which mattered to the Admiralty, to senior naval officers and generally speaking to the public at large. Battleships still furnished a world of dreams, dreams which were to become nightmares in the Second World War.

Not everyone, however, shared this belief in the battleship as the prime naval weapon at sea. The revolutionary effect of air power now began to be debated. Here again progress was hampered, as steam had been in its taking over from sail, by the innate conservatism of Admirals and Admiralty alike bemused by the majesty of their capital ships. Just as Dr Lardner in the early 1830s had declared a steamship voyage from Liverpool to New York to be 'perfectly chimerical' so did Their Lordships initially and somewhat haughtily reject the Wright Brothers' offer of help by retorting that they saw no possible naval use for aircraft.

A few years later, however, other views prevailed. Murray Sueter, the Inspecting Captain of Airships from 1908 to 1911, was then appointed the first Director of the Air Department in the Admiralty. Largely as a result of Sueter's drive and enthusiasm, backed by the support of the Second Sea Lord, Prince Louis of Battenberg, the Royal Naval Air Service came into being and achieved a proud record in the First World War. Indeed the Fleet Air Arm had so far developed that when amalgamated into the Royal Air Force together with the Royal Flying Corps in April 1918, the joint outfit comprised, by the end of the war, 20,000 aircraft staffed by 290,000 personnel and cost the country a million pounds a day. Even the most bigoted big-ship men were forced to admit that there could now be no turning back.

The first scheduled London to Paris flight in a De Havilland 16 took place on 25th August 1919. In that same year Alcock and Brown flew the Atlantic in 16 hours 27 minutes and Ross Smith flew from London to Australia in 135 hours. These and other pointers to the way things were going came about within nine months of the Armistice. Their significance did not pass unnoticed by the visionaries. These included the outspoken Murray Sueter himself who had been Superintendent of Aircraft Construction and a member of the Joint Air War Committee, Sir Murray Sueter's views on the future dominance of the air, published in his book *Airmen or Noahs?* successfully barred him from promotion to Flag Rank. Instead, he became a Member of Parliament from 1921 to 1945, was knighted in 1934 and died in 1960 at the age of eight-eight. Admiral Sir Percy Scott, one of the most influential big-ship gunnery experts, turned round after the war and launched a vigorous attack on the battleship, claiming that submarines and aircraft had rendered it obsolete; Jackie Fisher, the prime creator of the Dreadnought declared, shortly before his death in 1920, that 'to build battleships so long as cheaper aircraft can destroy them . . . is merely to breed Kilkenny cats unable to catch rats or mice'. Moreover, and to the dismay of hardcore reactionaries, even David Beatty, the First Sea Lord, prophesied in a Mansion House speech in 1923 that 'the fleets of the future will be commanded by officers with as intimate knowledge of the air as of the gun and the submarine . . . it may well be that in the future the Commander-in-Chief of a fleet with his staff may be quartered on board

Even as late as 1929 aircraft carriers were still being reconverted from battleships which had actually served as such in the First World War. Apart from the enormous expense of conversion, H.M.S. "Courageous" and H.M.S. "Glorious" demonstrate the unsuitability of trying to use this new power of the air without thinking through from scratch all its requirements.

an aircraft carrier, during operations his staff officers being in the air, far in advance of the fleet, giving information which will enable him to dispose his forces to obtain strategic and tactical advantages which would culminate in great victory.' At that time his voice was not heeded.

The controversy continued to rage until the outbreak of the Second World War, both sides being forced to admit that only practical experience under war conditions would decide the full effect of air power at sea. In the meantime none of the other great powers abandoned their capital ships. The guns of the Royal Navy, it was pointed out, had defended Britain for four hundred years. No one disputed this but if critics then pointed out that the torpedo and not the gun had been the dominant weapon in the First World War, battleship men quickly countered that to fire a torpedo, you had first to deliver it by air, submarine or fast torpedo boat well within range of the enemy's guns and that the great guns of the battle fleet still had a far longer range than anything else. This, of course, was true. It was also true that these expensive capital ships required increasing armour, built-in anti-torpedo bulges and flotillas of destroyers to screen and to hunt submarines whenever they put to sea. More significant, though less noticed, perhaps, was another indisputable fact – that more and more of the power resources of the capital ship had perforce to be devoted to its own defence. Shades of the brontosaurus! The battleship's vulnerability, when protecting ships were not available, came to be tragically demonstrated in the Second World War.

There is ironic truth in the saying that Britain goes into each war she fights prepared – more or less – to win the last one in which she was engaged. There is also, of course, a natural tendency after every major war to forget the horrors and ghastliness of it all, and to revert to the comfortable ways of peace as soon as possible. Unfortunately in the process a number of lessons get forgotten and have to be expensively relearnt when the next great struggle begins. The sad but outstanding feature of British seapower at the start of the Second World war lay in its irrelevance to the task it had to undertake. We had too many of the wrong ships and not nearly enough of what was essential.

There were several reasons for this, some of them comprehensible, some of them even valid, but all stemmed from the attitudes with which the Admiralty and senior naval officers of pre-First World War vintage attacked the problems which the Ten Year Rule, the various treaty obligations and the rise of Mussolini and Hitler provoked.

However, not everything swirled down the drain when the bath was unplugged. The necessity of a competent naval staff so hotly resisted by Fisher, Jellicoe and even Churchill had now been generally accepted. By the end of the First World War the naval staff numbered 336 officers in twelve divisions, yet the 'intellectual capital to float an efficient staff' remained in short supply and control of naval operations continued to be semi-amateur and quirkish. In the Admiralty women typists had come to stay. This revolution had taken place despite staunch pre-war Admiralty opposition which had declared to the Treasury that 'Their Lordships cannot conceal their decided preference for the boys'. Incidentally, the first 'lady typewriters' had been securely locked away in a guarded room, women being forbidden entry to the

Compass Department in case the steel ribs of their corsets might upset the compasses and 'derange the Navy's navigation'.

By the end of the war Admiralty administrative and operational autonomy, until then a law unto itself, had perforce to be brought under Cabinet control together with the other Service Ministries. This was achieved in 1918 after the Admiralty had seen fit to mount a strategic offensive from France without bothering to inform the War Office or the General Staff. With the peace an era of inter-departmental committee rule began.

In effect the Chief of the Imperial General Staff and the First Sea Lord became Commanders-in-Chief subordinate to the Cabinet Committee of Imperial Defence whose job it was to blend all aspects of national defence into one viable whole. In 1923 the Chiefs of Staff Committee (of the Committee of Imperial Defence) became the principal advisers to the Cabinet and not the Service Ministers as they had been previously.

Meanwhile the Naval Staff, now slimmed down into eight divisions together with over forty distinct Admiralty departments, buckled down bravely to peacetime conditions, contriving to resist and/or come to terms with pernickety Treasury control and not allowing themselves to be drugged into slumber behind 'a deceptive façade of hard work'. Under Beatty and Murray they succeeded with a liveliness, almost a brilliance, for which the Navy and indeed the whole country had cause to be grateful when the Second World War began.

' "The Naval Staff", wrote Murray, "is the Alpha and Omega of the Admiralty alphabet", while "The Child's Guide to the Admiralty" prepared in 1941 for newcomers to the Admiralty, described the Naval Staff as "the dynamo of the naval war machine." For men trained by Fisher, with his belief that a staff was useful, if at all, only to ameliorate the effects of a fool as First Sea Lord, this was a rapid reversal of opinion.'[1]

In addition to aviation, there was another area affecting the Navy in which revolutionary advances were made in the 1920s and 30s. This was communication, a word to be taken – in this context – in its widest sense. Until 'the wireless' was invented, communication between Admiralty and the fleet and between individual ships in the fleet depended upon the handwritten word, flag signalling, the searchlight or signalling lamp and the semaphore. On board ship orders were 'piped', that is conveyed by voice after attention had been called by a bugle or bos'n's pipe or whistle to what was to follow, different cadences on the bos'n's pipe being used to identify particular orders.

The electric telegraph, and the code devised by its inventor Samuel Morse, was first used in Washington D.C. in 1844 and thereafter internationally. In 1895 Marconi invented Wireless Telegraphy (W/T) using the Morse Code to communicate through 'the ether' and in 1901 he succeeded in beaming a message across the Atlantic from Cornwall to Newfoundland. The effects were profound. W/T went into general fleet use in 1904, prior to the battle of Tsushima, and had a great bearing on the outcome of the First World War, in particular Jutland. Then in 1920 broadcasting began. In February of that year Marconi opened the first public broadcasting station in Britain at Writtle and in November the Westinghouse Company inaugurated the first similar station in the United States at East Pittsburgh in order to disseminate the Presidential election results.

By the early 1930s reproduction and amplification of the voice by microphone, loudspeaker and radiotelephone were facts of life. Tannoy systems were being installed in H.M. ships so that for the first time it became possible for the Captain of even the largest battlecruiser to be in instant communication with his whole ship's company of perhaps 1500 men. This, too, had a revolutionary effect which was entirely beneficial.

I remember some years ago asking an Admiral with whom I served in the Second World War and who later became Director of Naval Intelligence what in his opinion were the main differences in life at sea in the two world wars. He replied at once 'Communications' and then amplified it by saying that in the 1914–18 war 'no one knew a thing'. Secrecy existed for secrecy's sake. Even in action only those on the bridge or on deck were aware of what was happening and sometimes then only the Captain and his immediate staff would be in the know. The stoker in the boiler room, the Surgeon Commander in his sick bay or the cook in his galley might just as well have been deaf, dumb and blind for all the information they were given. Sailors asked no questions and simply did as they were told.

In my early days at sea I actually heard a sailor who was being questioned as to why he had done something say: 'Sir, I thought it the best thing to do at the time.' 'You thought?' said the officer, 'You're an Able Seaman, you're not paid to think.' Things had changed dramatically by the time the Second World War broke out and the mutiny at Invergordon in 1931 helped to speed up the process, since the mutiny itself came about as the direct result of faulty communication.

In the Second World War Commanding Officers brought their ships' companies into their confidence, without revealing essential secret orders, at the very earliest opportunity they could. Incredible as it may seem today, it took a world war and a mutiny for the Admiralty and senior naval officers to appreciate that the more a ship's company knows of the reason for any course of action, the more is morale improved. Almost any endurance or bravery is possible once people are told the truth. But this was a lesson which rigidly trained officers of the first three decades of the century had particular difficulty in learning. Could the lower deck be trusted with the truth? Such doubts were caused, perhaps, by a fear of losing authority. No one could be certain where risky ideas might take them, much as those in authority objected to the Penny Post in 1840 because the 'lower classes' might start writing letters.

The Invergordon mutiny, the first time the Royal Navy had struck since 1797, exemplifies the above. It occurred in September 1931 at Cromarty Firth on the north-east coast of Scotland when seamen of certain Atlantic Fleet battleships refused to take their ships to sea. The reason for this was inept handling by the Admiralty of a delicate matter at a sensitive time, neither the delicacy nor the sensitivity being apparent to Their Lordships until it was all too late and irreparable damage had been done.

The National Government under Ramsay Macdonald, which had been elected in the pit of the world depression, had decided that the Navy (and not for some reason the Army or the Air Force) should take a ten per cent cut in pay. This, of course, struck hardest at the most poorly paid seamen, whose wives could in any case scarcely make ends meet. Politically the Admiralty at that time was headed by an inexperienced First Lord, Sir Austen Chamberlain, complemented by a weak and sickly First Sea Lord, Sir Frederick Field. The Permanent Secretary, Sir Oswyn Murray, who alone could have brought sense into the matter, happened to be on leave.

This combination of events allowed the ten per cent cut to be announced without any warning. It was also to take immediate effect, the first that anyone in the fleet knew about it being an order pinned up on ships' notice boards. There was already a slow-burning feeling in the fleet that the Admiralty was 'a thing apart from the sailor, a body that wore top hats and was their permanent enemy'. This sudden cut turned up the flame. 'Many decent men', the First Lord was later to admit, 'were driven to distraction by anxiety about their homes and were swept off their feet by this anxiety.' It required but a handful of agitators (one of whom later took refuge in Moscow for life) on board ship or in the canteen ashore to stimulate this discontent and resentment to the point of a mass, dumb refusal to weigh anchor when the fleet was next ordered to sea. The repercussions were staggering. A few days later the Admiralty withdrew the offensive order and the mutiny subsided. However, enormous damage had been done to the national image. In less than a week Britain abandoned the Gold Standard, the pound sterling falling in value from $4.86 to $3.49.

But there were benefits as well as disasters deriving from the Invergordon mutiny. If the lower deck did not exactly come into its own overnight, the relationship between officers and men took a great and common-sense turn for the better. The mutiny had really been against the workings of a quasi-mechanical and distant bureaucracy rather than against officers on the spot. In the fifty years since Invergordon our self-perpetuating bureaucracy has, of course, grown infinitely worse, so that today, whether in Whitehall, local government or the unions, its sludge is the worst blot on the nation's escutcheon. In the seagoing Royal Navy, however, the working interdependence of officer and rating has steadily improved, rigid class distinctions have to a great extent disappeared and the entire personnel of the Navy today feels itself a cohesive but in no way self-important élite.

This amour-propre had exhibited itself during crises in the past and in spite of appalling conditions (notably in the Seven Years War 1756–63 and in Nelson's fleet). Its present strength can be traced back in this century to the increased care and attention given by Divisional Officers to their men, to better communications and mutual understanding which resulted from a self-help process after the Invergordon mutiny. So far as the Navy was concerned, whilst respect for rank in no way diminished, there did come about a great lessening of the divine right of class and of the arrogance which had previously gone with it. Instead, officers and ship's companies of 'happy ships' (and these were, perhaps surprisingly, in a large majority in the Navy of the 1930s) seemed to draw together in self-respecting comradeship. This may have been in unconscious anticipation of the second armageddon which was to blight us all from 1939 to 1945.

The sombre thirties are as depressing in retrospect as they were to live through at

Nazi Germany's observance of the checks and limits imposed by Treaty on naval rearmament was perfunctory at best and non-existent at worst. Once the decision to rearm had been taken, the only problem from the German point of view was that of playing for time. The building of the 'pocket-battleships' was declared officially to be within the limits imposed (the photograph shows the "Admiral Scheer"). An 'accidental' transposition of figures put the super-spectacular battleship "Bismarck's" tonnage as 35,000, when in fact it was 53,000. She was thus the largest warship then building in the world.

the time. Despair seemed to stalk the entire world and although in Britain people still believed what they read in the papers or heard over the wireless, they increasingly distrusted the country's leadership which they took to be incompetent if not actually dishonest. The 'powers that be', the establishment, the ruling classes – indeed even the monarchy until after the Abdication – were suspect. The socialist tide which was to engulf the country after the 1945 election rose all through the thirties but its power remained diffuse and as yet only partially channelled. Political facts such as the above need to be considered together with events and movements elsewhere in the world if the state of the Navy at the start of the Second World War is to be properly understood. We got the equations, the priorities and the psychology wrong because no one, except for Churchill and his clique, could peer far enough through the fog or had the ability to rise above it in order to regain some sort of vision.

The phenomenon of the fascist dictators, Mussolini, Franco and Hitler on the one hand and the corruption and unreliability of France on the other were patently obvious at the time to all who travelled or even read the papers. Yet we stubbornly continued to believe in the Maginot line and the dependability of Hitler's word. This despite the fact that, as Prime Minister Baldwin said in 1935, 'our frontier had moved from Dover to the Rhine'. We dithered and delayed because frankly it was inconvenient to do anything else.

Even as late as 1936, when we began seriously to rearm, doubt, uncertainty and a

Above: The Battle of Navarino in the Greek War of Independence, 1827, by Thomas Luny.

Right: Shipboard life in the nineteenth century, by T. Sutherland.

Right: Queen Victoria's Diamond Jubilee Review, 1897, by Charles Dixon.

Below: The Battle of Jutland, 1916, by R. Smith.

Withdrawal from Dunkirk, 1940, by C. Cundall.

The Sea Harrier, victor in the Falklands, 1982.

'…a security for such as pass on the seas upon their lawful occasions.'

kind of creeping indolence beset us. 'A democracy is always two years behind a dictator,' Stanley Baldwin said complacently as if this excused the sloth of his government. Indeed eighteen months after Neville Chamberlain had succeeded Baldwin as Prime Minister and had returned from his meeting with Hitler waving a piece of paper which, he claimed, represented peace in our time, a fair proportion of the electorate still refused to consider the facts or face the fearful consequences which then lay a mere twelve months ahead. How did this come about and how did it affect the Royal Navy?

'The age of Locarno' (from the Treaty signed in 1925), the Ten Year Rule, the shipbuilding restrictions of the Washington Conference of 1922, lip service to the League of Nations and a decade of endeavour by British politicians to isolate the country from political or military commitments to the continent all came to an abrupt end in September 1931 (co-incidentally with Invergordon) when Japan began her conquest of Manchuria, reducing it within two years to a puppet state. A month later Hitler secured German industrial backing for his Nazi party. The writing was on the wall. A month after that Franklin D. Roosevelt became President of the United States in a landslide victory over Herbert Hoover of 472 electoral votes to 59.

No equivalent stimulus to awakening and change occurred in the United Kingdom and British Empire. In that same year construction of the naval base at Singapore had been halted, British power in the Far East was seen to be neutered by the Washington Conference and, thanks to the economy drives of the 1920s, the Admiralty reported in April that 'in certain circumstances our naval strength is definitely below that required to keep our sea communications open in the event of our being drawn into war'. We possessed only 120 destroyers, well below the number necessary for escort and anti-submarine duties and our 50 cruisers would have been completely inadequate to protect imperial trade routes. It was small wonder that British reaction to Japan's aggression consisted of a weak diplomatic protest and that the whole world shivered for a while after Britain's abandonment of the Gold Standard with all the financial insecurity which that implied.

Two years later, with Hitler firmly in power, reassessment began. Sir Austen Chamberlain had resigned as First Lord after Invergordon and Sir Bolton Eyres-Monsell, who replaced him, though not perhaps a politician of the first rank nevertheless exhibited skill, tact, patience and loyalty, to which was added first-hand knowledge of the Navy since he had once been a naval officer himself. Indeed Eyres-Monsell was the first naval officer to be appointed First Lord of the Admiralty since the Duke of Northumberland in 1852. To complement his arrival at the seat of power Admiral Sir Ernle Chatfield (later to be Lord Chatfield) became First Sea Lord, a man of quiet distinction who soon made it clear that he had the finest mind and the strongest character of any First Sea Lord since Beatty. With the pulling out of retirement of the lantern-jawed Admiral Joe Kelly and his appointment as Commander-in-Chief to revitalise the Home Fleet after Invergordon, a new spirit began to be felt in the Navy at home and abroad. The country might be in terrible shape: the Navy had begun to pick itself up.

The Cabinet abandoned the Ten Year Rule in 1932 but, nudged by the Treasury, gave out that 'this must not be taken to justify an expanding expenditure by the

RADAR AND SONAR

Radar, an abbreviation of 'Radio Direction and Range' is a method of detecting objects by sending out pulses of radio waves. When these waves strike anything they are reflected back and the time taken for these echoes to return is measured. Since the speed of radio waves is known, this time can be automatically translated into distance.

Although radio detection is almost as old as radio itself, the first experiments being made by Hulsmeyer of Dusseldorf in 1903, it was not until the 1930–40 decade that serious development work began in Britain, Germany and France. The breakthrough for shipborne radar came in 1940 with the British invention of the magnotron which produced very short wavelengths and was used to detect U-boat periscopes during the Second World War. With the invention of the semiconductor and later the microchip, signal processing of all kinds has become extremely sophisticated with a language of its own and able to code and decode information for high integrity communication. The effectiveness of modern defence systems relies increasingly on the subtlety, complexity and above all on the extremely high speed of signal processing and modern shipborne and airborne radar is at the heart of these systems. Depending upon the height of its aerials, the range that a modern vessel can 'see' is seldom less than twenty-five miles and from an aircraft this ability can be extended to hundreds of square miles.

Sonar, formerly Asdic (Anti-Submarine Detection Investigation Committee, set up in 1918) is the apparatus used to detect submerged submarines, and was originally a French invention. Today sonar comprises a transducer and a receiver attached to the hull of a ship or lowered to the required depth from a ship or helicopter. The transducer, using the vibrating properties of quartz, emits pulses of high frequency sound which pass unimpeded through water but reflect from any solid object encountered. As in radar the accurate measurement of the time between the emission of a pulse and the arrival of the returning echo gives the range of the object. By using a narrow sweeping beam pulse, bearings can also be obtained and when trained on a moving submarine, the Doppler effect or change of note will indicate the direction of the movement.

A British development of sonar for mine detection is now in use and the system is also used by the fishing industry to locate shoals of fish and also in marine archaeology as in the 1982 recovery of the "Mary Rose".

The weapon control and target designation consoles forming part of a Modular Combat System. In these days of missiles, supersonic aircraft and nuclear submarines, speedy and adequate detection is vital if effective countermeasures are to be taken in time.

Defence Services without regard to the very serious financial and economic situation which still obtains'. This evasive point of view was endorsed by the Liberal and Labour parties, both of whom fiercely opposed rearmament, preferring to rely upon the collective security system of the League of Nations, though how this was supposed to work without armaments was never clear.

Nor did the Labour and Liberal parties care to be reminded of the complete ineffectiveness of the League of Nations over the Japanese invasion of Manchuria. In some magic way an ideal world would establish itself if only people kept still and did not annoy the aggressors, just as there are people today, incredible as it may seem after the experience of Hungary, Czechoslovakia and Afghanistan, who sincerely continue to believe that if we abandon the nuclear deterrent and reduce our conventional armaments the Russians will follow suit rather than take advantage

of the West whenever it happens to suit them. So was it in the thirties with Hitler and Mussolini. Treat them properly, the appeasers said, and they will surely behave themselves with us. Had not Hitler brought a new self-respect back to Germany and did not Mussolini make the Italian trains run on time?

Fate, however, decreed otherwise. Hitler and Mussolini first met each other in Venice in June 1934 but were unable to agree owing to differences over control of the Danube valley. However their interests clearly complemented each other north and south of the Alps and in November 1936, with Roosevelt overwhelmingly re-elected for a second term and the news about King Edward VIII and Mrs Simpson becoming public, the two Dictators announced the Rome-Berlin axis. From then on hostilities became virtually certain. By that time Mussolini had already brought Europe to the brink of war in October 1935 with his invasion of Abyssinia, and Franco had opened

H.M.S. "Nelson", flagship of the Home Fleet, leads other battleships on manoeuvres in 1936. Between the wars Great Britain built only two battleships, H.M.S. "Nelson" and H.M.S. "Rodney", both shortened 'by Treaty', so that all main armament (nine 16-in guns in three turrets) had to be forward of the bridge. Both ships were difficult to steer at slow speed and H.M.S. "Nelson" went aground three times during the commission in which I served in her.

up the Spanish Civil War in July 1936, a contest used by Germany, Italy and Russia as a testing ground for their armaments. Hitler annexed Austria in 1938, dismembered Czechoslovakia in the spring of 1939 and then entered into a pact of friendship and non-aggression with Soviet Russia. A mere three months of tawdry peace remained.

Eyres-Monsell and Chatfield had continued in office until 1936 and 1938 respectively and were able to give the Admiralty and the seagoing fleet most of the firm leadership required. The Admiralty War Registry was expanded in 1934 and reorganised in 1937. A register of scientists whose services could be called upon was established and the whole Wireless Telegraphy network brought up to date.

Perhaps the most significant organisational improvement in the Admiralty, however, was the setting up in 1937 of the Operational Intelligence Centre by Admiral Sir William James, at that time Deputy Chief of Naval Staff and a former member of the famous Room 40 in the First World War, then so restricted and under-used. The O.I.C. took over the former War Room, its chief feature becoming a huge well-lit plotting table on to which all intelligence and information was fed

and upon which all operational orders would be based. At last the higher direction of the Navy had a unified central grip on the war at sea, a control it had not acquired – and then only in part – until 1918.

The Permanent Secretary, Sir Oswyn Murray, who had seen the Navy through so much stress and strain, died in 1936. He was replaced by Sir Archibald Carter from the India Office, who was neither liked nor admired. Then when Lord Chatfield departed in November 1938, the rot set in. The new First Sea Lord, Sir Roger Backhouse, late Commander-in-Chief of the Home Fleet, was a compulsive centraliser whom the staff found almost impossible to serve and whose health broke down in under a year. Another 'workaholic' centraliser, Admiral of the Fleet Sir Dudley Pound, then took his place. Some observers saw Pound as embodying in himself most of the faults which had proved so disastrous in the previous war. Lacking in humour, set in his ways and afflicted by several serious illnesses, including a tumour on the brain which affected his concentration, Pound believed in bullying or driving people rather than in leading, lacked the character to stand up to Churchill when the latter came back as First Lord on the outbreak of war, never allowed his Commanders-in-Chief to get on with the job unhampered and finally seemed often reluctant to defend his subordinates against outside attacks.

Other observers were more kindly in their assessment of the elderly Admiral who had only been in office three months when war broke out and who had never had 'small-ship' experience during the whole of his naval career. John Colville, for instance, one of Churchill's secretaries at the time, judged him to be 'a naval officer of the highest worth: courageous, matter of fact in thought and word and gifted with a fine precision of mind . . . a wholesome check on impetuosity.'[2] Hindsight depends so often on a subjective attitude of criticism or support but however much you credit Pound with success in 'impressing on Churchill the principle that the First Sea Lord was the final arbiter in technical and professional matters'[3] there seems to be little doubt that Churchill, in fact, did much as he pleased during the first nine months of the war. This may or may not have been a good thing. At all events it was with Churchill and Pound at the helm that Their Lordships went into the Second World War and whilst the Admiralty was undoubtedly an efficient, well-geared administrative machine, its operational control left those in the know dismayed by its weakness and lack of panache.

What about the fleet itself? With what effective naval strength did the British Empire enter the Second World War? And what German and Italian forces did it face? In 1933 when Hitler came to power, the Germans at once began rebuilding their navy. Britain, still treaty-bound, retorted by modernising old ships but did not lay down new ones until 1936/7 when war already seemed to be inevitable, so that in one sense the 'go-ahead' already came too late.

However in those two years the Admiralty ordered 5 new battleships, 3 aircraft carriers, 12 cruisers, 25 destroyers, 11 submarines and, incredible as it may seem, a mere 9 escort vessels, 20 of which could have been built for the cost of one battleship. Income tax was raised from 4/6d in the pound in 1934 to 7/6d in 1939 and the strain on British shipyards and industry became such that Czech and other foreign steel had to be bought. This in turn further worsened our balance of payments deficit,

Destroyers like these were the navy's maids-of-all-work well into the Second World War. Lack of them and American willingness to help, led to the famous 'lease-lend' agreement and the use of fifty over-age but valuable American destroyers.

though it was inevitable since in 1939 German steel production exceeded that of Great Britain and France combined by over a quarter. Apart from the fifteen-year gap in shipbuilding, with German inventiveness and techniques already in the lead, a much more significant fact was that Germany had already been building a large fleet of submarines. Indeed, although in September 1939 both the British Empire and Germany entered the war each with 58 operational submarines, by the end of 1940, whereas British yards had completed another 12 boats, Germany had leapt ahead with a further 58 finished after the outbreak of war.

Only by tallying surface ships on the old-fashioned 'Blue water' school basis could it be made to appear that the Royal Navy had an adequate superiority. The British Empire entered the war with 12 battleships, 3 battlecruisers, 7 aircraft carriers, 64 cruisers, 184 destroyers and 38 sloops. Against them the Germans had 2 battlecruisers, 3 pocket battleships, 6 cruisers and 17 destroyers. The Italians had 6 battleships, 19 cruisers, 61 destroyers and 105 submarines. Until the fall of France in June 1940, it was considered that the French fleet more or less balanced the Italian with 5 battleships and battlecruisers, 1 carrier, 15 cruisers, 75 destroyers and 59 submarines, but doubts about this caused the Admiralty to base a considerable part of the British battle fleet at Alexandria where it could also keep an eye on the Suez Canal.

None of the above, however, took into consideration the greatest naval threat of all. This was Japan with her 10 battleships, 10 aircraft carriers, 36 cruisers, 113 destroyers and 63 submarines plus the huge Yamato class battleships already on the stocks. To see this in perspective, the entire Royal Navy would have had its hands overfull taking on the Japanese alone.

An interwar picture of units of the Mediterranean Fleet in Grand Harbour, Valletta, Malta. Halfway between Gibraltar and Suez, Malta occupied the key position in control of the Mediterranean. This control was only lost when the Luftwaffe installed itself in Sicily and the intensive siege of the 'George Cross Island' began. Until this happened, Malta with its magnificent harbour and full-facility dockyard was considered to be virtually impregnable.

The real calamity lay in finance. By the summer of 1939 it was clear that Britain must prepare herself for another long war. This time there could be no illusions about a victory by Christmas as there had been in 1914 and 'if we were under the impression that we were as well able as in 1914 to conduct a long war, we were burying our heads in the sand' the Treasury observed to the Cabinet. It was a grim prospect for a proud nation once called 'the workshop of the world'. Yet there was no option, however soon financial collapse might come. The twilight war, as Churchill dubbed it, began after the second and final ultimatum to Germany over her invasion of Poland expired without reply on 3rd September 1939.

CHAPTER X

THE SECOND WORLD WAR

TO PEARL HARBOR

1939–1941

CHRONOLOGICAL COMPENDIUM

General

The events of the first part of the Second World War, i.e. until the Japanese attack on Pearl Harbor and the entry of the United States into the war, can be summarised as follows. The first six months, from September 1939 to the beginning of April 1940, referred to at the time as the 'Phoney War', was a period when little of note happened on land and the French and British armies considered themselves secure behind the great forts of the Maginot line. Neville Chamberlain was Prime Minister and Winston Churchill was back at the Admiralty as First Lord. The war had begun when Germany invaded Poland on 1st September 1939 and annexed Danzig. On 3rd September France and Britain declared war on Germany. By the end of September when Germany had conquered Poland and settled its partition with the U.S.S.R., the French army had some seventy-six divisions facing the German threat to which were added the token British Expeditionary Force of four divisions (some 158,000 men). Belgian and Dutch neutrality had so far been respected and the peace-feelers which Hitler had made early in October had been summarily rejected by both Britain and France.

Then on the 9th April 1940 Germany invaded Norway and Denmark. The blitzkrieg had begun. It was an astonishing success. On 10th May Germany invaded Holland, Luxembourg and Belgium and in Britain Churchill replaced Chamberlain as Prime Minister. By the end of the month Holland, Belgium and Luxembourg had all capitulated and the evacuation of British forces from Dunkirk had begun (29th May to 3rd June). On 14th June the Germans entered Paris and on the 22nd France concluded an armistice with Germany. Great Britain now stood alone against Nazi Germany and Fascist Italy which had declared war (after the fall of France) on the German side.

As summer lengthened into autumn, the invasion of southern England became more and more probable, the air blitz on London began and it was not until the 'Battle of Britain' had been won by the R.A.F. on 17th September that invasion of the island was postponed, and finally called off until the following spring, on 12th October.

Meanwhile the 'Battle of the Atlantic' between German U-boats and supply convoys from the United States had begun. In November Franklin D. Roosevelt, the American President, was re-elected for a third term and in December the Eighth Army in Egypt opened the Desert War against the Italians, driving them back across the Libyan border.

During the first half of 1941 the situation worsened for Britain. Merchant ship losses in the Atlantic mounted and control of the Mediterranean began to be lost. German Panzer divisions under Rommel entered the North African war and the Eighth Army was driven back to the frontiers of Egypt. Greece and Crete were evacuated and Luftwaffe raids on London had recommenced. Malta came under siege and for all practical purposes the Mediterranean was closed to through traffic, supplies for the British forces in the middle east having to be sent round the Cape of Good Hope.

Then on 22nd June 1941 Germany invaded Russia and a new phase of the war began. On 12th August Churchill and Roosevelt met in the western Atlantic to sign the Atlantic Charter and on the following day an Anglo-Soviet trade agreement was also signed. By 16th October the German army was only sixty miles from Moscow; Kharkov and Odessa were in German hands but the German offensive against Russia had already begun to fail.

In December Britain declared war against Finland, Hungary and Roumania on their refusing to withdraw from the war against the U.S.S.R. and on the 5th December the British Foreign Secretary (Anthony Eden) visited Moscow.

This first period of the war ended with the Japanese attack on Pearl Harbor, Hawaii and British Malaya on 7th December and the declaration of war by the United States on Japan on the 8th December and on Germany and Italy on the 10th December. Terrible disasters still lay ahead, but from then on the tide had begun to turn.

Naval

1939

3 September	Winston Churchill returns as First Lord of the Admiralty. U-boat sinks "Athenia"
19 September	H.M.S. "Courageous" sunk
14 October	H.M.S. "Royal Oak" sunk in Scapa Flow
18 November	Magnetic mines, laid by U-boats, sink 60,000 tons of shipping on English east coast in one week.
13 December	Battle of River Plate – "Graf Spee" v H.M.S. "Exeter", "Ajax" and "Achilles". Ends 17 December with scuttling of "Graf Spee".

1940

16 February	H.M.S. "Cossack" rescues British prisoners from German supply ship "Altmark" in Norwegian waters
14 April	British naval forces land in Norway: fail to take Trondheim (lack of air power)
3 May	Royal Navy evacuates Namsos
26 May–3 June	Dunkirk evacuation
3–5 July	Force H (Admiral Somerville) destroys French Atlantic Fleet at Mers-el-Kebir (Oran)
3 September	Britain-US Lend-Lease agreement by which fifty destroyers traded to Britain in return for bases in Newfoundland and Caribbean
22 October	Intensification of U-boat warfare
26 October	"Empress of Britain" with P.O.W.s for Canada sunk
3 November	British forces occupy Suda Bay, Crete
4 November	H.M.S. "Jervis Bay" sunk
11 November	Taranto. Aircraft from H.M.S. "Illustrious" and "Eagle" torpedo and sink new battleship "Littorio" and two older ones "Conte di Cavour" and "Caio Duilio" for loss of two aircraft
20 November	Anglo-U.S. agreement for partial standardisation of weapons and pooling of technical knowledge

1941

10 January	H.M.S. "Southampton" and "Illustrious" crippled by German bombers on convoy to Greece
4 March	Royal Navy raids Lofoten Islands
28 March	Cape Matapan. Italian battleship "Vittorio Veneto" damaged and three cruisers "Pola", "Fiume" and "Zara" plus two destroyers sunk
6 April	Royal Navy lands 60,000 men in Greece
22 April–5 May	Greece evacuated
20 May	Germans invade Crete
24 May	H.M.S. "Hood" sunk by "Bismarck"
27 May	"Bismarck" sunk: "Prinz Eugen" escapes
29 May	Royal Navy evacuates Candia, Crete
12 August	Roosevelt and Churchill sign Atlantic Charter on board H.M.S. "Prince of Wales"
12 November	H.M.S. "Ark Royal" sunk near Gibraltar
25 November	H.M.S. "Barham" sunk in Mediterranean
10 December	H.M.S. "Prince of Wales" and "Repulse" sunk by Japanese aircraft in Far East
25 December	Hong Kong surrenders to Japanese

People

Sir Dudley Pound
1877–1943

Admiral of the Fleet and First Sea Lord at outbreak of Second World War. Commanding Officer H.M.S. "Colossus" at Jutland, Battle Cruiser Squadron, Atlantic Fleet, 1929–31, Second Sea Lord 1932–5, C. in C. Mediterranean 1936–9.

Andrew Cunningham
1883–1963

Admiral of the Fleet and First Viscount Cunningham of Hyndhope (known as A.B.C.). Flag Captain to Admiral Cowan on America and West Indies Station 1926–8, Captain H.M.S. "Rodney", C. in C. Mediterranean 1939–42. 1942 Washington as Head of British Admiralty Delegation. November 1942 C. in C. Mediterranean for North African landings. 1943 Accepted surrender of Italian fleet. On death of Admiral Pound in 1943 became First Sea Lord.

Sir Charles Forbes
1881–1960

Admiral of the Fleet. C. in C. Home Fleet on outbreak of war till October 1940. C. in C. Plymouth 1941–3.

John Tovey
1885–1971

Admiral of the Fleet and First Baron Tovey of Langton Matravers. Second-in-command, Mediterranean Fleet on outbreak of war. Relieved Forbes as C. in C. Home Fleet October 1940–3, C. in C. the Nore 1943–6.

Sir James Somerville
1882–1949

Admiral of the Fleet, C. in C. East Indies 1938 but invalided with pulmonary tuberculosis. Volunteered to help Dunkirk evacuation and returned on last ship from Calais, later taking control of operation to give Admiral Sir Bertram Ramsay a chance of occasional rest. June 1940 officially recalled to active service in command of Force H and first task was the agonizing one of bombarding the French fleet at Mers-el-Kebir. Commander Force H when "Bismarck" was sunk. 1942 given task of asembling fleet in Indian ocean and in 1944 delivered successful air strikes on Sumatra and Java. 1944–5 Head of British Admiralty Mission, Washington.

Bruce Fraser
1888–1980

Admiral of the Fleet, First Baron Fraser of North Cape. Third Sea Lord and Controller 1939, C. in C. Home fleet 1943, relieved Somerville in command of Eastern Fleet 1944 and served with the C. in C. U.S. Admiral Nimitz, C. in C. Portsmouth 1947–8, First Sea Lord 1948–51.

Sir Henry Harwood
1888–1959

Admiral, Commodore, South America Station on outbreak of war and commanded the cruiser squadron at the battle of the River Plate. After service as assistant chief of the naval staff, relieved Cunningham as C. in C. Mediterranean 1942 but had to relinquish the appointment due to ill health. Then commanded the Orkneys and Shetlands station being invalided in October 1945.

Sir Max Horton
1883–1951

Admiral, in command of the Reserve Fleet when the Second World War broke out. After a few months in command of the Northern Patrol became Vice Admiral Submarines for three years. In 1942 took over from Admiral Sir Percy Noble as C. in C. Western Approaches at the most critical phase of the Battle of the Atlantic. At the end of the war took the surrender of a group of German U-boats at Londonderry.

Sir William James
1881–1973

Admiral. As a small boy was the model for the well-known painting "Bubbles" by his grandfather, Sir John Millais. C. in C. Portsmouth 1939–42, subsequently Chief of Naval Information and from 1943–5 represented North Portsmouth in Parliament.

Technical advances

Degaussing

A method of reversing the magnetic field of a ship by passing a current through an electric cable encircling the hull. This prevented magnetic mines from being activated.

Radar

(an abbreviation of Radio Direction and Range) grew out of Radio Direction Finding. Originally suggested by Marconi, serious work on the problem only began in the decade 1930–40. In 1940 the British invention of the Magnetron allowed very short wavelengths of under ten centimetres to be produced. First gunnery use of radar was during the night of 26–27 May 1941 by the German battleship "Bismarck" against British destroyer attacks. By 1943 1·9 centimetre wavelength sets could detect the periscopes of U-boats.

In the First World War it was the British Army which bore the brunt of the slaughter, suffering the most grievous casualties in its entire history. In the second great struggle it was the turn of the Royal Air Force and the Royal Navy. That ordeal and the resulting changes have made the Navy of today as different from that of the mid-century as the Second World War Navy was from that of Trafalgar. Where do these differences lie and how did they come about?

First of all seapower for which the Navy exists. As in the First World War the Navy's principal task continued to be the keeping open of global sea routes, the breaking of any blockade of the British Isles and the denial to the enemy of essential war materials. Circumstances differed, the means employed varied but the prime task remained the same. In the Second World War the scale simply widened. More was at stake. The determining watershed, however, remained the same in both wars and that was the entry of the United States into the contest. Without the United States both wars, in all likelihood, would have been lost.

Moreover, although victory was achieved in both wars, the price which the British had to pay crippled the nation in the first war and bankrupted her in the second, in addition to which the British Empire was effectively destroyed. No one cared to think about this at the time. It was enough to have won the war, to have annihilated one dictatorship and to start the rebuilding process before confronting another. Forty years on and we are still none too eager to face up to the facts. For the country in general, therefore, and for the Navy in particular, the Second World War stands as the ultimate trial.

In both wars the Navy went in convinced that we were bound to win. It could only be a matter of time. There might be one or two setbacks and shocks on the way – in the event both were appalling – but the outcome could never really be in doubt. Even after the fall of France in June 1940, when invasion was very much in the air and it was conceivable that the war might have to be continued from Canada, the British sailor, regular or volunteer, never gave a moment's thought to the possibility of defeat. And it may be that this ancient island-certainty-in-the-blood was, when all is said and done, the main psychological weapon which won us the war.

Certainly the seagoing Navy took a poor view of the popular label pinned on the first winter of the war as 'phoney'. There was nothing phoney about the battle of the River Plate. Politicians at home might be – and were – complacently optimistic, 'What we ought to do is just to throw back the peace offers and continue the blockade', Chamberlain, the Prime Minister, noted, 'I do not believe holocausts are required: the Allies are bound to win in the end.' Idiotic propaganda songs such as 'We're going to hang out the washing on the Siegfried Line' might be sung in music halls whilst stalemate continued across the Channel behind the delusive protection of the Maginot Line. Life differed sharply at sea. Certainly those in the know realised that inter-war economy measures and the weakness of British finance and industry had left serious fleet deficiencies in the rearmament programme. The truth was, though efforts were made to disguise it, that the Navy entered the war in its most parlous condition since the American War of Independence. The right ships and matériel were plainly not there and everyone at sea sensed that in reality the British would be fighting for their lives.

'Winston is back' the Admiralty signalled on the first day of hostilities and I well remember the fillip that Churchill's return as First Lord gave us in the Sixth Submarine Flotilla at Blyth in Northumberland, an encouragement which reverberated right through the fleet. At least, we said, there would now be one strong politician at the head of naval affairs who knew his own mind. The other first day news struck a more sombre note.

Out in the Atlantic the Donaldson liner "Athenia" had been torpedoed by U.30 without warning and in disregard of orders. This caused the loss of 112 lives and scarcely prejudiced neutral opinion in favour of the Reich. Nine days later the 22,000-ton aircraft carrier "Courageous" was sunk by U.29 whilst herself hunting U-boats. The third of the early disasters then took place on the 14th October 1939. This was the most humiliating of all. A daring U-boat Captain, Gunther Prien, quietly worked U.47 through the defences of Scapa Flow, torpedoed the battleship "Royal Oak" and crept out again unscathed to return to a hero's welcome in Germany. Given that attackers always have the advantage, the loss of an unarmed liner and of two capital ships without a shot being fired and within six weeks of the declaration of war could not be considered a good omen. The battle of the River Plate, therefore, did a great deal to restore both naval and national morale.

Within a few days of the outbreak of war German merchant shipping vanished from the oceans of the world. German raiders, however, as in the First World War, had already been stationed in readiness, far out of sight of land, keeping radio silence and, therefore, in the days before radar, successfully hidden from British intelligence. These sea wolves initially comprised the pocket battleships "Deutschland" and "Graf Spee" and each had a supply ship to increase endurance. "Deutschland" was to operate in the North and "Graf Spee" in the South Atlantic, but both were ordered to keep off the trade routes whilst Hitler still nursed a hope of patching things up with the Allies after his onslaught on Poland.

When this proved to be an illusion, the raiders were given the 'go ahead'. The "Deutschland" had little success, her total bag in October being three ships, two sunk and one – an American – made prize. "Deutschland" then returned north of Iceland to Germany whereupon Hitler changed her name to "Lutzow" because of the psychological effect he feared if "Deutschland" were ever to be sunk. The "Graf Spee" fared better. She captured one ship off Pernambuco, sank four ships on the Cape route and then, to throw the scent, operated for ten days off Madagascar in the Indian Ocean.

In November and December 1939 the "Graf Spee" returned to the Atlantic, sank the liner "Doric Star" (which revealed her position) on the Cape–Sierra Leone route and then set off west bent on more ambitious hunting off the busy River Plate. At that point her luck turned and she ran into three of the four cruisers of the British South American Squadron, H.M.S. "Exeter", "Ajax" and "Achilles". "Exeter" had 8-inch guns, "Ajax" and "Achilles" 6-inch, whereas "Graf Spee" was not only more heavily armoured but had 11-inch guns directed by radar, a refinement no British cruiser as yet possessed. The result was predictable.

"Exeter" first drew the "Graf Spee's" fire, thus allowing "Ajax" and "Achilles" to close the range until they were scoring hits on the pocket battleship; hits which,

The "Graf Spee", one of Germany's pocket battleships, began the Second World War with three months of successful commerce-raiding in the Atlantic, but was run to ground by three cruisers of the South American Squadron, H.M.S. "Exeter", "Ajax" and "Achilles", off the River Plate. Though greatly inferior to the "Graf Spee" in fire power, these cruisers managed to inflict sufficient damage to the German pocket battleship to cause her to seek shelter in Montevideo. Here rumours that the "Hood" and other capital ships were about to appear on the scene drove the "Graf Spee's" Captain to take his ship out of Montevideo and scuttle her.

alas, did no visible damage. "Exeter", badly mauled, with two of her turrets out of action and losing speed, then fell out of the fight. So "Graf Spee" turned her big guns on the flagship "Ajax", destroying her turrets. "Achilles" clearly unable to continue the engagement alone with any hope of success then decided to shadow the "Graf Spee" in company with the damaged "Ajax" and signal for reinforcements.

Although the British squadron expected a drawn-out chase, they had done more damage than they thought. "Graf Spee" headed for the mouth of the River Plate, taking refuge in the neutral port of Montevideo. Here some nasty rumours were put about to the effect that overwhelming British forces were on the point of arrival. In fact the nearest ships, the aircraft carrier "Ark Royal" and the battlecruiser "Renown", were over a thousand miles away at Rio de Janeiro. But rumour allied to despair, did its work. Four days later the German Captain took his ship down to the river mouth, scuttled her and then committed suicide.

This was the first restorative victory of the war, although with the mutual respect for each other which fighting sailors have always had, the Navy was distressed by the German Captain's death. The British would much have preferred to have fought it out again at sea. This action had a sequel early in 1940. The "Altmark", the "Graf Spee's" supply ship, found herself caught in a Norwegian fiord on her way back to Germany with three hundred prisoners battened down in the hold. These were released in an old-fashioned way by a boarding party from a British destroyer, H.M.S. "Cossack", the news being passed down to the prisoners with a rousing shout of 'The Navy's here!' This gave new life to an old legend which people were only too eager to believe, namely that whenever the Navy was around, effective action would always result.

Until the spring of 1940 the general naval situation was considered by the Admiralty to be similar to that of 1914. Italy and Japan still remained neutral and there could be no doubt that the Anglo-French fleets were decisively superior to Admiral Raeder's force in which Hitler, a land animal like Napoleon, took but a

'The Navy's here!' Reminiscent of earlier cutting-out operations in the Royal Navy's history, this cry rang out when a boarding party from H.M.S. "Cossack" stormed the supply ship "Altmark" (employed in servicing commerce raiders and at that time carrying prisoners from the ships she had sunk) and released 299 British prisoners then in the hold. It was a highly enspiriting event at a time when the 'Phoney War' had begun to make people wonder if the real war would ever begin.

passing interest. As in 1914 the strategic problem continued to be that of enticing the enemy's small surface fleet to come out and give battle. With this end in view and a feeling that history surely repeats itself, the Admiralty concentrated the main Home Fleet at Scapa Flow, organised blockade patrols and sent a small Expeditionary Force without incident across the Channel to France. This apparent similarity to 1914 was yet further increased by the "Graf Spee" defeat appearing to be a repetition of Admiral Sturdee's success at the Falklands, a quarter of a century before.

To cement these ideas together the Chiefs of Staff then added a firm and declared belief in the efficacy of a naval blockade. In 1939 Germany's dependence on vital raw materials from abroad was universally accepted as fact. 66 per cent of ores for the Reich's steel production came from abroad as did 25 per cent zinc, 50 per cent lead, 70 per cent copper, 90 per cent tin, 95 per cent nickel, 99 per cent bauxite, 66 per cent oil, 80 per cent rubber and even between 10 and 20 per cent of food. Such figures were apt to be bemusing. It was small wonder, then, that 'both Government and country regarded the blockade as Britain's chief offensive weapon and looked to it for decisive, or at any rate dramatic, results'.[1]

A terrible awakening lay ahead. In the summer of 1940 the whole of western Europe, except for Sweden, Switzerland and the Iberian peninsula, fell to the German army through a new and deadly process known as 'blitzkrieg', the audacity of which was staggering. In this lightning war speed was of the essence – the Maginot Line merely being turned and then ignored, entire countries being overrun before governments caught their collective breath. Paralysing shock gave way to daunting collapse, the results to begin with being beyond calculation. By July Great Britain stood stripped and alone. What had actually come about could then be seen to be far worse than the blackest nightmare anyone had previously suffered.

The blitzkrieg began on 9th April 1940 with the simultaneous air and sea invasion of Denmark and Norway, in defiance of British seapower, an invasion accomplished with such success that by the end of that very first day the capital cities and every main port including Narvik in the far north had been taken into German hands. The Royal Navy had been present in strength covering minelaying operations off the Norwegian coast, so how, people asked, did the Germans get through? Disillusionment was then followed by a brand new fantasy generated by Churchill himself who maintained in Parliament that Hitler had made a grave strategic blunder for which he would now have to pay by fighting 'vastly superior naval forces' during the whole summer. In the event this turned out to be a somewhat naive notion since the British forces which were landed in Norway five to nine days later – too little, too late and unprotected from air attack – had to be evacuated with difficulty and loss scarcely a fortnight later. This was humiliating in itself and reflected on the real value of seapower in such circumstances. 'When it came to the point of action, the Admiralty despite its prewar disdain for air power became extremely cautious and shrank from risking ships at places where their intervention could have been decisive.'[2]

Norway and Denmark soon came to be seen as no more than the overture. On 10th May 1940 General Guderian's panzer corps crossed the Meuse at Sedan, breaking through the defences of the West, and soon expanded their narrow breach into an enormous gap. 'The decisive act of world-shaking drama' had begun. Four days later the Netherlands surrendered and, on the 28th May, Belgium followed suit. Between then and the fall of France less than a month later (the Germans entered Paris on 14th June) 338,000 British and French troops were evacuated from the beaches and port of Dunkirk.

This extraordinary naval feat, codenamed 'Dynamo', was put under the operational control of Admiral Sir Bertram Ramsay, the Flag Officer at Dover, who was later to plan and execute the major Anglo-American landings in North Africa, Sicily and Normandy. The Dunkirk evacuation began on the afternoon of the 26th May and ended some nine days later on the 4th June, only 2,000 men being lost in ships of every shape and size en route to England. A total of 860 vessels took part, 700 British and the rest Allied. This 'Mosquito Armada' as Churchill called it included lifeboats from liners in the London docks, tugs, yachts, trawlers, drifters, barges and pleasure boats, all of them assisting 39 destroyers (the largest warships which could be risked in-shore and of which 6 were sunk and 19 damaged), 7 sloops and 36 minesweepers.

Dunkirk has gone down in history as a most brilliant improvisation by volunteers on an amazing scale never previously seen at sea. It turned defeat, if not into victory, at least into an event which enthralled the whole nation and fortified the national spirit for the increasing rigours ahead. Churchill who had replaced Neville Chamberlain as Prime Minister on the 10th May, the day the blitzkrieg began, declared with appropriate magniloquence that 'In the midst of our defeat, glory came to the island people, united and unconquerable, and the tale of the Dunkirk beaches will shine in whatever records are preserved of our affairs.'

As the hot sunny summer of 1940 went on and Hitler was now seen to control a huge arc of coastline from the Arctic to the Bay of Biscay, the Admiralty was forced into a basic and rapid re-appraisal of the naval situation. As in 1805, invasion now became the next likely step the enemy would take and soon the question would be not 'if' but 'when'. 'We must by very careful', Churchill said, 'not to assign to this deliverance (Dunkirk) the attributes of a victory. Wars are not won by evacuations.' Moreover a new and worrying factor had begun to show itself significantly at Dunkirk as it had first done in Norway the previous month. That factor was air power, the use of which in the Second World War was to demonstrate beyond doubt that command of the sea had now become dependent upon a prior command of the air. This of course did not accord well in 1940 with the big-ship lobby.

Two swallows might not make a summer but the implications were clear for all to see. 'It was the threat from German air power, effective against smaller ships in the narrow waters of the leads and fiords, which prevented our naval superiority from exercising its accustomed influence on the operations', the official historian wrote.[3] The same thing happened at Dunkirk and tactical and strategic air power had now to be given prime importance by the Royal Navy, as the later successes and losses of Atlantic, Mediterranean and Arctic convoys were to prove.

On land, of course, the close working relationship of Luftwaffe and Wehrmacht had enabled Hitler to conquer Europe at very small cost. In the later summer of 1940, it could only be England's turn next and the whole of the south-eastern part of the country began tensing itself for the onslaught which people then felt was sure to come. Had the Battle of Britain not been won, invasion would have been certain and

St Vincent's famous dictum, quoted defiantly by Churchill—'I do not say they cannot come, only that they cannot come by sea' – would have been put to the test.

For the Navy it was an extraordinary time. The collapse of France caused a deep numbing trauma and scarcely had that passed before the Navy was suddenly required to execute one of the most distasteful acts of its entire history. This was to destroy the French Atlantic fleet in order to prevent it from falling into German hands. This dire, unexpected tragedy happened at Mers-el-Kebir (Oran) in French North Africa on the 3rd and 5th July 1940 and seemed to the British fleet which had to do the job to be as stunning a calamity as the overrunning of Europe had been to the whole British nation.

Indeed every long summer day appeared to bring fresh shock and perplexity to us all. Churchill alone imperturbably maintained the country's morale – and to understand the emotional impact of what was, perhaps, the most dangerous year in the country's history, the rousing speech he made to Parliament on the 4th June

The evacuation from Dunkirk, May–June 1940 has become one of the epics in naval history. Although technically a defeat, since British forces were driven to leave the continent of Europe, the operation itself, involving an armada of small vessels of all types manned largely by amateurs, succeeded in bringing back to England nearly 340,000 fighting men who had been pinned down on the coast by the German Army. The operation lasted nine days.

220

SUBMARINES

Although Europeans, notably William Bourne, Cornelius van Drebble, de Son and Symons designed primitive, hand-operated submarines during the two centuries after 1578, it was left to two Americans, David Bushnell and Robert Fulton, the first in the American War of Independence and the second in the Napoleonic Wars, to demonstrate that the submarine could one day become a viable warship. Neither was much heeded.

At the end of the nineteenth century another American, J. P. Holland, seeing the possibilities of combining the internal combustion engine, the electric motor and the Whitehead torpedo, designed a submarine which was accepted by the U.S. and later the Royal Navy. The first five submarines built in England in the first decade of the twentieth century displaced 105 tons, had surface and submerged speeds of 8½ and 7 knots respectively and a surface endurance of 500 miles.

At the outbreak of the First World War some 400 submarines existed,

distributed among sixteen navies and by the end of that war not only had the German U-boat had a devastating effect on allied merchant shipping, there were also being built submarines which carried a single 12-inch gun and in one instance an aircraft.

In the Second World War the submarine proved itself to be a vital weapon, the battle of the Atlantic, as it came to be called, becoming one of the most crucial of the entire struggle.

Then in 1952 the true submarine (i.e. one which could operate submerged almost indefinitely) became a reality when the U.S.S. "Nautilus" was launched. A new era began. Because a nuclear reactor consumes no oxygen, the only effective limitation of a nuclear-powered submarine lies in the endurance of her crew. On one occasion "Nautilus" covered 91,324 nautical miles, 78,885 of them submerged, without refuelling, and she could dive to a depth of 720 feet. Later nuclear submarines, of course, have improved performances. By

employing an inertial navigation system a submarine can fix its position with great accuracy without the necessity of coming to the surface from time to time in order to take conventional observations of heavenly bodies. The "Nautilus" had a sustained submerged speed of twenty knots and more recent submarines have exceeded thirty knots. Since a submarine does not roll or pitch under water and suffers none of the stresses of a surface ship in a heavy sea, the possible development of the submarine is today almost unlimited.

H.M.S. "Porpoise" had an all too typical career for a thirties submarine – built by Vickers Armstrong at Barrow, launched in August 1932, laid mines during the Second World War and was sunk by Japanese aircraft in January 1945 in the Malacca Strait. This picture, however, shows her peacefully entering Dartmouth in 1934.

1940, after Dunkirk but before the fall of France, should be allowed to reverberate again. This speech instantly became a symbol of the time, and its power and nobility have in no way diminished with the passing years. 'Even though large tracts of Europe', Churchill declared, 'and many old and famous states have fallen or may fall into the grip of the Gestapo [which he pronounced Jest a Poe] and all the odious apparatus of Nazi rule, we shall not flag or fail. We shall go on to the end. We shall fight in France, we shall fight in the seas and oceans, we shall fight with growing confidence and growing strength in the air; we shall defend our Island whatever the cost may be. We shall fight on the beaches, we shall fight on the landing grounds, we shall fight in the fields and in the streets, we shall fight in the hills; we shall never surrender; and even if, which I do not for a moment believe, this Island or a large part of it were subjugated and starving, then our Empire beyond the seas, armed and

guarded by the British fleet, would carry on the struggle, until in God's good time, the New World, with all its power and might, steps forth to the rescue and the liberation of the old.' These measured and magnificent phrases inspired the entire free world. Even today they can move the heart.

The Battle of Britain, which occasioned another Churchillian axiom, 'Never in the field of human conflict was so much owed by so many to so few', next raged in the air space over Kent from June to September 1940 and on the 23rd August the Blitz on London began. It was now becoming painfully clear to everyone in the United Kingdom that the British nation really was alone and at bay. The menace of invasion hung sombrely over the east and south coasts like a thunder cloud. 'Armed and guarded by the British fleet', the country nevertheless found itself beleaguered as it never had been before. Now, when the Nazi industrial machine not only showed no

signs of faltering but had in fact been immeasurably strengthened by what amounted
to the loot of Europe, it was the British Isles and not the Reich which came under
blockade.

In the one month of September 1940 British shipping losses amounted to 160,000
tons. A great flaw in our seapower – or rather in the way we thought about seapower
– was coming to light. Not only had we seriously overestimated the effect of our
blockade on Germany, we had also assumed that the superior economic resources of
the British Empire could readily be assembled to bring retribution on the enemy and
that our control of raw materials and especially of finance equipped us to withstand
war as it had done during our rise to economic supremacy in the late nineteenth
century. This proved to be a dangerous fallacy.

Even in February 1940 before Europe had been overrun, the British Treasury
estimated an adverse trade balance for 1940 of £400 million at a time when our total
gold and dollar reserves stood at £700 million: by August the Chancellor of the
Exchequer was warning the Cabinet that our reserves would be exhausted by
Christmas. By the end of 1940 we had run up a bill for munitions from the U.S.A.
amounting to $10,000 million, far more than our total debts for the whole of the First
World War. This sum was quite beyond our capacity to pay. In 1941 immediately
before Roosevelt managed to persuade Congress to pass the Lend/Lease Act, British
reserves had dipped to a disastrous $12 million.

Bankruptcy stared us in the face, and we were now dependent for life itself on the
United States. It might be true that we were sacrificing our post-war future for the
sake of the world, we still had to have the tools with which to finish the job. It was
also true, as Keynes was quick to point out, that we had thrown good housekeeping
to the winds. The reality of the situation which the western world lived through
until Pearl Harbor on 7th December 1941 was that the collapse of Great Britain
would have been as disastrous to the United States as the fall of France had been to
Great Britain. American generosity, therefore, was naturally tempered with a certain
amount of self-interest. By 1945 when our housing and industrial property had been
wrecked by six years of bombing, when we had lost eleven-and-a-half million tons
of shipping and when our export trade had almost completely collapsed, we British
found ourselves in the unenviable position of being the world's largest debtor nation.

This, then, was the Whitehall background, so to speak, to a sea change in the
Royal Navy which took place after Dunkirk. This change centred on the urgent
necessity of building and putting into service a vast armada of small fighting ships
and of finding and training the officers and men to staff them. Motor torpedo boats,
gunboats, launches and later combined operations craft, together with escort vessels,
minesweepers and anti-submarine ships now became a top priority and the twentieth-
century equivalent of the 'sea fencibles' leapt at the chance of early command even if
it had to be only a fishing boat with guns.

The Navy had already used up its regular reserve of merchant service officers (the
Royal Naval Reserve) and now began to train a large number of young civilian
volunteers (the Royal Naval Volunteer Reserve) who had not been reservists or
seamen of any kind before the war. These Wavy Navy officers (they wore wavy
stripes instead of the regular officers' straight ones) served six months or more on the

lower deck and then trained for three months on board H.M.S. "King Alfred", a 'stone frigate' or disused holiday building on the seafront near Brighton.

Here, in addition to the bare essentials of seamanship, navigation and signals, they became imbued with the high traditions of the Navy, emerging as Sub-Lieutenants with a determination and a pride in the service which often outshone that of the regulars whose ranks were steadily thinning and who sometimes treated the Wavy Navy with a slight and wholly indefensible arrogance. Whenever this happened, however, regulars were apt to be reminded that the R.N.V.R.s had been invited to join in order to show straight stripers how to run their ships. In general, however, the blending was excellent and as the war went on, R.N.V.R.s rose in rank and experience until they commanded almost every small ship or craft the Navy built. Together with the invaluable Women's Royal Naval Service, the R.N.V.R. provided the country with its first full and complete Citizens' Navy.

If 1940 goes into the record as the blackest year of the century, there were nevertheless occasional flashes of hope, as if a lighthouse could be glimpsed from time to time through swirling fog. One of these was the steady behind-the-scenes support of President Roosevelt, re-elected for a third unprecedented term in November 1940. This support expressed itself in the secret interchanges between this extraordinary President and the equally exceptional British Prime Minister which continued throughout the war.

Both Churchill and Roosevelt were what would later be called 'hung-up' on their respective navies. Roosevelt had once been Secretary of the U.S. Navy and Churchill had been First Lord of the Admiralty at the start of both world wars. Each valued and looked with slight nostalgia on his past naval connection and after Churchill became Prime Minister in May 1940, he referred to himself in his exchanges with Roosevelt as 'Former Naval Person'. In Churchill's own words, 'My relations with the President gradually became so close that the chief business between our two countries was virtually conducted by these personal interchanges between him and me. In this way our perfect understanding was gained. As Head of the State as well as Head of the Government, Roosevelt spoke and acted with authority in every sphere and, carrying the War Cabinet with me, I represented Great Britain with almost equal latitude.'[4]

More to the point were the various practical manifestations of this friendship, beginning with the despatch to the United Kingdom the very day after Dunkirk of half a million rifles, 900 field-guns and 800,000 machine-guns. Churchill declared this to be 'a supreme act of faith and leadership for the United States to deprive themselves of this very considerable mass of arms for the sake of a country which many deemed already beaten'. Yet more important from the Royal Navy's point of view were the fifty over-age American destroyers loaned in return for ninety-nine-year leases of air and naval bases in the British West Indies and Newfoundland.

This deal, which Churchill preferred to call 'a parallel transaction and act of goodwill rather than a bargain', was so skilfully managed that the sensibilities and prejudices of the public, both in the United States and in Britain, were set at rest, and a highly dangerous, potentially fatal gap in the provision of escort vessels was bridged for the six months from September 1940 to February 1941, when new

NAVAL AIR POWER

The notion of flying off aircraft from the decks of H.M. ships originated in 1911 when Commander Samson took off in a Short biplane from the foc'sle of the battleship "Africa", but he could not land. Indeed it was not until 1918, when H.M.S. "Argus" came into service, that an unobstructed deck over the whole length of a ship allowed this problem to be solved.

The idea of warships carrying aircraft, other than for spotting purposes, had a rough passage in the naval thinking of the inter-war years. The Fleet Air Arm, as such, only came into existence in 1924 and then its training and the procurement of its aircraft remained the responsibility of the R.A.F. In 1937, however, with the Second World war in sight, naval aviation came under the direct control of the Admiralty. Even then the Fleet Air Arm was one of the Navy's poorer relations. Events in the Second World War changed all that. The aircraft carrier – and there were never enough of them – proved to be invaluable. Moreover the Fleet Air Arm's heroic feats were often accomplished with ancient aircraft such as the Swordfish.

Aircraft carriers built up to the end of the Second World War were of three main types. Large fleet carriers with up to one hundred aircraft operated with the battle fleet (and required the same expensive destroyer protection). Light fleet carriers with some forty aircraft provided search and strike for lesser squadrons and finally slow-moving merchant ship convoys came to be protected by escort carriers of moderate speed operating twenty to thirty-five aircraft.

Today the missile age has changed everything yet again. Now only the U.S. Navy keeps a number of front line aircraft carriers in commission. These are called attack carriers and the largest of these in existence, the U.S.S. "Nimitz", displaces 95,000 tons and operates about 100 aircraft.

So far as the Royal Navy is concerned, the Sea Harrier working from carriers which, until the Falklands crisis, were due to be sold or scrapped, has shown itself to be the wonder aircraft of the eighties. The Sea Harrier is a maritime jump jet which can, if necessary, take off and land vertically and is therefore capable of being carried by almost any ship with a platform or length of unobstructed deck. The Harrier came into front line service in 1980 and has not only introduced a new concept into naval fixed wing flying, it has proved itself to be the most effective manned weapon now available to the Royal Navy. Helicopters, too, have played an invaluable role in the Falklands campaign.

A Swordfish Mk III bombed up and on patrol during the Second World War. It was these 'Stringbags' that virtually put the Italian Navy out of the war at Taranto, although in terms of landbased planes these desperately slow biplanes were already obsolete. Now, with the Sea Harrier the balance between land and sea based aircraft has become more even, since it combines high performance in the air (including 'dodging' on its jets) with an almost vertical take-off requiring only a short tilted deck.

British-built destroyers, corvettes and other anti-submarine patrol boats began to come into service. How different were the relationships between Hitler, Mussolini and Franco who met severally and together in October 1940 with no result other than mutual dislike. Indeed after Hitler had spent nine fruitless hours with the Spanish dictator he remarked that 'rather than go through that again, I would prefer to have three or four of my teeth out'.

Mussolini, as expected, had declared war on France and Britain on 10th June 1940 in order to share in the spoil (on the same sly basis Stalin took over the Baltic states between 17th and 23rd June when the attention of his German partner and of the world was on France). In September 1940 the war in North Africa began. Marshal Graziani opened with a lunge towards Egypt from Italian Libya in which he reached Sidi Barrani before meeting serious opposition. In October 1940 Mussolini decided

to make an attack of 'both a maritime and territorial character' against Greece in order to put her out of action and to ensure that in all circumstances 'she will remain in our politico-economic sphere'.

British reaction to this was to occupy Suda Bay in Crete in order to secure the Eastern Mediterranean, to plan a surprise attack on the Italians in the Western Desert from the rear and thirdly to cripple the main Italian fleet at Taranto. This action at Taranto on 11th November 1940, like the battle of the River Plate a year before, did a very great deal to boost naval and national morale. It provided further dramatic proof of the value of air strikes against capital ships. Two waves of 21 aircraft, of which 11 carried torpedoes, took off from the carrier H.M.S. "Illustrious" 170 miles away from Taranto and for an hour rained fire and destruction on the Italian ships. Despite heavy flak all but two of the aircraft flew safely back to "Illustrious" having, by this single stroke, decisively altered the balance of naval power in the Mediterranean. Three battleships, one of them the new "Littorio", were torpedoed, one cruiser was hit and much damage inflicted on the dockyard. Half the Italian battle fleet had thus been put out of action for at least six months, the remaining undamaged ships being withdrawn a few days later to Trieste.

Taranto was the first major victory over the Italian navy achieved under the direction of Admiral Sir Andrew Browne Cunningham, (nicknamed A.B.C.), the Commander-in-Chief of the Eastern Mediterranean Fleet. The second took place on 28th March 1941 off Cape Matapan when three Italian cruisers were sunk and the Italian fleet was prevented from interfering with convoys from Egypt to Greece. Matapan, however, became the last spectacular piece of good news in a period of gathering storm. Hitler's immediate reaction was to send the Luftwaffe to aid his feckless ally and from then on, until the invasion of North Africa in November 1942, the stream set strongly against the British war effort in the Mediterranean. Things continued to go from bad to worse and by the end of 1941 Cunningham's entire battle squadron had been temporarily put out of action.

The first evidence of German air presence in the Mediterranean had been the concentrated attack on the new aircraft carrier, "Illustrious". Thanks to her armoured flight deck, the ship survived in spite of serious damage and was repaired at Malta through what the brave inhabitants of that stony island would soon come to know as continuous siege by air assault.

Malta holds a key position in the Mediterranean, being almost equidistant from Gibraltar and Alexandria, and possessing a large, well fortified harbour with excellent docks and repair facilities. Also – and less fortunately in 1941 – Malta lies only ninety miles from Sicily. So, as soon as the Luftwaffe had established itself in that island, Malta came under blockade with, as it seemed at the time, the grave probability of airborne invasion.

Another endurance trial for the Navy began with the unexpected stiffening of the Italian army which had invaded Greece. Until the Wehrmacht took a hand, the Italians could scarcely be said to have achieved impressive results. This German intervention, however, proved to be of such strength and effectiveness that the British contingent helping the Greeks had to be hurriedly withdrawn by sea under extreme difficulty caused by a lack of air cover. This situation was then made worse in May 1941 when the Germans captured Crete by airborne assault. British ship losses now became critical. 3 cruisers and 6 destroyers were sunk and 2 battleships, 7 destroyers and over 30 transports and fleet auxiliaries severely damaged. Yet when it was suggested to Cunningham that enough was enough and that remaining troops would have to be left to surrender, he ordered the fleet rescue operation to continue. Whatever the cost might be, A.B.C. was not going to have it said that the Navy would ever abandon the Army ashore. 'It takes the Navy three years to build a ship', he observed, 'it would take three hundred to rebuild a tradition.'

Meanwhile out in the Atlantic the "Bismarck" saga was under way. The "Bismarck" had been laid down on 1st July 1936, launched on 14th February 1939 and began her trials in September 1940. Officially rated for 'evasion of treaty purposes' at 35,000 tons, a neat transposition of figures made her, in fact, the largest battleship in the world at that time, her real tonnage being 53,000. She was also the ultimate in design, guns and equipment, far in advance of H.M.S. "Hood" the 42,000-ton battlecruiser, then thought to be the mightiest warship afloat, but which had been laid down in the First World War.

Accompanied by the heavy cruiser "Prinz Eugen", "Bismarck" left German waters on 18th May 1941 with orders to sink as many allied ships on the transatlantic routes as she could find. Such commerce raiding could be and usually was more economically effected by U-boats but the despatch of one german battleship or cruiser into this vital Atlantic area inevitably caused at least a dozen similar British ships to be occupied in searching for the raider. Thus began what has come to be known as the most dramatic seahunt of the twentieth century. Nine days later, and after sinking H.M.S. "Hood" in a matter of minutes with the loss of all but three out of 1,500 men, "Bismarck" herself disappeared beneath the waves, a shattered wreck but one which it took an entire British fleet to sink. From the "Bismarck" only 115 survived out of a crew of 2,200.

The sinking of the "Bismarck", in perspective merely an incident in the battle of the Atlantic,★ distracted attention from the debacle of Crete. In fact the loss of Crete marked the opening of a period of maximum danger in the Mediterranean. This lasted until the tide turned after success in the Western Desert and the complementary Anglo-American invasion of North Africa in November 1942. During this critical period of eighteen months, and except for the heroic and extremely costly succour of Malta, the Mediterranean remained virtually closed to allied shipping. Immediately after Crete Admiral Cunningham had only two battleships, three cruisers and 17 destroyers ready for service. Nine other cruisers and destroyers were under repair in

One of the saddest shocks of the Second World War was the sinking of H.M.S. "Hood" ('the Mighty Hood') in a matter of minutes whilst in action with the German battleship "Bismarck", which was later sunk in the same action. A lucky salvo of shells struck "Hood's" magazine and she literally blew herself up.

★ The Battle of the Atlantic was officially so named by the Minister of Defence on 6th March 1941 and his Ministry set up a Standing Committee to review the problem of sinkings and convoy protection daily until the danger had passed.

Egypt, but the battleships "Warspite" and "Barham" and his only aircraft carrier "Formidable", together with other lesser warships, were forced to sail to the United Kingdom and the United States for repair after long, hazardous journeys round the Cape of Good Hope.

A footnote to Crete was the sinking on 22nd May of the famous but luckless destroyer H.M.S. "Kelly" whose story inspired Noel Coward to write, act in and direct the film *In which we serve*. H.M.S. "Kelly" was commanded by Captain the Lord Louis Mountbatten, Captain (D), 5th Destroyer Flotilla, and its sinking – after very active service and much damage in the English Channel, Atlantic, North Sea (Norwegian campaign) and now at the battle of Crete in the Mediterranean – released Mountbatten for other duties. Though never again to fight at sea, he was to advance from Chief of Combined Operations via Supreme Allied Commander, South East Asia, to appointment as the last Viceroy of India and finally First Sea Lord.

This 'Hero of our Time' will figure later in the story but the full account of the "Kelly's" end, which Coward extracted after a dinner party, was told by Mountbatten 'without apparent emotion but the emotion was there, poignantly behind every word he uttered' and in it Coward recognised 'all the true sentiment, the comedy, the tragedy, the casual valiance, the unvaunted heroism, the sadness without tears and the pride without end' which make *In which we serve* the most famous and moving of war films even to this day.[5]

Then on 22nd June 1941 what Churchill called 'The Soviet Nemesis' began. Those who lived through it saw the invasion of Soviet Russia by its erstwhile ally as one of the most astonishing events of the war. Nemesis is the Goddess of Retribution and the reaction of the non-communist majority in the United Kingdom was 'and about time too!' As became known from German archives after the war, Hitler was strongly and responsibly warned against the adventure by his professional advisers. However, like Napoleon, Hitler always knew best and now the hour had struck.

Although the opening of the Eastern Front brought long wanted relief to the country from the switching of the Luftwaffe to distant targets, it added appallingly to the burden the Royal Navy had to bear at a time when we were still taking on Hitler alone and had been so doing for exactly a year (the French armistice had been signed on 22nd June 1940). The Russians demanded supplies and these could only reach them by the Arctic route. A long series of convoy operations began. These had to run the gauntlet not only of vile weather conditions but also of German air attack from bases in Norway.

In running these convoys through, we received no help but only surly abuse from the Russians themselves. Indeed, as Churchill observed, 'The Soviet Government had the impression that they were conferring a great favour on us by fighting in their own country for their own lives.' This was not a point of view appreciated by ill-used sailors carrying supplies to Murmansk and Archangel at enormous risk.

It took ten days of acute danger for ships to reach Russia from the United Kingdom. Of 811 merchant ships which sailed in 40 convoys, 92 or one in nine were sunk on the way. Then, of course, they had to face the return journey in empty ships. It was a thankless task. In the continuous daylight of summer, they withstood attack throughout the twenty-four hours. In winter there would be freezing fog, snow and

ice on the rigging and guns, plus the knowledge that if you fell overboard, the sea was so cold your endurance could only be a matter of minutes. The worst loss occurred in the mid-summer of 1942 when Convoy P.Q.17, now marked down in history as a victim of the British Admiralty, lost 24 out of the 35 ships which sailed, but throughout these arctic operations there was evidence of the greatest gallantry from all who took part.

The first period of the war ends, so far as this story is concerned, with Pearl Harbor and the entry of the United States into the war. This took place on 7th December 1941 and was the culmination of six to nine months of a continuously growing Japanese threat in the Far East. So far as Great Britain was concerned, American intervention came at the eleventh hour, though only Churchill and the Cabinet were aware of the appalling facts and how very near we were to a fatal exhaustion.

It has been said, rightly in my opinion, that Churchill's most important

Pearl Harbor, 7th December 1941. Japan demonstrates in shattering fashion the strength of a naval air strike, allied to surprise. It was no surprise, however, that this action brought the United States into the Second World War thus making victory against Germany, Italy and Japan not only possible but virtually inevitable.

contribution to British war strategy was to realise from the start, as did cool and calculating opinion in Germany, that American partnership was absolutely essential if we were to last the course. Accordingly Churchill used all his charm and political expertise to maximum effect in order to secure this backing in the way best suited to the interests of the whole British Empire.

The Atlantic Charter, signed by the American President and the British Prime Minister on board the battleship H.M.S. "Prince of Wales" in Placentia Bay, Newfoundland on 12th August 1941, defined this partnership and its aims but it was only when the United States actually declared war on Germany, Italy and Japan that the world could see clearly that, however long it took, the outcome of the war was no longer in doubt. Churchill's reaction, despite the horrors of Pearl Harbor and the British disasters which immediately followed, such as the fall of the Far East, is moving in the clarity of its simple relief. 'So we had won after all!' he wrote,[6] 'Yes, after Dunkirk; after the fall of France; after the horrible episode of Oran; after the threat of invasion, when, apart from the Air and Navy, we were an almost unarmed people; after the deadly struggle of the U-boat in the Battle of the Atlantic, gained by a hand's breadth; after seventeen months of lonely fighting and nineteen months of my responsibility in dire stress, we had won the war. England would live; Britain would live; the Commonwealth of Nations and the Empire would live.'

CHAPTER XI

THE SECOND WORLD WAR

FROM PEARL HARBOR TO HIROSHIMA

1941 - 1945

CHRONOLOGICAL COMPENDIUM

General

The surprise attack by Japan on the U.S. Fleet at Pearl Harbor on 7th December 1941 moved the centre of gravity of the war to the Pacific so far as Americans were concerned. Luckily for Europe Churchill and Roosevelt realised that the war could only be ended by the physical occupation of Germany and by its unconditional surrender.

During the first six months of 1942, whilst the United States was gearing her vast economy to war, things went from bad to worse for Britain and the handful of ex-patriate governments sheltering in London. Britain and her allies pledged themselves to make no separate peace with the enemy and the United Nations was born. This was not enough, however, to stem the impetus of Japanese expansion, and in January 1942 the Dutch East Indies, Malaya and Burma were all invaded. In North Africa the Eighth Army was on the retreat and on 15th February Singapore surrendered. By the end of March Japanese successes in Burma and the Andaman Islands threatened the east coast of India.

May saw Malta under continuous air attack whilst vital reinforcements from Italy were being sent to Rommel in North Africa, the Japanese took Mandalay and Corregidor surrendered. By June the Nile Delta was under threat, the British having lost two hundred and thirty tanks in desert fighting, with Rommel in possession of Tobruk. In the Atlantic allied shipping losses reached their peak with German U-boats even operating off the eastern seaboard of the United States and what the Japanese were pleased to call their 'co-prosperity sphere' – in other words the empire they had conquered – reached its maximum extent.

Then, imperceptibly at first, the scene began to change. In Britain there had been considerable Communist pressure for a 'Second Front Now' to assist the beleaguered Soviet Union. Except for a disastrous foray to Dieppe, this had been resisted to allow secret preparations to be made for Operation Torch, under the supreme command of American general, Dwight D. Eisenhower. This was to be the invasion (by the largest armada which, at that time, had yet put to sea) of Morocco and Algeria. This successful operation in November 1942 was timed to coincide with General Montgomery's onslaught on Rommel at the battle of El Alamein and the effect of both was a pincer movement which compressed the German and Italian forces into Tunisia, denied them reinforcements and caused their surrender in April 1943 after which there were no Axis forces left in the whole of North Africa.

The tide had also begun to turn in the Pacific. The U.S. navy first crippled the Japanese fleet at the battle of the Coral Sea and then defeated it at the battle of Midway in 1942 and the following year recaptured Guadalcanal, the Aleutians and other Pacific islands.

The conquest of North Africa was followed, in 1943, by the relief of Malta, the opening-up once more of the Mediterranean and, in July, the invasion of Sicily. On 3rd September 1943, Italy surrendered unconditionally.

In the meantime preparations for D-Day began. This was the Anglo-American assault on Normandy on 6th June 1944 and the subsequent liberation of France, Charles de Gaulle transferring his Provisional Government from Algiers to Paris on 30th August 1944.

Throughout the autumn, winter and early spring of 1944–5 German armed forces, ferociously fighting to the end, were driven back steadily until on 13th March 1945 the Allies commanded the west bank of the Rhine. Despite the bombing of London by Hitler's last secret weapon, the V.1 and V.2 rockets, the end in Europe was now in sight. On 1st May 1945 the German army on the Italian front surrendered and a week later the final capitulation of Nazi Germany took place.

Three months later the United States dropped the first atomic bomb on Hiroshima and on 2nd September Japan capitulated.

Naval

1942

11 February German battlecruisers "Scharnhorst" and "Gneisenau" escape from Brest and make a daring dash up the Channel, very nearly reaching Kiel before being mined. Once docked for repairs both were attacked from the air, the "Gneisenau" being so seriously damaged that she was never operational again. The "Scharnhorst" completed repairs in January 1943 and was then based in northern Norway.

28 March British commando raid on St Nazaire. This was the only dock reachable from the Atlantic where the German battleship "Tirpitz" could be repaired, if damaged. The dock gates were rammed by an over-age ex-U.S. destroyer the "Campbelltown" and destroyed when the ship blew up with delayed charges the next day.

21 June Heavy losses on convoy of supplies to Malta.

27 June–5 July Most famous of the convoys to Russia PQ.17 – 24 out of 35 ships sunk.

10–15 August H.M.S. "Eagle" and "Manchester" lost escorting convoy to Malta, codenamed Operation Pedestal. The "Ohio", an American tanker on loan to British Ministry of War Transport and manned by a British crew, was torpedoed, set on fire and stopped. She nevertheless got under way again with a minesweeper towing and destroyers lashed on either side. She arrived in a sinking condition in Malta's Grand Harbour but the 10,000 tons of fuel she carried were a decisive factor in enabling Malta to hold out against further Italian and German air attacks.

19 August Commando raid on Dieppe. Heavy casualties including 3,500 Canadians.

8 November Allied invasion of French North Africa (Operation Torch). The assault required 200 warships, 1,000 aircraft, 70,000 troops and 350 merchant ships. There were three Naval Task Forces, the Eastern (Algiers) and Centre (Oran) being under British command and the Western (Casablanca) under American.

1943

By May Malta relieved and Mediterranean re-opened, the U-boat menace at last coming under control. Also turning point in battle of the Atlantic when sufficient aircraft, ship-based and land-based, became available to supplement surface escort of convoys. Total losses over whole war in Atlantic and Arctic: 2,828 merchant ships of a total tonnage of 14,687,231 while 782 German and 85 Italian U-boats were destroyed.

10 July Allied invasion of Sicily. Seaborne landings at Syracuse and Pachino (British), Licata and Gela (U.S.).

17 August Last German soldier flung out of Sicily and the island now in allied hands.

3 September Allies invade Italy.

8 September Landings in Salerno Bay.

30 September U.S. Fifth Army takes Naples.

26 December "Scharnhorst" sunk off north Norway by gunfire and torpedoes, a battle fought almost entirely in darkness. British force comprised battleship "Duke of York" and three cruisers.

1944

6 June D-Day (Operation Overlord) in Normandy. In the first twenty-four hours the Allies flew 14,600 air sorties dropping 5,200 tons of bombs. From midnight three airborne divisions (one British two American) between Caen and the Cotentin peninsula (20,000 airborne troops). By end of first day nearly 250,000 troops landed with tanks. Two synthetic harbours (Mulberries) taken across and emplaced (one subsequently blowing away in storm). Five beaches were assaulted – three to the east, 'Sword', 'Juno' and 'Gold' – British, two to the west, 'Omaha' and 'Utah' – American. Warships involved – 243 British, 48 U.S., plus 19 patrol craft, 9

French, 3 Polish, 3 Norwegian, 2 Greek and 2 Dutch plus 4,126 Landing Ships and Craft, 736 Ancillary Ships and Craft, 864 Merchant Ships – a total of 6,055 *ships of war*.

12 November   "Tirpitz" (sister ship of the "Bismarck" and completed in 1941) sunk in Norwegian fiord.

1945

January   Renewed U-boat attacks in Atlantic using homing torpedoes.

28 March   Last of 1,050 V-rockets falls on Britain.

People

Louis Mountbatten   Admiral of the Fleet and First Earl Mountbatten of Burma. On outbreak of war Captain in
1900–1979   command of 5th Destroyer Flotilla in H.M.S. "Kelly" in which he was sunk, 23 May 1941.
Appointed as adviser on Combined Operations with the rank of commodore, later becoming Chief of Combined Operations in April 1942 with concurrent ranks of Vice-Admiral, Air Marshal and Lieutenant-General. Responsible for raids on St Nazaire, Vaagso and Bruneval, also Dieppe. Played large part in planning growth of combined operations technology. October 1943 appointed Supreme Allied Commander, South-East Asia. First defensive battles in the Arakan and at Imphal and Kohima. Reconquered Burma during 1945. Accepted formal surrender of the Japanese expeditionary force, Southern Region, in the Municipal Building, Singapore. February 1947, Viceroy of India, appointed to organise transfer of sovereignty from British crown to people of India. Then Governor-General till June 1948. Reverted to Rear Admiral in command of First Cruiser Squadron in Mediterranean. Fourth Sea Lord 1950–2. C. in C. Mediterranean (and C. in C. Allied Forces Mediterranean) 1953–4, First Sea Lord 1955–9 and Chief of Defence Staff 1959–64. Principally responsible for reorganising Admiralty, War Office and Air Ministry into a single, co-ordinated Ministry of Defence in 1964. Murdered by terrorists at Mullaghmore, Co. Sligo, Eire, 27 August 1979.

Sir Bertram   Admiral, on retired list at outbreak of war (since 1935) through disagreement with his
Ramsay   commander-in-chief, when Chief of Staff, Home Fleet. Flag Officer, Dover 1939 – 42
1883–1945   (responsible for the evacuation from Dunkirk), 1942 Naval C. in C. Expeditionary Force
planning Operation Torch (invasion of French North Africa), 1943 planned operation Husky (invasion of Sicily) with General Montgomery in Cairo. 1944 Re-instated on active list as Admiral and became Allied Naval Commander, Expeditionary Force for the invasion of Normandy (D-Day).

Sir Philip Vian   Admiral of the Fleet, and one of the most successful tactical commanders of the Second World
1894–1968   War. Captain of H.M.S. "Cossack" rescuing prisoners from the "Altmark" (in the action
against the "Bismarck"), then Rear Admiral, Cruiser Squadron in Mediterranean bringing supplies to Malta 1942. Commanded aircraft carrier force in Italian landings, commanded Eastern Task Force on D-Day landings June 1944, then commanded British aircraft carrier force in Far East for final operations against Japan. After war, Fifth Sea Lord and then C. in C. Home Fleet.

Technical advances

Development of specialised Landing Ships and Craft for combined operations. This began in 1941 and came to a climax with the Normandy invasion.

The aircraft carrier and the increasingly sophisticated aeroplanes working from it.

Refinements in radar.

The 'schnorkel' system allowing a submarine to recharge its batteries whilst still submerged just below the surface of the sea (German).

The second part of the Second World War story opens at the turn of the year 1941/2 with the proclamation by the American President and the British Prime Minister of the Grand Alliance which from then on structured the conduct of the war. It had no easy ride. Strategy, even in theory, became difficult to agree and proved to be still more hazardous in its execution. The conquest of Europe by Nazi Germany and the 'unflinching resistance of Britain alone' had brought the British nation to the point of physical and financial exhaustion. Light at the end of the tunnel might just be discerned by Churchill: more immediately it was clear that worse must necessarily come.

At the beginning of 1942 we, the British, were no longer alone in that we now had two massive allies – Russia and the United States – irrevocably committed to fighting it out to the death in concert with ourselves. However, the quality of that alliance differed seriously and at times dangerously as between the Soviet and American war effort. In the early days, indeed, the Russian alliance seemed to be merely another drain on our painfully limited resources. Moreover, all the allies were not compelled to suffer in impotence the barbaric onslaught of Japan.

Hong Kong had surrendered to the Japanese on Christmas Day 1941. Japanese forces had also invaded Luzon in the Philippines on the 10th December three days after the assault on Pearl Harbor. On 10th January 1942 Japanese forces started to occupy the Dutch East Indies, on the 11th Kuala Lumpur in Malaya fell and on the 19th the invasion of Burma began. From then on it was only a matter of time before Singapore was forced to surrender and Japan became possessed of the largest empire yet known to the orient which they named, with disarming hypocrisy, 'the Co-Prosperity Sphere'.

Singapore duly capitulated on 15th February 1942; on the 28th of that month the Japanese landed in Java and by the end of March their successes in Burma (Rangoon fell on 8th March) and the Andaman Islands were threatening the east coast of India. They could scarcely have achieved more in a shorter time. Moreover this concatenation of disaster numbed us all as if we had been continuously and heavily bruised. It distressed the Navy in particular because maritime command of the Far East had vanished for the foreseeable future in no more than weeks and this debacle had been preceded by a shock equivalent to the loss of H.M.S. "Hood". This was the sinking in the South China Sea on the 10th December 1941 of H.M.S. "Prince of Wales", one of our newest battleships (of which there were only three in service) and of H.M.S. "Repulse", an elderly but prestigious 32,000-ton battlecruiser.

These two great ships, with a small destroyer screen but no air cover of any kind, were under the command of Vice Admiral Sir Tom Phillips, who as Vice Chief of the Naval Staff had been largely responsible for sending them out to Singapore in the first place and who had been a strong believer in the superiority of the capital ship over any air attack which a Japanese striking force, known not to have radar, could mount. In fact the only aircraft carrier which might have provided this cover, H.M.S. "Ark Royal", had been sunk in the Mediterranean on 14th November 1941.

With hindsight it is easy now to deplore the folly of not holding back unprotected heavy ships from attempting what Admiral Phillips envisaged as a possibly decisive blow against the Japanese invasion of Malaya. Phillips was an officer of high courage, intellectual power and firm determination. At the time he saw it as his duty to risk his ships. If he held back, would it not be a tacit admission of their uselessness? Alas, their uselessness in these circumstances was manifestly proved, nearly a thousand officers and men being killed in the action. Admiral Phillips' decision can now be seen as a grievous under-estimation of the efficiency of the Japanese in air warfare. The death knell of the battleship had begun to sound.

Churchill, on being told the news on the telephone by the First Sea Lord, recorded that he was thankful to be alone. 'In all the war I never received a more direct shock.'

Back in the Atlantic the scene became equally grey and grim. Fresh into the war, Americans showed an understandable reluctance to apply lessons learnt by the British in more than two years of slogging it out alone. Like most newcomers to a complicated fray, they thought they knew better, a notion they were to repeat later in the year in North Africa. It did not then seem to matter just how expensively acquired the British experience had been. Fleet Admiral E. J. King, head of the U.S. Navy, was both 'Pacific minded' and as much an anglophobe as his President was anglophile. 'I fought under the goddam British in the First World War and if I can help it no ship of mine will fight under them again', he is on record as saying, a point of view which did not make liaison between the two navies any the easier.

The head of the German Navy, Admiral Donitz himself an ex-U-boat commander, was quick to cash in on this early disarray, sending some of his most experienced submarine commanders to prey on unescorted shipping off the eastern seaboard of the United States. They had a sensational success. By the end of one month, January 1942, the German 'Paukenschlag' (Roll of Drums) had reverberated to the tune of 31 ships of nearly 200,000 tons sunk off the U.S. and Canadian coasts.

These attacks later spread southwards to Hampton Roads, Cape Hatteras, the coast of Florida and the Gulf of Mexico, causing a serious interruption of oil tanker traffic with Venezuela and totting up the score in February to 71 ships of 384,000

A convoy of British and American ships at anchor in Hvalfiord, Iceland May–June 1942. During the first six months of 1942 before the effect of the U.S.A. entering the war began to be felt 568 merchant ships of a tonnage of 3,116,703 were sunk by U-boats, operating in what were known as 'wolf packs'. The remedy was to surround each convoy not only with surface escorts but also with a screen of aircraft sufficient to find and force any U-boats nearby to dive but the right Support Group ships and long distance aircraft did not become available until 1943 when the tide at last began to turn.

tons. This was the highest rate of loss so far endured in the battle of the Atlantic and it was soon to be surpassed. What made it worse was the fact that these losses were inflicted by no more than twelve to fifteen U-boats working in the area at any one time. The situation was not to improve in any substantial way until Admiral Sir Max Horton, also a First World War 'submariner' and for the first three years of the second war Vice Admiral (Submarines), had been appointed Commander-in-Chief, Western Approaches with headquarters at Liverpool. But this did not take place until November 1942.

Meanwhile the darkening scene in the spring and summer of that anxious year was to be further complicated by Hitler's decision in January to send his only super battleship, the "Tirpitz", sister ship to the "Bismarck" and then the most powerful capital ship in the world, to Trondheim in Norway from which port she was to overshadow and to an extent dominate the North Atlantic theatre of operations. All went to show, as Churchill had remarked after the fall of France, that the battle would be long and hard. There was to be no respite until the success of Operation Torch in November 1942.

We come now to the revival of a British nautical skill which had not been much

One disaster followed another. Only a few days after Pearl Harbor, Japan's naval air power inflicted another crushing blow, this time on the new British battleship "Prince of Wales" (seen here at Singapore) and the more elderly battle-cruiser "Renown". These two great ships escorted by destroyers but without air cover were sunk in the China Sea by aerial bombardment, thus putting into question the whole value of the capital ship. This was a lesson which had yet to be learnt.

in evidence since the Seven Years War. This was Combined Operations and here Mountbatten enters the scene. With the exception of the raid on Dieppe in August 1942, the Combined Operations story is one of astonishing ingenuity, courage and success. Mountbatten replaced the sixty-nine-year-old Admiral of the Fleet, Sir Roger Keyes, as Chief of Combined Operations in the autumn of 1941.

The appointment of a Captain R.N. – who was also a cousin of the King – with the acting rank of Vice Admiral and membership of the Chiefs of Staff Committee, had a mixed reception. Mountbatten inherited 'an uneasy and unloved organisation that was neither fish nor flesh nor fowl and it was distasteful to lovers of all three. If the Combined Ops dish had not yet gone bad, it was widely regarded as "going off" ... the staff including messengers and typists numbered around twenty and most of the officers were superannuated. Mountbatten was appalled and amazed that anything had so far been accomplished (Keyes, a straight talker, had made numerous enemies and left behind him a "formidable inheritance of feuds"). Mountbatten inspected this set-up and its establishments for a single whirlwind month and reported back to the Chiefs of Staff. His suggestions were accepted without question and he began his appointments, expansion and reorganisation.'[1]

The results were electrifying as I can vouch from personal experience. I joined the organisation in February 1942 as temporary Secretary to Admiral Sir Bertram Ramsay, then Naval Commander-in-Chief of the Expeditionary Force, and four years later returned to Whitehall to end my service career as Deputy Secretary of Combined Operations Headquarters. In the interim the growth and achievements of Combined Operations in all its ramifications, culminating as it did in the invasion of Normandy (D-Day) in June 1944, can be seen as nothing short of astounding and the impulse behind it all was Mountbatten's energy, charm and ruthlessness. He had, moreover, 'the priceless asset of access. He could talk on equal terms to George VI *and* his Prime Minister *and* his Foreign Secretary. He had the ear of anyone whom he wished to complain to, acquire something from or praise.'[2]

At different periods of the war I had the good fortune to serve on the staff of four Admirals, each of whom in a distinct way played a major part in the winning of the war. These were Sir Max Horton when Admiral (Submarines), Sir Bertram Ramsay who planned the invasion of North Africa, Sicily and Normandy, Sir Andrew Cunningham, Commander-in-Chief of the Mediterranean Fleet after the North African landings and Lord Louis Mountbatten, as he then was, both at Combined Operations and also briefly when he became 'Supremo' of South East Asia.

Each Admiral was possessed of very different qualities and temperament but Mountbatten was the only one with the understanding, power of leadership and charisma comparable – in quality though not perhaps in degree – with that of Nelson. No man is a hero to his valet, it used to be said, and in naval terms few Captains or Admirals are heroes to their Secretaries or staffs. Of course Mountbatten had faults. He believed he could never make a mistake. He took a childlike pleasure in himself, was intensely ambitious, aroused the jealousy of his peers and, as St Vincent said of Nelson, 'his zeal does now and then (not often) outrun his discretion but his zeal and activity cannot be exceeded.'[3]

But so far as this junior officer was concerned, no other Captain or Admiral was more of a delight to serve nor demanded and received a greater loyalty. He had that magic ability, as Quakers say, 'to speak to the condition' of each individual he met whether Able Seaman, Commander or Prime Minister. He had the presence and flair of royalty. It must be remembered that Dickie Battenberg was born a Serene Highness, scion of the oldest traceable Protestant reigning family in the world yet he seemed always and genuinely to be interested in you yourself whatever you were and whatever job you were doing. He stands in my opinion as the outstanding naval personality of the Second World War and of its aftermath. By any scale of measurement, he was a very rare man.

In 1942 we had need of every ounce of leadership and drive that was going. On the home front Communist agitation – aided regrettably by Beaverbrook and the *Daily Express* – for a 'Second Front Now' (which would have been fatal had we embarked on such a folly) distracted attention from the strategic realities which Great Britain and the United States had perforce to face. Both Churchill and Roosevelt were well aware that in the end the war could only be won by returning to the continent of Europe in force and conquering the heartland of Germany.

To attempt this before being sure of success would have prolonged the war by, perhaps, another five years. But in 1942 there were strong pressures to attempt just such an invasion. It was a near thing. In the event wiser counsels prevailed and the raid on Dieppe in August 1942 proved the point. There the losses were excessive when set against the advantage gained. In the first six months of 1942 ten Commando raids had been made, mostly on a very small scale. Bruneval on 27th February yielded vital information about enemy radar in the face of intensive local opposition. At St Nazaire on 27th and 28th March the lock gates shielding the "Tirpitz" were rammed by an ancient and expendable U.S. destroyer with delayed charges on board. This was a complete success and the operation was signalised by the award of five V.C.s.

At Dieppe, however, on 18th and 19th August a raid in unusual strength was made upon what was coming to be known as Hitler's Atlantic Wall. This raid, about which Mountbatten remained defensive till the end of his life, has been generally regarded as ill-conceived, poorly carried out, of needless cost and dubious in its lessons. The world saw it also as undeniably 'Mountbatten's show'. It was, in fact, a fiasco.

Of the 5,000 Canadians engaged on the operation, nearly 1,000 were killed and 2,000 made Prisoners of War. Of the 2,000 who returned, some 500 were wounded. A destroyer and 33 valuable landing craft were sunk. 106 R.A.F. Fighters were shot down. Apart from the Canadians over 1,000 further casualties were recorded. The Germans suffered a total of 591 casualties and rightly claimed an enormous propaganda victory.

To those urging 'a Second Front Now' it was a sizeable and salutary shock, yet the truth was that, on the scale of the Second World War, the casualties were negligible and the real lessons learnt of much greater value than they would have been had the raid been a walk-over. These experiences took time to digest but all had been thoroughly absorbed by the time of D-Day two years later. They included the fact that a defended coast requires a much more powerful bombardment than that of the 4.5-inch guns of destroyers. This led to the multiple rocket bombardment ship which could drench its target with 1,000 shells at a time.

It also came to be realised that deadly beach obstacles must be neutralised before tanks went ashore: that landing craft needed to be precisely piloted and that assault parties must know in detail their points of attack on the beach assigned. The most significant lesson of all, however, was that an assault on a port is likely to entail the total destruction of that port and therefore invaders must either capture the installations intact, which is always unlikely, or take their own harbours with them. Hence 'Mulberry', the renowned artificial port which was first used and shown to be invaluable on the Normandy coast two years later. These Dieppe post-mortems, some of which, like those on Jutland, continue to this day, were agonising to Mountbatten himself who took them personally. Yet undoubtedly they played an essential part in the vast preparations which then got under way for the greatest amphibious operation in the history of the world, that of the Normandy assault on 6th June 1944.

S.S. "Empire Tide" with a seaplane on its catapult ready to be launched. Certain merchant ships and troopships were fitted later in the war with a seaplane to aid in the spotting of U-boats.

H.M.S. "Duke of York", a Second World War battleship, fires a broadside from her 14-inch guns. The day of the big gun battleship may well have been ending, its majestic firepower could nevertheless hypnotise opinion so that the battle fleet remained the symbol of the fleet in being and of the sea power it was considered to provide.

    In any case, during the latter part of 1942, a more immediate and important Anglo-American operation was being planned which was to change the whole direction of the war. This operation, codenamed 'Torch', was put under the overall command of an American General, Dwight D. Eisenhower, planned, prepared and executed in total secrecy and, as a result, took the Germans completely by surprise. In the context of the time the scale of 'Torch' was breathtaking. At one time over 800 ships were at sea, their destination unsuspected by the Germans, having sailed from such diverse places as the north of Scotland and the eastern seaboard of the United States. For the assault alone over 200 warships, 1,000 aircraft, 70,000 troops and 350 merchant ships, including transports and landing ships, were required, the object of the operation being simply 'the occupation of Algeria and French Morocco by combined British and American forces with a view to the early occupation of Tunisia'. The force had also to be strong enough to move into Spanish Morocco if Spain turned hostile.

    The North African landings were the first of the three great European-ended invasions of the war, the others being Sicily and Italy in 1943 and Normandy in

1944. Thanks to meticulous planning at Norfolk House in St James Square, London and equally skilled and secret preparatory work behind the scenes in Algeria and Morocco, led by Robert Murphy, a U.S. diplomat accredited to the Vichy Government, the execution of 'Torch' was achieved almost without bloodshed. Three Naval Task Forces were involved, the Eastern (Algiers) and the Centre (Oran) being British, the Western (Casablanca) coming directly across the Atlantic under U.S. command.

The grand strategy behind 'Torch' was a pincer movement to squeeze out and eject the German and Italian forces from Libya and Tunisia thus putting the entire southern coast of the Mediterranean under Allied control. This objective was achieved between 23rd October 1942 (Battle of Alamein) and 12th May 1943 when the German army in Tunisia surrendered. Thereafter Malta was relieved, the Mediterranean opened up and the passage of ships from the United Kingdom to the Far East restarted through the Suez Canal. 'The Hinge of Fate', as Churchill called it, marks the turning point for the Allies from almost uninterrupted disaster to almost unbroken success. The invasion of Sicily, planned by Admiral Ramsay and General Montgomery in Cairo during the early summer of 1943, took place on the 10th July. This struck a fatal blow on the 'soft underbelly of the Axis' and led to the later overrunning of the mainland, the fall from power of Mussolini and the declaration of war by Italy on its late partner on 13th October 1943.

A German type IX C U-boat leaves Kiel for its operational area in the Atlantic. This was the weapon which all but won the Battle of the Atlantic for Germany.

During the summer of 1943 a great Allied Air-Sea offensive was mounted in the Atlantic under the overall direction of Admiral Horton, the Commander-in-Chief, Western Approaches. The rewards were spectacular. The Battle of the Atlantic had become a remote control chess game between two Admirals who were essentially submariners to the end of their days. Both German and British Commanders-in-Chief were equally skilled, inventive and quick to apply new equipment and techniques as soon as they became available. On the British side more powerful escorts, longer ranged aircraft, more sophisticated anti-submarine weapons and above all radar in which Britain had the lead, came into effective use in 1943. The German invention of the schnorkel, an air pipe device which allowed a U-boat to charge its batteries whilst almost entirely submerged, did much to restore advantage to the Kriegsmarine.

The Battle itself, however, did not reach its climax until the four months from 22 May to 18 September 1943. During that period British and other merchant ship

The Battle of the Atlantic, the name given to the Second World War campaign against German and Italian U-boats, was controlled on the British side from this Operation Room into which all available information from sea and air was fed. During this campaign, U-boats sank 2,828 merchant ships of a total tonnage of 14,687,231. In turn 782 German and 85 Italian U-boats were destroyed.

losses dropped to 207,227 tons. Considering that from the date the United States entered the war on 11th December 1941 to 21st May 1943, approximately eighteen months, seven *million* tons of allied shipping had been torpedoed by U-boats, the drop was sensational and this improvement continued through the following eight months to 15th May 1944 when no more than 314,790 tons were sunk.

The Battle of the Atlantic was the only major long term confrontation which on his own admission had Churchill worried in its early and middle stages in spite of the impressive mastery which Hunting Group Commanders, such as Captain F. J. Walker, achieved. This outstanding 'U-boat killer' at one time destroyed six U-boats in a single cruise. Churchill's anxiety was to continue until the French Atlantic ports could be finally denied to the U-boat command in the autumn of 1944. Until then Admiral Donitz certainly did not despair. As late in the war as 20th January 1944 he said, 'The enemy has succeeded in gaining the advantage in defence. The day will come when I shall offer Churchill a first-rate submarine war. The submarine weapon has not been broken by the setbacks of 1943. On the contrary, it has become stronger. In 1944 which will be a successful but a hard year, we shall smash Britain's supply line with a new submarine weapon.' This was no idle threat. Early in 1944 Donitz introduced a new type of U-boat with greater underwater speed and increased range. Combined with the schnorkel advantage – and had the war continued – this could have turned the U-boat campaign if not into a German victory then at least into a draw.

This new German submarine was known as the Type XXI. There had been considerable development delays between 1943 when the design was first adopted, and 1945 when the first Type XXI went to sea in March. Moreover this first Type XXI U-boat had to return to Trondheim on its way to its patrol area due to breakdown. The only Type XXI which became fully operational reached its patrol area on 8th May 1945, the day Germany surrendered. The schnorkel, incidentally, was a Dutch invention taken over by the Germans when they overran Holland.

During 1943 the immense United States war production gathered momentum. Long-range aircraft, escort ships and above all the mass-produced 10,000-ton Henry Kaiser Liberty ships poured out of American yards and workshops and completely altered the scene so far as the Atlantic and the supply of food and matériel to Europe was concerned. In the Pacific the U.S. Navy had gone into the attack since the Battle of Midway in June 1942 and with the appointment of Mountbatten as Supreme Allied Commander, South East Asia – in the later summer of 1943 with his H.Q. first at Delhi and then in Ceylon – the Japanese threat to India was held and preparations begun for the reconquest of Burma.

In October 1943 Admiral of the Fleet Sir Dudley Pound, the quiet overworked First Sea Lord, died in office of a tumour on the brain. He had not been especially popular with the fleet because of his inability to delegate and an unhappy tendency to give Admiralty instructions directly to sea commanders, by-passing normal channels. The most glaring example of this had been the destruction in 1942 of Convoy P.Q. 17 to Russia. Pound ordered this convoy of thirty-five ships to scatter because of an unconfirmed threat from a German squadron thought to include the "Tirpitz" and he gave these orders over the head and against the advice of the

Commander-in-Chief of the Home Fleet. As a result twenty-four defenceless merchant ships were picked off and sunk, and some hard things were said by those who survived about lack of naval support.

A great deal has been written about these convoys to Russia in general and about P.Q.17 in particular (notably *Convoy is to Scatter* by Captain Jack Broome who was in command of P.Q.17). The general background, as Pound had pointed out to the government, was that considered purely as naval operations, they were not feasible. However if they were *politically* necessary, then they were a job that the Navy would of course do but heavy warship and merchant ship losses would have to be accepted.

On the night in question, Peter Kemp was Duty Commander at the Operational Intelligence Centre and remembers thinking, when the scatter signal was sent, that it was a mistake. After the war, however, when he was head of Historical Branch at the Admiralty, he was asked to write a staff appreciation of the operation and went into it in great detail, using all the information that had been available to the Admiralty that night. Kemp came to the conclusion that there was no other course of action than for the convoy to be scattered. 'Of course it is easy to be wise with hindsight', he says, 'but with all the intelligence available in the Admiralty at the time, I am convinced that Pound had no alternative but to order the convoy to scatter.'

Kemp saw a lot of Pound during the first four years of the war, had a great admiration for him and feels he deserves better treatment from historians than he has had and certainly, on the positive side, Pound undoubtedly stands as a good if not great wartime First Sea Lord because of his willingness to accept responsibility for disasters, his refusal to react to uninformed press attacks, his ceaseless hard work and his ability to restrain Churchill from implementing some of his more unsound naval ideas.

Pound was replaced by A.B.C. – Admiral of the Fleet Sir Andrew Browne Cunningham – in many respects his very opposite. Pound had been a 'big-ship' man. Cunningham's early career had been in destroyers and to the end of his life A.B.C.'s outlook was basically that of a 'small-ship' man, much as Horton thought as a submariner. Like Nelson, Cunningham was an aggressive operational commander always ready, perhaps overready, to risk lives for the sake of an idea. Again unlike Pound, A.B.C. delegated wherever and whenever he could, being basically bored by administration in all its forms. Valiant in action, staunch in adversity, he relied, when Commander-in-Chief of the Mediterranean Fleet after the invasion of North Africa, upon an operational cabal of subordinates whom he trusted implicitly and from whom he received loyal and unceasing support. To his administrative staff, whom he avoided whenever possible, he was a pain in the neck.

As First Sea Lord he had neither the warmth nor the personality to endear himself to Churchill and there will always be two points of view as to whether this was a good or a bad thing so far as the war effort was concerned. However, there is no question but that he was the outstanding seagoing Admiral of the Second World War and although he was buried at sea he is commemorated, as such, with other national heroes in the crypt of St Paul's. His character compares with that of Horton and both are well described by a flag officer who served with distinction under each of them. Horton, this Admiral said, worked through 'humane discipline, a most unusual knowledge of matériel and, on the spiritual side – vision'. Cunningham, on the other hand, applied 'humane discipline, vigilance and an appeal to tradition'.[4] The distinction is succinct.

Another great Admiral of the Second World War was Bruce Austin Fraser, later Baron Fraser of the North Cape. A brilliant Gunnery Officer in the First World War, Bruce Fraser, when Executive Officer of the battleship "Resolution" – during operations in the Black Sea in support of White Russian forces at the end of 1918 – had been arrested by the Bolsheviks and imprisoned for eight months. Fraser was to have a further connection with Russia in the Second World War. Appointed Commander-in-Chief, Home Fleet, in May 1943 in succession to Admiral Sir John Tovey and thus, among other things, responsible for running convoys to North Russia, he commanded operations at Christmas 1943 which resulted in the sinking of the German battlecruiser, "Scharnhorst". This was the last action between battleships in European waters.

Only the continuing but diminishing threat of the "Tirpitz" remained, after the ending of which all British heavy ships would be free to move to the Far East. The mighty "Tirpitz", having been badly damaged in her Norwegian fiord by mines laid beneath her by two British midget submarines on 22nd September 1943, was then put out of action once more by aircraft of the Fleet Air Arm on 3rd April 1944 and finally sunk by R.A.F. bombers on 12th November 1944.

Although the Battle of Leyte Gulf in the Pacific, from the 23rd to the 26th October 1944, between the main Japanese fleet and the Third and Seventh U.S. Fleets was to be the last heavy ship encounter in the Second World War and also the biggest naval battle in history, the sinking of the "Tirpitz" marked the end of an era in European sea warfare.

It was a sad curtain to lower on a superb warship which had never been able to operate at sea in her proper role, could not in her final stage go back to Germany for the refit she needed and ended by capsizing at her moorings, after being hit by 12,000 lb bombs, and sinking upside down in the shallow, icy waters of a Norwegian fiord with more than half of her 1,900 officers and men being killed. After a quarter of a century the old air-versus-battleship debate had been finally resolved. Only one further British battleship, H.M.S. "Vanguard", was completed – shortly after the war – and she in turn was broken up in 1960, the last of her breed to serve in the Royal Navy.

By the end of 1943 the Japanese were in retreat in the Pacific, the 'Co-Prosperity Sphere' perimeter steadily shrinking under assault from island-hopping U.S. Marines. In Europe, Operation 'Overlord', the invasion and re-investment by the Allies of France and later of the continent had gone into active planning. This was to be the supreme Anglo-American effort, designed to thrust hard into the heart of Germany, a policy known to be the only practicable way of ending the war with the Nazi Reich.

Under the overall command of General Eisenhower, the naval assault, codenamed 'Operation Neptune', was to be planned and commanded by Admiral Sir Bertram

Ramsay. Having served with him in varying junior capacities on the two previous expeditions (North Africa and Sicily), I was delighted to be appointed Force Supply Officer to Force G, one of the five Assault Forces for D-Day, three of which were to be under British and two under American command. The planning, the build-up and the execution of this extraordinary operation was, certainly to me and, I fancy, to everyone who took part, the epitome of all we had been working towards since the fall of France four long years before.

Everything about Operation Overlord from the smallest landing craft to the largest supporting battleship seemed from the start to be part of a secret cosmos, almost an Arabian Nights' world, for which there were no points of reference. We were about to reach what the Western Powers correctly assumed to be the supreme climax of the war. Nothing like it had been seen before in the history of the world.

The forces afloat involved 125,000 officers and men, 6,055 ships including 6 battleships, 23 cruisers, 104 destroyers and over 4,000 landing craft. Midget submarines had to be in position two days before H hour to pinpoint the targets each Force would assault, two mobile harbours ('Mulberries'), their breakwaters composed of ancient vessels to be sunk on site, would be created off the beaches (one Mulberry blew away in a subsequent storm) and 'Pluto' (Pipeline under the Ocean) would be run on the seabed from England to France to provide uninterrupted supplies of fuel.

The arrival of this gigantic armada and of its supporting vessels was to be preceded by saturation bombing of the defences by the R.A.F. and given air cover of a strength which again had never been mounted before. Even the deception plan which necessitated dummy landing craft grouped in the Thames Estuary, squadrons of wooden tanks in Kent meadows and Army signal traffic sent by landline from genuine Headquarters to be broadcast from Kent, worked so successfully (German

The return to mainland Europe. D-Day, 6th June 1944. The assault, preceded by the biggest naval bombardment in history, was made at dawn on five beaches – three British and two U.S. – between Le Havre and the Cotentin peninsula. Over 6,000 ships and 11,000 aircraft were involved, two artificial harbours (Mulberries) were towed across (the photograph shows the one at Arromanches), and a pipeline to supply fuel was laid on the seabed from England to Normandy.

DUNKIRK AND D-DAY

'Of course whatever happens at Dunkirk, we shall fight on,' Churchill said on 28th May 1940 but it was not until 4th June when Operation Dynamo was declared completed, that the world realised what an extraordinary feat the evacuation of British and Allied troops from the harbour and beaches of Dunkirk had proved to be.

The evacuation from Dunkirk began on the evening of the 26th May under the control of Admiral Ramsay who commanded at Dover. At that time it was thought no more than 45,000 men could be rescued in two days but immediate emergency measures were taken to find additional small craft 'for a special requirement'. Boatyards from Teddington to Brightlingsea were searched and upwards of forty serviceable motor boats were assembled at Sheerness the following day. At the same time lifeboats from liners in the London docks, tugs from the Thames, yachts, fishing-craft, lighters, barges and pleasure-boats were called into service from the eastern and southern coasts of England and a most brilliant improvisation of volunteers on an amazing scale began. Altogether some 860 vessels (of which 243 were sunk) evacuated 338,226 men and delivered them safely in England.

Four years later, 'we cannot afford to fail', said General Eisenhower, the Supreme Commander of the Allied Expeditionary Force, when the greatest Armada the world has seen sailed for the Normandy beaches, the naval content of this being again under the command of Admiral Ramsay. The return blow delivered against the Nazi war machine consisted of a staggering 130,000 men landed across five beaches (all of them thickly mined and otherwise defended) in one day. 14,600 air sorties had been flown to cover these landings and 5,200 tons of bombs had been dropped. Two artificial harbours, codenamed 'Mulberry', were towed across the Channel (one of them later became unusable in a storm) and a Pipe Line Under the Ocean (PLUTO) was laid from the Isle of Wight to Cherbourg to pump fuel to the invasion force without providing the enemy with tanker targets off open beaches.

Altogether in the invasion of the Normandy beaches over 6,000 ships, landing ships and craft were involved.

The return. Supplies pour ashore on one of the American beaches during the height of the Normany landings after D-Day. This was of course the greatest Combined Forces exercise of all time, in which British, American and French forces together with contingents from many other countries were landed under the vigilant eyes of a combined Naval Force. The planning of Operation Overlord was complete down to the provision of paper bags for the use of seasick soldiers.

reconnaissance aircraft were allowed 'accidentally' to penetrate normal air defences to photograph these massive concentrations) that von Rundstedt and Rommel, the German Commanders-in-Chief, were able to assure Hitler that the main assault would take place in the obvious area of the Pas de Calais, where the sea crossing was shortest, any other landings in Normandy being merely a diversion for decoy purposes.

Operation Overlord became from beginning to end a feat – not *incredible*, since it was planned, happened and was seen to happen – but of such scale and tension as to make it seem to those who took part that we were living through a legend in the making. Overlord was quite simply the most massive and complicated operation in naval history, executed by the largest fleet that had ever put to sea for any purpose at any time in any part of the world.

By now the 'Brits' and the 'Yanks' had taught themselves to work together in comparative harmony all over the world. For Normandy eighty per cent of the ships were British and/or British Commonwealth: in the Pacific the Royal Navy could offer no more than a token presence until the autumn of 1944 when, except for the damaged "Tirpitz", there no longer existed any serious surface ship threat in Europe. By then Allied armies were back in force on the continent of Europe. France had been freed. De Gaulle had entered Paris in the wake of Allied troops on 25th August 1944 and the seat of the French Provisional Government had been transferred from Algiers to Paris on 30th August 1944. It was time to turn once more to the East.

To begin with, the American High Command appeared neither to need nor to want British assistance in the full-scale naval operations then in progress in the area of the Spice Islands. But by quiet insistent pressure from Churchill in London,

Mountbatten in Asia and later on from Admirals on the spot, the Royal Navy made itself first acceptable and then welcomed so that the last actions of the war were fought by British battleships and aircraft carriers as a Task Force under supreme American command, the principal British fleet being commanded by Admiral Sir Bruce Fraser, the carriers by Admiral Vian.

Indeed, as David Howarth remarks, 'never since the early eighteenth century before the Americans declared their independence, had they fought in such close combination with a navy as strong as their own. Both navies were shocked, or pretended to be, at the customs, manners and equipment of the other. But it was certainly time the British discovered there could be other ways of doing things at sea, which might sometimes seem to them bizarre or inartistic, but undeniably worked. And it was not a bad time to remember that most of the history of the British at sea was American history too.'[5]

The war in Europe ended on 8th May 1945. Three months later, on 6th August, the first Atomic Bomb fell on Hiroshima to be followed on the 9th by another on Nagasaki. Five days after that Japan surrendered unconditionally and the Second World War came to an end. The nuclear age had begun, an era in which we have lived ever since under conditions so different as to be all but incomprehensible to those of us who were born before the 'Great War', as it was then called, began in 1914, an event which itself changed civilisation for ever.

The composition of the Royal Navy when demobilisation got under way in the autumn of 1945 highlights in a striking way the evolution in ships which had taken place since the ending of the First World War. Then over 70 battleships had been in commission. In 1945 when decommissioning began only 14 of the dinosaurs remained, most of them in any case earmarked for reserve. But 52 aircraft carriers, 62 cruisers, 257 destroyers, 131 submarines and some 9,000 other smaller craft from frigates and corvettes to landing craft, together with 70 strike and fighter squadrons of the Fleet Air Arm, showed to what an extraordinary degree the fleet had revolutionised itself.

But at what a cost and after what shuddering reverses had the war been won! 4,786 Allied vessels had been sunk, double the tonnage lost in the First World War. 69 per cent of these had been destroyed by U-boats or by mines: 16 per cent by air attack and a mere 7 per cent by conventional gunnery or torpedoing from surface ships. The remaining 8 per cent were chalked up to the usual hazards of the sea, enhanced of course by wartime conditions. How Jackie Fisher would have smiled!

Yet the Royal Navy, in partnership with the R.A.F., had continued to be the nation's main defence throughout the blackest years. It had kept the island people supplied, had transported armies overseas to successful landings and subsequent victories on a breathtaking scale. All in all it had surmounted dangers, obstructions and crises in a way which no one, expert or layman, would have considered believable on the outbreak of war and for over two critical years of the struggle it had been the only significant maritime force engaged against Germany and Italy. Now after six years, its victory was complete and the seas were once again freed for the commerce of the world.

CHAPTER XII

1945
TO THE
PRESENT DAY

CHRONOLOGICAL COMPENDIUM

General

President Roosevelt died on 12th April 1945, less than a month before Germany surrendered, his place at the Potsdam Conference (17th July to 2nd August) being taken by President Truman. During the course of this same conference, which determined the future of Europe from that day to this, an event of even deeper significance for Great Britain took place. This was the General Election on 26th July when Labour was returned to power with a landslide 412 seats against Conservatives and supporters 213 and Liberals 12. Winston Churchill, the heroic wartime Prime Minister, was rejected by the electorate in favour of his deputy, Clement Attlee, and the vast social revolution began through which we have lived ever since.

The improvement in our living standards, a surge of growth in higher education, and the gradual breakdown of class barriers at home, were matched abroad by the dissolution of the British Empire, indeed by a general retreat from empire undertaken by those western nations which had – until the Second World War – comprised the colonial powers. India, Africa, and those countries of the Far East and Caribbean which had previously been dominions or colonies now gained their independence and the Third World was born.

These profound changes, such as the advent of the Welfare State in Britain, were accompanied by a quickening in communication – air travel, an enormous worldwide increase of the telephone network, radio and television – but only, for practical purposes, in the non-communist world. Soviet Russia and her satellite countries in Europe entrenched themselves under Stalin and his successors into a fortress such as the world has never seen before. Tyranically governed, and complete with slave labour camps, no one could nor can get into or out of that fortress, which extends from the Baltic to the borders of China, without the direct or indirect imprimatur of the Kremlin.

This process, and the 'Cold War' which followed, began immediately after the Potsdam Conference. The U.S.S.R. regarded the territorial changes, tentatively agreed, as final and flouted the cardinal decision that Germany should be treated as a single economic unit. This led to the fusion of the U.S., British and French zones of occupation into the Federal Republic of Germany in September 1949 and those under Russian control into the communist German Democratic Republic in October 1949. This had followed an unsuccessful attempt by the U.S.S.R. to stop road and rail traffic between Berlin (which was and is under four power occupation) and the West which became known as the Berlin Air-Lift of 1948–9. In 1961 the building of the infamous Berlin Wall began and the 'age of bipolarity' has turned the world of today into two armed camps between which the Cold War waxes and wanes. Meanwhile the peace of the world has depended and continues to depend upon the understanding by both sides of the nuclear deterrent and the willingness of the West to subsidise with American grain and European food surpluses the economic dereliction of the U.S.S.R. and the 'empire' it controls.

Naval

The Communist Bloc has no fundamental need for maritime strength. All its important lines of communication – roads, railways and canals – are internal and at the end of the Second World War, the Soviet Navy was organised almost entirely for coastal defence with a negligible amphibious capability. Today the Soviet Navy is the second largest in the world and her cargo fleet the largest with all the newest roll-on roll-off ships adapted to carry military equipment anywhere in the world.

To counter the threat implied by the above, the maritime nations of the West, all of whose important lines of communication depend upon the sea, have had to adapt their navies and plan their disposition and use so that the technological superiority which the West possesses can counteract and overcome the numerical strength of the Soviet Navy. Ships and the weapons they carry have changed, almost beyond recognition, since the ending of the Second World War, and in the van of this technology stands the Polaris submarine, and the missiles it carries.

A Miscellany of dates affecting the Royal Navy

1945 Dropping of the atomic bomb (6th August) reveals discovery of releasing and controlling atomic energy
Developments in radar and other wartime scientific inventions become more generally known

1946 Edward Appleton and Donald Hay discover that sun-spots emit radio waves
Discovery of Carbon-13 isotope
Fairey Aviation construct a pilotless radio-controlled rocket missile
Chester Carlson invents xerography
The magnetic north pole observed by aircraft to be 250 miles north of charted position
Britain and U.S. restore Azores bases to Portugal

1947 Britain's first atomic pile at Harwell comes into operation
L. Essen determines speed of radio waves in a vacuum
First supersonic air flight
First transatlantic automatic flight

1948 Transistor invented by Bell Telephone scientists
Preparation of antibiotics, aureomycin and chloromycetin
Auguste Piccard constructs bathyscaphe for deep ocean descents

1949 North Atlantic Treaty Organisation comes into being (4th April)
Cortisone and neomycin discovered
U.S.S.R. carries out first atomic bomb tests
South Africa begins policy of apartheid
Chinese nationalists under Chiang Kai-shek withdraw to Formosa and Communist People's Republic proclaimed at Peiping under Mao Tse-tung

1950 U.S. Atomic Energy Commission separates plutonium from pitchblende concentrates
New calculations for speed of light obtained through radio waves at National Physical Laboratory, Teddington and Stanford University, California
Thor Heyerdahl publishes *The Kon-Tiki Expedition*
N.A.T.O. bilateral agreement by which United States provides arms to its associates ·
U.S.S.R. announce possession of atomic bomb
Communist North Korean forces invade South Korea: U.N. forces land at Inchon, South Korea and Korean war begins
N.A.T.O. Council decides to form an integrated European defence force

1951 Electric power satisfactorily produced from atomic energy at Arcon, Idaho
Second British plutonium pile in operation at Sellafield, Cumberland
John Brown Ltd make a peat-fired gas turbine on Clydebank
France, West Germany, Italy, Belgium, Netherlands and Luxembourg ('the Six') sign Paris Treaty embodying Schuman plan for single coal and steel authority
Peace Treaty with Japan signed though boycotted by U.S.S.R.

1952 Rapid extension of use of radio-isotopes in scientific research, medicine and industry, Britain becoming chief exporter of isotopes
Britain's first atomic bomb tests in Monte Bello Islands, N.W. Australia
U.S. explodes first hydrogen bomb at Eniwetok Atoll, Pacific
President Truman lays keel of first atomic-powered submarine "Nautilus"
Death of George VI and accession of Elizabeth II

1953   Astronomers in Australia, South Africa and the United States discover a new scale of space outside solar system
Cosmic ray laboratory established Mount Wrangell, Alaska
Royal Observatory moves from Greenwich to Herstmonceux, Sussex
Experimental colour T.V. in U.S.
Council of Europe meets in Strasbourg to draft constitution
President Eisenhower proposes to U.N. General Assembly an international control of atomic energy

1954   Bell Telephone Company develops solar battery capable of converting the sun's radiation into electricity
First 'flying bedstead' aircraft with vertical take-off
South East Asian Defence Treaty and Pacific Charter signed by Britain, France, U.S., Australia, New Zealand, Pakistan, Thailand and Philippines
West Germany enters N.A.T.O.
Anglo-Egyptian agreement for British troops to leave Suez Canal zone. General Nasser becomes head of state in Egypt.

1955   Dolfus ascends four and a half miles above the earth to make photo-electric observations of Mars
Radio-physicists of Massachusetts Institute of Technology develop Ultra High-Frequency waves
First use of atomically generated power in the U.S.
European Union agreement ratified
Britain and U.S. sign atomic energy agreement
Britain returns Simonstown naval base in South Africa to S.A. government whilst retaining right to use it
Goodwill visits of Royal Navy to Leningrad and of U.S.S.R. Navy to Portsmouth. Disappearance of Commander Crabbe, frogman, at Portsmouth during Russian visit
South Africa withdraws from U.N. General Assembly over apartheid

1956   Detection of the 'neutrino' (a particle of no electric charge) at Los Alamos Laboratory, U.S.
Discovery of anti-neutron at California University
'Dido' reactor at Harwell opened
Calder Hall, largest nuclear power station, opened
F. W. Muller develops the ion microscope
First multi-purpose industrial high-energy plant in Europe developed by Tube Investments Ltd
Mullard image-dissector camera, capable of taking very rapid photographs
Transatlantic telephone service inaugurated
Peter Twiss flies at 1,132 m.p.h. in a Fairey Delta
H.M.S. "Girdle Ness", Royal Navy's first guided missile vessel, commissioned
President Nasser seizes Suez Canal provoking Anglo-French Suez War. British paratroopers land at Port Said. Truce negotiated in November and in December Anglo-French forces withdraw from Egypt

1957   International Geophysical Year begins in July with scientists concentrating on Antarctic exploration, oceanographic and meteorological research and launching of satellites into space
U.S.S.R. launches Sputnik I (4th October) tracked by Jodrell Bank radio telescope under Bernard Lovell
H.M.C.S. "Labrador" discovers new north-west passage
U.S. expedition is flown in to South Pole
U.S.S.R. non-magnetic ship "Star" on expedition to take magnetic recordings
At Bermuda Conference (March) President Eisenhower and Prime Minister Macmillan re-establish special relationship which was strained by Suez Crisis. U.S. makes certain guided missiles available to Britain

'The Six' sign Treaty of Rome establishing Common Market and Euratom
U.S. Sixth Fleet sails for Mediterranean despite Soviet protest (April)
Britain explodes first British thermonuclear bomb in megaton range in Central Pacific

1958 U.S. artificial earth satellite 'Explorer I' launched at Cape Canaveral (31st January) to study cosmic rays, 'Vanguard I' to test solar cells (17th March) and 'Atlas' to investigate radio relay (18th December)
U.S.S.R. launches 'Sputnik III' for aerodynamic studies and puts two dogs in a rocket to height of 279 miles (27th August)
U.S. nuclear submarine "Nautilus" passes under ice cap at North Pole (4th March)
U.S.S.R. launches nuclear-powered ice-breaker "Lenin"
Submarine current discovered in equatorial Pacific
British section of Commonwealth Transantarctic Expedition under Vivian Fuchs reaches South Pole (20th January)
Iceland extends fishery limits to twelve miles (1st June)

1959 More U.S. and U.S.S.R. rocket launchings
First atomic submarine and first atomic-powered passenger-cargo ship "Savannah" launched by U.S.
British hovercraft crosses the Channel in two hours
Anglo-U.S. agreement enables Britain to purchase components of atomic weapons other than warheads from U.S.
Queen Elizabeth opens St Lawrence seaway

1960 Twenty satellites are in orbit
R. L. Mossbauer's discoveries in gamma rays
An optical micro-wave laser is constructed
U.S. bathyscaphe "Trieste" designed by Professor Piccard dives to the bottom of the Challenger Deep, 35,800 feet
U.S.-Britain build ballistic missile early warning station at Fylingdales (17th February)
U.2 aircraft, flown by Francis Powers, shot down in Urals by U.S.S.R.
U.S.S.R. protests at U.S. proposal to arm Bundeswehr with Polaris missiles
Facilities for U.S. Polaris submarines made available at Holy Loch, Scotland

1961 Major Yuri Gagarin of U.S.S.R. becomes first man in space being orbited in a six ton satellite (12th April)
Alan Shepard of the United States makes re-entry in capsule through atmosphere (5th May)
The Atlas computer, the world's largest, is installed at Harwell to aid atomic research and weather forecasting
Britain and Iceland settle fisheries dispute

1962 U.S. spacemen John Glenn (Feb) and Malcolm Scott (May) are put in orbit
Satellite 'Telstar' put in orbit from Cape Canaveral (10th July) circles earth every 157·8 minutes enabling live T.V. pictures transmitted from Andover, Maine to be received at Goonhilly Down, Cornwall and in Brittany
U.S. also launch the rocket 'Mariner' to explore Venus and the British satellite 'Aerial' to study cosmic radiation
Twenty years after beginning of nuclear age U.S. has 200 atomic reactors in operation, Great Britain 39 and U.S.S.R. 39
U.S. blockade of Cuba following installation of U.S.S.R. missile base (24th October) which ends 20th November with withdrawal of Ilyushin bombers from Cuba by U.S.S.R.

1963 Britain is refused entry into Common Market
U.S. recommends that surface ships should carry Polaris missiles on N.A.T.O. force
6th April Britain-U.S. sign Polaris missile agreement
Friction welding is invented
Natural gas deposits in Groningen are developed which presages North Sea gas and oil
21st June France withdraws naval Atlantic forces from N.A.T.O.
Britain, U.S. and U.S.S.R. sign nuclear test-ban treaty
22nd November President Kennedy assassinated in Dallas, Texas

1964 First close-up photographs of moon's surface obtained
Britain's 'Blue Streak' is launched
U.S. divers live in "Sealab" for nine days 192 feet down off Bermuda coast to study effects of depth on man
Britain grants first licences to drill for gas and oil in North Sea
Vietnam war increase in fighting

1965 First walks in space by U.S. and U.S.S.R. cosmonauts
U.S. 'Mariner IV' satellite transmits first close-up photographs of Mars
'Early Bird', U.S. commercial communications satellite, first used by T.V.
British Petroleum strikes oil in North Sea but rig collapses
Sir Winston Churchill dies. (State Funeral 30th January)
Vietnam War escalates
Death penalty abolished (November)

1966 First moon landings (unmanned)

1967 France launches her first nuclear submarine "La Redoutable"
Six Day War between Israel and Arab nations
People's Republic of China explodes its first hydrogen bomb
U.S. has 74 nuclear powered submarines in commission

1968 Pulsars discovered by Hewish and Bell, Mullard Observatory, Cambridge
Upheavals in Czechoslovakia and student riots in Paris

1969 Anglo-French Concorde makes first test flight
'Apollo II' launched from Cape Kennedy, lands on surface of moon 20th July. Neil Armstrong steps out on moon 21st July and 'Apollo II' returns with crew 24th July
Gravitational waves, first postulated by Einstein in 1916, observed by J. Weber of University of Maryland

1970 150-inch reflecting telescopes completed at Kitt Peak Observatory, Tucson, Arizona and at Cerro Tololo, Chile

1971 Largest tanker yet built, 372,400 ton "Nisseki Maru" – Japan
U.S. and U.S.S.R. sign treaty banning nuclear weapons on ocean floor

1972 Britain imposes direct rule on Northern Ireland (476 killed during year)
Watergate scandal breaks in U.S.
Britain, Denmark and Ireland join Common Market

1973 American space probe transmits pictures within 81,000 miles of Jupiter
Cease-fire agreement signed in Vietnam
Middle-east oil embargo precipitates energy crisis which has continued ever since

1974–82 During the last decade microchip technology has arrived: so also has the glass fibre optical cable which will replace the conventional insulated copper cable

1982 The Falkland Islands war

Definitions

Cruise Missile — A guided missile launched at a ship or other surface target. It flies at speeds similar to supersonic aircraft, using a high or low flight path, to home on to its target.

Ballistic Missile — A guided missile or rocket, launched at a surface target, which follows a ballistic trajectory through the outer atmosphere to reach its target. It attains speeds five or ten times that of a cruise missile.

Strategic Nuclear Weapon — A long range weapon, usually a ballistic missile armed with a nuclear warhead, which can be launched at targets deep in the enemy's homeland.

Tactical Nuclear Weapon — A medium or short range nuclear-tipped weapon used in the battle zone, or at sea.

Conventional Weapon — Any weapon e.g. missile, bomb or shell, fitted with a non-nuclear warhead.

Sonar — A sensor using high frequency sound in water to detect submarines.

Warsaw Pact countries — Russia and her satellites, East Germany, Poland, Czechoslovakia, Hungary, Romania and Bulgaria.

Over thirty-five years have now passed since the ending of the Second World War. During this time there have been confrontations and localised wars but no general showdown between the U.S.S.R. and the West. The nuclear deterrent, in fact, expensive and terrible though it is, has successfully maintained world peace. How has the Royal Navy weathered this period? What changes have taken place? In what way can its present usefulness best be judged? And what of the future?

The problems involved were epitomised on the day I began writing this final chapter by the Prime Minister's dismissal of her Under Secretary of Defence for the Navy. This crisis arose from a speech made by Mr Keith Speed in which he claimed that if the Navy were downgraded to any great extent it would be a danger to national security. At the heart of the controversy lay the Government's decision to go ahead with the American Trident system to replace the Polaris nuclear deterrent at a cost of more than £5,000 million over the next ten years from 1981. To make an outlay of this size possible, the argument ran, conventional forces must be cut and here the Navy tops the list. In view of the conflict with Argentina over the Falkland Islands in 1982, the reader can judge for himself the validity or otherwise of this argument.

What does all this amount to? Is it simply a matter of prudent housekeeping? Or are the fears valid that one naval correspondent expressed, with slight exaggeration, when he described the Royal Navy as being reduced, in effect, to a rowing boat on the Serpentine? And what of another correspondent's suggestion that if the Royal Marines, our Commando Assault Force, were disbanded, the Navy without aircraft carriers would amount to little more than a coastal defence force? It seems that the capital ship versus aircraft debate continues in an updated form.

We live in a nuclear, electronic age. To grasp, let alone understand, what is going on a new language has to be learnt. Since I retired from the Navy in 1946 technological advance has been such that at times I confess to being as bemused as the newest Dartmouth midshipman by such things as influence mines, proximity fuses, supersonic backfire bombers and the like. What does it all mean? And above all how can the layman, who is paying for it, gauge its significance?

The essence, from which all else derives, is that the nature of seapower has changed. Whilst the key role of every national navy remains, as it always has been, the maritime defence of the homeland, the securing of free movement over the oceans of the world for oneself and the inhibiting, if need be, of a similar capacity in others, no one navy can now dominate and police the world in the manner the Royal Navy did in the nineteenth and early part of the twentieth centuries. The atom bomb and its progeny, satellites and electronics have altered all that.

Gone now for ever are the dinosaur battle fleets of the two World Wars. Moreover, whilst both the United States and Soviet navies maintain powerful aircraft carriers and the defence systems associated with these monster ships, the ultimate weapon is now the nuclear submarine with its incredibly accurate missiles. Though launched at sea, these are basically land weapons and are really no part of conventional naval forces as such.

These weapons, perhaps the most important development in sea warfare since Hawkins designed the low-charged galleon in the sixteenth century, relate to

seapower only in that they are launched from a seaborne platform. They cannot be used in naval operations aimed at keeping or restoring freedom of the seas for trade and supply. Their value lies purely in the fact that they are at present the only 'fully credible second-strike' weapons available and therefore the only 'fully credible deterrent' against what has come to be known as 'first strike capability.'

In other words if Soviet Russia were to contemplate launching its nuclear missiles against Europe or the United States, it would be deterred from so doing by the knowledge that it would invite instant destruction from the submarine-borne Polaris-Poseidon-Trident missiles lurking in readiness in undiscoverable depths in the oceans of the world. On that sombre equation the peace of the world continues to depend.

How has this come about and where does the Royal Navy stand in this virtual stalemate between the super powers? To begin with, a brief look at the uses which have been made of British naval forces since 1945 will serve as a reminder that Defence must always be dominated by geography and by the unchangeable fact that

By June 1953 the Coronation Naval Review at Spithead shows a navy composed of aircraft carriers, cruisers and smaller ships. The battle fleet has gone. Soon the emphasis will change again as nuclear submarines and missile ships come into service.

nearly three quarters of the earth's surface is water. The Royal Navy has been actively employed in the following trouble-spots since the ending of World War II:

Corfu Straits 1946
Palestine 1946/7
China 1948/9
Korea 1950/3
Gulf of Aqaba 1951
Cyprus 1955/9 and 1974
Suez 1956
Iceland (Cod War) 1958/9, 1973/6
Kuwait 1961
British Guiana 1962
Indonesia 1962/6
Bahamas Patrol 1959/73
Tanzania 1964
Beira Patrol 1965/75
Aden 1967/8
Mauritius 1968
Belize 1977 and 1980
Falkland Islands 1982

Carrier operations in Korean waters during the Korean War of 1950–3. Servicing aircraft on board the Australian Navy's H.M.A.S. "Sydney".

and continuously over the whole period at Gibraltar and in Northern Ireland. In all these running events, with the exception of Suez and the Falkland Islands, only single ships or small squadrons have been involved. Conventional fleet actions are a thing of the past.

Behind all the above lies a principal feature of the global maritime scene. During the past thirty-five years a major shift has taken place in the role Great Britain plays in the world. In 1945 we were still a great imperial power. Today, whilst our world *influence* remains considerable, we have become at heart a European power. This metamorphosis has naturally been accompanied by dramatic and necessary changes in the country's defence policy.

All three of our military forces – Navy, Army and Air Force – have been reduced in size, their functions now being directed primarily to the shared defence of Europe within the framework of the North Atlantic Treaty Organisation which came into being on 4th April 1949. The Western Nations involved in N.A.T.O. with the United States of America were originally Belgium, Denmark, France, Great Britain, Italy, Luxembourg, the Netherlands, Norway and Sweden but Eire refused to participate whilst Ireland remains divided; Greece, Iceland and Turkey joined later; West Germany entered in 1955 and France withdrew her fleet in 1963 whilst at the same time vetoing British entry into the Common Market.

The Royal Navy, however, is still the strongest maritime force in the world after the navies of the United States and Russia, but it is a navy of intricate and complex seaborne machines run by officers and ratings who, in addition to seamanship, must acquire and keep up to date an increasingly sophisticated technology. Naval personnel in 1981 comprised 62,000 men and 4,000 women, all of whom were volunteers. These minuscule numbers out of a population of nearly 56 million underline the intense specialisation which the Royal Navy has been forced to undertake. The sailor, too, has changed. The social gap between the sailor of 1914 and of today is greater by far than that between the Tudor sailor and the Jack Tar of 1914.

As for the sailor so for the ships in which he serves. Size, purpose, weaponry and propulsion – all have undergone revolutionary changes. The warships of the nineteen eighties, some of them driven by gas turbine aircraft engines now rely on missiles rather than guns, their hulls in some cases being no longer of steel but of glass fibre. Ships can now navigate by satellite when necessary and are so crammed with what we used to call 'the shape of things to come' as to be all but unrecognisable as conventional warships to someone like myself who retired from active service thirty-five years ago. Yet the links and traditions are all of them there.

The Falkland Islands imbroglio of 1982 has made the British aware of the Royal Navy in a manner and to a degree not seen since the Second World War. It has also revealed the huge importance in modern sea warfare of the role which radar and sonar play in the tracking and the engagement of potential enemies, from Nimrod up in the air with its surveillance range of 300 miles to the shipborne sonars and radars with a sub-surface and surface range of about twenty miles plus.

This, allied to active homers in torpedoes and missiles which can be guided to within lock-on range of the target, whether airborne, surface or submerged, is the main ingredient of the modern sea battle.

THE COMING OF MISSILES

Today target-seeking weapons such as missiles and anti-missile missiles have almost entirely replaced the gun as the prime naval weapon and the success of the French designed Exocet missile, for instance, has been only too well demonstrated in the Falklands campaign.

The present range of missiles is as follows:

Polaris A submarine launched ballistic missile fitted with a nuclear warhead. It has a range of 2,500 nautical miles with solid fuel propulsion and is guided by an inertial system.

Exocet A medium-range missile, originally surface-to-surface but now launchable from an aircraft, with a very low trajectory and a radar homing head.

Sea Dart A ship-to-air medium-range missile with an anti-ship capability, propelled by ramjets.

Sea Slug A medium-range ship-to-air missile with four solid propellant boosters which jettison after burn out. Guidance is by 'beam-riding'.

Sea Cat A close-range anti-aircraft missile which can also be used in an anti-ship role. Guidance is by radio-controlled visual tracking and propulsion is by solid fuel.

Sea Wolf A high-speed, close-range anti-missile and anti-aircraft missile with fully automatic radar control and guidance

Sidewinder An infra-red homing air-to-air boost guide missile. It has a solid fuel propellant motor and a high explosive warhead.

Ikara A rocket-propelled anti-submarine missile designed to deliver homing torpedoes at long range.

SS11 An assault missile used in the Royal Marines Commando helicopters. It has a range of over 2743 metres and can achieve high penetration.

AS 12 An air-to-surface wire guided and spin stabilised missile developed from the SS 11, with a range of 6000 metres. Carried in Wasp and Wessex helicopters it is used mainly as an anti-patrol boat missile.

Sea Skua An anti-surface ship missile carried by the Lynx helicopter.

Sub Harpoon A long-range anti-ship missile launched from a submerged submarine and today the principal anti-surface ship armament of Fleet Class Submarines.

An Exocet surface-to-surface missile being fired from the guided-missile destroyer H.M.S. "Norfolk". Only war proves the efficacy of weapons and the weaknesses of defence systems. In the Falklands Campaign the Exocet proved itself extremely effective and at the same time raised grave doubts as to whether some of the new, lighter materials used recently in naval construction might not leave warships too exposed to fire hazards. These experiences will no doubt soon be incorporated in new planning for the future.

The paramount factor in battle today is that the warship relies on its radar and sonar not only in defence but also in attack as a guidance system for its missiles and torpedoes. In this factor are also comprised the electronic countermeasures now available in modern sea warfare, which we have seen used in the South Atlantic in 1982, such as radar decoys, jamming and the anti-missile missile.

The anti-missile missile is perhaps the most extraordinary development of the whole range of weaponry and one of the most arresting facts about it came to light during the trials of Seawolf when one of these anti-missile missiles tracked and intercepted a 4.5 inch shell fired from a gun – to the amazement of the American officers who were witnessing the trial.

The other ingredient of sea warfare today in which the Royal Navy and in particular the Royal Marines have proved themselves supreme is amphibious

operations. These, too, have been demonstrated in the Falkland Islands engagements. The skills, training and sophisticated operation of these special commando parties (though their methods remain largely secret and unknown except to the Task Force command) seem to have advanced so far since the commando raids of the Second World War as to be almost unrecognisable.

Of course, because a ship is a ship and all who sail in her sink or survive together, the ancient skills of the sea have still to be learnt anew by the micro-electronically minded sailor of today. The psychology of a modern ship's company, even though its internal relationships may have adapted to the times, remains very much what it has always been. The hierarchy and the discipline, differently accepted perhaps, are still essentially there and in working order as before.

The Royal Navy's fortitude and constancy in battle, so dramatically declared in

1982 in the South Atlantic, has restored to the nation its ancient belief in the greatness of the country, so long derided in the Marxist infected age through which we have been passing. This tradition is still a matter of pride to the sailor of today. More particularly an innate assuredness that the ship in which he serves is without any doubt superior to all others in the fleet continues to animate the individual sailor today as it once drew together 'the people' or the ships' companies of a bygone age. 'Aft the more honour: for'ard the better man' our most famous Admiral declared and the prestige which Nelson's victories established still heartens the fleet today. *Plus ça change, plus c'est la même chose.*

The changes in the greater world of which the Navy is a part have indeed been revolutionary and not only in the political sense. Confucius declared a very long time ago that revolution is only believed in when it has been accomplished, though whether what has happened in Russia, Eastern Europe, China and other parts of the world overtaken by Marxism is 'believed in' may, perhaps, be questioned. However the titanic struggle between collectivism and capitalism which has gone on throughout the twentieth century is the prime fact of life in the world of today, and it is that same dreary Marxist theory of its own inevitable success, now seen to be an illusion except when maintained by armed suppression, which breeds like a nuclear reactor and which is at the core of the main threat to world peace. This brings us back to the Navy with a dramatic jolt. Why is this?

At the end of the Second World War the Soviet Navy was organised almost entirely for coastal defence. Its amphibious capability was negligible. Today the Soviet naval presence in the Mediterranean consists of over fifty ships. The U.S.S.R. also deploys her warships permanently in the Indian ocean and the South Atlantic. In addition the Soviet Navy regularly visits the Caribbean. Russia now possesses a well-balanced, modern and effective fleet fully capable of worldwide operations. But Russia needs no such fleet for defence alone. It is therefore clear that the U.S.S.R. continues to build up this formidable weapon as a key element in her foreign policy.

And what a weapon it is! Russia now has the largest submarine force ever seen in the world. Close on 500 boats will soon be in service, of which over 150 are nuclear powered. Since it takes five years of skilled building to make a modern submarine and since the Soviet Union is currently turning one out every five weeks, these figures are alarming. Soviet growth is more than twice that of N.A.T.O. and the costs, the 'megabucks' or 'megaroubles' involved, are likewise immense. Between 11 and 13 per cent of Russia's Gross National Product goes on defence and a quarter of that is put into research and development. The rates in the U.S.A. and the U.K. are 5.7 per cent and 5 per cent respectively. We need to be blind or bigoted or both not to suspect what Russia intends to do.

However, not all the trumps are in the Soviet hand. Geography remains on our side. The coast of the U.S.S.R. is divided into five distinct regions, of which the arctic coastline of Siberia can be ignored because of its ice conditions. In each of the other four regions, separate fleets are maintained . . . Murmansk, the Baltic, the Black Sea and the Far Eastern Pacific Coast. From these bases come the threats which the United States and European navies have to oppose.

But except for the Pacific force, these Soviet fleets are compelled by geography to pass through what are known as 'choke points' on their way to the oceans of the world. The Murmansk fleet has first to penetrate the Svalbad-Norwegian-North Cape gap and then the Greenland-Iceland-United Kingdom gap. The Baltic fleet can only emerge through the Kattegat between Sweden and Denmark. The Black Sea fleet must pass through the Bosporus and Dardanelles before reaching the Mediterranean, the exit from which in turn is controlled by the Suez Canal in the east and by the Straits of Gibraltar in the west. Such inescapable exigencies somewhat ease the problems of surveillance.

Once at large in the oceans of the world, however, the naval scene and its assessment changes again. Pitched battles, such as at Jutland or Leyte Gulf, are now unlikely. Today missiles and anti-missile techniques write the scenario, tactics being decreed by electronic and satellite intelligence, which, of course, includes radar, sonar and radar counter-measures.

The launching of H.M.S. "Dreadnought", Britain's first nuclear powered submarine, in 1960. This type of 3,500 ton boat, often referred to as a 'hunter-killer', ushered in a new age in naval affairs. Since nuclear propulsion is silent and requires no oxygen, such submarines can remain submerged for very long periods and can move about the oceans of the world undetected. A most formidable weapon.

The outstanding factor is that now both the United States and Soviet navies can and do maintain a world presence and both are in more or less permanent confrontation in sensitive areas such as the Mediterranean or the Persian Gulf. Nuclear submarines can circle the globe without surfacing. A Polaris missile can be fired from under the sea, say in the Caribbean and three minutes later will hit its target in the South Atlantic with an accuracy of fifty yards, having travelled over 3,000 miles. It must again be stressed, however, that these nuclear missiles have no relation to sea warfare and would never be used against ships even in a state of all out nuclear war.

'Send deterrents out to sea, where the real estate is free', said a distinguished American Admiral,[1] adding under his breath 'and far away from me.' The speed at which things will happen if a Third World War ever comes is all but unimaginable and this means that the highly trained officer on watch must now be capable of a 'Command reaction' with an instant readiness never before contemplated or necessary.

The weight of responsibility is daunting. There is no time now to go through the hallowed formalities of bringing a warship to her action state. Correct response in a matter of seconds and without orders from above will alone allow a ship to be saved. Today the computer and what navies call 'its interface with man' dictate this reaction.

There is a common misconception that navies somehow protect 'sea lanes' or 'lines of communication' but seapower is primarily about protecting ships. To do this we must be able to sink the ships and shoot down the aircraft and missiles of those who would prevent our lawful use of the sea. That outcome decrees whether N.A.T.O. armies and air forces can be reinforced – and reinforced in time – thus measuring up to the vastly more numerous forces of the Warsaw Pact countries. This requirement has again been dramatically demonstrated in 1982 in the South Atlantic.

Moreover the timing of everything has changed. Just as weapons are now brought into use in a matter of seconds, so today the making and preparation of ships and weapons takes longer than ever before. Consistency in our maritime affairs is therefore of paramount importance. It now takes some ten years to design and produce a new warship. This will then remain in service for up to thirty years. A lifetime of forty years from conception to scrapyard requires naval planning of a high order. This planning must be based on a realistic long-term appreciation of the threat involved: it cannot respond to short-term political changes of policy which only hinder and weaken the implementing of what is ultimately necessary.

In any long drawn-out confrontation, such as has been in progress between East and West since the Second World War, the ability of democracies to stand up to a ruthless, doctrinaire, totalitarian foe requires extremely demanding efforts. The Royal Navy has to be there in the right place with the right ships and equipment every day of every week in the year.

Defeat can come in only three ways: by being struck down in combat, by not fighting at all or by not being in a state of adequate preparedness to be able to fight. The constantly escalating Russian effort, therefore, can only be met by a determination to demonstrate in ways which cannot be misunderstood that if the Soviets go beyond a certain point (and as I write today that point seems, with Afghanistan and

Poland in mind, to be dangerously nearer than it has ever been before), then they enter a situation in which they are *not necessarily* going to win and would almost certainly suffer severe consequences if they proceeded further.

For the Royal Navy to achieve the above capability requires an investment in men, resources and training which might well have unnerved Jackie Fisher. Yet however arresting the finances may be, the present day Royal Navy stands out as one of the most cost-effective elements of defence in the western world. 'Despite a succession of Defence Reviews', Admiral Sir Raymond Lygo wrote,[2] 'the span of capability in our own Navy from air power through surface ships, amphibious forces and minesweepers to some of the most advanced nuclear submarines in the world encompasses a range of capabilities for a modest cost which must be one of the bargains of the present day military scene.'

Perhaps the most remarkable change in the British naval scene of today has been the disappearance of the Admiralty, its functions now being merged into a set of

The Silver Jubilee Review of the Fleet in June 1977. H.M.S. "Ark Royal", "Hermes" and "Fearless" form part of the line steaming past the Chief of Defence Staff and First Sea Lord.

initials, the M.O.D. or Ministry of Defence. On 31st March 1964 the Board of Admiralty met for the last time, surrendered its patent and hauled down its flag. On the following 'All Fools Day' – a date much remarked on at the time – Her Majesty's ships, vessels and shore establishments came under the charge of the 'Admiralty Board of the Defence Council'.

Their Lordships, no longer Lords Commissioners, resumed their duties as members of this Board. The Queen again assumed the *title* of Lord High Admiral (the *office* being firmly vested in the person of the Minister of Defence) and thus ended a unique feature of British government life after 336 turbulent years. This event – and it was arrived at after a series of monumental rows which raged throughout 1962–3 – took place at the prime instigation of Mountbatten, nicknamed by those who opposed the change as 'the Hound of the Battenbergs'. As N. A. M. Rodger remarks in his excellent book *The Admiralty* – 'a project to abolish the Roman Curia would scarcely have met with less enthusiasm in the Vatican'.

Whether or not it is and will continue to be a successful innovation remains for the future to judge. Mountbatten himself had no doubts at all. His experience, first at Combined Operations, later as Supreme Commander in South East Asia and lastly as First Sea Lord had convinced him that only a closely unified command and administration could match the demands of modern war. He may well have been right. But the Admiralty's antiquity was always deceptive.

Given that its constitutional form was a façade behind which its actual power, position and character repeatedly changed, the dear old Admiralty proved itself at crucial moments throughout its history to be surprisingly modern both in outlook and method. I, for one, regret its departure from the naval scene. As serving officers we were all uncomfortably aware of its overstaffing and of its manifest follies, highlighted in my time by the Invergordon mutiny. It might also be true to say – and it was said – that whereas we possessed a seagoing fleet of diminishing importance immediately after the Second World War, we yet continued to maintain a splendid Admiralty. Nevertheless the paradox remained that no department of state had survived for so long through so many *bouleversements* of trouble and change.

Again its epitaph is well stated by Dr Rodger: 'When most of the great departments of state were born, it was already ancient, and yet it never lost a certain chameleon-like quality, ever changing and never quite matching its background. In spite, or perhaps because of its strong regard for its own history, it neither became set in its own ways, nor easily adopted those of others. Monarchs and dynasties, statesmen and ministries came and went, the tides of war and revolution washed over and around, constantly altering but never submerging the Admiralty and it survived them all counter, original, spare and strange to the last.'[3] Pepys could not have put it more succinctly and who knows, now that the 'small is beautiful' idea is gaining general acceptance, the Admiralty may yet rise again in its well-known phoenix-like way.

So where do we stand today? The nature of seapower may alter, basic parameters, however, remain timeless and unchangeable. The 'three dimensional' character of the marine environment, the necessity to operate on, above and under the surface of the sea, and the need above all for ships to co-ordinate the whole, continues to be central to our conduct of maritime affairs. What is now called the interface area remains the key to it all and that is the surface of the sea. Vulnerability has become relative. We now appreciate fairly well that anything fixed is more at risk than things which move. In defence, therefore, the navies of the world and especially their submarines have become the least vulnerable of all elements of military power however disposed.

We also contrive to remember, though at times only by chance, that history has a clear lesson for any island folk such as the British. That lesson is that once control of the sea is lost, or an essentially maritime strategy is abandoned, decline inevitably sets in. All major conflicts in recent history declare that victory on land without control of the seas can never last for long. The nation or nations which enjoy freedom of the seas and operate from safe industrial bases are bound to win in the end. It is axiomatic that battles may be won or lost in any environment. Wars on the other hand can only be lost at sea.

The odds, however, have changed. On land it seems to be generally accepted that a ratio of 3 to 1 against defenders is fair enough if you can hold your ground for a reasonable time. At sea the balance needs to be 6 or 8 to 1 *in favour of* a defending force. This can be readily understood once the problem of defending a large group of surface ships against one lurking submarine is visualised. That is a prime factor conditioning the real balance of power, and in addition it must also be remembered that the U.S.S.R. is completely independent of any need for overseas commerce in order to sustain a war effort. The West, on the other hand, has perforce to put total reliance on the free flow of raw and manufactured materials, men and machines if it is to sustain its own capacity and capability for any length of time. The Russians are well aware of this imbalance, hence their heavy investment in maritime muscle. It is that which enables them to exploit and perhaps to dominate an area vital to us, negligible to them. Those are the facts of life which confront us today.

In the end readiness and presence are what matter most. To keep the peace, the Royal Navy, in concert with its allies, must always be ready, must always be there. The nuclear submarine is the most significant development in naval warfare since the Second World War. Anti-submarine measures, therefore, require to be available in a continuing state of almost instant readiness. This in turn requires manpower and training of a quality never even imagined before. 'We have developed a navy throughout our long maritime history', Admiral Lygo writes, 'which is a sharp and effective tool of military and political management but it is now of a size from which it must only expand. The possibilities of contraction could only mean the loss of one of those elements or arms which are vital to sustain the whole. It is equipped with some of the finest weapon systems that exist in the world today and it is manned by, I am quite sure, the finest collection of free men available for this purpose in society as a whole. Put these two priceless assets together and then only one thing is necessary, the national will and resolve to support it.'[4]

What sort of navy, then, do we have in this post atomic age? And what sort of changes in ships, weapons and personnel have taken place comparable to the transition from 'wooden wall' to ironclad and from sail to steam?

In 1945 a British naval pilot made the world's first deck landing in a jet aircraft. Today with modern jet fighters, the vertical take-off Sea Harrier and strike aircraft

BLOCKADE BY SEAPOWER

Blockade in maritime warfare is a legal declaration by a belligerent power denying seaborne trade to an enemy. In sailing ship days and up to the end of the Napoleonic war, the short range of guns made blockade into much the same thing as the investment of a harbour. In other words, blockading enemy ports such as Toulon and Brest required a squadron of ships to be almost permanently on hand.

With the invention of long range guns, mines, torpedoes and aircraft, such close blockade ceased to be feasible, being replaced by a more distant one in which enemy seaborne trade was intercepted on the high seas. In the recent Falklands campaign a blockade was declared by Great Britain initially within the radius of two hundred miles of the islands and later extended to twelve miles off the coast of Argentina.

In the Napoleonic war, the whole of the British Isles were declared by Napoleon to be under blockade but he had no means of enforcing this and it became known as a 'paper blockade'. The British counter blockade, on the other hand, by Cornwallis off Brest and by Nelson off Toulon, backed up by other squadrons off Carthagena, Cadiz, Coruña and Rochefort, alone stood between Napoleon and his domination of the world.

A century later international agreement was reached at a conference called by Great Britain in 1908 that for a blockade to be binding, it must be effective and from then on that principle has constituted the law of naval blockade as we know it today.

In the First World War both Germany and Britain blockaded each other, although the German blockade did not really come into effect until the spring of 1915 when intensive U-boat warfare began.

Two years later when Germany began unrestricted U-boat attacks not only on British but on neutral shipping, the whole civilised world was appalled and largely because of this the United States entered the war in April 1917. By then the stranglehold over the British Isles was such that the country's survival was in question, food supplies having been reduced to a matter of weeks.

In much the same way the Battle of the Atlantic in the Second World War showed that the German U-boat could achieve at sea almost as much as Panzer divisions did on land.

Today, as has just been demonstrated in the Falklands, although a naval blockade can never be completely successful so long as it can be breached by air, it is nevertheless a major factor in the bringing of matters to a head.

To sit within sight of the French coast, virtually on a lee shore, for years at a time and in all weathers was the fate of Nelson's Navy during the Napoleonic Wars. There were few dramatic moments like this capture (off Brest) of the French ships "Resistance" and "Constance" by "San Fiorenzo" and "Nymphe". Yet it was this fleet and its command of the sea that defeated Napoleon.

equipped with nuclear weapons, three inventions, later adapted to all N.A.T.O. aircraft carriers, have revolutionised the scene. These inventions are the angled deck which allows more aircraft to be operated at any one time: the steam catapult which launches aircraft more smoothly and with greater acceleration and the mirror landing sight which makes deck landings safer than they have ever been before. To these must now be added the variable angle 'ski jump' launching ramp as fitted in anti-submarine cruisers such as H.M.S. "Invincible", "Illustrious" and "Ark Royal" which has proved to be an effortless method of launching aircraft and has greatly reduced catapult reverberation. This is such a success that it is said that the 'grocers' and the 'greasers' below decks scarcely realise that aircraft are being operated.

The key to understanding the role which the Royal Navy plays today is to appreciate that whilst it is the strongest navy in Western Europe, it is still only part

of a greater whole. However the Royal Navy takes a major part in facing the challenges of each new decade with a modern fleet of surface warships, fixed-wing aircraft and helicopters supported by a large number of repair, maintenance and replenishment vessels. It is also equally formidable under water.

At present the Royal Navy has four Polaris submarines, H.M.S. "Resolution", "Renown", "Repulse" and "Revenge". These submarines are all nuclear powered and each carries sixteen missiles. These 7,000 ton submarines, one of which is constantly on patrol, comprise the United Kingdom's contribution to N.A.T.O.'s strategic nuclear deterrent. Three decks offer unusually spacious crew accommodation for a submarine and they can remain submerged for long periods without any outside support. Each submarine has two crews, known as Port and Starboard, so that when one is away on patrol, the other is training or taking leave.

In addition to the Polaris submarines, the Royal Navy has ten Fleet submarines with three more building. These, too, are nuclear powered and used to be known as 'Hunter-Killer' submarines (nicknamed in 1982 with the usual naval irreverence as 'Junta-Killers'). These submarines are armed with homing torpedoes which can be used against other submarines or surface vessels. The Sub-Harpoon long range anti-ship missile will be the principal anti-surface ship weapon these submarines carry. Capable of continuous patrolling at high underwater speed, they are independent of base support and can circumnavigate the globe without surfacing. Although only half the displacement of Polaris submarines, Fleet submarines also have three decks and although space is restricted, living conditions are relatively comfortable.

Then there are sixteen conventional submarines with diesel-electric power units, armed with torpedoes, which with less endurance than that of nuclear submarines, nevertheless, are fast, silent and difficult to detect.

Three Anti-Submarine Cruisers, one of which is still building, have the primary task of acting as command ships for anti-submarine warfare forces. They operate the Sea King anti-submarine helicopter and also carry Sea Harrier aircraft and the Sea Dart surface to air missile for air defence and anti-ship operations.

Perhaps the most versatile vessels yet built for amphibious warfare are the two Assault Ships, H.M.S. "Fearless" and "Intrepid". Each ship displaces some 11,500 tons and is fitted out as a Naval Assault Group / Brigade HQ from which naval and military personnel, working in close co-operation can mount and control an amphibious operation. They can transport a military force complete with supporting armour. Landing craft capable of carrying heavy tanks are housed in the ship's dock and can be launched from the open stern. The ships also operate a flight of assault helicopters and are armed with the Seacat guided missile and two 40mm Bofors guns. At present one of these ships is also used as the Dartmouth Training Ship, providing young officers with their first sea experience.

Then there are H.M.S. "Hermes" and "Bulwark" which double as Anti-Submarine Carriers and as Commando Carriers. These displace approximately 24,000 tons, are 750 feet long with a beam of 90 feet and have a complement of 980 men.

The rest of the major surface fleet comprises eleven Sheffield class Destroyers (Type 42) whose primary role is to provide air defence for task group operations, six County Class destroyers and one Type 82 destroyer, H.M.S. "Bristol" which was built as a proving ship for the Sea Dart missile, and fifty-six Frigates of varying types, sizes and capabilities. Many of these, in addition to having conventional steam propulsion, are powered by Rolls-Royce Olympus and Tyne gas turbines and have controllable-pitch propellers. These frigates are the general purpose ships of the modern navy, have speeds in excess of thirty knots and are known for their excellent sea keeping qualities and their ability to perform in the worst weather.

The rest of the fleet is made up of Mine Countermeasures Vessels, an Exercise Minelayer and a class of Edats Minesweepers, Fishery Protection and Offshore Patrol Vessels, Far East Patrol Boats (operating from Hong Kong), Survey Ships, an Ice Patrol ship, Trials and Training Ships and Fast Training Boats, Helicopter Support Ships, Hydrofoils and a fleet of Royal Fleet Auxiliaries for replenishment at sea. All in all the Royal Naval Fleet of today is a formidable maritime force.

Any navy, however, is only as good as the men and women who man it. Here, too, great changes have taken place in the personnel of the Royal Navy and the conditions under which they serve. A vast improvement in living conditions at sea during the last thirty-five years, since the ending of the Second World War, is taken for granted by the highly specialised volunteers who now enter the Navy on short and long term service contracts. Individual bunks have replaced the old-time hammocks, there are air-conditioned messing and recreational spaces reasonably furnished and decorated, and high quality food is now served on the cafeteria system. The rum ration was abolished in 1970 and beer is now available from ships' canteens. This is a far cry from the salt junk and weevil-filled hard tack of sailing ship days: it is also a great improvement on the general messing arrangements which obtained in H.M. ships when I first went to sea.

Exercises involving only the Royal Navy have now largely given way to joint N.A.T.O. occasions. In this Sea Day Exercise in 1978 the Royal Navy frigate "Phoebe" is followed (left) by the "Schleswig-Holstein" from West Germany, the "Tjerk Hiddes" from Holland and (right) Norway's "Trondheim".

Pay, allowances and pensions have also necessarily been greatly improved, not least because the navy now has to compete with industry ashore for the highly skilled talent it needs. My pay as a Midshipman in my first seagoing appointment was five shillings a day (25p in the currency of today) and from that I had also to pay for my mess bill and uniform. Today a Midshipman on entry gets £4,201 per annum and after one year £5,205. An Ordinary Seaman on entry at 17½ years on a short service option is paid at the rate of £76 a week and since April 1981 all ratings are paid monthly through their banks. Personnel serving ashore now pay for a proportion of their food and accommodation charges.

The use of microform at sea has also gone ahead with on-board stores documentation now being supplied entirely in microfiche form. Not only is this system quicker and more efficient, it also provides a considerable saving in space. This logical progression is especially valuable in a submarine's documentation where space is at a premium.

Altogether life at sea has changed greatly. The nomenclature of rank and rating has remained as before – from Midshipman to Admiral for officers and from Ordinary Seaman to Fleet Chief Petty Officer for ratings but Gunrooms and Warrant Officers' messes have gone. Within the old established hierarchy of rank and command, there is now a new classlessness which reflects the social changes taking place in the country. Wardroom life today has a very different feel about it but at sea the old

The tragic end of H.M.S. "Sheffield", the famous destroyer sunk in the 1982 Falklands Campaign, brings a reminder of the high price which still has to be paid for control of the seas and that there are always new and sometimes unforeseen defence problems to be solved. The Falklands Campaign saw the Royal Navy's first encounter with missile warfare and the acquisition of much valuable and unique experience in actual combat.

camaraderie or ésprit-de-corps, as it was once called, is as evident as it ever has been.

The last fifteen years, as the Director of Naval Public Relations has remarked, have seen profound changes both in the Fleet and in the type of young person who enters Dartmouth – or to give it its full name the Britannia Royal Naval College, Dartmouth – bound for a naval career. The College's task is to match these variables whilst maintaining traditional standards of self-discipline, professionalism and leadership. Today virtually all Royal Naval officers (and over one hundred officers per term from foreign and Commonwealth nations) come through the College, including the future Seaman (including aviators), Engineer, Supply and Instructor Officers of the General and Supplementary Lists; Special Duties Officers; Doctors, Dentists and Nursing Sisters, Royal Marines, W.R.N.S., Chaplains and Reserve Officers.

Academic backgrounds range from five 'O' levels to second university degrees but the great majority enter Dartmouth with their eyes wide open, intent on making a success of a naval career for as long as that may be. Questioning and critical, they are far more broad minded and receptive to new ideas than their predecessors of even twenty years ago. Today valued traditions are often questioned. However they are quickly accepted when seen to be sensible.

Steady pressure for economy has reduced Naval General Training to one term at Dartmouth. Priorities have had to be sharply defined. However with such a varied entry the first requirement is the development of leadership, and here the theme of 'functional leadership' – that is learning by doing – pervades all training. Thus the first four tough weeks are devoted to the rudiments, such as living and working together, being at the right place, in the right rig and at the right time and to becoming physically fit.

The individual is given a brief introduction to the principles of leadership, but mostly by practical exercises in the classroom, on College 'cliffs and chasms' and, most effectively, in the challenging conditions of cold, wet nights on Dartmooor. Over one hundred College boats of all types and two Bird-class Patrol Vessels "Petrel" and "Sandpiper" are extensively used for leadership practice as well as for teaching the first professional skills of seamanship.

At the other end of the training spectrum, but equally important, is the development of latent officer-like conduct. Dress, wardroom customs and manners form an essential part of the syllabus. As one young man disarmingly put it to a College wife at a Divisional coffee morning 'This is the first time I've had to make polite conversation to anyone!' Naval vessels are, after all, often our 'ambassadors' in foreign ports.

As always there never seems to be enough time. Much fundamental training in self-discipline is consolidated in the Training Ship but the Midshipman's professional knowledge when he later joins the Fleet is still very limited. The College sets the standards and points the way but much responsibility devolves upon the ships of the Fleet, as it always has done, to continue the long process of moulding the character and quality of our future officers.

This story of the Royal Navy over a thousand years is now all but told. I wish it could be summed up and left 'all ship-shape and Bristol fashion' but in casting around

*The new age of technology
in which the Royal Navy
now has its being is
symbolised by this April
1982 picture taken on
board H.M.S. "Hermes",
flagship of the Falkland
Islands Task Force.
Against a crowded
background of Sea
Harriers and Sea King
helicopters, Royal
Marines line up for a
weapons check prior to a
possible assault. As
always, the essence of sea
power in this connection is
to be able to deliver troops
and their armament where
and when they are
wanted. This ability was
again clearly demonstrated
in the Falkland Islands
Campaign.*

for a way to do this, it seems to me that in this micro-chip electronic age, inventions and developments come upon us at such a pace and leave us in such a flux that even the mildest generalisation seems to be out of date or inappropriate as soon as it has been formed in the mind.

Except, perhaps, for those sailing about the world in small boats for adventure and pleasure, the nature of life at sea – certainly of naval life at sea – has basically changed. We no longer breed a race of seafarers as such, instinctively sniffing the wind; we watch dials and television screens and react to computers which tell us what we can or cannot do. A great skill is clearly necessary in doing this but so far as the weapons of today are concerned, and to a certain extent the ships in which they are carried, naval personnel at the sharp end of any action – with the exception of combined operations which is a world of its own – are very much in the hands of the scientists who design and programme their equipment.

Even as recently as the Second World War, the Royal Navy's research and development establishments were comparatively small, their status secondary to that of shipbuilding and armaments firms such as Vickers and the Royal Dockyards whose job it was to build the great capital ships of the Navy and subsequently maintain them in A.1 fighting condition.

Today the Fleet could not be kept at sea achieving one hundred per cent performance for one hundred per cent of the required time without the facilities of conventional dockyards and bases plus the essential and organic work of the Admiralty Marine Technology Establishment, the Atomic Weapons Research Establishment, the Royal Signals and Radar Establishment, and the Admiralty Underwater Weapons Establishment.

However, the Royal Navy is not primarily ships, weapons and supporting establishments, it is the men and women afloat and ashore who serve the Queen and the White Ensign her warships wear. The duties change, but the tradition of loyal and courageous service continues unbroken, as it has done for longer than in any other fighting service in the history of the world.

This tradition, well exemplified in the war with Argentina in 1982, is the essence of the Royal Naval story which I have tried to portray in this book. It holds through good times and bad, through victory and defeat, but I think it is always at its most potent when things are not going too well or when unexpected disaster has overtaken a particular ship, squadron or fleet. The unique qualities of the British sailor then glow out of the gloom and I can think of no better way of ending this account of the Royal Navy over a thousand years than by quoting from Stephen Roskill's excellent book *The War at Sea*.[5]

Captain Roskill was commenting on the tragic sinking of the battleship "Prince of Wales" and the battlecruiser "Repulse" on 8th December 1941 whilst trying to intercept a Japanese troop convoy reported to be approaching the Malayan coast. In this terrible attack by Japanese aircraft 876 officers and men in the two ships were killed and a fatal blow to our ability to defend Singapore and Hong Kong was struck, Churchill recording that in all the war, he never received a more direct shock.

'The only redeeming feature of the tragedy was the splendid conduct of the officers and men involved in it. The Royal Navy always seems to rise to its highest peaks of devotion and self-sacrifice in adversity. A young airman who flew over the scene while the destroyers were performing their work of rescue wrote to Admiral Layton these words: "During that hour I had seen many men in dire danger waving, cheering and joking as if they were holiday-makers at Brighton . . . It shook me, for here was something above human nature. I take my hat off to them, for in them I saw the spirit which wins wars." The last prophetic sentence was, indeed, true as all our enemies were to learn in due time . . .'

And finally as a valediction, Sir Alan Herbert's verse written for Warships' Week in 1942 when things were not going any too well:

> In every creek and river, wherever ships could ride,
> King Alfred's men built ships for him and sent them down the tide;
> And many a modest stream, boys, and many a humble street
> Were proud they'd sent a "Monarch" or a "Glory" to the fleet.
> Today the little places lay famous keels no more:
> No battleship is building from Chiswick to the Nore.
> But we can still contrive, boys, that every tiny town
> Shall help to make an "Exeter", a "Cossack" or "Renown".
> It may be 'ballyhoo,' boys, as clever people say:
> The Navy won't go short, maybe, if you refuse to pay.
> But we can all be partners in this tremendous thing;
> And I *like* to think I'm lending a "Cossack" to the King.

SELECTED BIBLIOGRAPHY

Ed. Peter Kemp. *The Oxford Companion to Ships and the Sea*, O.U.P. 1976
Paul M. Kennedy. *The Rise and Fall of British Naval Mastery*, Allen Lane 1976
Oliver Warner. *The British Navy – A Concise History*, Thames & Hudson 1975
David Howarth. *Sovereign of the Seas*, Collins 1974
Arthur J. Marder. *From the Dreadnought to Scapa Flow*, O.U.P. 1965
Julian Corbett. *Sir Francis Drake*, Macmillan 1890
J. A. Froude. *English Seamen in the 16th Century*, Longmans, Green 1895
Oliver Warner. *Great Sea Battles*, Weidenfeld 1963
William P. Mack and Royal W. Connell. *Naval Ceremonies, Customs and Traditions*, Naval Institute Press 1980
N. A. M. Rodger. *The Admiralty*, Dalton 1979
Peter Kemp. *The History of Ships*, Orbis 1978
Felix Barker and Peter Jackson. *London*, Cassell 1974
Sir Nicholas Nicolas. *A History of the Royal Navy*, Richard Bentley 1847
Ed. Captain Eric Wheeler Bush. *The Flowers of the Sea*, Allen & Unwin 1962
Captain S. W. G. Pack R.N. *Admiral Lord Anson*, Cassell 1960
Richard Hough. *First Sea Lord*, Allen & Unwin 1969
John Colville. *The Churchillians*, Weidenfeld 1981
B. H. Liddell Hart. *History of the Second World War*, Cassell 1970
Winston S. Churchill. *The Second World War*, Cassell 1949
Captain John Cresswell R.N. *Sea Warfare 1939–1945*, Longmans Green 1950
Richard Hough. *Hero of our Time*, Weidenfeld 1980
Baron Burkhard von Mullenheim-Rechberg. *Battleship Bismarck*, Bodley Head 1981
Evelyn Berckman. *Nelson's Dear Lord*, Macmillan 1962
Captain Stephen Roskill R.N. *The War at Sea*, H.M. Stationery Office 1954
Ian Hogg and John Batchelor. *Naval Gun*, Blandford 1978
Peter Hodges. *The Big Gun*, Conway Maritime 1981
B. B. Schofield. *British Sea Power*, Batsford 1967
Julian Corbett. *Signals & Instructions 1776–1794*, Navy Records Society 1908
Jack Broome. *Make Another Signal*, William Kimber 1973
J. L. Moulton. *The Royal Marines*, Leo Cooper 1972
Geoffrey Callender. *The Naval Side of British History*, Christophers 1924
Ruddock Mackay. *Fisher of Kilverstone*, Oxford 1973

REFERENCES

Chapter II
1 The Papal Bull 'Inter-Cetera Divina' 1493 and The Treaty of Tordesillas between Spain and Portugal 1494
2 Thomas Coventry, Lord Keeper of the Great Seal, 17th June 1635
3 Edmund Waller. *Of a War with Spain*
4 J. A. Froude. *English Seamen in the 16th century*

Chapter III
1 David Howarth. *Sovereign of the Seas*

Chapter IV
1 N. A. M. Rodger. *The Admiralty*
2 Peter Kemp. *The British Sailor*
3 Peter Kemp. *The British Sailor*
4 David Howarth. *Sovereign of the Seas*
5 David Howarth. *Sovereign of the Seas*

Chapter V
1 N. A. M. Rodger. *The Admiralty*
2 N. A. M. Rodger. *The Admiralty*
3 N. A. M. Rodger. *The Admiralty*
4 David Howarth. *Sovereign of the Seas*
5 Peter Kemp. *Oxford Companion to Ships and the Sea*
6 David Howarth. *Sovereign of the Seas*

Chapter VI
1 Winston S. Churchill. *A History of the English Speaking Peoples Vol. IV*
2 N. A. M. Rodger. *The Admiralty*
3 N. A. M. Rodger. *The Admiralty*
4 Christopher Lloyd *Mr Barrow*

Chapter VII
1 N. A. M. Rodger *The Admiralty*
2 N. A. M. Rodger. *The Admiralty*
3 N. A. M. Rodger. *The Admiralty*
4 Winston S. Churchill. *A History of the English Speaking Peoples Vol. IV*
5 N. A. M. Rodger. *The Admiralty*
6 Richard Hough. *First Sea Lord*
7 *The Times* – 14th July 1920

Chapter VIII
1 N. A. M. Rodger. *The Admiralty*
2 N. A. M. Rodger. *The Admiralty*
3 N. A. M. Rodger. *The Admiralty*

4 Harold Nicolson. *King George V: His Life and Reign*
5 Richard Hough. *First Sea Lord*
6 N. A. M. Rodger. *The Admiralty*
7 N. A. M. Rodger. *The Admiralty*
8 Peter Kemp. *Oxford Companion to Ships and the Sea*
9 N. A. M. Rodger. *The Admiralty*

Chapter IX
1 N. A. M. Rodger. *The Admiralty*
2 John Colville. *The Churchillians*
3 Peter Kemp. *Oxford Companion to Ships and the Sea*

Chapter X
1 Medlicott. *The Economic Blockade*
2 B. H. Liddell Hart. *History of the Second World War*
3 T. K. Derry. *The Campaign in Norway*
4 Winston S. Churchill. *The Second World War Vol. II & III*
5 Richard Hough. *Mountbatten: Hero of our Time*
6 Winston S. Churchill. *The Second World War Vol. III*

Chapter XI
1 Richard Hough. *Mountbatten: Hero of our Time*
2 Richard Hough. *Mountbatten: Hero of our Time*
3 Evelyn Berckman *Nelson's Dear Lord*
4 Oliver Warner. *The British Navy*
5 David Howarth. *Sovereign of the Seas*

Chapter XII
1 Arleigh Burke, Chief of Naval Operations, United States Navy.
2 Ian Allan Ltd. *Armed Forces No. 1*
3 N. A. M. Rodger *The Admiralty*
4 Ian Allan Ltd. *Armed Forces No. 1*
5 Stephen Roskill. *The War at Sea*

INDEX

N.B. Numerals in *italics* refer to captions, and the abbreviations FWW and SWW to the First World War and Second World War respectively.

ARCTIC CIRCLE

1C

1c

Unalaska
Aleutian Is.
Nootka SD
Vancouver

NORTH
AMERICA

NORTH

ATLANTIC

OCEAN

1a

1C

Plymouth

Madeira

Canary Is.

1c

Sandwich Is.
(Hawaiian Islands)

TROPIC OF CANCER

PACIFIC

OCEAN

Cape
Verde
Is.

1b

1b

Marshall Is.

Christmas Is.

Galapagos Is.

0

1c

Marquesas Is.

1b

SOUTH
AMERICA

1b

Samoa

Tuamotu Is.

Friendly Is.
(Tonga?)

Society Is.

Tahiti

TROPIC OF CAPRICORN

1a

1c

Cook Is.

(Austral Is.)

Pitcairn

Easter

Montevideo

Oct 1773

1a

1a

Juan Fernández Is.

1a

40

1c

ATLANTIC OCEAN

July 1773

1b

Patagonia

Falkland Islands

South Georgia

Nov 1774

1b

1b

Dec
1773

1b

1b

C. Horn

1b

ANTARCTIC CIRCLE

160

120

80

40

0